# CHINA AT A TURNING POINT

*Perspectives after the 19th Party Congress*

# CHINA AT A TURNING POINT

*Perspectives after the 19th Party Congress*

Edited by

Manoranjan Mohanty

Institute of Chinese Studies, Delhi

PENTAGON PRESS LLP

CHINA AT A TURNING POINT
**Perspectives after the 19th Party Congress**
***Editor: Manoranjan Mohanty***

First Published in 2019



ISBN 978-93-86618-63-4



Published by
PENTAGON PRESS LLP
206, Peacock Lane, Shahpur Jat
New Delhi-110049
Phones: 011-64706243, 26491568
Telefax: 011-26490600
email: rajan@pentagonpress.in
website: www.pentagonpress.in

Printed at Aegean Offset Printers, Greater Noida, U.P.

*To the memory of the departed colleagues*
*who built the foundations of what is today the*
***Institute of Chinese Studies***

Huang I-shu (1932-2018)
Rajni Kothari (1928-2015)
G P Deshpande (1938-2013)
K Subrahmanyam (1929-2011)
Mira Sinha-Bhattacharjea (1930-2009)
Giri Deshingkar (1932-2000)
C R M Rao (1929-1995)

# Contents

## IV. Ethnic Question



## V. Ideology, Culture and History

# Acknowledgements

The collective and committed efforts of colleagues and friends have enabled this publication project to come to a successful conclusion. We faced many roadblocks along the way, which could be crossed only because associates came forward to share the responsibilities and push it forward. The support of the ICS stalwarts, Patricia Uberoi, Kishan S Rana, Ravi Bhoothalingam and Alka Acharya as referees, reviewers and editors of many of the papers was most valuable. The advice of another ICS pillar, Sabaree Mitra, as an expert in Chinese language and literature, was of utmost help. Ashok K Kantha, ICS Director, provided full assistance and encouragement at every stage.

The colleague who discharged the day-to-day academic monitoring of this project, pursuing the contributors, checking facts cited in papers, pointing out gaps in references and in most cases completing them, and leading the entire effort to its conclusion was Bhim B Subba, ICS Research Associate, himself a contributor to the volume. He deserves our sincere appreciation for all this as well as compiling the valuable documentation. He was assisted by four bright interns in ICS, Saurav Sarkar, Shristi Singh, Surbhi Lohia and Navreet Kullar.

Jabin T Jacob, who had been part of the group which first discussed the idea of launching this project nearly two years ago, garnered the intellectual resources, especially from the newly trained China scholars in India and abroad, bringing together contributions from three generations of Indian scholars of China. He had also undertaken the lion's share of the responsibility of planning the first workshop in September 2017 and the follow-up seminar after the 19th Party Congress in December. Even after leaving ICS he continued to support this initiative as a contributor. We warmly acknowledge his contribution to this effort.

We thank the participants in the workshop and the seminar, especially those who acted as discussants on the papers. Shyam Saran's participation and comments on several papers were of great value. Comments on various contributions by Imrana Qadir, Bidyut Mohanty, Hemant Adlakha and M V Rappai also proved invaluable in giving them final shape.

The India International Centre has been a valuable and cherished partner of the Institute of Chinese Studies in most of its important programmes. We thank the IIC for co-hosting the workshop and the seminar on this project.

The ICS faculty, Madhurima Nundy, Tshering Chonzom, Nirmola Sharma and P K Anand, besides Bhim Subba, contributors themselves, were always available to lend their shoulder to the wheel. The ICS staff, particularly Kripal Singh Rawat, P R Singh, Ram Singh and Ramji Lal, provided the much needed behind the scenes support and succour.

Most importantly, I thank the contributors whose cooperation in making this volume possible cannot be overstated. I am personally grateful to them for placing their trust in me in this final leg of the journey.

We were also fortunate to get a competent editorial consultant in the well-known journalist Seema Guha, who deserves our sincere thanks. Rajan Arya of Pentagon Press cheerfully endured the shifting deadlines in finalising the manuscript, presenting multiple options in the technical sections and so on. We thank him for respecting this partnership with ICS in the publication programme.

Patricia Uberoi, the Chairperson of ICS, has blessed this effort with a Foreword which only she could write. We are truly indebted to her for her gracious and experienced hand guiding us.

As is customary, with all the best efforts and will, the editor must needs take responsibility for such gaps and oversights that may have remained in this publication.

October 2018 **Manoranjan Mohanty**

# Foreword
# China Studies in India: Then and Now

By happy coincidence more than by conscious design, this collective publication by members and associates of the Institute of Chinese Studies (ICS) coincides with the golden jubilee of the ICS or, to be more precise, with the initiation of the self-styled 'China Study Group', the kernel out of which the ICS was eventually to take shape. In this sense, it invites reflection on the broader field of China Studies as this has evolved in India over the last half-century or so: its locations, practitioners, preoccupations and methodologies and, more broadly, the changing landscape of local and global social science knowledge in which it is embedded as a (non-Western) species of what is commonly known as 'Area Studies'. So, just as the contributors to this volume venture to speculate on whether or not the build-up to the 19th Congress of the Communist Party of China (18-24 October 2017), its actual proceedings and its follow-up together mark a 'turning point' in China's developmental trajectory, we may also take the opportunity to ask whether the practice of China Studies in India is now at some sort of 'turning point'. In either case, the answer might be a qualified affirmative.

The China Study Group originally comprised a heterogeneous set of teachers and researchers, diplomats and journalists from different institutions across Delhi who, from 1969, met regularly on Wednesday afternoons to discuss current developments in China. Recall that this was at the height of China's baffling Great Proletarian Cultural Revolution, and that India–China relations were still at a very low ebb following the 1962 border war. Though we called ourselves a 'group', there was no political or ideological unanimity among the participants – in fact, arguments were often quite heated, even acrimonious, given the personalities involved and their various political persuasions. But there was also a shared commitment to trying to understand China better with whatever academic tools and methods we could muster while parrying the unfortunate perception in some quarters that, by so doing, we were merely acting as 'pro-China' analysts. Our collective command of Chinese language, spoken and written, ranged from fluent through patchy to effectively non-existent, but all were agreed that, looking ahead, access to Chinese language materials should be an important component of our tool-kit and, moreover, that understanding China's present – both its domestic and foreign policy aspects – required a much broader and more holistic understanding of her civilisational past.

For many years, the venue for these animated discussions was the centrally located Indian Council of World Affairs (ICWA), known familiarly as 'Sapru House' after one of its eminent founders. In winter months the China Study Group, along with various other gaggles of engaged citizens, met on the expansive sun-bathed Sapru House lawns, fringed by pots of giant chrysanthemums. In inclement weather the group retreated to somebody's office in the main building or its precincts, or even to the noisy and insanitary canteen at the back. At that time, the general Mandi House area where the ICWA is located was the acknowledged cultural centre of Delhi, with theatres, art galleries and museums; state-run academies of literature, fine art and the performing arts; schools, colleges, hostels and educational institutions (including the office of the bi-monthly *China Report*, which subsequently became the flagship journal of the ICS); and all this within close proximity to the gourmand's delights of the Bengali Market sweets shops.

From today's perspective, the singular history of the ICWA as an independent institution in a non-governmental political space would appear to have surrendered to collective amnesia. A sort of local equivalent of London's Chatham House (the Royal Institute of International Affairs), the ICWA was co-founded in 1943 by two eminent 'Liberal' jurists / parliamentarians, Sir Tej Bahadur Sapru and Hridya Nath ('H.N.') Kunzru. In March–April 1947, the fledgling ICWA played host to the historic Asian Relations Conference. That so-called 'unofficial' gathering on the eve of Indian independence was the brain-child of Pandit Jawaharlal Nehru, then head of India's interim government, and its aim was to bring together national leaders and leaders of freedom movements throughout Asia to discuss matters of common interest and the potential role of a united Asia in post-colonial world affairs. Even then, and despite the organisers' intention to avoid tricky issues of defence and security, which they naively perceived as being merely the disruptive legacy of rival imperialisms, the tension between pan-Asian utopianism and the emerging nationalist sentiments of new nation-states coloured the Conference proceedings. Notable in fact was the controversial presence on this occasion of delegates from Tibet, to the manifest chagrin of the Chinese (ROC) representatives.

As far as I know, few if any of the China Study Group ever entered the imposing Sapru House building through the grand portico or climbed the stately white marble steps framed by a huge tablet listing the names of donors to the building's construction: eminent jurists, freedom fighters, politicians of different persuasions, Indian princes, captains of industry, notable philanthropists, and so on. Our magnet was the elegantly spacious library on the ground floor where, when they were not airing their views loudly in the famous Indian Coffee House in Connaught Place, the cream of Delhi's journalist community, recognised 'public intellectuals' and All India Radio commentators on current affairs could be observed consulting the fine archive and book collections and scribbling opinion pieces. Somewhere in the back-rooms, unknown persons were assiduously engaged in the work of 'clipping' from the daily newspapers, a practice that continued in ICS too till the advent of the internet, this being our local supplement to the off-shore China-Watchers' staple diet of *Survey of China Mainland Press*, the *Foreign Broadcast Information Service*, the *BBC Summary of World Broadcasts* and the Hong Kong–based *China News Analysis*.

Apart from being a congenial public space open for reading, writing and spirited intellectual disputation, the ICWA was of course a substantial research institute in its own right, producing over the years numerous publications on subjects deemed to be germane to independent India's assumption of its rightful place in Asian and world affairs. The pioneering *India Quarterly*, an academic journal focusing on India's relations with its Asian neighbourhood, was published by the Council from 1945, continuing to this day. Equally significantly, the ICWA spawned and provided a temporary home to several other institutions. While the nascent Asian Relations Organisation, an abortive attempt to institutionalise the Asian Relations Conference, was quietly dissolved in 1955, this same year saw the foundation under ICWA auspices of the largest and most prestigious centre of international and area studies in the country, the Indian School of International Studies (ISIS), which shared and augmented the ICWA library resources. The multi-talented G.P. Deshpande, a faculty member of the ISIS, was among the founding members of the China Study Group. In 1968, the ISIS moved into its own premises nearby in Ferozeshah Road, shortly afterwards merging with the newly established Jawaharlal Nehru University. Also quartered in the ICWA premises for some time was the Institute for Defence Studies and Analyses, founded in 1965. IDSA's Director, K. Subrahmanyam, the brilliant and prolific strategic expert and advocate of Indian nuclearisation, along with historian Bharat Wariavwalla, also on the IDSA faculty and a close associate of the China Report editor, C.R.M. Rao, were generous hosts and spirited sparring partners of members of the China Study Group, Giri Deshingkar and Mira Sinha Bhattacharjea in particular. In fact, K. Subrahmanyam often made his office available for our discussions, predictably adding his own realpolitik spice to the proceedings.

This very simplified re-telling of the history of the ICWA through the first quarter century of its existence exemplifies the dynamics of successive but overlapping conceptions of the role of China Studies in the Indian setting, modulated by the changing contexts of colonial rule, preparation for statehood, and independent nationhood. Thus, the tone of Pandit Nehru's speech at the 1947 Asian Relations Conference recalls the spirit underlying Rabindranath Tagore's establishment of the Cheena Bhavana in the Visva-Bharati University at Santiniketan (1937) and the academic labours of early 'Sino-Tibetan-Indological' scholars such as P.C. Bagchi who had sought to locate India's pre-colonial past within a dense web of inter-Asian cultural and commercial connectivities. The founders of the ISIS, on the other hand, essentially conceived China Studies as one among many 'area' specialisms within an overall project of establishing International Relations as an independent academic discipline in its own right, and of tooling this body of knowledge-in-the-making to the theory and practice of Indian diplomacy. It was admittedly a rather narrow agenda.

It was following the 1962 Sino-Indian border war, and not unconnected with that traumatic event, that the University Grants Commission proposed the introduction of Area Studies programmes in select Indian universities. Of course, China Studies was only one among several planned UGC Area Studies programmes, but it was certainly an important one. Unlike the conflation of Area Studies with International Relations in the ISIS, UGC Area Studies programmes were re-conceived along the lines of current practice in U.S. universities, that is, as multi-disciplinary programmes involving the collaboration of scholars from different humanities and social science backgrounds seeking to promote a holistic understanding of the society, culture, history, economy and politics of the countries / regions involved. (This, of course, was in the days of innocence before the horrors of the Vietnam war forced 'concerned Asia Scholars' to acknowledge the witting and unwitting contribution of Area Studies specialists to the promotion of American national interests in war theatres in Asia and elsewhere.) A component of the official UGC perspective on the conduct of Area Studies was emphasis on mastery of the language(s) of the respective regions, aided and supplemented by 'fieldwork' (with a minimum of two weeks and a maximum of sixty days as the bureaucratically determined time-frame of exposure to the culture area!).

But in 1969, history was against us. While India was the first non-Communist country to recognise the People's Republic as the legitimate government of China (1 December 1950), the political and cultural bonhomie of the first decade of post-colonial Asian solidarity was soon to evaporate. Thereafter, for almost two decades, academic exchange between India and China was negligible. In the process, China Studies in India lost a whole generation of potential practitioners, along with recall of the singular labours of the pioneers of China Studies in the colonial period. Meanwhile, whatever their academic backgrounds and personal political proclivities, Indian China Studies scholars found themselves effectively confined to the role of 'China-Watchers' (in the Cold War sense), dedicated to the task of de-coding Chinese ideological statements and official policy pronouncements, and otherwise dependent on secondary sources and perspectives relayed through the Western media and academies. In those pre-internet days, access to Chinese language sources was severely limited and, for all but the most dedicated of Indian China scholars, hard-won language skills were slowly evaporating. It was only in the late 1970s as the post-Mao 'reform era' unfolded that India–China academic contacts gradually resumed, picking up pace a decade later. One after another, members of the China Study Group and other Indian academics were able to make brief and tightly monitored 'study visits' to China. The experience was sufficiently novel that, in the early 1980s at least, each such visit was recounted in intimate detail in a Wednesday seminar, and received with rapt attention.

This volume of essays on the significance of the Nineteenth Party Congress of the Communist Party of China bears witness to the long overdue coming into being of a third generation of post-Independence China scholars of more varied academic and professional backgrounds, superior language skills, and in many cases first-hand experience of living and working in China. Certainly, there are now many more 'feet on the ground' of China Studies, and a welcome (if still limited) dispersion of China Studies activities outside the older academic centres of Kolkata and Delhi. Superficially it might appear that this volume simply follows the format of many ICS group discussions over the last half century, taking as its starting point the intensive scrutiny of a major policy document or set of documents such as the General Secretary's Political Report to the quinquennial Party Congress, the Premier's Work Report to annual sessions of the National People's Congress, Communiqués of Party Plenums, etc., along with Chinese White Papers on important themes. In other words, then and now, a main focus was on continuities and changes in the Party leadership for what they might reveal of behind-the-scenes factional, regional, personal and ideological frictions, for what they might portend for the line of political succession going forward, and for the potential impact of domestic political developments and economic compulsions on China's foreign policy, India–China relations in particular.

While these remain important issues of self-evident relevance to Indian foreign policy and national defence, robustly addressed in this volume, the field of inquiry has certainly broadened. For obvious reasons, issues concerning the Chinese economy have come increasingly to the fore, along with questions of regional, social and gender inequality, social welfare, ethnicity, urbanism, rural development, environment and culture. Implied here also is a critical engagement with the human and social sciences, rather than confinement within the exotic silo of China exceptionalism.

Does this imply that China Studies in India is finally reaching a turning point, a coming of age? Perhaps it does. But looking back a half century, one is also reminded of a question that was animatedly discussed, if never actually 'minuted' so to speak, in meetings of the China Study Group: Is there, or can there be, an 'Indian perspective' on China, or is our knowledge of China to be forever subordinated to, or relayed through the Western academies? In this globalised world it appears that, except in the crassest geo-political frame of 'national interest', this question is no longer considered worth asking.

This volume, carrying 'perspectives' of Indian scholars on what will surely prove to be an important phase of the Chinese development process, is a timely offering at this special moment in the history of the ICS. We owe our collective thanks to Manoranjan Mohanty, himself one of the ICS pioneers, for steering this project to its successful conclusion; to Jabin T Jacob of the promising second generation of ICS scholars for setting the process in motion; and to Bhim B Subba for his multifold contribution to all aspects of this collective publication.

**Institute of Chinese Studies** **Patricia Uberoi**

# Introduction
# China Again at a Turning Point

*Manoranjan Mohanty*

The People's Republic of China (PRC) has been at turning points many times before. But the Nineteenth Congress of the Communist Party of China (CPC) in October 2017 marked a very special point in the history of the PRC. It declared the ushering of a 'New Era' (*xin shidai*) almost rivalling the concept of 'New China' (*Xinhua*) that the CPC-led New Democratic Revolution popularised in the course of the movement that culminated in the establishment of the PRC in 1949. This new period that China had entered, the 19$^{th}$ Congress claimed, recorded, among other things, the achievement of economic goals of living standards of a moderately 'well-off society' and higher levels of infrastructure on the one hand and new global standing as a major country on the other. In this volume of essays, a group of Indian scholars associated with the Institute of Chinese Studies examines the nature of this turning point and scrutinises the policies, trends and their implications on many important aspects. They do so from a number of vantage points and range of perspectives. Understanding closely the formulations, examining the context and underlying factors and their dimensions and interconnections, characterise this effort by scholars who have been engaged in research on these issues for a long time.

## New Era Initiatives of Xi Jinping

Heralding this 'New Era' was the emergence and consolidation of position of CPC leader, Xi Jinping whose first term of five years since 2012 was interpreted as addressing boldly questions that were side-lined for a long time. Xi Jinping's package of policies not only presented an overall perspective, but also touched almost every arena of society, economy, polity, culture, ecology and above all China's global role. The proclamation of 'Xi Jinping Thought for building

Socialism with Chinese characteristics for a New Era' was the single most striking summation of the new orientation, marking the new turning point for China. Inevitably, the significance of this formulation was seen in comparative reference to the proclamation of Mao Zedong Thought in the 1960s. The period preceding the Nineteenth Congress and the months following it showed centralisation of power and authority of Xi Jinping in Party, State and Army through a number of political and administrative decisions. Declaring him as the 'core' at the Sixth Plenum in 2016, calling for 'aligning all behaviour and policies at all levels with the core', amending the PRC Constitution at the 13th NPC removing the term limits for the President and Vice-President in March 2018 and promulgating new rules for enforcing discipline in the Party that came into force on the 1st of October 2018 were some of the political and organisational measures to firmly establish the personal command of Xi Jinping. Essays in this volume deal with the implications of this development, asking whether such a form of centralised governance and authoritarianism would enable China to acquire new elements to foster a fresh wave of nationalist upsurge with global aspirations, or whether it reflected political uncertainties within the system, or whether it was a mode of firmly implementing a certain set of policies in various fields.

Among the policy initiatives under the new 'governance philosophy', the anti-corruption campaign loomed large. With new institutional initiatives and widespread campaigns, Xi Jinping launched measures to expose and punish both 'tigers and flies'– high-and-low-level officials who engaged in corrupt practices. This drive against corruption, together with the so-called 'four comprehensives' – comprehensively achieve a well-off society, deepen reforms, promote rule of law and enforce strict Party discipline – constituted Xi Jinping's approach to governance. Several contributors examine the effects of the anti-corruption campaign and its results. According to some observers, there is a climate of growing transparency and rule-abiding behaviour in some spheres in contemporary China. But there is also evidence that this campaign has been used to handle various factions in the party, neutralise opponents or prosecute and isolate or jail rival leaders. The media, in its new, advanced technological avatar and growing constantly into new modes including social media, served the politics of the regime comprehensively. Has this governance perspective brought new elements in handling the persisting challenges in the minority nationality regions such as Xinjiang and Tibet? Contributors to the volume point out the continuation of the familiar approach of the CPC leaders for long, focusing on economic development of these regions with some cultural accommodation, while pursuing the policy of 'hard strike' against dissidents in the minority regions. Enforcing the centralised authority of the Party leadership in every sphere and at every level throughout the country is the evident trend in Xi Jinping's framework of governance.

Equally important was the much publicised focus on a 'new development philosophy' that stressed the quality of development rather than quantity of growth. The stress on achieving economic growth that Deng Xiaoping had laid by setting targets to double the 1980 level of GDP by 2000, doubling that by 2010 and further doubling it by 2020 drove China's four decades of reforms since 1978. That perspective was a continuing thread with Deng's successors. This process had in fact secured high rates of economic growth making China the world's second largest economy in 2010 and raising per capita income from about US$250 in 1980 to over US$8000 in 2017. But this scenario also brought many problems that were recognised by Hu Jintao in the early 2000s and have now become the central preoccupation of Xi Jinping. Issues such as inequality of income and wealth, regional disparities, urban-rural gaps, environmental crisis, social alienation, corruption, difficulties faced by common people in availing public utilities and social security have been widely discussed in the past decade and more in contemporary China. Hence Xi Jinping's stress on opting for a 'reduced rate of growth as the new normal', shifting of focus from 'quantity of growth to quality of development'. Xi's development mantra seems to be based on 'innovation' through state of the art science and technology in a digital age. Backed by adequate investment and a new governance system he called for achieving new targets of 'abolishing absolute poverty by 2020', achieving modernisation by 2035 and building a 'great modern socialist country' by 2049 when the PRC turns 100.

In this volume the authors take these questions for in-depth treatment by taking up specific vantage points of study. For example, an attempt is made to find out how the workers are treated in terms of wages and welfare in the current regime and how the poor regions have faired in relation to the advanced regions? In both cases the picture is full of challenges. The gender dimensions of this development process show that the Chinese women have a long way to go to achieve equality in political, economic and social space. As for the environmental policy under the Xi regime, there has been no doubt some breakthrough in enforcing emission standards, but the dominant pattern of the growth process has its serious consequences in pollution and depletion of natural resources. In the same way, the targets of the new urbanisation policy may appear carefully balanced, but beneath lie new challenges of environmental, cultural and political risks and social costs.

Besides, the announcement of a New Era, the proclamation of Xi Jinping Thought, the unfolding of a new governance perspective and a development policy package, Xi Jinping's global strategy marks another major turning point.

Early in his tenure Xi announced 'new principles governing relations among major powers in the 21st century'. Then came his notion of a new security doctrine. But the two key formulations that came to be publicised as Xi Jinping's signature concepts were the Belt and Road Initiative (BRI) and the Common Destiny of Humankind the former being proclaimed as the more significant. Together these elements composed his global outlook shaping his diplomatic strategy on the one hand and linking his domestic policies with international initiatives on the other. Essays in this volume deconstruct, contextualise and critically examine these policies and raise questions as to whether they mainly served China's great power ambitions or they also reflected responses to a set of complex historical forces in the emerging world or were meant to address major domestic concerns. The authors discuss the implications of these policies for the world as a whole and for neighbouring countries in particular.

Xi Jinping had started his term of Party leadership in 2012 by announcing the task of 'realising the Chinese dream of national rejuvenation'. Since then his emphasis on leveraging the Chinese civilisational and cultural heritage as a springboard of a new wave of national mobilisation has been conspicuous. There is thus a simultaneous invocation of tradition, nationalist goals of the past century, Party ideology and organisational mobilisation as well as science and technology. Contributors try to capture this combination by analysing history, culture and ideology.

## Perspectives and Issues

Discussion on these issues in the volume begins in **Section I** with analysis of the party leadership and organisational initiatives. Not all Party Congresses have been equally historic. But, as Sreemati Chakrabarti points out, some are marked out for the crystallisation of important policy perspectives even though some major formulations may have come out in preceding plenums. C V Ranganathan highlights the ambitious agenda of the Xi Jinping leadership both in the domestic and the international spheres and wonders if conditions at home and abroad are ripe to fulfil all of them. Anurag Viswanath points out that the personalisation of the leadership role under Xi Jinping in effect has reversed the trend of political reforms that Deng Xiaoping had set in motion (followed by Jiang Zemin and Hu Jintao) which were meant to avoid the emergence of a personality cult and the undermining of institutions. Ritu Agarwal shows that the measures taken by Xi Jinping in enforcing fresh canons of discipline, exercising Party leadership in all spheres of society and state as per the central guidelines and above all, asking the cadres to demonstrate communist values in day-to-day conduct have amounted to 'reinventing' the Party, thus reversing several trends of the recent years. Bhim B Subba goes into the modalities of Xi Jinping's political management by showing the way he built up a new team of loyal colleagues by reorganising the Central Committee and Politburo and choosing certain regional leaders and professionals to implement his agenda. This is followed by B R Deepak's further identification of factions and factional politics that represent both interest groups and policy advocates operating within the Party. Raviprasad Narayanan provides further evidence to show how the anti-corruption campaign is also a power struggle to sideline or neutralise opponents of the leader. At the same time, the anti-corruption campaign is raised to the level of a legal framework, but as Santosh Pai points out, the law has so many discretionary provisions that it hardly certifies as 'rule of law' in the sense that is understood in a liberal democracy, for purposes of handling the cases of corruption. All this required a new communication system to legitimise the leadership's policies and Xi Jinping's personal aura. This was evident to the world as well to the Chinese people in the part played by the media during the Nineteenth Congress as detailed by Tilak Jha.

Xi Jinping's global initiatives have been his most talked about in China and abroad as they have made a departure from the earlier international line laid down by Deng Xiaoping. From a policy of 'lying low and biding your time', China under Xi Jinping unfurled a new and pro-active global outlook. In **Section II**, Kishan S Rana profiles Xi Jinping's diplomatic strategy in its major dimensions and predicts that the consequences may not unfold as stipulated in the policy statements of China. Alka Acharya deconstructs Xi's prominent formulations in the Political Report and suggests that much of the foreign policy initiatives of Xi Jinping were actually propelled by serious domestic compulsions. Backing the new global perspective, Xi Jinping has announced a plan to develop the PLA into an advanced level force of the 21st century that can 'fight modern wars and can win'. For that purpose, as spelled out by Atul Kumar, the Xi regime has put in place a new system of PLA capability to fight a 'joint war'.

We then move to specific dimensions of the socio-economic policies in **Section III**. The focus of Xi Jinping's overall transformation strategy is admittedly 'innovation', a dimension which is discussed in-depth by Ravi Bhoothalingam in both historical and contemporary global perspectives. According to him, the Chinese case shows how culture and politics of various kinds can facilitate, not merely constrain, manifold innovations in the fields of science, technology, management and social orientation. Innovation is one aspect of the larger strategy which at the Nineteenth Congress, as shown by Aravind Yelery, emphasised supply side structural reforms to ensure quality and responsiveness to market demand and also put in place a set of carefully formulated financial reforms to address the concerns arising from the global economy.

The earlier way of looking at the economy in a disaggregated frame through regions underwent a significant change under Xi Jinping. Analysing this trend, Jabin T Jacob underlines a movement in the direction of greater centralisation of economic management. This puts the initiatives such as BRI in a different perspective. To what extent has the centralised Party-State followed policies to provide social security and welfare to the vast body of workers is examined by P K Anand who shows that despite many new measures causes of dissatisfaction among them persist. The Chinese development orientation throughout the reform period has actually kept the Western pattern of urban development during the last two hundred years as its reference point if not its explicit model. Under Xi Jinping this orientation got a further fillip, as argued by T G Suresh, with the announcement of a 'New Urbanisation' policy and launching of many new urban zones, most prominent of them being Xiong'an New Area near Beijing. No doubt, as Madhurima Nundy shows, steps were also taken in the recent years that resulted in significant achievements in the provision of healthcare both in urban and rural China moving towards universal coverage. She points out that despite steady increase in privatisation, the state role in maintaining the public health system remained prominent. But when we ask whether healthcare, education, employment and social security in rural and urban areas, among men and women, among minority population and backward regions were equitable the answer is that clearly there was a long way to go. It is also true that the regime was conscious of the prevailing disparities and took measures to address them. In the case of women, Usha Chandran argues, this inequality was evident in the social and economic sphere and more so in institutions of political power, even though the CPC still upheld the slogan, 'Women hold up half the sky'. In another area, namely the much discussed environmental crisis where much attention in policies and strong regulations had been initiated under the Xi Jinping regime, Rajiv Ranjan argues that many serious problems remain to be tackled.

Continuing the discussion of specific areas and the unfolding situation on the ground, the two essays in **Section IV**, on the minority ethnic regions, show how the government policies remained inadequate to address the anxieties and aspirations of the people of Xinjiang and Tibet. Debasish Chaudhuri examines the evolution of the nationalities policy of the CPC and concludes that co-option and development assistance accompanied by firm suppression of dissent have not yielded the desired results. Tshering Chonzom explains the Tibet policy by stating that while the traditional approach of clubbing security measures with development initiatives continued, the Xi regime had expanded the work of the Party's United Front Department to promote 'patriotic Buddhism'. Despite this, the phenomenon of alienation and dissent in Tibet persisted showing weaknesses in the regime's Tibet policy.

The volume ends with reflections on ideology, culture and history in

**Section V** followed by an Appendix (some valuable information on Party structure and personnel). Xi Jinping Thought is still a project in the making, according to Mohanty, as the clarifications and principles articulated in the Political Report mainly contained some policy statements and even the mention of the principal contradiction did not present a core theoretical formulation. He argues that this body of thought failed to address the crucial issues of the 21st century. Efforts were, however, not lacking in seriously articulating a cultural perspective. As Sabaree Mitra points out Xi Jinping had tried to put together multiple sources, Confucianism, Marxism, Western modernity and innovative additions to promote a perspective that aided his agenda. Xi Jinping's agenda is put in the context of China's five-thousand-year history by the veteran scholar Tan Chung, a teacher of many of the contributors. Analysing phases of the rise and fall of different regimes in Chinese history, he registers a warning, arguing that, whenever a Chinese regime pursued the path of hegemony, it eventually collapsed. He hoped that Xi Jinping's commitment to promoting the 'common destiny of humankind' would take a path that avoided hegemony and benefited the people of China and the whole world.

## The Turning Point

A wide range of issues has been taken up in this volume, analysed through a variety of perspectives. Some issues have been treated in greater detail, even with some repetition, than have others. Even then, this volume is by no means a comprehensive account of contemporary China after the 19th Party Congress. Many important aspects of China's economy, society and international relations could not be taken up during the period of preparation of this volume. But the ICS scholars and associates writing here on China before and after the 19th Party Congress from the perspective of their individual research interests have collectively decided to focus on the present turning point in the history of China's development process. They have tried to capture the nature of the long-term vision for China, declared by Xi Jinping at the Party Congress, of building a '*great modern socialist country that is prosperous, strong, democratic, culturally advanced, harmonious, and beautiful*' over the next several decades. At the same time they have tried to examine to what extent some of Xi's specific policies were capable of taking China in that direction. The contributions suggest that the emerging scenario is complex, and by no means appears unfolding on the desired path. China is very likely poised to emerge as a strong country, industrially and militarily, but whether the goals embodied in the 'new development philosophy' will also be realised with the present path of development is far from certain.

While China can see itself at a turning point in moving to a new stage of history, the world is no doubt experiencing a transition to a new epoch of civilisational movement. In this transition the history of the economic growth and development process of recent centuries is under serious scrutiny. That this historical pattern produced wealth and improved life conditions across the world is no doubt true, but it is being increasingly acknowledged that this development trajectory has also been destructive of the environment, and created new inequalities and inequities and new sources of alienation. This past epoch has mainly seen Grand Drivers such as state, capital, science and technology using market, management, communication and political organisation or party carrying out a transformation process. That process now confronts Ground Drivers of knowledge, culture and power in all parts of the world which also have in them new forms of politics, capital, science and technology to generate freedom, equality, dignity and happiness for every individual, group and region. The struggle for freedom and happiness has acquired more intensity with strong forces active on both sides or multiple sites. The struggle for transformation today has far more complex dimensions than ever before, with many new catalysts all over the world. A phase of civilisational movement to address these questions on a global scale has begun, as the debate on the Anthropocene Age intensifies. Some of the familiar goals and targets of the age of hegemony, doggedly pursued by many global leaders, have begun to look increasingly outmoded. To what extent the leaders guiding China's new Turning Point are consciously responding to this historical moment is an open question.

# I. PARTY, LEADERSHIP AND GOVERNANCE

# 1

# CPC Congresses in Historical Perspective

*Sreemati Chakrabarti*

The 19th Congress of the Communist Party of China (CPC) was held from 18–25 October 2017. A major achievement of the CPC in the post-Mao era has been the regularity with which the Party Congresses have been held. Since 1977 when the 11th Party Congress took place we see a Congress being held every five years as per the Party Constitution. Holding of a Congress indicates political stabilty, discipline and consensus among Party members and the consolidation of the policies pursued in the five years before the Congress as well as drawing a roadmap for the future. With each Congress, particularly in the post-Deng Xiaoping era, one notices that the international media has been increasingly paying more and more attention through news reports, comments and analyses.

However, a survey of the history of the CPC shows that the first five decades of the Party's life has been marked with uncertainty, instability and turbulence. Only after Mao Zedong's exit the Party and the state winessed relative stability as evident from the fact that Congresses are taking place at regular five-year intervals. This paper will briefly review the Party Congresses by dividing them into three periods:

1. Early Years: Pursuing an Urban Strategy (First to Fifth Congress, 1921 to 1926)
2. Era of Turbulence and Revolution (Sixth to the Tenth Congress, 1928 to 1973)
3. Period of Relative Stability (Eleventh to the Nineteenth Congress, 1977–present)

Each period will be analysed and the main political events will be highlighted. The paper also shows that even though the Congresses reveal much about the ideology, organisation and leadership of the CPC but most significant decisions of the Party have been taken either in the plenums or at other fora. The Party Congresses, particularly in the present era showcases to the people of China and to the world the stabilty and consensus within the Party.

## Early Years: Pursuing an Urban Strategy (1921–27)

After the Lenin initiated Karakhan Declaration in 1918 whereby the new Soviet state unilaterally revoked all the unequal treaties which the Chinese were forced to sign with Czarist Russia, a large number of young intellectuals got attracted towards the Soviet leader and his ideology. Small socialist groups had appeared around the time of the May Fourth Incident but it was only on 1 July 1921 that the Communist Party of China was formally established with the first Congress in Shanghai. There were 12 members including Mao Zedong. Chen Duxiu was elected Chairman. No documentary evidence in English has so far been found regarding any resolution, etc. At the first Congress perhaps due to the threat from Shanghai police which raided the building where the meeting had started. The members disappeared from Shanghai and a few days later the inconclusive session was concluded on a boat in a lake.

Soon after the Secretariat of the Chinese Labour Union was set up in Shanghai with Zhang Guotao as its head and a few months later the Party's Hunan branch was formed with Mao Zedong as Secretary. The 1921–26 period is marked by upholding the cause of the urban proletariat – very much in line with classical Marxism. However, Peng Pai and later Mao Zedong urged the Party to bring the peasant question within their radar.

The earliest public statements of the Communist Party are available from 1922 onwards (Brandt et al. 1959). The two documents produced at the second Congress held that year were the *First Manifesto of the Current Situation* and the *Manifesto of the Second Congress.* These manifestos call for a "democratic united front of workers, poor peasants and petty bourgeoisie." In the same year the Hong Kong seamen's strike happened where the Communist members took active part. It was in this year that the Communist Youth Corp had its first Congress. It was, however, at a Special Session of the CPC Central Committee in August 1922, the decision to ally with the Kuomintang *(Guomindang)* was taken. In June 1923 when the third Congress of the CPC met it resolved to cooperate with the KMT but in August at a plenum the important decision was taken: to keep the labour movement outside the KMT (Brandt 1959: 31). No Congress was held in 1924 but the year was significant as in the month of May the Whampoa Military Academy was set up with Chiang Kai-shek as its President and Zhou Enlai as head of the Political Department. The Fourth Congress in January 1925 had no major significance except that a North China Bureau and a Yangtze Bureau were created. However, Sun Yat-sen's death that year changed the direction of Chinese politics. In this period when the Communists allied with the KMT the CPC gained visibility but lost autonomy. The fifth Party Congress in 1926, held in aftermath of Chiang Kai-shek's clampdown on Communists, on the one hand, stresses on the struggle against feudalism (read warlordism) and imperialism, and on the other, attacked the right-wing KMT but maintained a soft attitude towards the Wuhan faction. The Congress documents give no evidence of any likelihood of the break-up of the United Front which happened shortly after. The CPC plunged into a long period of uncertainty, instability and turbulence.

The first five Congresses (except the first one) were normal yearly events with the number of Party members increasing with each meet. The Party was involved in organising a strong labour movement in most of the urban centres which were not under the control of warlords. To its credit go several successful strikes and in the May 30th Movement it was very active. It set up labour unions, peasant associations and women's organisations at many levels. Although Peng Pai in Guangdong and Mao Zedong in Hunan organised resilient peasant movements the Party's ideology upheld proletarian revolution as its main task and goal. In other words, even though China was not ideally suited for the application of classical Marxism the Party believed in concentrating on the urban labour. In this period the leadership showed no charisma – perhaps the overarching personality of Sun Yat-sen came in the way. Chen Duxiu was popular among the youth but he was purged in the aftermath of the Shanghai Massacre. Mao was not considered among the top rung perhaps due to his rural background and other factors (Spence 1999). The CPC's close ties with the Soviet Union and the Communist International is yet another factor which impacted on the CPC in its formative years. To sum up, one can say that the Party was unable to stand on its feet in this initial phase.

## Era of Turbulence: Sixth to the Tenth Congress (1928-73)

After the Shanghai massacre the CPC was in disarray for some time. Those who could flee to the Soviet Union organised the Sixth Congress in Moscow in 1928. This Congress urged greater emphasis on the agrarian revolution 'under the leadership of the proletariat'. Zhou Enlai, Qu Qiubai, Liu Shaoqi, Peng Pai and Li Lisan were given responsibilities to head different bureaus but it is not clear if all of them were present at the Congress.

It was at this time that the Communist revolution in China gained momentum. After his Hunan experience where Mao realised the revolutionary potential of the peasants it became clear to Mao that China's impoverished and exploited peasantry was his main constituency. Moreover, the assault by the Kuomintang also made it amply evident that there was no question of sharing power with them, power has to be wrested by force and so an armed revolution was the only alternative. With no military training behind him Mao began organising the peasants into small bands of an insurrectionist army. Soon, he and Zhu De joined forces at Jinggangshan in Hunan. This group of armed peasant guerrillas eventually came to be known as the People's Liberation Army (PLA). This begins Mao's ascendance both as a leader as well as an ideologue. While Chiang Kai-shek was busy with the Northern Expedition, Mao Zedong, Zhu De along with the small peasant army were able to get control of some territories in the southern part of China in Jiangxi province. The Communists settled there for a period of three years and established a government which was named the Jiangxi-Soviet base area government. Here agrarian and labour reforms were introduced but no Party Congress could be held as Chiang Kai-shek after being victorious in the Northern Expedition made many attempts to destroy the base area. It was in the fifth attempt that he was successful. The entire Communist paraphernalia abandoned the Jiangxi-Soviet and moved towards northern China with the Kuomintang troops after them. Called the Long March this is celebrated by the Chinese Communists as a saga of bravery, resilience and determination. The Long March made Mao the undisputed leader of the CPC. The Communists settled in Yanan in Shaanxi province in 1935 where they continued with their agrarian and other reforms. A conference held in Zunyi in the same year made Mao the supreme leader. However, the situation was never stable enough to call a Party Congress as within two years of the setting up of the base area in Yanan, Japan attacked China.

The war continued from 1937 to 1945 and ended with Japan's defeat in World War II. During this period Mao entered into a 'Patriotic United Front' with the Kuomintang which happened despite Chiang's initial reluctance. If the first United Front (1923–27) proved to be a setback for the Communists the second one gave them an opportunity to penetrate into those areas of China where hitherto they were not visible and in this way they were able to disseminate their ideology almost all over China. Mao's PLA is said to have come very close to the large masses of the Chinese peasantry during the war years. PLA grew in size and put up stiff resistance to the Japanese aggressors. In comparison the Kuomintang army left many villages at the mercy of the Japanese and fled when attacked. In this period the Kuomintang's fortunes too began to dip because as a government it failed to deliver. China's social and economic condition was appalling. The middle-classes who were the main support base of the Kuomintang lost confidence in the Party and many shifted their loyalty to the Communists. The size of the CPC increased phenomenally. While this was a welcome development for the Communists Mao was uneasy about the entry of a large number of 'bourgeios intellectuals' in the organisation. This, in his view, would take the Party away from its path. To counter the influence of right-wing elements Mao initiated a Rectifcation Campaign in Yanan which lasted from 1942 to 1944. It was after eliminating his prospective enemies and achieving substantial all round stability within the Party that Mao called for the next Party Congress after a gap of 17 years.

In 1945 the Seventh Congress was held in Yanan. Between 1928–45 is the era when the Chinese revolution takes-off. The major significance of this Congress was Mao's Report, which later came to be known as 'On Coalition Government' which lays out the roadmap for a post-revolution China. The Report expresses Mao's concerns as Japan had not still been defeated and large parts of China were under enemy control. However, this Report also makes it abundantly clear that the United Front with the Kuomintang was collapsing but Mao did not give up hope, he called for the abolition of the Kuomintang's 'one-party dictatorship' and establishing a democratic coalition government. Till this period, Mao and the Party hoped for a continuation of the United Front. A new constitution was also promulgated which superceded the earlier one enacted at the Sixth Congress. With the end of World War II and Japan's surrender, the alliance of the two parties broke formally and China slipped into a civil war. Four years later the PLA defeated the Kuomintang army and took control of the Chinese mainland.

Liberation in 1949 did not bring stability and consolidation of the gains of revolution in the short-term and hence Party Congresses were held erratically. Itself a war-ravaged country, China decided to get involved with the Korean war within months of liberation. Land reforms in the entire coutryside was one of the important measures taken up by the government and Party in the early years, and for industrial growth and development the Soviet-directed First Five year Plan was implemented. Land reforms implementation was accompanied by large-scale violence. The Eighth Congress which should have been held in 1950 was held in 1956 but major disagreements occurred between leaders and so it could not be concluded. It was in 1958 – two years later – that this Congress was concluded in the 'second session'. Differences arose over the Soviet model of development and agricultural policies. The fiasco of the Eighth Congress, which clearly revealed the disunity and factionalism in the Party, has not happened in the later period. Henceforth, unless there was substantial unity and consensus among the top leaders Congresses have not been held.

The Hundred Flowers Campaign, the Great Leap Forward, the Socialist Education Movement and the Great Proletarian Cultural Revolution intervened in the period before the Ninth Party Congress. This could, therefore, be held only in 1969 by which time Mao was able to eliminate or neutralise his rivals. The 'two-line struggle' as the Maoists preferred to call it or the ideological dispute between the pro-egalitarian lobby led by Mao and the pro-development faction led by other senior leaders from the mid-1950s to late 1960s was disruptive, destabilising and unproductive. Defence Minister Peng Dehuai was purged in 1959 and Liu Shaoqi and Deng Xiaoping also lost power in the mid-sixties. Lin Biao, the Defence Minister who replaced Marshall Peng had emerged as a prominent leader and proved himself to be a staunch Maoist by initiating within the PLA what is called a 'Mini-Cultural Revolution.' The Ninth Party Congress was Lin Biao's Congress. He read the Report where he strongly condemned the 'revisionist line' of Liu Shaoqi, who, throughout the report, was accused of being Capitalist Roader No.1, hidden traitor, renegade and scab, etc. The turbulent part of the Cultural Revolution was over and the leadership believed that Mao's enemies have been eliminated. Earlier in 1968 Lin Biao was declared 'comrade-in arms and successor to Chairman Mao.'

Within four years (1973) the Tenth Congress was held. There is no official explanation why this event was held a year in advance. However, in all likelihood it was the events of 1971–2 which necessitated bringing back Zhou Enlai into the scene (it was he who read the Report at the Tenth Congress). In September 1971 Lin Biao, accused of planning a coup against Mao died in a plane crash, Mao was left without a leader who was an organisation man. Moreover, relations with the United States were thawing with Kissinger's secret visit to Beijing. The PRC was also admitted to the UN. No one was better in international diplomacy than Zhou Enlai. This Congress marked the unannounced reinstatement of Zhou Enlai who since 1966 was completely sidelined though not purged. At this Congress Lin Biao was severely attacked and condemned by Zhou, exactly in the same language Lin attacked Liu Shaoqi in his Ninth Congress Report.

To sum up this phase it can be said with certainty that Mao was not only the unquestioned leader but Maoism became a cult. No leader remained the number two man for long. Organisationally the Party did not grow and during the Cultural Revolution it was in shambles for some time. Marxism-Leninism-Mao Zedong Thought was the ideology to be upheld, so continuous indoctrination became the norm. The theory of 'continuing the revolution under the dictatorship of the proletariat' gained prominence.

## Period of Relative Stability: Eleventh to the Nineteenth Party Congress

With the 11$^{th}$ Party Congress begins the era of stability and consensual politics in China. Any major confrontation or strife within the Party was handled well by the leadership as it did not lead to any major disruption.

The 11$^{th}$ Congress, the first one after Mao's death, remained Maoist in essence. Hua Guofeng as Party Chairman read the Political Report but the main position he stuck to was that 'class struggle is the key link' thereby not deviating from the Maoist line even though he stressed discipline and economic matters.

His Report criticised the 'Gang of Four' who were then in jail. A new constitution of the CPC was promulgated at this Congress. The closing Report was read by Deng Xiaoping who put emphasis on key phrases like 'less empty talk and more hard work' and 'seeking truth from facts' (Waller 1981: 82). Hua Guofeng, Mao's chosen successor held the position of Party Chairman, Premier of the State Council and Chairman of the Military Affairs Commission (now the Central Military Commission). Retrospectively, this Congress was criticised by the Chinese officially as being one which upheld the Cultural Revolution. Gradually, Hua Guofeng had nominal presence in the organisation and Deng Xiaoping emerged as the paramount leader. In fact, it was the Third Plenum of the 11$^{th}$ Party Congress, held in December 1978, which is the path-breaking, landmark event where Deng announced reforms for China through the slogan Four Modernisations. The Third Plenum established Deng as China's unquestioned leader and he remained so till his death in 1997. The Sixth Plenum held in 1981, was another significant event as it made a thorough criticism of the Cultural Revolution through a document titled 'On Certain Questions of Party History.' The 11$^{th}$ Congress though held after Mao Zedong's death cannot be called *per se* a transitional Congress due to Hua Guofeng's dominant role but the plenary sessions, third to sixth, were certainly transitional.

It was the 12$^{th}$ Congress, held in the aftermath of the very important plenums that marked a clear break with Maoist policies. With this begins a period marked by unparalleled political stability as well as economic growth in the CPC's history. Deng Xiaoping called it the most important Congress after the Seventh Congress in 1945. The earlier constitution was replaced by a new one. The position of chairperson was done away with and replaced by General Secretary – a clear departure from the Mao era. Deng's idea of a collective leadership was seen to be practised at this Congress. Deng's opening speech was as presiding chairman but along with him there were nine other presiding chairmen (Dittmer 1983).

Also three important measures were introduced:

- Structural Changes in the Central Political Organs as outlined by the new Constitution
- New Policy Agenda
- Personnel Changes

Hua Guofeng was demoted to the Central Committee and Deng himself vacated the position of Party Vice-Chairman but retained membership of the Politburo Standing Committee and remained Chairman of the CMC. Emphasising separation and division of powers, Hu Yaobang, erstwhile Chairman and later General Secretary, said, 'Party gives ideological and political leadership and does not administer'. In his opening speech Deng criticised egalitarianism. He said,

'Historical experiences show that egalitarianism will emerge in our country once it has a chance and disguise itself as something Communist to confuse people. Therefore, we must continue to combat the egalitarian tendency and never allow it to wreck havoc again' (cited in Dittmer 1983).

The 13th Congress was held in the aftermath of the disturbances of 1986–7 followed by Hu Yaobang's exit. Expectations were therefore somewhat subdued. In Zhao Ziyang's Report we see a major ideological reformulation in the form of 'primary stage of socialism'. However, the speech also indicates major differences among the leadership and understandably so. Zhao Ziyang as the new Party General Secretary faced a very difficult task as he had to placate leftist demands without giving up reform policies. Zhao refers to 'Right Deviationists' and 'Left Utopians' indicating the continuation of intra-party policy disputes as well as factionalism. Months before the Congress, Deng Xiaoping had to come to the defence of Zhao and he did so by dismissing a few powerful 'leftists' from their posts which prevented them from direct participation of day-to-day politics. To balance this Deng himself quit all posts except that of Chairman of the Military Affairs Commission (now called the CMC). These changes were confirmed in the 13th Congress (Vohra 1990). The new Central Committee reflected Deng's desire for younger and better educated leaders. Almost 73 percent of the CC members had college degrees (twice as many as the earlier Central Committee) and the average age was less by 11 years. Zhao made it clear that neither the Right Deviationists who want to speed up reform measures nor the Left Utopians who supported the idea of maintaining egalitarian principles are correct as China was in the primary stage of socialism. Pre-1949 China was extremely backward and 'leftist' errors between 1950 to 1970 did not help China get out of the backwardness (Goodman 1988; Young 1989). However, Zhao Ziyang had to quit the scene in 1989 for his open sympathies with the demonstrating students.

The 14th Congress may be called a path-breaking event. Jiang Zemin was at the helm. 'Socialist market economy' becomes the new *mantra.* Taking place within three years of the Tiananmen Square student protest this Congress had the imprint of Deng Xiaoping's second phase of reforms. The first decade of reforms created wealth to some extent in rural China but rapid industrialisation had not taken place and the aspirations of the newly emerging middle classes though small in numbers, were not being met by the state. The resurgence of the economic programme linking China's future with capitalist development led to the inclusion of Zhu Rongji in the Politburo Standing Committee (PBSC). Hu Jintao then aged 49 was the youngest PBSC member. Major reforms that were undertaken included the phasing out of price control, establishment of stock exchanges, the commercialisation of urban housing and the sale of land-use rights to foreign investors. After about three years of retreat the reformers were in the process of resurgence (Cheng 1994). Stress on economic growth rather than ideology become a prominent feature at the 14th Party Congress and years following it.

The 15th Party Congress was clearly Jiang Zemin's show. Deng Xiaoping, Chen Yun and Peng Zhen were all gone. Jiang's position as the legitimate heir of Deng Xiaoping was secured. Also by the 15th Congress in 1997, the second phase of reforms initiated in the earlier Congress begin to show some results. For instance, the State Owned Enterprises showed impressive growth without privatisation. This Congress, therefore, gave Jiang Zemin an opportunity to set forth his own agenda for China's development on his initiatives (Zhang and Zou 1998). Jiang Zemins's report stresses on Deng Xiaoping theory and was titled 'Hold High the Great Banner of Deng Xiaoping Theory for an all-round advancement of the cause of building socialism with Chinese characteristics.' This Congress is also seen as one where privatisation was accepted. According to one author even though without privatisation there was significant growth and productivity gains yet privatisation grew phenomenally – it reached a milestone at the Party's 15th National Congress (Lau 1999).

Strictly speaking the 16th Congress (2002) was the first Congress of the post-Deng era but it showed no major change in the general direction of the policies. However, it was significant in the sense that there was a change in top leadership following Deng's directive of term-based positions. Jiang Zemin stepped down as General Secretary amidst speculation that he may continue as CMC Chairman beyond March 2003 when the next National People's Congress was to meet. Hu Jintao was the new General Secretary. With this 16th Congress corporate leaders begin to assume independent identities in view of Jiang's 'Three Represents' which was added to the CPC Constitution through an amendment. This was necessary as the Party needed to broaden its social base and change its anti-capitalist stance in view of the fact that workers and peasants, two social groups whose interests were undermined, were strongly opposing economic reforms. Factionalism was visible as the Politburo had Communist Youth League affiliates as the biggest group, followed by the Qinghua and Shanghai factions. Princelings were relegated to the fourth position. This Congress begins transformation in the types of factions. In the 14th and 15th Congresses the opposing factions were described as leftists or rightists but with the 16th Congress the factions are from different category of backgrounds. However, the 16th Congress failed to launch major new initiatives in the much anticipated political reform, as Jiang Zemin's continuation as the CMC Chairman did cast a shadow on the real power of Hu Jintao. It was clear that Hu's style will differ from that of Jiang and there was less likelihood of him becoming the next strongman of China or even a charismatic leader (Gao 2003). Retrospectively, it can be said that it was with this Congress that institutionalised power transfer takes place making it a remarkable accomplishment in the Party's history.

Substantive policy decisions remained more or less the same as before at the 17th Congress. Hu Jintao's report repeated the catch-phrases: 'to build a well off society in an all-round way' and to adhere to the concept of 'Scientific Development'. The latter was included in the Party Constitution thus giving Hu the status of his predecessors. The new Politburo Standing Committee gave indication that Xi Jinping and Li Keqiang are to take over the two important positions after the next Congress. Many observers wrongly predicted that Li and not Xi would take over as Party General Secretary. In fact, Xi Jinping, former Governor of Fujian and Party Secretary of Zhejiang, 'helicoptered' to a position that should have been Li's. Multiple explanations were given for this: being a 'princeling' he could be trusted more, having been a sent-down youth to the countryside for seven years he had a better understanding of rural issues, his years in Fujian gave him more knowledge of issues pertaining to Taiwan, his experience in Zhejiang where economic growth has been phenomenal (Liu 2007). Before the Congress PRC intellectuals – academics and scholars – debated publicly about political reforms. They called for greater political pluralism but the Congress endorsed no significant political reform and made clear that the CPC's complete monopoly of power would continue (Dumbaugh 2007). The post-17th Congress period developments seemed positive for Hu Jintao. The Beijing Olympics were held with plenty of grandeur and became the mega-event of Twenty-First Century China. The financial crisis and slowing down of the US and other western economies made very little difference to China with its economy growing and it was in this period that China achieves the position of becoming the world's second largest economy relegating Japan to the third position. In practical terms none of these made a lot of difference but they certainly added to China's and Hu's prestige.

Amidst much speculation and rumours the 18th Party Congress was held couple of months later than usual. The Bo Xilai affair was on everyone's mind. Xi Jinping was out of public view for a few months before the Congress. It revealed serious factional rivalry at the highest levels. At the Beidaihe conclave differences were sorted out. Hu Jintao, unlike his predecessor, handed over both positions to Xi Jinping – Party General Secretary and Chairman, Central Military Commission – thereby ensuring a peaceful transition of power. Only for the second time in PRC history did an ostensibly smooth succession took place. This is remarkable in view of the fact that China is an authoritarian system. A notable departure at this Congress was that PBSC membership was reduced to 7 from 9. Jiang Zemin's continued influence was evident as of the seven members of the PBSC six (Xi Jinping, Zhang Dejiang, Yu Zhengsheng, Liu Yunshan,

Wang Qishan and Zhang Gaoli) were Jiang's men. This shows that nominally retired party elders remain powerful behind the scenes. This Congress too made no departure from the past by not introducing any new reforms. It was clear that the new group of leaders would neither initiate any measures to reduce state control over the econmy nor ease the CPC's grip on political power. Influence of party elders and powerful interest groups like the PLA and the SOEs will restrain the new leadership from initiating changes (Dotson 2012). The main message that Hu gave in his Report was the need to crack down on corruption. According to him the 'class-enemy' of the CPC was none other than graft. Within days of the Congress Xi Jinping began the crackdown on corruption. In November itself three senior officials were including one from the police were ousted from their positions (*The SCMP* 2013).

## Conclusion

On the whole the Congresses since 1982 demonstrate a peaceful and institutional succession while dissent and power struggle remain behind the scenes. The post-Mao era Congresses reflect a transformed China where power is wielded by a middle-class – urban, educated and technically skilled – through the Communist Party. Peasants and workers, the two main traditional constituents of the Party – the classes that brought the Party to power in 1949 have no real control over the reigns of power. Nonetheless, the Party remains very well organised and disciplined. The leadership has tried to give the appearance of being collective though one-man has been at the helm. (This is also the case in the most liberal of democracies across the world). Ideology has undergone a metmorphosis. To Marxism-Leninism-Mao Zedong Thought the ideas of the top leaders of the second, third, fourth and fifth generations have been added making it an eclectic ideology bearing little resemblence with Marxism-Leninism.

The first six Congresses indicate the efforts of the CPC to survive as an entity. The seventh to the eleventh Congresses strongly bear the imprint of Mao. The 12$^{th}$ Congress onwards are focused on reforms. However, one can arguably say that the Party Congresses *per se* are not really important. The events and policies pursued before and after the Congresses reveal much more about the workings of Chinese politics than the holding of the Congresses. None of the important events or decisions have happened during the Congresses. In the pre-Liberation period from the decision in 1922 to join the Kuomintang to the decision to set up the PLA in 1927, the Zunyi Conference, the decision to form the Second United Front, Yanan Rectification Campaign, and other important policies were not announced in any of the Party Congresses. Similarly in the post-revolution era from the Hundred flowers Campaign, Great Leap Forward, Cultural Revolution to the policy of Reforms and Opening Up, assessment of the Cultural Revolution to the Three Represents, Scientific Development, China

Dream and One Belt, One Road, etc. were not initiated at the Party Congresses. The one week or 10 days long congregation held in Beijing since the birth of the PRC are grand mega-events with much fanfare and glamour observed by the international community and media. It will not be an overstatement if it is compared to a carnival or festival for the 2000 plus members of the Party. The entire event is wonderfully stage-managed, well rehearsed in Beidaihe, well-organised and efficiently executed.

## REFERENCES

Brandt, C. Fairbank, J. Schwartz, B. 1959. *A Documentary History of Chinese Communism.* London: George Allen & Unwin.

Cheng, Chu-yuan. 1994. 'China's Economic Policy After the CCP 14th Party Congress,' in D.K. Vajpayee (ed.) *Modernizing China*, New York: E.J. Brill.

Dittmer, Lowell. 1983. 'The 12th Congress of the Communist Party of China', *China Quarterly,* Vol. 93, March, 108–24.

Dotson, John. 2012. 'Outcome of the CCP's 18th National Congress', *USCC,* 21 December, https://www.uscc.gov/sites/default/files/Research/18th-CCP_PartyCongress_ Overview.pdf (accessed on 22 February 2018).

Dumbaugh, Kerry. 2007. 'China's 17th Communist Party Congress, 2007: Leadership and Policy Implications', *CRS Report for Congress,* 5 December, https://fas.org/sgp/crs/ row/RS22767.pdf ( accessed on 18 January 2018).

Gao, Baogang. 2003. 'The 16th Party Congress: The Beginning of a New Era?', *China Currents,* Vol. 2, No. 1.

Goodman, David S.G. 1988.'Political Reform and Technocracy', *Pacific Review,* Vol. 8, No.1, 20–23, http://journals.sagepub.com/doi/abs/10.1111/j.1467-9256.1988.tb00231.x (accessed on 18 November 2017).

Lau, W.K. 1999. 'The 15th Congress of the CCP: Milestone in China's Privatization', *Capital and Class,* Vol. 23, Issue 2, http://journals.sagepub.com/doi/abs/10.1177/030981689906800105 (accessed on 16 September 2017).

Liu, Yawei. 2007. 'The Road Ahead: A Preliminary Assessment of the 17th Congress of the Chinese Communist Party,' *China Research Center,* August 28, Vol. 6, No. 3, https://www.chinacenter.net/tag/chinese-communist-party/ (on 20 October 2017).

Spence, Jonathan. 1999. *Mao Zedong.* New York: Viking.

Vohra, Ranbir. 1992. *China: Search for Democracy and Socialism.* New Delhi: Penguin.

Waller, Derek J. 1981. *The Government and Politics of the People's Republic of China.* New York and London: New York University Press.

Young, Graham. 1989. 'The 13th National Congress of the Chinese Communist Party and the Agenda of Chinese Politics', *Politics,* Vol. 24, No. 1, 85–91, https://www.tandf online.com/doi/abs/10.1080/00323268908402080 (accessed on 17 September 2017).

Zheng, Yongnian and Zou, Ziyang. 1998. 'Power to set own Agenda: Jiang Zemin's New Political Initiatives at China's 15th Party Congress,' in *China after the 15th Party Congress: New Initiatives, EAI Occasional Paper No.1,* National University of Singapore.

# 2

# Xi Jinping's Leadership:
## The Man and the Mission

*C V Ranganathan*

Xi Jinping succeeded Hu Jintao as General Secretary of the Communist Party of China (CPC) in 2012 at the conclusion of the 18th National Party Congress. While various policy guidelines were laid down in the customary Report to the Congress by the outgoing leader, it was soon evident from various public pronouncements of Xi Jinping that his approach and leadership style would be quite different from that of his predecessors. Xi's leadership style was characterised by populism; an unforgiving and well-publicised eradication of corruption at both high and low levels of the Party-State bureaucracy; far reaching reforms in the overall military field with a firm emphasis on undisputed Party leadership of the People's Liberation Army (PLA); and, importantly, the appeal for dedication of the entire nation to his call for accomplishing the dream of the rejuvenation of China by two important landmark dates: 2021 and 2049.

A few examples of his public statements may illustrate the above points.

> 'Peoples' longing for a good life is what we are fighting for. Our aim is to give them better education, more stable jobs, more income, greater social security, better medical care, improved housing and better environment. CPC faces severe challenges – corruption, cadres being divorced from people, some party officials indulging in bureaucratism and mere formalism. Party should supervise its own conduct' (Xi 2012).

An inspiring goal to be achieved by the whole nation was also formulated by Xi at the 'Road to Renewal' Exhibition at Beijing in the presence of the new members of the Politburo Standing Committee: 'achieving the rejuvenation of the Chinese nation is the greatest dream of the Chinese people since the advent of modern times'. This rejuvenation of the Chinese nation can be realised only when (i) 'the goal of bringing about a moderately prosperous society in all respects can be achieved by 2021,' the year of the CPC's 100th anniversary, and (ii) 'the goal of building China into a modern Socialist country that is prosperous, strong, democratic, culturally advanced and harmonious can be achieved by 2049', the year of the PRC's 100th founding anniversary (Xi 2012: 124–5). These Two Centenaries (两个一百年 *liang ge yi bai nian*) has today become the basic foundation of realising the Chinese Dream (中国梦 *zhongguo meng*).

While meeting Guangzhou Military Region Commanders in December 2012, Xi is quoted as having said: 'The PLA's core task is to develop the ability to wage regional wars in information age and conduct diversified military operations. The PLA must intensify combat readiness. Our dream can be said to be the dream for a strong nation; and for the military it is the dream for strong military. We must achieve the great revival of the Chinese nation and strong military.' In addition to these remarks during the very early days of his tenure, Xi also referred at a Politburo Study Group and at the Central Party School to 'reforms and opening up being implemented along the path of Socialism with Chinese characteristics, conducted on the premise of stability and carried out under the Party leadership while ensuring social equity' (Xi 2015).

A brief look at Xi's career trajectory would point to a wide network of elite relationships which he established on his way to the top rung of the Party hierarchy. He was a member of the Politburo Standing Committee since 2007, and also the Vice President of the PRC since 2010. Son of a comrade of Mao Zedong, Xi Zhongxun, Xi is a 'princeling', but like his father he was also a victim of Mao's 'Great Proletarian Cultural Revolution', and was a 'sent down youth' who spent time in the countryside. He has a doctorate degree in law from the Tsinghua University, and has worked in the Central Military Office (CMC), as a Secretary to then Defense Minister, Geng Biao. Xi's work experience with the Party has been in the Shaanxi, Fujian and Zhejiang Provinces and, along with one of his predecessors, Jiang Zemin, he built up a coterie of protégés from Provincial level leaders of these Provinces. Some of them have become members of the Politburo Standing Committee (PBSC), Politburo (PB) and the Central Committee (CC) formed at the 19th Party Congress.

At the 19th Congress of the CPC, Xi Jinping began his second five-year term as General Secretary of Party, President of PRC and Chairman of the Central Military Commission of the Party and the State. However, over his first term from 2012 to 2017, Xi had assumed top leadership positions either as Chair or Head of six important 'Leading Groups' and two other posts, Chair of the National Security Committee and Commander-in-Chief of the PLA Joint Operations Command Centre. Many of these posts were created and occupied by him within the first three years of his first tenure from 2012 (Li 2016: 12–3).

At the 19th Party Congress, Xi achieved a unique distinction. Portions of his lengthy Political Report to the Congress have been extracted and added as amendments to the constitution of the CPC but, unlike his immediate predecessors whose names were not affixed to their contributions to theory and practice, Xi's statements have been prefixed by his name. Only leaders of the first generation, Mao Zedong and Deng Xiaoping, have been honoured in this manner. Thus, what we have in Resolutions amending the Constitution of the Party, are appeals to all ranks of the CPC to take guidance from 'Xi Jinping Thought on Socialism with Chinese characteristics for a new era', to achieve the two centenary goals of 'national rejuvenation' and 'build China into a strong modern Socialist country'. This was to be done by following the leadership of the Party Central Committee with Xi Jinping at its core, and to realise the goals of the Belt and Road Initiative (BRI) as a shared destiny between China and the world.

From 2013 onwards, this initiative, which was first articulated by Xi in Kazakhstan, has become one of the dominant themes in Chinese foreign policy. Countries from Asia to Eurasia to East and West Europe and Africa have signaled their intention to join in this ambitious venture which seeks to bring about land and maritime connectivity by means of investments, to be made by Chinese-supported institutions, in road, rail, power and other projects stretching from Asia to Europe.

During the first three years of his leadership from 2012, Xi took several decisive actions, and made political and policy moves. Prior to the opening of the 18th Party Congress in 2012, there took place what was perhaps the biggest political crisis since the Tiananmen Square incidents of 1989. This was the arrest and trial of Bo Xilai, also a 'princeling', whose father was a close associate of Mao. Bo was accused of openly canvassing for a top position in the 18th Party Congress, of putting forth the so-called Chongqing model of development (Chongqing being the Municipality where he had previously been the Party Secretary), of encouragement of red revolutionary songs and of misusing the law to arrest and imprison alleged members of criminal gangs. When the former Police chief of Chongqing, Wang Lijun, sought asylum in the American Consulate in Chengdu and implicated Bo's wife, Gu Kailai, in the murder of a British national, the ambitions of Bo Xilai were laid to rest with his arrest, trial and eventual imprisonment. With the support of the then Premier, Wen Jiabao, Xi Jinping was praised for ordering a very transparent trial which exposed the decadent life styles of high ranking Party leaders. The social media on the net was used to publicise the trial, thus strengthening Xi's populist call for purity in the ranks of the high and low Party cadres.

The next major initiative of Xi Jinping from 2013 was the drive against corruption. With the help of Wang Qishan, a member of the Standing Committee of the Politburo and head of the Central Commission for Discipline Inspection along with the Ministry of Supervision, 172,000 corruption cases were handled and 182,000 officials investigated. By May 2016, the Xi leadership had purged some 160 leaders at Vice-Ministerial and Provincial levels on charges of corruption. Even members of the Central Committee of the 18th Party Congress were not spared, and 20 of them were purged. Also, leaders in higher positions were implicated. A member of the Politburo Standing Committee who controlled China's security and law enforcement institutions, Zhou Yongkang, and two Vice-Chairmen of the CMC, its highest-ranking generals, Xu Caihou and Guo Boxiong, were removed from their positions on charges of corruption, as was Ling Jihua, who was in charge of the General Office of the Central Committee working under Hu Jintao.

Next, Xi undertook a massive restructuring of the PLA, by revamping the PLA administrative lineup and its regional organisations and by reshuffling officers across departments, regions and services. To make the Chinese military prepared for modern warfare, these administrative measures are designed to contribute to the command and conduct of joint force operations. Some aspects of military reforms also alter the dominance of the Army through downgrading the four general departments – General Staff Headquarters (GSHq), General Political Department (GPD), General Logistics Department (GLD), General Armament Department (GAD) – thereby making the Army equal, instead of superior to, other services such as the Navy and Air Force. Another measure is the founding of the Strategic Support Force and the new emphasis attached to joint operations within the newly formed theatre-based commands. All these measures have induced foreign observers of China's military to comment that the reforms contribute to the new systems becoming like 'western style joint commands' (Li 2016: 8–11).

In keeping with the grand scheme of rejuvenating the Chinese nation by providing opportunities for all Chinese to achieve a middle-class lifestyle, at the Third Plenum of the 18th Central Committee held in November 2013, Xi announced economic policies to make the private sector the 'decisive driver' of the economy. These policies would include a roadmap for financial liberalisation, service sector development and environmentally friendly urbanisation. While the economic outlook for China in the recent past has pointed to the possibility of facing serious difficulties on account of rising domestic debt levels, the official reconciliation of what is referred to as the 'new normal' rate of growth around 7 percent (in contrast to earlier double digit rates of growth), shows that China still has one of the world's fastest growing and largest economies. According to the IMF World Economic Outlook, China is expected to grow at 6.5 percent or higher over the period 2017 to 2021. As for the problem of rising domestic debt, given the fact that banks in China are state-owned, debt restructuring is less difficult than in situations where private banks predominate.

Another major factor to be taken into consideration is that innovation-based movement up the value chain is being emphasised, over export-led growth. A 'Made in China, 2025' strategy aimed at achieving dominance in high tech industry identifies innovation as the motivating force. China's research and development investment has grown and, according to UNESCO data, China is the second largest spender in R&D, accounting for 20 percent of the world's R&D expenditure, second only to the US which accounts for 30 percent. In brief, sustained progress on the above measures would ensure China's strong growth with a concomitant rise of strategic influence.

In his Report at the Party Congress, Xi Jinping identifies the principal social contradiction to be faced in the new era is between unbalanced and inadequate development and people's ever growing needs for a better life. What this seems to indicate is that beyond making the necessary supply side structural adjustments to earlier models of development which have outlived their utility, demand side problems of urban and rural development, such as inadequate education and healthcare, housing shortages and similar micro-level issues which are critical to human wellbeing are weak areas of China's macroeconomic and social reform plans. A satisfactory balance between the two sides is a prerequisite for social stability in all regions of the vast country where past growth was dependent on state-owned enterprises and public investment, whereas the new model reflects a human capital-oriented approach. Thus, the vision of a 'people centered development' emphasised in the Report to the Congress, while accepting a lower rate of GDP growth, would be a challenging task nonetheless.

The first five years of Xi Jinping's dominance as General Secretary of CPC have resulted in the vast Party machinery exercising strict ideological oversight over liberal intellectuals and foreign NGOs. In Tibet and Xinjiang, religious and cultural activities on the part of ethnic minorities are seen as manifestations of demands for local autonomy, and all such activities are sought to be controlled. At the Fourth Plenum of the 18$^{th}$ Party Central Committee meeting in 2014, legal and judicial reforms were taken up. Surprisingly it was the first plenum in Party history that concentrated on the rule of law. While many important concrete measures were adopted, including the establishment of circuit courts and regulations for transparency in court proceedings, there was a mass persecution of human rights' lawyers and legal professionals on charges of threats to security. These are just a few examples of Xi's attempts at striking a difficult balance between various constituencies, plural socio-economic forces and the paramount preoccupation for the maintenance of stability (Li 2016).

Neighbours in South East and East Asia would view China as increasingly assertive – even belligerent – because of its extensive claims over oceanic space in the South and East China Seas. Within China, however, the Chinese public perhaps interprets Chinese actions through a patriotic prism, and Xi's proactive approach as a welcome departure from that of his predecessor, Hu Jintao. Indeed a few prominent academicians in China have questioned the continuing relevance of following Deng's advice to bide time till China became stronger and more prosperous – implying thereby that the time had come for China to become more assertive. Frequent summit-level diplomacy between Xi and Putin have placed Sino-Russian relations on a much enhanced political and economic footing. With a declaration at the Conference on Interaction and Confidence Building Measures in Asia, held in Shanghai in 2014, that 'ultimately Asian affairs should be decided by Asians, and Asian security should be protected by Asian nations' (*BBC Com* 2014), Xi Jinping seemed to assert China's right to influence regional and international issues. Such explicit global power ambitions are spelt out in his lengthy Report to the 19th Party Congress. A few examples of the above follow:

- 'We, the Chinese people, have greater confidence in our own culture. China's cultural soft power and the international influence of Chinese culture have increased significantly.'
- 'We have stepped up weapons and equipment development and made major progress in enhancing military preparedness.'
- 'We have made all round efforts in the pursuit of major country diplomacy with Chinese characteristics, thus advancing China's diplomatic agenda in a comprehensive, multilevel, multifaceted way and creating a favorable external environment for China's development.'
- 'Construction on islands and reefs in the South China Sea has seen steady progress.'
- With reference to the 'culture of Socialism with Chinese characteristics', China 'is blazing a new trail for other developing countries to achieve modernisation.'

In his Report to the Plenum of the Congress, Xi articulated what has become a national perception of China becoming a 'global leader of composite national strength and international influence', moving closer to the centre stage by mid-century. A *Xinhua* commentary refers explicitly to this ambition: '[B]y 2050…China is set to regain its might and re-ascend to the top of the world'. Complementing these thoughts in the military field, Xi has set the goal of completing the modernisation of the armed forces by 2035, with the expectation that the PLA would be transformed into a world class military by 2050.

Echoes of the role played during the Mao-inspired 'Cultural Revolution' of the 'little red book' containing miscellaneous quotes from Mao can be heard today, it seems. According to a notice issued by the CPC and carried by *Xinhua*, millions of officials across China have been asked to study President Xi Jinping's new book (his second) on governance, which contains his speeches, ideological thoughts and instructions (*Press Trust of India* 2017). From all the above material on Xi Jinping and his actions over his first term as General Secretary of the Party, including his Report to the 19th National Congress of the CPC, it would appear that there is strong resonance between his long-term mission for China, to be achieved both by domestic policies and by an increasingly assertive foreign policy. Undoubtedly there is growing asymmetry between China and almost all its neighbours in South and South-East Asia, whether from the economic or the military angles. This in turn has led to continuing dilemmas and problems between China and some of her neighbours in Asia.

As can be seen from the statements above there are obvious implications for China's international relations and their impact on China's neighbours in Asia and elsewhere. These needs to be examined objectively.

**(1) On the Chinese Model of Development and its Impact on the World**. The very Chinese model celebrated at the 19th Party Congress will perhaps hamper China's ability to lead the modern world, even if the nation's power continues to grow. China's role is restricted to 'economic globalisation' – to material and technological well being – but not to upholding certain established values which underlie international modernity, for example, free flow of information; respect for social, cultural and political pluralism; representative government; and an inclusive attitude to beneficial external influences. Irrespective of whether these values are or are not indigenous to individual countries, the revolution in communications has made them universally desirable. Also, few societies can adopt the system of a one-Party totally dominant rule, which matured in China over many decades in historical circumstances peculiar and exclusive to China.

**(2) On a Global Leader of Composite National Strength and International Influence Moving Closer to the Centre Stage by Mid-Century**: As contemporary historical experience has shown there are severe costs to be borne by great powers who are called upon to take centre stage. They are expected to uphold rules and norms that are applied and accepted universally. On quite a few occasions they are also required to subordinate their individual interests to those of the global system, and make sacrifices of lives if need be. However, the Chinese political culture seems to be averse to such unavoidable requirements. While articulations of foreign policy objectives tend to be made in highly moralistic terms, China's actual practice of its foreign relations (as with Pakistan, Zimbabwe, Maldives, etc.) is based on a value neutral approach.

(3) **On Major Country Diplomacy:** This term was first coined during the leadership of Jiang Zemin and has been in vogue since, largely to assuage the reservations that US leaders and establishments held about Chinese behaviour over a variety of issues in their bilateral and international agendas. With the advent of President Trump and his 'America first policy' and the imposition of dumping duties on Chinese high-tech products as well as difficulties faced by American investments in China acquiring the proportions of a growing US-China 'trade war', the situation in Korean Peninsula, where the American expectation of greater pressure being exercised by China on North Korea has shown some results such as the Trump-Kim summit but with little progress on the deliberations on denuclearisation, the Chinese emphasis on 'Great Power Relations' does not sound promising. In its annual 'National Security Report', the US identified China as a 'threat', a reversion to the Cold War perspective in the Chinese estimation.

(4) **On Building of Infrastructure on Islands and Reefs in the South China Sea and Chinese Military Growth:** Evidently, the building by China of infrastructure on islands and reefs in the South China Sea has no support from other littoral states of South East Asia. The rejection by China in 2016 of the decision of the Permanent Court of Arbitration involving the Philippines has added to the worsening of the disputes in the region. Referring to the Chinese approach to this dispute, a veteran diplomat from Singapore and former Foreign Secretary in the Foreign Office, Bilahari Kausikan, who has had ample negotiating experience with the Chinese said: 'China does not merely want consideration of its interests. China expects deference to its interests to be internalised by ASEAN members as a mode of thought' (Kausikan 2016: 69).

(5) **On the Expectation that the PLA would be Transformed to a World Class Military by 2050:** Through a series of assertive actions from 2012, when Xi Jinping assumed power, China's relations with major Asian powers (Japan, Vietnam, India, Indonesia, and even Australia) have worsened, leading these countries to seek mutual cooperation in the fields of defense, security, intelligence, etc. As pointed out by Edward N. Luttwak in his book, *The Rise of China Versus the Logic of Strategy* (2012): 'Other things being equal, when a state of China's magnitude pursues rapid military growth....it causes a general realignment of forces against it to coalesce in formal or informal alliances against the excessively risen power.'... 'These reactions which express the very logic of strategy ensure in themselves that China cannot concurrently increase its military strength and its diplomatic or political influence (Luttwak 2012: 257–58).

(6) **On India-China relations:** Both India and China are undergoing a process of power accumulation to establish themselves as great powers within the international system. However, it is difficult to see if either can succeed in this

exercise without the help of the other. We can expect that India-China relations will face some turbulence, given China's announced objectives of achieving the dream of rejuvenation, the strengthening of the Chinese military, and the frequency with which old differences in relations between India and China are revived. In addition the quality of China's growing relations with Pakistan in multiple civilian and military fields, despite the latter not eschewing the encouragement of terrorism against India and the conduct of military actions across the Line of Control and the international boundary in Jammu and Kashmir, shows that Beijing is reluctant to exercise its vast influence over the Pakistan establishment. Briefly put, at present the overall prevailing atmosphere for an amelioration of relations between India and China is sorely lacking. The media in both countries need to play an important role in this regard. An obsession with China on the part of India, where every foreign policy initiative by India is projected as China-centric, needs to be avoided. Similarly, on the part of China, patronising remarks about India, constant iterations of India's alleged interference in its neighbourhood and India's efforts to improve sorely lacking infrastructure within India, together do not contribute to creating favourable public opinion in either country. What is also urgently needed is to open up multiple channels for reasoned dialogues between academicians, intellectuals, businessmen, and military personnel from both sides to supplement the efforts of the two Governments through the existing mechanisms.

## REFERENCES

Li, Cheng. 2016. *Chinese Politics in the Xi Jinping Era: Reassessing Collective Leadership*. Washington: The Brookings Institution Press.

Kausikan, Bilahari. 2016. *Dealing with an Ambiguous World*. Singapore: World Scientific Publishers.

Luttwak, Edward N. 2012. *The Rise of China Versus the Logic of Strategy*. Cambridge, Mass.: Harvard University Press.

Press Trust of India. 2017. 'Millions of officials urged to read Xi's book', *The Hindu*, 24 November.

Xi Jinping. 2012. 'Remarks to Chinese and Foreign Press, *China.org.cn*, 16 November, http://www.china.org.cn/china/18th_cpc_congress/2012-11/16/content_27130032.htm (accessed on 12 December 2017).

____ . 2014. *The Governance of China*. Beijing: Foreign Language Press.

____. 2014. 'China President speaks out on security ties in Asia', *BBC News*, 21 May, https://www.bbc.com/news/world-asia-china-27498266 (accessed on 17 April 2018).

____ . 2015. 'Adhering to and developing socialism with Chinese characteristics', Politburo Joint Study Group, 19 November, http://cpc.people.com.cn/n/2012/1119/c64094-19615995.html (accessed on 16 August 2018).

# 3

# Mao to Xi Jinping:
## What happened to Deng Xiaoping's Political Reforms?

*Anurag Viswanath*

A recent phenomenon has been the rise of the 'strongman' leader – Donald Trump in America, Rodrigo Duterte in Philippines, Narendra Modi in India and Xi Jinping in China.

In India, the meteoric rise of two strong leaders, Indira Gandhi (1917-1984)[1] and Narendra Modi (1950-) was largely unanticipated. In China too, the rise of Xi Jinping (1953-) as the 'strongman' has been a surprise. Until the 2000s, Xi was the seemingly reticent leader serving in Provinces such as Hebei and Fujian and later, in Shanghai, until he came into political prominence as a member of the Politburo Standing Committee (PBSC) in 2008 and appointed as Vice-Chairperson of the Central Military Commission in 2010. At the 18th Party Congress (2012), despite being the 'heir apparent' Xi appeared the political underdog pitted against a particularly flamboyant adversary, the Party Secretary of Chongqing, Bo Xilai. In the manner that landslide victories of Gandhi in the 1980s and Modi (2014) changed the direction of Indian politics, Xi won decisively against Bo and has not looked back. This has had far reaching implications on politics in China.

As in the case of 'strongman' leaders in India in two different time periods (Gandhi and Modi), Xi has gone from strength to strength since the assumption of office. Unlike his predecessors, Xi was lucky to don all 'three hats' (General Secretary, President and Chairperson of the CMC) at one go, given that Hu Jintao (2002-2012) relinquished all positions, what has been called 'naked retirement' when he stepped down – a departure from earlier times when the departing leaders did not unequivocally relinquish one of the positions, that of the CMC.

Following his visible political triumph, Xi initiated a severe anti-corruption campaign (that many interpret as a 'purge') directed (selectively) against established cliques and adversaries. Many heads rolled including those regarded as 'political untouchables'. Several changes were made, such as the establishment of leading groups with Xi as the central figure, the increasing fusion of the Party-State and the designation of Xi as the 'core' of the leadership consolidating Xi's position.

Then came the circumscription of 'Xi Jinping Thought on Socialism with Chinese Characteristics for a New Era' into the Party Constitution at the 19th Party Congress (2017) along with Marxism-Leninism, Mao Zedong Thought, Deng Xiaoping Theory, and Theory of Three Represents. This marked a turning point as it placed Xi on par with Mao Zedong. China's reformer Deng Xiaoping had placed himself a rung lower than Mao with 'Deng Xiaoping Theory' (as opposed to 'thought'). 'For Deng it was theory (*lilun*) and for Mao, it was Mao Zedong Thought' (Mohanty 2003: 1369). In effect, Xi superseded Deng in the Communist pantheon.

In March 2018, at the National People's Congress, the stipulated two-term limit for President and Vice President (in the 1982 Constitution) was struck down paving the way for Xi's continued political presence. Indeed, observers began to liken Xi's pre-eminence as akin to the 'solitary tiger on the mountain top' – in China's competitive elite politics of several factions, an achievement of no mean significance.

Though the political dispositions of China and India are vastly different, what is causing concern in China is also what has been an issue in India – the increasing personalisation of power.

In private, Xi is said to have an enviable persona. No less enviable is Xi's carefully cultivated public profile. Xi is China's 'Number One Newsmaker', boasts a cyber-alter ego (*xuexi xiaozu*) and even has a fan club 'Learning from the Xi Fan Club' (*xue xi fensi tuan*) with 2.94 million members in 2016. Xi's is feted as a 'peoples' man 'Uncle Xi' (*Xi Dada*) and the song 'Grandfather Xi is our friend' (*Xi Yeye*) resounds in the countryside. A small book of Xi-speak called Xi's 'pocket book' is being quietly embraced alarming observers who view it as the return of Mao's 'red book'. Some cadre such as Ningbo Party chief Liu Qi have gone as far as 'issued (ing) an order to require Party members of Ningbo to always keep two booklets in their pockets' (Gore 2017a: 49). A familiar throwback from the past, the evergreen 'red' revolutionary song of the Mao years 'The East is Red' has made a comeback as 'The East is Red Once Again.'

But whether Xi's 'new era' is on the ashes of reformer Deng's era (beginning of reform, 1978 until 2012), and at the expense of reversal of several measures taken by Deng to prevent the rise of a solitary locus of power – is the question.

## Deng era – Departure from Mao

The Deng era was in itself a grand break from the Mao years (1949-1976) with '30 percent errors' such as of centralisation, personalisation and arbitrary exercise of powers. Deng sought to amend and rectify the system to prevent the recurrence of the same. In 1980, a piece entitled 'On the Reform of the System of Party and State Leadership' decried 'patriarchal traditions and over concentration of powers' calling them 'a tool for a dictator' (Lam 2015: 9; Brodsgaard 2016).

Deng sought to fine-tune and lead the system away from a 'strongman' (Mao) toward a 'collective and consensual leadership,' buffered with unwritten norms, conventions and informal rules that were followed in spirit. Deng also made a case for separation of the Party from the State, until Tiananmen in 1989 where the separation between Party and the State led to a crisis and forced a reconsideration. But many of these gradual steps were important and described as constituting 'quasi-formal' institutionalisation of the Chinese political system.

It was Deng who brought the Congresses back in. During the Mao years, Congresses failed to convene on schedule. By way of example, there was a ten-year gap between the Eighth Congress (1959) and the Ninth Congress (1969). 'Since the Eleventh Party Congress (in 1977) and the subsequent convocation of the Twelfth Party Congress (in 1982, after 5 years), Party Congresses have been held on schedule' (Fewsmith 2010: 41). They began a 'regular, evaluative function, introducing constitutional changes' (Brown 2015: 70).

Deng sought to accommodate elites, particularly Party elders by giving them a say in a new outfit, the Central Advisory Commission (CAC in 1982). The Central Commission for Discipline Inspection (CCDI in 1978) was created. Given the number of Party elders, Deng had to perforce play consummate balancer and deemed that every leadership had to have a 'core' (*lingdao hexin*) – a final arbitrator amongst equals.

## Deng's Lead to Collective Decision-making

Deng led the shift to collective decision-making (over and above a singular locus of power) because of the manner in which the Communist Party of China (CPC) is organised and the manner in which the Chinese political system is stacked.

The CPC as a mass-based, mobilisational Party achieved organisational dominance or 'hard power' through a 2000 odd network of Party Schools (under the Central Party School, CPS) which churns China's administrative elite – equivalent to écoles (France) and Oxbridge (UK) (Brown 2015: 74). This is quite different in India with different channels of appointment of the administrative elite and the political elite.

A further difference between India and China is discernable through the CPC control over the State and government through a 'control cartel' (propaganda, appointments and police) (Shirk 2007: 42) – the Party over State through the management of cadres (the nomenklatura system), and on the government through the Central Leading Small Groups (CLSG) and through the systems (*xitong*). Parallel systems shadow the other from the county to the township, namely, the Party affairs system (*dangwu xitong*) and government (*zhengwu xitong*) (Zheng 2010: 99, 103-9).

Political scientist John Burns told us that the nomenklatura system is most significant, 'because it is *the* instrument of Party control of leadership selection in institutions throughout the country' (Burns 1989: xxi). The fact that all top government officials are selected by the Party, the Party maneuvers the 'cadre-exchange system' helps gauge the primacy of the Party (Zheng 2010: 104).

Here, Deng perceived a need for Chinese-style 'checks and balances' by way of 'collective leadership' at the top and check on arbitrary exercise through the modicum of what has been called 'quasi-formal' institutionalisation.

## Deng's 'quasi-formal' Institutionalisation

Deng 'put the system back together' (Fewsmith 2010: 42) as the Party evolved into a 3-tier pyramidal hierarchy with the Central Committee (CC) of the CPC, of 200 members and alternate members, who are elected by the National Party Congress (altogether 370 odd members) (Gore 2014: 233-52).

Unlike the Mao years where revolutionary credentials were necessary and sufficient, membership became procedural. Newcomers could 'helicopter in' but only to the CC and not the hierarchies within.

The membership of the CC is again, procedural, by job-slot. CC represents a formidable 'power elite' of Provincial leaders, heads of 27 ministries, military leaders, and heads of State Owned Enterprises (SOEs). Studies reveal that every Province has two representatives, every central department is represented and that the biggest bloc in the CC is the People's Liberation Army (PLA). Deng ensured that the CC elects two other bodies: Central Commission for Discipline Inspection (CCDI) and the Central Military Committee (CMC) (Shirk 2007: 40-2).

The CC elects the 'elite within the elite,' the 25-member Politburo. The composition of the Politburo indicates the weight given to Provincial leadership, political factions, and the next generation of successors.

At the apex, is the Politburo Standing Committee (PBSC) whose membership varies between 5 to 9 members. PBSC is premised to function, 'on consensus and collective leadership.' At the 19$^{th}$ Party Congress, the PBSC line-up consists of 7 members.

Susan Shirk tells us that Party leaders do not have to stand for elections, but 'neither are they absolute dictators'. There is no electorate, but the higher echelons of the Party members and the General Secretary have to win the support of the 'selectorate' (where the election is by secret ballot). In that sense, power flows in both directions – top down and bottom up, what has been called 'reciprocal accountability' (Shirk 2007: 40).

In recent times, the Chinese press has referred to the election process within the Party with several references to a 'Straw Poll' in 2007 and in 2012 where the 400 members (full and alternate members of the 16th Party Congress and 'relevant responsible comrades') were asked to choose from a 200-odd list of names for the Politburo and PBSC (Miller 2017).

This system is underscored by retirement rules and functional responsibilities. The 13th Party Congress (1987) is considered a landmark as Party octogenarians had to relinquish their positions in the PBSC and Politburo, including Deng. This set a precedent about age requirements. This has evolved into two terms in office or what is called 'honourable' retirement (Wang and Vangeli 2016: 30). The Party does not favour those older than 68 years (or *qi shang, ba xia* 'seven up, eight down' meaning if you are 67 years old, you may go up the hierarchy, but if you are 68 years you have to come down or retire) has also become the norm. These rules and norms have ensured a steady turnover within the Party what has been called 'circulation of elites' or 'revolving elites'.

## In Xi's 'new era'

### *Leading Groups (Committees)*

Xi's 'new era' where China is no longer 'getting rich' (as was in the Deng era) but definitively 'rising' is factoring in key changes and adaptations. It appears that Deng's norms are being significantly re-shaped and re-fashioned. American scholar Andrew Walder has indicated the shift from the Deng era calling out the 'end' of 'collective leadership' replaced by a concentration of power in a singular executive (Walder 2016).

Within the locus of the Party that has been restored to primacy. 'Party as leader of everything' a theme reinforced by Xi in his Political Report (2017), Xi is in charge. Since 2012, Xi has gathered a number of institutional titles heading notably the Central Leading Group (CLG) that oversees the economy, namely Central Leading Group of Comprehensively Deepening Reform and the Central Leading Group of Finance and Economy. New ones such as Central Leading Group for Cyber Security and Informatisation, Central Military Commission Leading Group for Military Reform have mushroomed.

Formerly, CLGs were 'temporary, ad-hoc, supra-ministerial bodies understood as 'tools for individual leaders to exercise their personal preferences over different policies' (Zheng 2010: 108). The formal head of all of the CLGs was Xi, including that of economic matters considered the bastion of the Premier thereby upstaging the Premier. Of them, the Central National Security Commission (CNSC) aimed at 'mega-security' is at the apex of the army, police, foreign policy and domestic security enforcement agencies (Lam 2015: 20, 78, 121). Xi's lead over the CNSC marks the apogee of control, of the Party 'over the gun'.

There has been a change after the 19th Party Congress with the Central Leading Groups for Deepening Overall Reforms, Cyberspace Affairs, Financial and Economic Affairs, and Foreign Affairs becoming formal committees. The newly established committees have Xi Jinping and Li Keqiang at the helm. Other members of the PBSC are assigned different groups.

### *Xi's 'Kitchen cabinet'*

Xi's 'China Dream' team is manned by several of Xi's close associates, a 'kitchen cabinet' in the sense that is understood in India. Several of Xi's chosen associates bypass the Politburo and the State Council.

In fact, it has been said as much that 'Xi, Wang and Li' are China's holy trinity. Wang refers to Wang Qishan the former head of CCDI; Li to Li Zhanshu, an old colleague. The Xi-Li friendship goes back to the time when they were secretaries of two adjoining counties, Zhengding and Wuji in Hebei between 1983-1985.

Besides, Xi depends on a small inner circle of people which includes Liu He (economic advisor, Vice-Premier 2018) and Wang Huning (Party Theoretician, credited with Jiang's theoretical 'Three Represents' and Hu's 'Scientific Development' and PBSC member 2017).

It has been noted that Li Zhanshu acted as a Special envoy preparing for Xi's visit to Russia (in 2015) superseding the State Councilor; economic hand Liu He exchanged notes with U.S Treasury Secretary (in 2016) breaking the traditional hierarchy in China (Shan 2016: 47-8).

### *Corruption – 'purge' in disguise?*

Xi's anti-corruption against 'three spends' vehicles, banquets and trips of cadre (*san ge xiaofei*), against 'flies' 'tigers' and 'foxes' who have been identified as 'cauldron destroyers' (*za guo dang*) (Zhao 2016: 1168-93). Indeed, Xi's Political Report (2017) claims to have netted 1 million cases and 1.34 million Party cadres. But the general perception is that the campaign was directed against foes not friends, rivals not relatives and that it has led to policy paralysis.

In contrast, it has been said that Xi's inner circle has gone scot free[2]. Journalist Shirley Lam's article in the *South China Morning Post* on 'Mysterious Connections' (2017) which spelt out allegations against Li Zhanshu's daughter, Li Qianxin went missing (Gore 2017: 52). A mysterious America-based tycoon Guo Wenghui appeared out of the blue, hurling accusations of corruption against Wang Qishan's nephew indicating that factionalism is not dead, yet.

The campaign may have netted former security Czar Zhou Yongkang, Presidential aide Ling Jihua, military chief Xu Caihou and Party Secretary of Chongqing, Bo Xilai but as Willy Lam has noted, Xi's three richest relatives are Xi's sister Qiaoqiao, her husband Deng Jiagui and their daughter Zhang Yanan[3] who have not been under the scanner.

Disturbingly, anti-corruption fell on an antiquated extra-legal procedure called '*shuanggui*' in which individuals were 'detained and interrogated during a designated time and at a designated place' giving few opportunities for self defence (Bo 2007: 36).

**Xi has followed precedents and yet, departures from precedents:** Xi's 'new era' is of several continuities, but also several departures.

Some of the norms of entry and of exit were followed. For e.g. the retirement age currently pegged at 68 years was followed. Xi's right-hand man Wang Qishan (age 69) did not get an extension as many predicted. However, in a break from the past, Wang was given the privilege of attending PBSC meetings (as a non-voting member) and further, entered China's parliament, National People's Congress (30 January 2018). In March 2018, Wang was appointed as the Vice-President seen as a consolidation of Xi's power.

There have been notable departures the most prominent being the change in the election system to the higher echelons of the Party via a 'Straw Poll' in 2007 and in 2012. In 2017, the 'bottom-up consultative process' replaced 'a vote-based system that was open to abuse.' *Xinhua* said that the 'excessive emphasis on votes' was 'susceptible to the influence of *guanxi*, or personal connections, and often led to cronyism' (*The Straits Times,* 2017). This is seen as a political rollback.

The other departure is a delayed transition to the 'sixth generation' leadership (born in the 1960s). The PBSC continues to be dominated by the 'fifth-generation' cohort (born in 1950s). In the 25 member Politburo, there are only three members from the 'sixth-generation' cohort, namely Ding Xuexiang, Chen Min'er and Hu Chunhua. The 'sixth-generation' line-up is more prominent at the provincial but not at national level – in that sense, transition to sixth generation is inevitable, but delayed.

Finally, despite flawed successional transition in the 1980s, a 'cross-generation designation of successor' was somewhat put in place by Deng where a hand-picked successor is placed in the political limelight and prepared for the top job. In 1992, at the 14th Party Congress, Deng elevated 49 year old Hu Jintao into the apex PBSC (Lam 2015: 15) who occupied the top job in 2002 (a decade before). But the absence of a 'sixth-generation' successor designate has led to predictions that Xi may continue beyond 2022 or that succession may prove rocky – run counter to what Deng had sought to achieve.

## Lessons from India

Indian history offers valuable lessons on personalisation of power. The Gandhi years were known for the rise of the 'kitchen cabinet' and dysfunctional institutions. Mrs Gandhi was 'not (as) an institution builder but one who finds easier the personalised methods of a courtly circle' (Morris Jones 1975: 451-461; Weiner 1976: 898). The current government and ruling party under Modi have been under fire too, for peddling disinformation to obliterating opposition to blurring the lines between the party and the government.

While the General Elections in India (2019) is around the corner, the misfortunes of absolute power is best exemplified by Mrs Gandhi's dramatic fall from grace. It was not for nothing that historian Sudipta Kaviraj said, that we all remember not how Indira rose (to legitimacy) but how she fell (Kaviraj 1986: 1697-1708).

## Assessing Xi's 'new era'

How should Xi's 'new era' be assessed? There are two ways of looking at Xi's rise.

On one hand, Xi's supporters articulate a similar argument that Modi's supporters in India do – that great or momentous economic changes need stable leadership and continuity. A strong political mandate is said to be the necessary foundation for economic gains. In China, Xi holds the promise, and in India, Modi. The justification rests in China's current economic situation where the miraculous double-digit growth has slowed, and India is still playing 'catch-up'.

Historians have said that strong leadership has played a critical role at key junctures in Chinese history – and given the pressing needs of the day, Xi is no exception.

Another argument that explains Xi's rise alludes to China's elephantine bureaucracy, which demands a 'strongman'. Chinese bureaucracy has embedded interests and is characterised by lines of vertical authority (*tiao*) and lines of horizontal authority *(kuai)* where the horizontal line *(kuai,* local) is deemed stronger. Xi's centralisation of power is seen to counter vested bureaucratic interests and ensure that economic reforms stay on track. Kjeld Brodsgaard (2016) has also explained that where the legal system and disciplinary systems are concerned, the vertical line of authority (*tiao*) has undercut local lines of authority (*kuai*) tilting the balance and control in favour of the centre. In effect, what Xi may have done is hone the 'organisational ability and political reach of the CPC' – to address the laxity and ensure speedy implementation of reforms.

As for removing the term limit on the President, there are no term limits for General Secretary and Chairman of the CMC. Removing the stipulation on State President was to align all three positions. Further, the 'power reshuffle' at the leading groups may prevent entrenched interests and improve coordination as Zheng Yongnian has recently put forth (2018).

On the other hand, a scholar like Fewsmith who previously articulated 'quasi-formal' institutionalisation of the Chinese system has revised the earlier stand to argue that reading institutionalisation in the Chinese context would be erroneous because CPC is a mobilisational Party that has operated under 'domination', and yet to resolve succession issue in an orderly, institutional manner.

The Deng days of talk of the separation of Party and State seem to be over too – there is only 'division of labour' as Wang Qishan recently said.

Thus 'Xi's new era' is complex – with continuities and adaptations, seemingly an enhanced Deng Xiaoping model in the new times which combines both Mao and Deng precepts – though some have likened it as'Mao measures to walk on the Deng road' (Xiao Gongqin 2013: cited in Zhao 2016: 1187).

The rise of Xi as 'strongman', as with Duterte, Trump and Modi may have a strong economic rationale but comes ridden with inherent dangers and contradictions. Across these countries, millions are better educated netizens who access varied channels of information. Dangers stems from superseding established institutions, norms and a solitary leader at the top as the 'fountainhead' over and above institutions can be detrimental.

In China, netizens have shown their teeth briefly, and historically, there have been challengers and contenders for the leadership from within the elite circles and as China's experience with the previous strongman Mao shows, mistakes can happen. With China's control over communication channels, mistakes can be big and left unaddressed for longer than in democratic societies. With the final buck stopping at Xi, Xi's position is in itself unenviable. Nobody would know these challenges better than Xi who has indeed conceded that 'governing a big country is as delicate as frying fish'.

## NOTES

1. 'Indira is India and India is Indira,' wisecracked Deba Kanta Baruah in the 1970s, presumably, in a fit of sycophancy. Indira Gandhi is no more nor is Deba Kanta Baruah but the disturbing essence and ethos of the statement, interpreted largely as a euphemism for extraordinary personalization of power may *again* be ticking just across the Himalayan borders – in China.
2. Based on *Apple Daily*, 'Daughter of Xi Jinping's Trust Aide Active in Hong Kong As Red Second Generation Hong Konger' 10th September 2012 (accessed by Gore 2 March 2017) and *Boxun News Net*, 'Daughter of Li Zhanshu: Vice CEO of China Trust Capital in her 20s' *Boxun News Net* (accessed by Gore, 4th March 2017), Gore informs us that Li Zhanshu's daughter, Li Qianxin is the vice-president of China Trust Capital and Vice President of Huaqing Association of HK. As Gore writes, 'Huaqing is an organization consisting of children of senior officials and rich businessmen of China....They form part of a privileged class who have obtained Hong Kong residency; they are wheeler dealers between China and Hong Kong'(Gore 2017b: 52).
3. Xi's siblings 'investments in companies with total assets of $376 million; an 18 percent indirect stake in a rare earth company with $1.73 billion in assets; and a $20.2 million holding in a publicly traded technology company' (Willy Lam 2015: 38).

## REFERENCES

19th CPC National Congress: Full Text of Xi Jinping's report at the 19th CPC National Congress. 3 November 2018, http://www.xinhuanet.com/english/special/2017-11/03/c_136725942.htm (accessed on 29 January 2018).

Bo Zhiyue. 2007. *China's Elite Politics: Political Transition and Power Balancing*. Singapore: World Scientific, p.36. p.49.

Brodsgaard, Kjeld. 2016. 'China's Political Order under Xi Jinping: Concept and Perspectives,' paper presented at the *International Conference on China's Neo-socialism under Xi Jinping*, 18-19th August.

Brown, Kerry. 2015. *Contemporary China*. (Second Edition) London: Palgrave, pp.70-4.

Burns, John. 1989. *The Chinese Communist Party's Nomenklatura System*. Armonk, NY: M.E. Sharpe, p.xxi.

Fewsmith, Joseph. 2010. Elite Politics: The Struggle for Normality in David Shambaugh (ed), *The China Reader: Rising Power*. Sixth Edition (2016), New York: Oxford University Press.

Fewsmith, Joseph. 2018. Authoritarian Resilience Re-visited. paper presented at the *International Conference on China 2035: Xi Jinping's Vision for Modernization*, 24 May.

Gore, Lance L.P. 2017a. 'Rebuilding the Leninist Party,' *East Asian Policy*, Vol.9, No.1, January/March, pp. 40-9

Gore, Lance L.P. 2017b. 'Li Zhanshu to Play Key Role in Xi Jinping's Second Term,' *East Asian Policy*, Vol.9. No.3, July/September.

Kaviraj, Sudipta. 1986. 'Indira Gandhi and Indian Politics', *Economic and Political Weekly*, Vol.21, No38/39, Sep.20-27, pp.1697-1708.

Lam, Willy Wo-lap. 2015. *Chinese Politics in the Era of Xi Jinping: Renaissance, Reform or Retrogression*? New York: Routledge p.9, p.20, p. 78, p.121.

Miller, Alice. 2017. How to Read Xi Jinping's 19th Party Congress Political Report, http://www.hoover.org/research/road-19th-party-congress (accessed 20th September 2017).

Mohanty, Manoranjan. 2003. 'CPC's Fourth Generation Ideology', *Economic and Political Weekly*, Vol.38, No.14, Apri 5-11, p.1369

Morris Jones, W. 1975. 'Whose Emergency – India's or Indira's?' *World Today*, Vol.31, No.11, November pp.451-61.

Shan Wei, 2016. 'Xi Jinping's Leadership Style,' *East Asian Policy*, Vol.8, No.3, July/September, pp.47-8

Shirk, Susan. 2007. *China: Fragile Superpower.* Oxford: Oxford University Press, pp. 38-42.

*The Straits Times.* 2017. 'Revealed: How China picks its top leadership, 28 October, p. A 13

Viswanath, Anurag. 2017. 'Five Years of Xi Jinping,' *Economic and Political Weekly*, Vol.52, Issue no.41, 14th October.

——. 2017. Xi Jinping's thought raised to level of Mao, but Deng may have the last word – the wisdom of future generations may decide status, *The Financial Express*, October 30.

Vogel, Ezra. 2011. *Deng Xiaoping And the Transformation of China.* Cambridge, Massachusetts: Belknap Press of the Harvard University Press, pp.388-9

Walder, Andrew. 2016. 'Back to the Future? Xi Jinping as an Anti-Bureaucratic Crusader', paper presented at the *International Conference on China's Neo-Socialism under Xi Jinping*, 18-19.

Wang, Zhengxu. and Anastas Vangeli. 2016. The Rules and Norms of Leadership Succession in China: From Deng Xiaoping to Xi Jinping and Beyond, *The China Journal*, Issue 76, July, p.30.

Weiner, Myron. 1976. 'India's New Political Institutions,' *Asian Survey*, Vol.16, No.9, September, p.898

Zhao Suisheng. 2016. 'The Ideological campaign in Xi's China: Rebuilding Regime Legitimacy,' *Asian Survey*, Vol.56, Number 6, pp.1168-93.

Zheng, Yongnian. 2010. *The Chinese Communist Party as Organizational Emperor: Culture, Reproduction, and Transformation*, Abingdon, Oxon: Routledge, p. 99, pp.103-9.

# 4

# Xi Jinping and the Reinvention of the CPC

*Ritu Agarwal*

The 19th Congress of the Communist Party of China (CPC) has presented a new vision and outlined long term goals for both the CPC and the nation. One of the important goals set out by the Congress is to create a norm based government mechanism and the national rejuvenation of China. Since CPC is the decisive institutional agency through which these twin objectives are to be achieved, the Congress has recognised, the rejuvenation of the Party is an essential task. For the General Secretary Xi Jinping, a rectified Party that comes out of the 'struggle' within, will be more efficient and committed to serving the people as China enters a new era of socialism with Chinese Characteristics. The goal was to create an effective and strong governance and achieve people-centred development. Party leadership was projected as above the authority of any individual leader. Thus, Party building was set as an important agenda for the next five years. In this context, this paper tries to examine the new political ideas being projected by the CPC, and how these ideas address new realities of the times. Why has Party building been set as an important agenda? At this critical juncture when CPC has already completed more than 90 years since its foundation, why is there a need to rectify the 'critical mistakes' being committed in the last few years? Lastly, what is the Party's approach to governance? By including people-friendly growth and people-centred development, is the CPC poised for a new era of authoritarian Party rule?

## The 19th Party Congress: Bringing the Party Back In

The 19th Party Congress Political Report begins with introspection about the work-style and functioning of the Party in the last five years. There is a tone of self-criticism for the mistakes committed in the last years. As it was put very clearly in these words, the Party is committed to 'examining ourselves in the mirror, tidying our attire, taking a bath, and treating our ailments'. Several measurers were launched to activate the Party's mass line and initiate a campaign for the observance of the 'Three Stricts and Three Earnests' (Xi Jinping 2017a: 6). The Three Stricts and Three Earnests are: to be strict with oneself in practicing self-cultivation, using power and exercising self-discipline and to be earnest in one's thinking, work and behaviour.

The political move to strengthen governance of the CPC, began from the 18th Party Congress, when Xi Jinping took over in 2012. It means that all the Party organisations and other bodies from top to the bottom, from the Provincial to the lower levels have to be responsible to the Central Party organs. The strict adherence to Party rules is considered to be the main challenge since the Sixth Plenum of the CPC which was held in 2016 before the 19th Party Congress. During the Sixth Plenum, a document was issued concerning the nature of political life in the Party (*Xinhua* 2016). It specifically mentions that there are problems, like lack of discipline, nepotism and corruption which requires immediate attention. Each Party member should adhere to Party's theory, path, principle and its policy. To strengthen the Party leadership, it requires a critical assessment of Party's style of functioning and the behaviour of cadres. There is a need to establish strict norms and rules to be followed in the work-style and functioning of the Party which can cleanse the system and thus strengthen the Party's grip over the country. The 19th Party Congress is itself a culmination of the reinventing process, which began when President Xi Jinping took over in 2012. There is an urgent need to make CPC not simply a ruling Party of China, but to make it popular with the cadres setting the standards as role models for ordinary citizens.

CPC has started a massive anti-corruption drive in last three years of Xi's first term which resulted in political reshuffling of leaders holding important positions at the Provincial level. It was followed by the removal of many Provincial leaders from their official positions either under corruption charges or for official misconduct. The Central Commission for Discipline Inspection (CCDI) became a very powerful agency. Wang Qishan was the key person in charge of examining political misconduct or indiscipline. Ironically most of the Party officials removed, were Party Secretaries or Provincial Governor's in their respective Provinces. It was made clear that any kind of threat will be strictly dealt with. Xi mentioned that the anti-corruption campaign had built into a crushing tide, and was being consolidated and developed (Xi Jinping 2017a: 7). The main characteristics of the anti-corruption drive has been the change in the local officials position. In the last six months, almost 230 Provincial level officials were changed mainly at the Deputy level (*China News* 2016). Besides, there were a shuffle of provincial party secretaries mainly in Qinghai, Jiangxi, Shanxi and

Jiangsu. Wang Guosheng was transferred to Henan as Party Secretary from Qinghai in place of Luo Huining, who was transferred to Shanxi in place of Wang Rulin. Wang retired from the Party post in 2016 (*Caixin* 2016), and became the Deputy Director, Committee of Cultural History and Research in the Standing Committee of the 13$^{th}$ CPPCC National Committee in March 2018. Lu Xinshe, who was appointed as Jiangxi Party Secretary in place of Qiang Wei was again transferred to Guangxi Autonomous Region as a Party secretary in March 2018. Li Qiang was appointed as Jiangsu Party Secretary in place of Luo Zhijun in 2016, but transferred to Shanghai as the new Party Secretary after the incumbent Han Zheng was promoted as one of the seven members of the Politburo Standing Committee in 2017. Luo Zhijun was made the Deputy Director of Environment and Resources Protection Committee. Lou Qinjian was appointed as the Party Secretary of Shaanxi succeeding Zhao Zhengyong in 2016. In 2017, Luo Qinjian was appointed as the new Party Secretary of Jiangsu Province succeeding Li Qiang.

In less than two years in 2016, the Provinces which had regular adjustment in the Party Secretary official position are Shanxi, Jilin, Yunnan, Tianjin, Liaoning, Anhui, Guizhou, Hebei, Henan, Shanxi, Qinghai and Jiangxi. In these Provinces, the Party Secretaries were transferred as Governors to different Provinces. Too much changes at the higher positions led to ambiguity in policy formulation and inadequate implementation at the local and regional level.

The removal of high level officials at the Provincial levels led to speculation that Xi Jinping was trying to centralise power in his hands and bringing in people of his choice to important positions. There is a system of patronage based on loyalty which was clearly reflected in appointing his allies to powerful positions. However, this is not the case as corruption has never been legally defined in China. Rather corruption has been used as a double-edged sword. Its defining features is labelling somebody as corrupt by putting some charges against him. In case of the anti-corruption campaign of Xi Jinping, political indiscipline has been the key criterion in corruption charges. The scale on which this campaign was carried out, clearly gives an impression that there is a widespread notion that there has to be certain defining features to prove your credibility as a Party cadre. Earlier, most of the Provincial leaders got promotions to higher positions either by making a breakthrough in bringing economic development to the region they have been appointed or bringing political stability to the most troubled regions. Now, involvement in any kind of economic projects is considered to be the main benchmark to put cadres under corruption charges. The number of powerful Provincial leaders ranging from Bo Xilai, Zhou Yongkang and Sun Zhengcai, who were initially removed from Chongqing were virtually running independent political kingdoms in their locality (Gan 2017). To argue that they were removed without resistance is unconvincing. It seems that there is a conscious attempt to bring individuals trusted by the CPC into political positions. Their performance was not the main criteria. So, my argument is that Xi Jinping alone cannot bring in these major changes without political backing. Removal of cadres has been a part of China's political history, but it was mainly due to differences in ideological line. But now there is widespread political consensus that the Party is the leading force in China. So Party building is an important step in leading China to the future. Xi Jinping is very much the political man of CPC and cannot be seen as separate from the Party. He has been projected as a CPC leader and carries along the directives from within. To further substantiate this, the six members of PBSC are not all his political loyalists. It seems that there is an evolving political consensus within the Party to build a new political system by appointing new cadres at important official position.

## Party Building a Key to National Rejuvenation

The need for Party building is considered an important project, as China enters a new era of Socialism with Chinese Characteristics and it is linked with achieving the vision of prosperous society and national rejuvenation. People were asked to participate actively once again in the process of national rejuvenation under the leadership of the CPC. The Chinese nation has been termed as a strong and mighty force which has all the potential to go for rejuvenation. But Xi also mentioned that 'achieving national rejuvenation will be no walk in the park; it will take more than drum beating and gong clanging to get there' (Xi Jinping 2017a:13).

The national rejuvenation has been the main objectives of the Party especially during revolutionary times when Mao Zedong gave a call for building a strong and modern nation and thus united the entire country to fight a battle against the feudal and imperialistic forces. There was an attempt to mobilise people at a large scale to make them participate in the revolutionary struggles. The main idea was also to build new China away from western influences and thus devised its own national strategy to continue struggle from within and outside. Now, after many decades, there is again a call for national rejuvenation for building a new China. This new China requires zeal and enthusiasm of the people to shape it. One does not know why China at this particular point of time requires such huge mass participation for this great project or the objectives it wants to achieve. Is it using national rejuvenation as a unifying force for the people? Though people's participation is important, Xi Jinping mentioned that Party has to be the guiding force, as it has been the case in the past to realise the dream of national rejuvenation. National rejuvenation has been introduced at this stage as a force to induce the vast energies and enthusiasm among the people for the country. CPC has given once again the vision of New China which requires the CPC leadership as the single and most powerful Party all the more important. Thus, the Political Report calls for a nation-wide struggle for Party building and for national rejuvenation, to realise the China Dream of prosperity for the large sections of society.

## Xi Jinping Regime: A move towards norm based governance in China

The guiding ideology of Xi Jinping era regarding revival of the Party is more in consonance with the modern times rather than going back to Maoist ideology. One more important fact is that Mao was an important leader who tried to control Party and his words were more important than any other institutional politics. But that does not seem to be so with the current regime as Xi Jinping is trying to build more norm, rules and law based governance for present day China. The self-criticism and the rectification campaign initiated by President Xi Jinping is not just a moral campaign as in the past, rather it is a reaction and an opposition to certain tendencies among the Party cadres. CPC is not going for any institutional and organisational reform from within, rather it is sort of filling the institutional vacuum which has been created in the last few years.

The Political Report has clearly spelt out that the Party has taken tough action against the practice of formalities like bureaucratism, hedonism, and extravagance, and have staunchly opposed privilege seeking (Xi Jinping 2017a: 60). He seems to be concerned that public money is losing accountability, especially among officials holding offices in Party, Government and Military and state owned enterprises involved in misusing of public funds. In one of his speeches, Xi defined extravagance as waste, squandering of resources, expensive building programmes, endless festivals and ceremonies, a luxurious and decadent life-style, and abuse of power. He warned Party officials that 'hedonism and extravagance' will lead to decline and demise. Therefore, he has emphasised the need of selecting trained and good officials who can work as leaders of the country. He has cited corruption, extravagance, indiscipline and lack of commitment as some of the problems which are the biggest challenges to the governance of the country (Xi Jinping 2014b: 407). In speaking of achievements, Xi mentioned that the Party has made tremendous progress in curbing corruption by conducting disciplinary inspection at every Party committee in all departments at the Central and Provincial levels. Nobody was above the strict policies on corruption.

Since the reform and opening-up, China has been experiencing impressive economic development, creating wealth and improving people's living standards. Within China and outside, the CPC's role in the economic miracle has been well recognised. In recent decades, the Chinese people seem to have developed greater confidence and trust in the CPC and the national leaders as the reform policies are instrumental in the positive transformation of their lives. While it appears that the CPC enjoys popular legitimacy and general societal support to its policies, it would still be a challenge in the long run to maintain legitimacy and at the same time sustain national economic development. It can easily be seen that prosperity has become a collective pursuit and a national obsession and the ill effects of prosperity has already started showing up in Chinese social life. Decadence, wastage and mindless consumption are becoming the life styles of not only the economic elites, but the CPC leaders as well. Xi Jinping finds these tendencies as portent forces which can erode the legitimacy of the CPC leadership and degenerate China's social relations. For him, therefore, regeneration of China is not possible without changing the CPC from within. He then calls upon the cadres to embrace the true Party spirit and engage in hard work while serving the people. He is emphasising that people need to work hard once again to make their dreams of prosperity and happiness come true. It applies to the CPC itself where the Party cadres need to rethink their leadership style. Perhaps he has felt that the CPC which has governed the country for long decades is becoming yet another political Party devoid of the ideals and visions that sustained its existence until now. The time has come where the CPC has to pay attention to the public delivery of development, prosperity and happiness, but without being decadent, wasteful and corrupt. He emphasised that the time has come for the CPC to strengthen its social base once again. The question is whether the CPC becomes yet another political Party in power enjoying the privileges of office, or will it reorient to become a Party engaged with masses.

## Portrayal of Xi Jinping as a Popular Leader

Chinese President Xi Jinping has been portrayed as a popular global leader for his innovative ideas and distinctive style of political leadership by the Party. There has been a conscious attempt by the CPC to put him at the helm of political affairs. His idea of 'China Dream' envisions making China a powerful nation on the world stage and achieving a moderately prosperous society domestically. During the last five years, the world has watched Xi Jinping's constructive engagements with the ever changing global economic and political scenario with great interest. He has been dubbed as a 'reformer' who wants to deepen financial and economic reforms which is reflected in his visit to Shenzhen, the first Province to experience the Special Economic Zones during the Deng Xiaoping era. His appearance at the World Economic Summit in Davos in 2017, where he set economic liberalisation as a priority, at a time when the world is turning protectionist, grabbed international headlines. Secondly, his visit to mountainous villages in Hebei and Gansu, and meeting with common peasants helped his image as a popular leader. His economic vision for China combines national economic growth with improving living standards of the people.

Xi Jinping has been portrayed as a popular leader within China and abroad. Most of his ideas have come from his personal inter interaction and knowledge of the country as he has travelled widely around China. The experience he gained, during the various positions he held in his political career is a major plus point. His rise to power also came after doing commendable work in improving the living standard of people, whether it is poverty stricken Zhengding County in Hebei Province, Ningde Prefecture in Fujian Province (Xi Jinping 2014b: 481). Born in Shaanxi Province, he served as a Party Secretary in different Provinces and understood the complexities of China from within. He has been hailed as the man of the people and he emphasised that the Party leadership needs to engage with the masses to get the true picture of what is happening. Thus, he has set as an example for Party cadres to follow.

He has been portrayed as just another common man who has suffered all the turmoil of the Cultural Revolution very much like other Chinese citizens. During his tenure as a Party Secretary in Zhengding county, Hebei Province, he was known for setting up official initiative to collect opinions of local residents. He is also like any other common man, cycling with his daughter, giving time to his ailing father and taking a stroll with his mother. He is projected as a man with a pleasing personality.

## CPC's New Approach to Governance: Promoting People Friendly Development

The issue is, whether the CPC is using a new mask of people-friendly development to project itself as the single most capable and efficient political Party? As mentioned in the Political Report, 'we must have the determination to get rid of all outdated thinking and ideas and all institutional ailments, and to break through the blockades of vested interests'. The Political Report emphasised people-centred development, a new strategy to make Party closer to people and the society at large.

While Xi Jinping talks about people-centred development, it should not be confused with any attempt at liberal democracy. No two political systems are entirely the same, and a political system cannot be judged in abstraction without regard to its social and political context, its history, and its cultural traditions. In China's political life, CPC leadership is the main political force and strengthening the centralised, unified leadership of the Party is the most important task.

Xi Jinping is responding to problems which he has inherited from the past and therefore he emphasised that the Party has to focus on serving public interests, make administrative procedures people-friendly and also keep business interests away from Party cadres. Party cadres need to fill the social responsibility of serving the people, which most of them seems to have forgotten. The People-centred development is a much higher task than fulfilling one's own personal interests (Xi Jinping 2017a: 40). Therefore, the greatest need of the hour is political discipline, in the sense of serving people's interests rather than oneself. Only a centralised and unified leadership can ensure development which is more people-centred.

It is a twin challenge for the CPC to maintain high levels of economic growth while at the same time ensure adherence to Party line and thought among the cadres. The discipline and loyalty are two important virtues which seem to be missing among the Party cadres. The people in power are busy in their personal ambitions and forgetting the larger goals of development and economic reconstruction. China has a huge task of building a prosperous society, which is possible only when continuous efforts are made by the CPC leadership. Therefore, corrupt practices need to be curbed immediately before it gets entrenched within the system. The Party cadres are concentrating more on their recruitment and mobility rather than delivery of shared benefits. The CPC has made the Central Commission for Disciplinary Inspection a powerful body, able to take action against Party cadres suspected to be guilty of corruption. The disciplinary actions against them are stricter in nature. It is an unprecedented moment in Party history where the CPC organisation at the Central and Provincial levels, state owned enterprises, central financial institutions and centrally administered universities have all undergone close supervision and investigation. Xi Jinping, emphasised that power needs to be exercised in a disciplined manner and it should come from within. The Party cadres need to exercise power in the interest of the people and people should work as a check against the arbitrariness of political power.

In a recent Work Report at 13$^{th}$ National People's Congress (NPC), Premier Li Keqiang has spoken of a new era in the history of the country where the development and growth of China will be governed by new thoughts of Xi Jinping, and the State will be governed by the leadership of the Chinese President. Moreover, he has also talked about a new model of governance, where the CPC discipline inspection agencies will exercise supervisory functions to prevent corruption within the government. The Party will expand the supervisory network over almost all state functionaries and most of the state agencies will function thus under the leadership of the Party. He clearly indicated Party supremacy over the state agencies (Li Keqiang 2018).

The Party has once again put forward its vision of 'China Dream' as a unifying force, and to achieve that, the Party leadership is the guiding force. CPC through its new political ideas of establishing norm based government, achieving people-centred development, and making the Party line, a guiding ideology, hopes to gain popular mass support and transcend from being yet another ruling Party. However, the only question is whether the China Dream will really be the vision of common prosperity and good governance. At a critical juncture when speculation about the Party losing its relevance is rife, the Party is becoming all powerful. It is actually over to the Party now.

## REFERENCES

湖北省长王国生任青海书记骆惠宁另有任用, *Hubei shengzhang Wang Guosheng ren Qinghai shuji Luo Huining lingyou renyong,* [Hubei Provincial Governor Wang Guosheng was appointed as Part Secretary of Qinghai instead of Luo Huining], *Caixin,* 29 June 2016 China.caixin.com/2016-06-29/110096026 (accessed on 9 February 2018).

上半年230名省部级官员履新 6省份调整 "一把手", *shang bannian 230 mingsheng buji guanyuan lux in 6 shengfen tiaozheng "yibashou",* [In the last six months, 230 provincial level officials were put under corruption charges and six provinces had a change in their Party Secretary level positions], 18 June 2016, *China News,* news.China.com.cn/2016-07/18/content-38909669_2.htm (accessed on 10 January 2018).

Gan, Nectar. 2017. 'Curse of Chongqing? Probe into Sun Zhengcai evokes memories of Bo Xilai's dramatic fall,' *South China Morning Post,* 18 July, https://www.scmp.com/news/china/policies-politics/article/2103007/curse-chongqing-probe-sun-zhengcai-evokes-memories-bo (accessed on 14 November 2017).

Premier Li Keqiang delivers Government Work Report 13th NPC Session, 4 March 2018, http://live.china.org.cn/2018/03/04/premier-li-keqiang-delivers-govt-work-report-at-13th-npc-session/ (accessed on 15 June 2018).

Xi Jinping. 2017. 'Secure a Decisive Victory in Building a Moderately Prosperous Society in All Respects and Strive for the Great Success of Socialism with Chinese Characteristics for a New Era', 19th National Congress of the Communist Party of China, *Xinhua,* 18 October, http://www.xinhuanet.com/english/download/Xi_Jinping's_report_at_19th_CPC_National_Congress.pdf (accessed on 19 October 2017).

____ 2014. *The Governance of China.* Beijing: Foreign language Press.

*Xinhua.* 2016. Sixth Plenary Session of the 18th CPC CC, 11 March, www.xinuanet.com/english/2016-11/03/c-129348224.htm (accessed on 9 February 2018).

# 5

# Central Committee for a New Era

*Bhim B Subba*

In Communist Party-States, the Party Congress has two primary functions. One is the Party leader or General Secretary laying a comprehensive Political Report, and the other is the leadership reshuffle that is election or selection of the new political elites. Here I refer 'political elites' as Central Committee (CC) members who among them are further chosen to hold and head positions in different Party organs in both Central and Provincial levels. In most of the Party-State systems, elections or appointments of the political elites are deemed to be 'promotion' in the Party bureaucracy based on 'meritocracy' and 'performance' of the incumbents (Bell 2016; Chu et al. 2008). Some empirical studies on Provincial politics – at the county and township levels, 'performance' become an important criterion from upward political mobility than in the Central Committee (Edin 2003; Chen et al. 2005; Victor Shi et al. 2012). At the same time, other authoritarian literature suggests that 'the top leadership is not only concerned with regime objectives such as economic performance and political stability but also internal political struggle within the Party leadership' (Bueno de Mesquita et al. 2003; MacFarquhar and Schoenhals 2006). However, apart from the 'performance' and 'merit' variables, there are also other factors for getting elevated into the CC. Incumbent's domicile, factional affiliation, inter-personal connections (关系 *guanxi*) and work-experiences also become necessary pre-requisites in getting elevated to the CC which is constituent of both full and alternate members. In fact, every Party Congress in the reform period have considered the role of these factors in appointing delegates to the Congress and subsequently promoting them as CC members.

The order of these factors may be reconsidered. As the top leadership is decided upon through the internal process of negotiations and factional compromises or victory or defeat of groups, this outcome and the process are reflected in the composition of CC and Politburo and Standing Committee and Military Affairs Committee. Performance and merit are the same kind of factors. Merit or performance, regional representation, perspective of building present and future generations and above all putting in place of authority a group of leaders who carry forward the Party's new agenda under the new leadership become important. At the 19th Party Congress, 204 full and 176 alternate members to the Central Committee were elected amongst 2287 delegates. These delegates represented diverse regions, institutions, age, gender, ethnicity, educational and work experiences. The 176 alternate members are promoted to CC full membership when vacancies arise. They are promoted during the plenary sessions of the CC held once every year or may be retained for full five-year term until the next Party Congress and promoted to the full membership or can be retired from the CC to head state or advisory positions in the Party-State political system.

## The Central Committee – a Stage for 'elite politics'

In the Chinese system of Party-State constitutionally the National People's Congress (NPC) Standing Committee is the highest organ of authority when the National People's Congress is not in session. In practice, however it is guided by the CPC Central Committee which first formulates the policies which are then translated into laws and decrees by the NPC Standing Committee and policies by the State Council (China's council of ministers).

According to the Party Constitution, the CC is elected by the National Party Congress and is the main power centre. It is vested with power to elect the General Secretary of the Party, Politburo and its Standing Committee, Discipline Inspection Commission and the Military Affairs Commission. As the Party Congress meets once in five years, the CC meets at least once a year. On the other hand, the Politburo meets once a month and its Standing Committee once every week. Apart from electing these functionaries, it is also a policy-making institution. Once passed the National People's Congress, the State's central legislature has no reason to vote down the legislation, but to approve. With such diverse powers and functions, the CC has become the main centre of elite politics. Chinese leaders have stacked the CC with their followers and 'yes men', and its annual plenums to demonstrate their control of the Party, institutions and policies. Lin Biao, once a designated successor had recruited more than 30 percent of the CC members from the People's Liberation Army at the Ninth Party Congress in 1969 to secure his own position in the Party legislature.

Similarly, Deng leadership post 1978 had substantial presence of Cultural Revolution victims and survivors in the Central Committee which mandated launching of watershed policies of reforms and opening-up at the Third Plenum of the 11th Central Committee in 1978. These policies and leadership decisions demonstrate the role of the Central Committee in the Chinese political system and other party-states. The 19th National Party Congress in 2017 also witnessed the reshuffling of the CC under Xi Jinping. Many sitting full members, lose their CC membership positions when they fall foul of the Party line or the leader. On the other hand, many lost out in the race because of the power shift of their political patrons or other criteria such as age and term limits. The CPC history is rife with such instances. The most recent prominent figure was Sun Zhengcai, once a designated successor, was shunted out from the Party because of alleged violation of Party discipline. Thus, CC is just not the Party legislature, but also a 'grand stage' of elite power politics. It saw almost 60 percent turnover which has been maintained since the 1980s. Though most people see the CPC as a monolith, but reading the Party pronouncements carefully, it is in fact a Party of diverse opinions and stake holders. The constant stress by the Party leadership on strengthening the Party centre and obeying the Party line do indicate the presence of divergent opinion makers such as regional representations, Party and State institutions, ethnicity and gender in the Party.

## Turnover in the 19th CPC Central Committee

Since the 1980s there have been regular election of CC members where new pool of elites are elected from 2300 odd Congress delegates. The meagre political reforms led to gradual institutionalisation of age limits and official norms for the cadres to hold office in both the Central and Provincial Party bodies. These norms led to 'circulation of elites' in the CC with constant change of the membership at every Congress. By 13th Party Congress in 1987, the CC had one of the highest turnover which was approximately 68 percent. Since then the turnover is fairly about 58-60 percent. In 2017, the turnover rate for both the full and alternate CC members were approximately 62 percent (Table 1). It was only in 1969 the total turnover was more than 80 percent when majority of leaders were purged during the Cultural Revolution. The turnover however did not cross more than 40 percent in the later period until 1982 where large number of leaders returned to the subsequent CCs in the reform period.

In 2017, 78 full members and 32 alternate members of the 18th CC were re-elected to the 19th CC, almost 54 percent of the total 204 members (*Caixin* 2017). In the Politburo and its standing committee (PBSC) there was substantial change in the personnel. PB had 9 members returning with 16 new members and 5 new members (71 percent) were elected to the PBSC in 2017 with Xi Jinping and Li Keqiang retaining their positions for the second five-year term.

**Table 1. Turnover in Central Committee and Politburo (1992–2017)**

| *Congress* | *Central Committee* | | | *Politburo* | | |
|---|---|---|---|---|---|---|
| *Years* | *Total* | *New* | *%* | *Total* | *New* | *%* |
| 14th/1992 | 319 | 181 | 57 | 22 | 15 | 68 |
| 15th/1997 | 344 | 215 | 63 | 24 | 8 | 68 |
| 16th/2002 | 356 | 220 | 61 | 25 | 15 | 60 |
| 17th/2007 | 372 | 232 | 63 | 25 | 9 | 36 |
| 18th/2012 | 376 | 242 | 64 | 25 | 15 | 60 |
| 19th/2017 | 376 | 243 | 64 | 25 | 16 | 64 |

*Source*: Compiled from various official sources, see also Li Cheng, *Chinese Politics in the Xi Jinping Era: Reassessing Collective Leadership*. Washington: Brookings Institution Press, 2016.

*Note:* The Total and New Central Committee includes both Full and Alternate members.

## Regional Representation in the Central Committee: *Continuity with Marginal Change*

The composition of Central Committee indicates the nature of leadership in the Party. With the gradual demise of prominent revolutionary leaders by 1990s, the third-generation leadership under Jiang Zemin made sure his fellows from native Jiangsu made to the CC. Especially after Deng's death in 1997 just before the 15th Party Congress, Jiang had a free hand to recruit many of his close associates. Besides, lacking aura like the Long March leaders, Jiang relied on cultivating patron-client relations. In 1997 Jiang had already promoted almost 34 individuals serving in different positions in the country. In 2002, by the time Jiang left, the CC members from Jiangsu were 28. Even in the 19th CC, the number of full members is at high of 19. Similarly, Hu Jintao hailing from Anhui, but some say Jiangsu, with a Communist Youth League (CYL) background promoted his native comrades. The 17th CC had 23 members from Anhui, a substantial increase from 11 members in 2002 when he succeeded Jiang Zemin. In 2012, it came down to 13 and further reduced to just 6 members in 2017 (See Table 2). In the case of Xi Jinping, born in Shaanxi and having served in various provinces in Hebei, Fujian, Zhejiang and Shanghai, the new CC shows only slight increase in membership from Fujian province. Overall, the numbers of native born members are constant to the earlier CCs. Native born CC members from Zhejiang, Shaanxi has remained 13 and 6 in the last two Congresses respectively. Fujian had an increase of 4 more than 5 in 2012. Hebei with 18 members, Jiangsu 19 and Shandong with 30 members has biggest representation in the CC. Jiangsu and Shandong have substantial PLA CC members. This trend shows that Xi Jinping has emerged as a 'unifying leader' and recruiting associates who had worked with him in the provinces.

**Table 2. Composition of Central Committee (1992–2017)**
***(place of origin/birth)***

| *Place of Birth* | *19th* | *18th* | *17th* | *16th* | *15th* | *14th* |
|---|---|---|---|---|---|---|
| Beijing | 5 | 6 | 2 | 7 | 6 | 4 |
| Tianjin | 0 | 4 | 2 | 3 | 4 | 4 |
| Hebei | 18 | 25 | 21 | 10 | 9 | 15 |
| Shanxi | 4 | 10 | 11 | 7 | 8 | 5 |
| Inner Mongolia | 4 | 4 | 3 | 0 | 1 | 1 |
| Liaoning | 17 | 13 | 13 | 13 | 15 | 9 |
| Jilin | 2 | 4 | 7 | 6 | 8 | 6 |
| Heilongjiang | 5 | 5 | 7 | 4 | 2 | 3 |
| Shanghai | 6 | 5 | 3 | 4 | 4 | 3 |
| Jiangsu | 23 | 19 | 21 | 28 | 34 | 22 |
| Zhejiang | 13 | 13 | 11 | 14 | 15 | 11 |
| Anhui | 6 | 13 | 23 | 11 | 11 | 5 |
| Fujian | 9 | 5 | 5 | 2 | 4 | 3 |
| Jiangxi | 4 | 6 | 3 | 3 | 5 | 2 |
| Shandong | 30 | 30 | 21 | 21 | 27 | 20 |
| Henan | 9 | 11 | 10 | 13 | 5 | 5 |
| Hubei | 11 | 4 | 11 | 11 | 7 | 7 |
| Hunan | 6 | 8 | 6 | 11 | 16 | 9 |
| Guangdong | 2 | 0 | 4 | 4 | 6 | 5 |
| Guangxi | 2 | 2 | 2 | 1 | 1 | 1 |
| Hainan | 0 | 0 | 0 | 0 | 0 | 0 |
| Sichuan | 6 | 0 | 6 | 5 | 6 | 7 |
| Chongqing | 4 | 5 | 4 | 3 | 1 | 1 |
| Yunnan | 0 | 0 | 0 | 2 | 0 | 1 |
| Guizhou | 2 | 1 | 2 | 3 | 3 | 1 |
| Tibet | 2 | 1 | 2 | 4 | 2 | 2 |
| Shaanxi | 6 | 6 | 7 | 9 | 5 | 3 |
| Ningxia | 1 | 2 | 3 | 2 | 0 | 0 |
| Gansu | 4 | 2 | 1 | 1 | 1 | 1 |
| Qinghai | 0 | 0 | 1 | 1 | 0 | 0 |
| Xinjiang | 3 | 1 | 3 | 2 | 2 | 2 |
| Taiwan | 0 | 0 | 0 | 0 | 1 | 1 |
| **Total (N)** | 204 | 205 | 208 | 205 | 209 | 159 |

*Sources*: Compiled from various biographical documents by the author. Note: This excludes the alternate Members of the CC.

On the other hand, Xi Jinping being himself nominated as a Party delegate from Guizhou, and other Politburo Standing Committee members also representing different provinces than earlier Congresses show that the Party under the Xi leadership has zero-tolerance against factions (mountain-top power bases) and social networks like the *Xishan* Society (*Duowei News* 2017). Alliances such as these were formed under Ling Jihua, former head of the United Front and Hu Jintao's chief of staff who also functioned as a parallel 'power centre' ensuring native loyalties for promotion and business opportunities. Xi Jinping's anti-corruption campaign led to investigations and arrests of many alliance leaders including Ling Jihua. Ling's expulsion also led to the demise of Communist Youth League (团派 *tuanpai*) faction in the CC. The relative decline of CC members from Shanxi from 10 in 18th CC to just 4 members in 2017 indicate Xi's fight against such alliances.

Many prominent full and alternate CC members of the group also lost their candidature and were not invited to the Party Congress. Qin Yizhi, Zhao Yong, Deng Kai, Nur Bekri were some of CYL stalwarts who could not retain their CC memberships. David Shambaugh argues that it is 'unusual, as once on the Central Committee, 99 percent of the time cadres remain there until retirement age' (Jun 2017). Besides, Xi has been successful in placing his 'trusted men' in various Party organs. Observing at the Politburo and its Standing Committee and other leaders in the CCDI and Party secretaries in the provinces, Xi not only has used his Shaanxi born leaders, but also promoted leaders with whom he had worked in Fujian and Zhejiang. Zhao Leji (赵乐际), He Yiting (合议庭), Wang Xia (王侠), Zhang Youxia (张又侠) are from Shaanxi. Chen Miner and Cai Qi, Party secretaries from Chongqing and Beijing were his deputies when Xi served in Zhejiang and Fujian. Both Chen and Cai are also PB members. Xi, thus being a 'core' has built a broad 'coalition' of protégés and allies to tighten his grip in the party-state far greater than Jiang Zemin and Hu Jintao, his immediate successors.

The data shows the place of birth of the CC members. However, many of these CC members do not serve in the same provinces of their birth. The presence of more CC members from the regions north of Yangtze river like Shandong, and less from provinces from Guangdong, Sichuan, Yunnan, indicate the geographical differentiation of the political elites' representation in China. Even economic powerhouse provinces like Guangdong do not have the same presence in the CC like other economically weaker hinterland provinces. These also indicates the sharp disparity of CC representation between the northern and southern provinces and likewise, there are more CC members from the eastern coastal regions than western hinterland and minority dominated provinces.

## **Institutional Representation:** *Less from SOEs, central government functionaries and more from Provincial leadership*

Membership to the Central Committee has also come from central Party apparatus, military and State-Owned Enterprises. During the last three Party Congresses, more than 600 delegates represented these institutions. They also form a large chunk in the composition of the CC since the reform period and leading members of these institutions are further elevated to Politburo. Party apparatchiks from both provinces and centre are recruited to national leadership position. Before their elevation to the PBSC, Wang Huning, Wang Yang, Zhao Leji and Li Zhanshu were working in central Party and state institutions. Wang Huning, a Party theoretician has risen to the current position from Central Policy Research Office. Similarly, Zhao Leji was the head of Organisation Department, Li Zhanshu was member of Guizhou provincial Congress from 2010–12, and later worked in the Secretariat. Wang Yang who served as Guangdong Party secretary in 2007–12, was a vice-premier and the head of the state-council leading group on poverty alleviation and development in the 18th CC from 2012–17. He was also a member of the Politburo. In the 18th CC, almost 85 members came from the Central Party organisation and government organisation. In 2017, the delegates from central and grassroots Party organisations were 109; state bodies 186; SOEs and financial institutions had 53 and 44 respectively. Similarly, there were 253 delegates from the PLA and 50 from the People's Armed Police. But with Xi Jinping at helm, there has been a major departure in the structure of CC representation (Table 3).

**Table 3. Institutional Representation in the Central Committee (Full Members)**

| *Representation Units* | *14th/1992* | *16th/2002* | *18th/2012* | *19th/2017* |
|---|---|---|---|---|
| Central Party Organisation | 17 | 20 | 25 | 26 |
| Central state Organisation | 75 | 58 | 59 | 38 |
| PLA/PAP | 43 | 43 | 41 | 41 |
| SOEs/Financial Institutions | 5 | 12 | 17 | 5 |
| Provinces | 49 | 65 | 63 | 81 |

*Source*: Compiled by the author from various official reports.

In 2017, there has been a rapid decline of the full members especially from the central state organisations (中央国家机关 *zhongyang guojia jiguan*) from 59 in 2012 to only 38 members and 13 alternate members. However, the membership decline of the central organisations have seen cumulative increase of full members from the provinces. The 19th CC has 81 full members chosen from the provinces. Hong Kong and Macau has Zhang Xiaoming (张晓明), Wang Zhimin (王志民) and Zheng Xiaosong (郑晓松) as full member of the CC respectively. Liu Jieyi (刘结一), who is a full member, is incumbent Director of the Taiwan Affairs Office (TAO) of the CPC Central Committee and the State Council. Moreover, one may argue that the reduction of the central state organs members can also be attributed to Party's anti-corruption campaign in the state institutions.

Likewise, military has a strong presence in the CC. This year 41 full members and 25 alternate CC members are from the military. This is approximately 22 percent of the total CC strength. Xu Qiliang (许其亮) and Zhang Youxia (张又侠) are Politburo members and Vice-Chairmen of the Central Military Commission. Unlike the pre-reform years, there has been a decline of the military strength in the Politburo. After Xi Jinping came to power, there is been a considerable pruning of the Central Military Commission with more civilian control or the so-called re-institutionalisation of 'CMC-Chairman responsibility system' which was not so during Hu Jintao's stewardship, when former vice-CMC chairmen Gen. Xu Caihuo and Guo Boxiong were more powerful than the chairman. However, both the former vice-CMC chairmen and many of their clients were investigated and arrested for corruption and violation of party discipline. Nevertheless, the overall CC membership from the PLA has not changed. The membership still is at the 18th CC level.

PRC's State-Owned Enterprises (中央企业系统 *zhongyang qiye xitong*) and central financial institutions (中央金融系统 *zhonyang jinrong xitong*) have become crucial actors in China's political economic landscape. Delegates from these institutions to the last two Congresses were approximately 100. In 2017 Party Congress, there were 53 delegates from the SOEs alone. Although there were 12 and 17 full members in 16th and 17th CC, there has been a sharp decline in the 19th CC which is just 5 members. However, there has been a substantial increase in the alternate members. The three full members are Wang Yupu (王玉普), the minister of Emergency Management; Xiao Yaqing (肖亚庆) the chairman of the State-Owned Assets Supervision and Administration Commission (SASAC); and Hao Peng (郝鹏) is the Party secretary of the SASAC. Wang Yupu was the chairman and Party secretary of China Petroleum and Chemical Corporation (Sinopec). Among the 53 delegates, 3 were elected as full CC members and 7 as alternate members.

From the financial institutions, only two delegates were elected as the full members – Guo Shuqing (郭树清), Party secretary of the China Bank Regulatory Commission and Liu Shiyu (刘士余), the chairman of the China Securities Regulatory Commission. Yi Gang (易纲) the governor of People's Bank of China is an alternate member, though his predecessor Zhou Xiaochuan (周小川) was full member since 16th CC in 2002 till he retired in 2017–18. There were 44 delegates among which 2 full members and 7 were elected as alternate members.

Both the SOEs and financial sector also underwent major reshuffle in the higher echelons after the anti-corruption campaign snared high ranking cadres especially after the 2015 stock market crash in China. This can be one of the reasons for the decline of full membership in the CC from the SOEs and financial sectors. Many party and state officials had connections and collusions with the big wigs from these two sectors. However, this does not mean that the

SOEs and financial sectors are losing their status. On the other hand, the increase in the number of alternate members shows their importance in the future. Most of the incumbents both full and alternate members come from military industry, Aerospace industry, Science & Technology Corporation, Shipbuilding, Regulatory commissions and financial institutions like China Construction Bank, Agriculture Bank and People's Bank of China.

## Average Age remains the same

Since the beginning of the reform period, the Party leadership sought to appoint more younger leaders for future successions. Leaders like Jiang Zemin, Hu Jintao, Wen Jiabao, Xi Jinping, Wang Qishan were recruited during the early reform period at the grassroots Party institutions. From the Central Committee level and above, there is no term limit, but on the contrary, have strictage-limits. In 2002, Organisation Department's guidelines also re-emphasised the age-criteria for nominating delegates for the CC membership. For election and re-election as full and alternate member, a delegate or candidate shall not be more than 64 years; full ministers and provincial chiefs delegated for new CC membership should be younger than 62 years and nominated vice-ministers and vice-governors should be younger than 57 years (Li 2016). Such guidelines have ensured the Party leadership to maintain uniformity and political expediency in the time of promotion and retirement of the leading cadres in the reform era. This has considerably changed the age structure of the CC and other leading party organs.

It was speculated that Wang Qishan, former CCDI head and Xi Jinping's right hand man would retain his position on the PBSC even after reaching 69 years of age. However, Wang's departure indicates that the Party has followed this age limit criteria. The *qisan baxia* rule (if 67 years you stay or promoted; if 68 years then an incumbent must retire) until the 2017 Congress has remained intact. However, Wang Qishan, called as Xi Jinping's 'crisis man' or 'fire brigade chief' (救火队长 *jiuhuo duizhang*) has been elected as the new vice-president, a state position. However, Wang's position in the Party has not dwindled as he is not only the former PBSC member but also one of the important members of the Central Leading Group on Party-building (党建设 *dang jianshe*). Table 4 shows the average age of the core party organs which have remained status quo since the 1990s.

**Table 4. Average Age of Core Leadership**

| *CC* | *Year* | *PBSC* | *Politburo* | *Secretariat* | *Central Committee* |
|---|---|---|---|---|---|
| 14th | 1992 | 63.4 | 61.9 | 59.3 | 56.3 |
| 15th | 1997 | 65.1 | 62.9 | 62.9 | 55.9 |
| 16th | 2002 | 62 | 60.4 | 59.4 | 55.4 |
| 17th | 2007 | 62.3 | 61.8 | 56.8 | 55.3 |
| 18th | 2012 | 63.4 | 61.2 | 61.9 | 56.1 |
| 19th | 2017 | 62.85 | 62.48 | 61.71 | 57.0 |

*Source*: Compiled from various official sources, see also Li Cheng, *Chinese Politics in the Xi Jinping Era*, 2016.

Apart from the civilian leaders, the age-limit also applies for military elites. With every position and rank having specific age limit, there is uniformity in retirement level. In 2015, some trial regulations regarding promotion and demotion of cadres in both civilian and military leadership have been initiated by the Party (Central Committee General Office 2015). Though a trial, it is speculated Xi had liberally used these regulations to expel large number of leaders who were presumed to be incapable, incompetent in their work and even inactive due to health reasons (Li 2016). Similarly, some of the SOEs and financial institutions CC members also follow this norm of retirement especially if mandated by the Organisation Department.

## Education: *University graduates more*

Since time immemorial, education has been an important criterion for political mobility in Chinese society. In the early PRC years, the legacy of the revolutionary struggle led to 'Red and Experts' (红专 *hongzhuan*) debates. But with changing times and demands, today's political elites are more of the experts. Deng's emphasis on education among the elites led to many early reform era leaders to study abroad. This continues even today, as some prominent national leaders like former vice-president Liu Yuanchao, and current PBSC members like Wang Huning and Wang Yi received their advanced education in the West as visiting scholars. Scores of leaders in the past, Jiang Zemin, Hu Jintao were highly educated technocrats. Xi Jinping, Li Keqiang, Wang Huning and Liu He are no different. Besides, many educationists, scientists, scholars have been appointed in the Central Committee. If the fourth-generation leaders were technocrats, then the fifth-generation leaders are mostly educated in social sciences, law and humanities have crucial policy implications for the future. The Politburo Study sessions (*jiti xuexi*) that began under Hu Jintao continues today where members of the Politburo are lectured by scholars of repute on different aspects of politics, economics and governance. Pan Yue, the legal expert from Peking University is a CC member had often lectured the Party custodians in these sessions. The college educated CC members in the reform period has doubled to 99 percent in 2012 from mere 53 percent (Li and Whyte 2003; Li 2016). Preliminary observations of education level of the 19th CC members also stand around 98.1 percent college educated and higher degrees. Among the 25-member Politburo, nearly 30 percent of them hold doctorate degrees, and almost 5 percent have completed their Master degrees (*News Sina.com.cn 2017*).

In China, foreign educated returnees have played important roles in decision making circles. Many of these returnees have also instituted think-tanks and research institutions. Intellectuals like Hu Angang, Zheng Yongnian, Yan Xuetong, Wang Hui, Shen Mingming, Yu Keping and many others have contributed positively through constructive criticism of the policies and issues of the party-state. These scholars through their research have helped the Party leadership to shape and formulate policies. With increasing global presence of China, the role of the foreign returnee – 'turtle' (海龟 *haigui*) will be a necessity even more in the coming years.

According to a survey conducted by the CPC Organisation Department (组织部 *zuzhibu*), in 2016 alone, more than 432,000 foreign educated Chinese returned to China which was 58.48 percent increase than 2012 (*Xinhua* 2017). These returnees availing fellowships from the central government and provincial governments to study and conduct research abroad came back to serve their home provinces and departments concerned. Even when many of these *haigui* may not make it to the CC, it is likely they play important role in provincial congresses and the National People's Congress and advisory bodies like Chinese People's Political Consultative Conference (CPPCC). In the 16th CC, the foreign returnees were approximately 22 members which rose to almost 55 members in the 18th CC.

## Women and Ethnic Nationalities: *tokenism?*

Like previous Congresses, the representation of women in the CC has been marginal. Only 10 out of 204 full members are women, which meant 95 percent of the members are men. Even after the Party's hype of increase in total female delegates, the number of total women CC membership is still not adequate (Linder 2017). With 10 full and 21 alternate members, women CC membership is meagre 8.24 percent. Similarly, the minorities strength is 16 full and 23 alternate members in a 376-member body which is also just 10 percent. This still is a very long way for 23.55 million (26.7 percent) and 6.52 million (7.3 percent) national minorities Party members to become national leaders in the Chinese party-state (Organisation Department 2018). However, one positive aspect among the women and minorities CC members is that they possess college degrees mostly with technical and professional education. Thus, it also implies that women and minorities with higher level of education can move up the political ladder.

## Conclusion: New Team in the New Era

Since October 2017, Xi armed with a new ideological formulation after his name, has emerged as the powerful leader after Mao, and much more than predecessors. Xi's Political Report at the Congress depicted the continuation of the past policy directives but under the strict control of the Party. The Party in Xi's New Era seems 'conservative' than reformative. Every unit (单位 *danwei*), whether a Party, government or joint venture with foreign entities required to have a Party committee. In analysing the 19th Party Congress leadership reshuffle, there were no substantial changes in the composition of the CC. Although there were rise in membership from the provinces at the cost of central state organisations, it is likely that Xi is building his own coalition at the provinces especially from regions he served like his predecessors. More CC members from Hebei, Shaanxi, Fujian and Zhejiang were elected. Likewise, minority and periphery provinces have almost equal number of full and alternate members. Guizhou, Ningxia, Sichuan, Tibet and Xinjiang have increased CC membership which shows that Party is concerned with the plight of these regions. Many of the prominent delegates to the Congress were nominated from poor and hinterland provinces. With Wang Qishan as the state vice-president and You Quan(尤权) a secretariat member and the secretary of the CC's United Front Work Department (UFWD), the team is a 'coalition of allies' that Xi leads for the New Era (Table 5). Wang Qishan, as a deputy-director of the CC Central leading group on Party building despite not being a CC member shows his influence in the Party hierarchy. With UFWD having wide ranging powers including the ethnic minorities, religious and overseas affairs have made You Quan's task important for the Xi leadership.

On the other hand, there is also a marked decline of the CC membership from Shanxi, Chongqing and Yunnan. Many of these provinces had strong factional links to the earlier leaders such as Bo Xilai, Zhou Yongkang and Ling Jihua. Similarly, Xi also ensured that many delegates from the CYL group did not make it to the Party Congress, thereby removing their chances of CC selection.

At the same time, Xi Jinping's consolidation of power and emerging 'cult status' have undermined many institutions, as he personally heads more than a dozen of supra-powerful small leading groups (小组 *xiaozu*). Many functions of the State Council is subsumed by these *xiaozu*, and Xi heading 'Leading Small Group for the Comprehensive Deepening of Reform' is the most important supra body of elite leaders (Huang 2014). Though these leading groups were in existence since 1958, but increasingly they have coopted policy functions and bypassed government agencies. On the other hand, Deng's the separation of the Party and government (党政分开 *dangzheng fenkai*) has merely been transformed into 'division of labour between the Party and government (党政分工 *dangzheng fengong*).

**Table 5. Xi Jinping's New Era team post 19th CPC Congress (Seven PBSC members, Vice-President and United Front Dept. Chair)**

| Incumbents | Academic Qualifications | Party (Current) | State (Current) | Previous Position (Pre-19th CPC) |
|---|---|---|---|---|
| Xi Jinping (1953) | PhD, Law, Tsinghua University | General Secretary, PBSC Member, CMC Chairman | State President CMC Chairman | Party General Secretary, State president |
| Li Keqiang (1955) | PhD, Economics, Peking University | PBSC Member | Premier, State Council | 18th PBSC Member Premier, State Council |
| Li Zhanshu (1950) | BA, Political Edu. Hebei Normal University | PBSC Member | Chairman, 13th NPC Standing Committee | 18th PB Member, Director, General Office of the CPC CC |
| Wang Yang (1955) | MSc. Eng. University of Sc. & Technology | PBSC Member | Chairman, 13th CPPCC Standing Committee | Vice-premier, 18th PB Member |
| Wang Huning (1955) | PhD, International Relations, Fudan University | PBSC Member Secretary, Party Secretariat | | 18th PB Member, Member of the Party Secretariat |
| Zhao Leji (1957) | MA, Politics Central Party School | PBSC Member, Head, CCDI | | 18th PB Member, Head, Organisation Dept. |
| Han Zheng (1954) | MA, Economics East China Normal University | PBSC Member | Executive Vice Premier, State Council | 18th Politburo Member Party Secretary, Shanghai, 2012–17 |
| Wang Qishan (1948) | MA, History Northwest University, Xi'an | Deputy-Director, Central LSG for Party Building (Even though not a CC member) | Vice-President | 18th PBSC Member Head, CCDI |
| You Quan (1954) | MA, Economics Renmin University | CC member, Party Secretariat Member, Chair of United Front Work Dept. | | 18th CC Member Party Secretary, Fujian Province |

*Source*: Compiled by author from various official sources.

The CC today also seems to adhere what the leader demands, and have become just an 'approving agency' of the whims of the leader. Thus, for CC to rejuvenate itself, it not only has to play the Party's legislature but also evolve as an institution of debate and discussion. The quest for political institutionalisation has taken a back seat once again. Hope the new team or 'coalition of allies' under Xi Jinping will march towards a future of shared prosperity not only in economic well-being but also socially and politically inclusive, representative and promoting predictable collective leadership in the new era.

## REFERENCES

25 位中央政治局委员近三成是博士超五成为硕士, *25 wei zhongyang zhengzhi ju weiyuan jin san cheng shi boshi chao wucheng wei shuoshi*, [Nearly 30 percent of the 25 Politburo members are doctorates and over 5 are post graduates], *News Sina.com.com.cn,* http://news.sina.com.cn/ china/xlxw/2017-10-25/doc-ifynfvar4039170.shtml (accessed on 29 October 2017).

2017 年中国共产党党内统计公报 2017 *nian zhongguo gongchan dang dangnei tongji gongbao* [Statistical Communique of the CPC in 2017], Organization Department of the CPC, http://news.12371.cn/2018/06/30/ARTI1530343889643695.shtml (accessed on 24 June 2018)

中国共产党第十九届中央委员会委员名单, *zhongguo gong chandang di shijiu jie zhongyang weiyuan huiweiyuan mingdan,* [List of the 19th Central Committee Members of the Communist Party of China], *Caixin,* 27 October 2017, http://china.caixin.com/2017-10-24/101160238.html (accessed on 22 November 2017).

推进领导干部能上能下若干规定（试行）*Tuijin lingdao ganbu nengshang nengxia ruogan guiding (shixing)* [A number of trial provisions to promote the mobility of cadres], General Office of the CCP Central Committee, *RenminNewsnet*, 29 July 2015, http://politics.people.com.cn/n/2015/0729/c1001-27375974.html (accessed on 25 November 2017).

Bell, Daniel A. 2016. *The China Model: Political Meritocracy and The Limits of Democracy.* Princeton University Press.

Chen, Ye, Hongbin Li, and Li-An Zhou. 2005. 'Relative performance evaluation and the turnover of provincial leaders in China', *Economics Letters,* Vol. 88, No. 3. 421–25.

Chu, Yun-han, Larry Diamond, Andrew J. Nathan, and DohChull Shin, eds. 2008. *How East Asians View Democracy*? New York: Columbia University Press.

De Mesquita, Bruce Bueno. 2003. *The Logic of Political Survival.* MIT press.

*Duowei News*. 2017. 'Revealed Nearly one-seventh of the 19th CC are from Shandong', 26 October, http://news.dwnews.com/china/news/2017-10-26/60019891.html (accessed on 22 November 2017).

Edin, Maria. 2003. 'State capacity and local agent control in China: CCP cadre management from a township perspective', *The China Quarterly*, Vol. 17, March, 35-52.

Huang, Cary. 2014. 'How Leading Small Groups Help Xi Jinping and Other Party Leaders Exert Power', *South China Morning Post,* 20 January, http://www.scmp.com/news/china/article/1409118/how-leading-small-groups-help-xi-jinping-and-other-party-leaders-exert (accessed on 16 November 2017).

Jun, Mai. 2017. 'Guess who's not invited to China's key Communist Party Congress', *South China Morning Post,* 31 July, http://www.scmp.com/news/china/policies-politics/article/

2103641/guess-whos-not-coming-chinas-key-communist-party (accessed on 29 October 2017).

Li, Cheng. 2016. *Chinese Politics in the Xi Jinping Era: Reassessing Collective Leadership.* Washington: Brookings Institution Press.

Li, Cheng and Lynn White. 2003. 'Sixteenth Central Committee of the Chinese Communist Party: Hu Gets What?', *Asian Survey,* Vol. 43, No. 4, July/August, 578.

Linder, Alex. 2017. 'Only 10 of the 204 members on new Communist Party Central Committee are women', *Shanghaiist.com,* 25 October, http://shanghaiist.com/2017/10/25/communist-party-central-committee-representation.php (accessed on 26 October 2017).

MacFarquhar, Roderick and Michael Schoenhals. 2009. *Mao's Last Revolution.* Cambrdge, MA: Harvard University Press.

*People's Daily,* Chinese Edition. 2017. 河北严格党代会代表人选条件 *Hebei yange dang dai hui daibiao renxuan tiaojian,* ['19th Party Congress Delegate Elections: Strict Selection of the Representatives in Hebei]', 20 March, http://paper.people.com.cn/rmrb/html/2017-03/20/nw.D110000renmrb_20170320_4-01.htm (accessed on 21 November 2017).

Shih, Victor, Christopher Adolph, and Mingxing Liu. 2012. 'Getting ahead in the communist party: explaining the advancement of central committee members in China', *American Political Science Review,* Vol. 106, No. 1, 166–87.

*Xinhua.* 2017. 'China Focus: China welcomes more overseas returnees', 12 September, http://www.xinhuanet.com/english/2017-09/12/c_136604325.htm (accessed on 21 March 2018).

# 6

# Factionalism in the Party

*B R Deepak*

Charles de Montesquieu (1689–1755), a French political thinker, famous for his separation of power theory says that 'Constant experience shows us that every man invested with power is apt to abuse it, and to carry his authority as far as it will go (Vile 1998)'. In 1887 Lord Acton wrote to Bishop Creighton a series of letters concerning the moral problem of writing history about the Inquisition. In one of the letters he wrote his famous phrase, 'power tends to corrupt and absolute power corrupts absolutely'.[1] Corruption throughout history has been both endemic and systemic, and China, where power is absolute is no exception.

## Corruption during Revolution, Reform and New Era

Corruption during the period of Revolution, which could be extended to Mao Zedong's demise in 1976, was in an embryonic stage. Political campaigns such as 'Three Antis' (*sanfan*) against corruption, waste, and red tape, and 'Five Antis' (*wufan*) targeting bribery, tax evasion, theft of state property, bid rigging, and stealing of state economic information etc. were launched. Furthermore, Socialist Education Movement (*shehui zhuyi jiaoyu yundong*) (1963–66) and the One Strike, Three Antis Campaign (*yida sanfan*) campaign (1970–72) in the middle of the Cultural Revolution dealt a heavy blow to corruption albeit favouritism through *guanxi* never died out.

During the reform era, – stretching from Deng Xiaoping's reign, through the Jiang Zemin era and ending with Hu Jintao – corruption raised its head as China underwent massive social transformation, brought on by opening up the market economy, urbanisation and industrialisation on an unprecedented scale. China showed its enthusiasm for merchandise and encouraged private enterprise and competition. China unflinchingly invited foreign capital and technology, as a result a new nexus between the village collectives and enterprises and officials from Provincial and Ministerial level more so the department or bureau level, came into vogue. These officials are major decision makers and implement every directive of the Central government. Various studies conclude that these are the people who are most corrupt and have been investigated and punished the most. According to Liu Hui (2017) of Fudan University who has extensively studied corruption at all levels, 'village committees are known hotbeds of graft, and village officials frequently conspire to skim off money intended for economic relief, poverty alleviation, development projects, and compensation payments'. For example, officials working with large quantities of cash or other financial resources more often engage in graft, as in the high-profile case of Liu Dawei, the former Party chief of a village under the jurisdiction of Huaibei, a coal-rich city in eastern China's Anhui Province, who fled to the U.S. in 2014 after pilfering 150 million yuan (US$23 million) from the village coffer. Bao Tong, a longtime advisor of Zhao Ziyang who was removed unceremoniously in the wake of 4 June 1989 Tiananmen incident says (2015) that it was Deng who by advocating 'let some people get rich first' and 'It doesn't matter if a cat is black or white; as long as it catches mice, it is a good cat' bred corruption in China in a big way. In his words, 'in the story of China's rise, the unsung heroes are Deng's 'good cats'. Whom should they pay? In the abstract, Party authority, and specifically, Party officials – from the former Politburo Standing Committee member Zhou Yongkang all the way down to county and village cadres'. Deng, according to him 'drew new demarcation lines to define enemies. The Party would protect corruption, and anyone who opposed Party – supported corruption was a deadly foe of both the Party and the army'.

According to professor Wedeman (2012) of Georgia State University, who tracks corruption in China, 'The Procuratorate 'filed' 9,000 corruption-related cases in 1980, the 1989 anti-corruption campaign yielded some 77,400 cases. Thereafter, the average number of cases hovered around 60,000 from 1991 to 1997'. He believes that the so-called 'two track' price system was responsible for fueling a wave of 'official profiteering' (*guandao*) during the late 1980s. The Supreme People's Procuratorate's Work Report points out that in a span of 20 years between 1993 and 2012, a total of 50,660 county-level cadres, 3,031 cadres at bureau level, and 102 at Provincial and Ministerial levels were investigated. Of these, 1120 officials at department or bureau level and 54 at Provincial level were punished. The figure between 2002 and 2011 has been given as 1881 at department levels and 82 at Provincial and Ministerial levels (*News QQ* 2014). This was the time when Chen Xitong, the then Party Secretary of Beijing, allegedly amassed millions of dollars from the realtors. Corruption reached its pinnacle as close associates of highest leadership were investigated. For example, Ling Jihua, former head of the Central Committee's United Front Work

Department, and once top aide of former President Hu Jintao was exposed in March 2012 when his son Ling Gu died in a Ferrari accident that has one nude and another semi-nude girl on board. A debate set the social media ablaze as to how a son of a Party official can afford US$800,000 car! (Deepak 2016: 287).

According to the Corruption Perception Index (2016) release by Transparency International, China ranked 79 out of 176 countries with severe corruption. It says that 'increasingly, people are turning to populist leaders who promise to break the cycle of corruption and privilege. Yet this is likely to exacerbate – rather than resolve – the tensions that fed the populist surge in the first place'. Xi Jinping, who is considered a populist leader in China, initiated unprecedented anti-corruption campaign ever since he took over the leadership at the 18th Party Congress (2012). He vowed to investigate 'tigers as well as flies' for 'serious disciplinary violations' an euphemism for corruption. During Xi Jinping era, officials as high as Politburo Standing Committee members and those from the Central Military Commissions were investigated and punished, thus showing 'zero tolerance' to Party and institutional corruption as mentioned in the 19th Party Congress in 2017 (Xi 2017: 23). Hundreds of 'tigers' as well as swarms of 'flies' at Central and Provincial levels were investigated and punished. Yang Xiaodu, Deputy Secretary of the Central Commission for Discipline Inspection (CCDI)[2] revealed during a news conference post-19th Party Congress that 'since the 18th Party Congress, a total of 43 Central Committee and alternate members, and 9 CCDI members were investigated, however, the names of only 18 Central Committees, 17 alternate Central Committees and 7 CCDI members were disclosed suggesting that there are 10 more senior officials whose names are being withheld.' Yang Xiaodu disclosed that since the 18th Party Congress, a total of 440 Provincial level officials have been investigated; of these 43 are the members of the 18th Central Committee and alternate members, 9 from CCDI. Besides, 8900 officials at department or bureau level, 63,000 at county levels and 278,000 at grassroots levels have been investigated[3] Recent figures released by China's state media, says that in the last five years, 1.4 million Party officials have been investigated for corruption. *ChinaFile's* infographic website (2017) which is updated daily, provides an excellent understanding of the anti-corruption drive in China. According to the website, 'Catching Tigers and Flies' is designed to give users a sense of the scope and character of the anti-corruption campaign by graphically rendering information about nearly 1,500 of its targets whose cases have been publicly announced either by the CCDI its official media partners, or related Chinese government organs.

The most high profile cases were those of Bo Xilai and Zhou Yongkang, China's former security chief and member of the Communist Party's Standing Committee of Political Bureau until his retirement in 2012. Even though Bo

Xilai was proved during the end of Hu Jintao's term, his close associates have been proved under Xi. It is amply clear that over ambitious Bo, a princeling pitched against Xi Jinping another princeling, could not succeed to the top post in China. Moreover, Zhou and Bo are said to have met several times when Bo was heading the CPC in Chongqing. It is believed that it was Zhou who apprised Bo about Wang Lijun's asylum in the US Consulate in Chengdu, which opened the lid on British businessman, Haywood's poisoning by Bo's wife and ultimately led to the fall of Bo Xilai. On March 18th Supreme People's Court (2015) in its White Paper, 6th since 2010, indicted Zhou Yongkang and Bo Xilai of 'Non organisational Political Activities' (非组织政治活动 *fei zuzhi zhengzhi huodong*). Also, not giving Zhou harsher punishment would mean that CCDI required Zhou for revealing details of other 'tigers' and 'flies' behind the scene whom the commission is intending to investigate for 'serious disciplinary violations'. Other people who have been indicted include Jiang Jiemin, China National Petroleum Corporation's (CNPC) Party chief between 2006 and 2012; Wu Bing, who allegedly served as proxy in business for Zhou Yongkang's son Zhou Bin; Ding Xuefeng, former mayor of Lüliang, Shanxi Province; Wen Qingshan, former chief accountant of the CNPC; and Zhou Hao, former Party chief of Liaohe oil field in Northeast China. In a closed door trial in Tianjin on 22 May 2015, Zhou Yongkang, was sentenced to life imprisonment. With this Zhou became the highest-level Communist official to be convicted after the 'Gang of Four' at the close of the Cultural Revolution.

## Taking on the Military 'tigers'

As the Chinese nation plunged into the ocean to make money (*xiahai*) in the wake of the reforms, the People's Liberation Army (PLA) was also allowed to pursue business activities and contribute to the growth story of China.In 1984, during the 9-day Central Military Commission session, Deng Xiaoping urged the PLA to play a bigger economic role including taking part in commercial ventures (Tai 2001: 27). Soon the PLA businesses thrived across entire sectors including hotels and discotheques. The growth between 1986 and 1993 has been pronounced as freewheeling years by Tai. The profit making bred bribery, graft, and smuggling, on the one hand and undermined the PLA's professionalism on the other. In the face of this menace, the then President Jiang Zemin ordered the PLA to divest most of its businesses in 1998. As a result, the armed forces, armed police and political and legal organs totally divested from 19,241 enterprises (*My Old Times* 2017). As of the end of November 2016, the paid services of the armed forces and the Armed Police Force have been suspended by 40 percent it is believed that the next step would be to suspend their businesses in real estate, agriculture and sideline productions, medicine and health sectors. The anti-corruption campaign of Xi Jinping has also been regarded as his power consolidation in the Party and army alike. And since people like Zhou Yongkang, Bo Xilai, Ling Jihua and General Xu Caihou were linked to the conspiracies to dislodge Xi Jinping, therefore, besides the political 'tigers' it was equally important to take on the military 'tigers' like Xu and his likes.

The biggest military 'tigers' fallen so far are General Xu Caihou, former Vice Chaiman of the Central Military Commission (CMC) and General Guo Boxiong both held for cash for rank in 2014 and 2015 respectively. Xu was in charge of appointments and promotions of high-ranking officers in the PLA between 1999 and 2012 and is believed to have promoted maximum numbers of high ranking officials than anyone else in the CMC. It has been reported that there are 38 more people being investigated for 'serious discipline breach.' Yang Jinshan, second in command of the Chengdu Military Division is another. There are other 'military tigers' that have benefited from Xu's and Guo's positions and are being investigated. Lt. General Gu Junshan, former Deputy Director of the logistics department of the PLA is just one of them. The removal of General Fang Fenghui, former head of the CMC's Joint Staff Department, and General Zhang Yang, former head of the Commission's Political Work Department demonstrates that it will be a long drawn battle. Xi has replaced General Fang with General Li Zuocheng, and appointed Admiral Miao Hua, as head of the Political Work Department thus further consolidating his position and hold over the PLA.

## 19th Party Congress and the Anti-Corruption Campaign

Anti-corruption issue has figured prominently in the 19th Party Congress, an indication that it will continue in Xi Jinping's second term as well. While talking about his achievements in the past five years, Xi reiterates his 'action to take out tigers,' 'swat flies,' and 'hunt down foxes.' He says (2017: 7) that 'the goal of creating a deterrent against corruption has been initially attained; the cage of institutions that prevents corruption strengthened; and moral defences against corruption are in the making'. In the 13th section of his speech titled 'Exercising Strict Governance over the Party and Improving the Party 's Ability to Govern and Lead' section 6 titled 'Securing a sweeping victory in the fight against corruption' has been devoted to anti-corruption drive. He says:

> "The people resent corruption most; and corruption is the greatest threat our Party faces. We must have the resolve and tenacity to persevere in the never-ending fight against corruption. Only by intensifying efforts to address both the symptoms and root causes of corruption – by making sure that officials are honest, government is clean, and political affairs are handled with integrity – can we avoid history's cycle of rise and fall and ensure the long-term stability of the Party and the country" (2017: 60–61).

As regards some of the measures, he speaks of instituting 'a system of disciplinary inspection for city and county level Party committees in an intensified effort to address corruption that occurs on the people's doorsteps. Wherever offenders may flee, they will be brought back and brought to justice. We will work for the adoption of national anti-corruption legislation and create a corruption reporting platform that covers both disciplinary inspection commissions and supervision agencies.' No wonder in early March this year, the National People's Congress (NPC), the Chinese legislature amended the 33-page Constitution of the People's Republic of China (PRC) literally making Xi Jinping President for the life and incorporating most of his vision for the governance of China. Chapter 3 under Article 62 at number 7, the amendment read, 'the NPC is also exercising the functions and power of electing the director of the National Supervisory Commission.' The same has been added in Article 63 and 67 and elaborated under Section 7 of the same chapter.

The establishment of the Supervisory Commission is a new State organ that will give it sweeping powers to supervise over the malpractices related to corruption and other misconduct not only within the Party but across the entire government machinery. Fighting the 'tigers and flies' during the last five years has been extremely successful. It's not that China is setting up such a commission all of a sudden, pilot work was going on in some areas including Beijing. A draft law was in circulation in 2017. Finally, the law was adopted by the 13th NPC in March 2018 under which the new National Supervision Commission was established as a state organ whose jurisdiction extended over the entire system including the Party. Once the organ is established across Provinces, municipalities and counties, various overlapping functions of other supervisory agencies would be done away with, thus bringing these functions under the ambit of one authority which would be more effective and efficient at the same time. Article 100 under Section 5 has an addition relating to formulating laws by provincial governments and reporting the same to higher levels.

## Combating Factionalism

The institutionalisation of certain norms has made the leadership succession more predictable in China of late. For example, Politburo membership is subject to a norm called 'seven up, eight down' – only Central Committee members who are 67 years old or younger can get elected or re-elected into the Politburo. Similarly, a norm called 'three up, four down' applies to Central Committee membership that 63 is the age threshold. Furthermore, the rule of avoidance makes it impossible to have a posting at your home Province. Xi Jinping has largely used this norm during the 19th Party Congress.

Many China scholars have utilised certain databases for their research. One notable example is Shi, Shan and Liu's (2008) Central Committee Database that quantifies the biographies of all the Central Committee members from 1992 to 2002. In the same vein, Zhang Yang (2016) in his Ph.D collected and coded the biographies for all the full Central Committee members between 2002 and 2012. The data makes it possible to examine recent factional networks and the dynamics of factional interactions over a longer period of time.

Since Confucian hierarchy based on interpersonal relationship is deeply rooted in Chinese society, strong family ties, connections and trust determine the elevation of cadres to higher positions, albeit economic performance at Provincial level is also one of the parameters. For example, Zhou Yongkang's faction had people from his family, those who worked under him during his days as Party chief in Sichuan, his career in the oil industry, and public security. Andrew Nathan (1973) who studied factional feud during the Cultural Revolution has argued that rather than subjecting the adversaries to harsh Stalinist purges, the factions in China used ideological institutions to settle scores. Tang (1995), calls it a zero-sum game, however, he agrees that institutionalisation of the leadership succession, will strike some balance amongst the factions. Xi Jinping after coming to power has made use of his connections as well as institutional mechanism such as Party 's internal investigative arm, the CCDI to combat both the factionalism and corruption as is evident from the Zhou and Xu-Guo investigations.

Although it may not be entirely correct to reduce the Chinese politics to binary factional power struggle, however, if we glance over the powerful Politburo Standing Committee constituted in the wake of the 18th National Congress of the CPC, we find Xi and Wang Qishan against heavy odds from 'Shanghai clique' once headed by Jiang Zemin. In the same vein, Xi battled it out in Politburo with the 'League faction' once headed by Hu Jintao. It becomes clear that factions are formulated by affiliation, patronage and experience. It is interesting to note that the existence of factions has been acknowledged by the CPC News Agency, *Xinhua* in some of its commentaries in January 2015. On 3 January 2015, the Agency flagged out three such factions, namely *'mishu bang'* (Secretaries gang), *'shiyou bang'* (Petroleum gang) and *'shanxi bang'* (Shanxi gang). It pointed out that while the man behind first two gangs was once powerful Petroleum and Security czar, Zhou Yongkang; Ling Jihua, former Director of the Central Committee General Office was behind the 'Shanxi gang'. Another commentary on CPC website on 5 January once again referred to these gangs and factions and stated that 'Beneath the old tigers, there are big tigers, and behind the big tigers there are foxes and rats. Where gangs form, there are also gang lords; where there are cliques, there are also 'mountain tops,' and these kinds of 'mountain tops' are very harmful to our Party'.

## Elimination of the 'New Gang of Four'

It had become clear prior to the 18th Party Congress that the Shanghai faction's appointees were in a power struggle with Xi Jinping. The 'New Gang of Four', Zhou Yongkang, Bo Xilai, Xu Caihou, and Ling Jihua allegedly planned to sabotage the leadership succession plan agreed upon by the senior Party leaders. The man behind the scene was pro Jiang heavyweight Zhou Yongkang, who after making it to the Politburo in 2002 was also made the Minister of Public Security the same year. In 2007, he made it to the Standing Committee of the Politburo, and also the Chairman of the Central Political and Legislative Affairs Commission, an organ that oversees all legal enforcement authorities, including the police. Zhou's power stretched into various state apparatuses including courts, police, paramilitary and intelligence. The defence budget of Public Security in 2014 reached $114 billion more than the declared defence budget of PLA. It was during this period that Zhou installed his own people at the Centre, provinces, and oil and gas industry. At Centre, he wished to promote Bo Xilai as the head of the Central Political and Legislative Affairs Commission, in oil and gas there was his son Zhou Bin, and others like Jiang Jiemin, and in the provinces primarily Sichuan he controlled politics and industry through a mining tycoon Liu Han who was executed early 2014 for corruption, underworld crimes, smuggling of arms and murder (Deepak 2016: 286). A recent editorial in *Chongqing Daily* published by *Sina News Centre* (2017) has further reminded people of the harm Zhou-Bo and Sun had caused the Party and people. It said, 'Bo Xilai tried to act independently, unconventionally in order to set up his own independent kingdom; Sun Zhengcai was indolent and indifferent towards politics, he deceived his superiors and deluded his subordinates, and responded negatively to decisions of the Central leadership. These gravely violated discipline and rules of the Party and caused grave harm to the Party and the people, and adversely affected Chongqing. At present, it is necessary to eliminate Sun Zhengcai's bad influence and eliminate the legacy of Bo Xilai's evil ideology so that a clear line of demarcation is drawn and deviational tendencies at work are rectified'.

Despite the factions, there are no clear cut demarcations between the rank and file of these factions. For example, Bo Xilai, one time contender to China's top post was from the 'princeling' faction but was a hard core neo-Maoist. It was he who initiated the so called 'singing red songs and strike hard the criminals' (唱红打黑 *chang hong da hei*) campaign in Sichuan, and perhaps became the second Lin Biao in Chinese history. This faction used Mao as their shield, and has extreme nationalistic tendencies. Bo Xilai and the so called angry youths or *fenqing* (愤青) is a point of reference. The omission of Mao Zedong's thought in their speeches and debates by Jiang Zemin, especially Hu Jintao and now by Xi has provided the 'Maoist' an opportunity to reemphasise values of Mao's revolution and dislodge the reformers. However, so far the reformers have had an upper hand. If Wang Yang could be considered a neo-liberal, he is also a *tuanpai*. It was under Hu Jintao's regime that he served in various Provinces such as Anhui, Chongqing, before Bo Xilai took over in 2007 and then Guangdong. Therefore, there are no clear cut distinctions between the factions, one may cross lines depending on the circumstances, for example Zhou Yongkang could be considered a Jiang protégée but Jiang agreed to penalise him when approached by Xi in the wake of Zhou-Bo expose.

Although Xi Jinping has not associated himself with any faction, yet analysts are of the view that Xi has gradually created a 'Fujian/Zhejiang faction.' The appointments of Wang Xiaohong, Vice Mayor of Beijing and since 2016 Vice-Minister of the Ministry of Public Security; Deng Weiping, Secretary of the Party Disciplinary Commission of the Public Security Ministry, and Chen Min'er, Party Secretary of Chongqing are some of the people who have worked for Xi Jinping in various capacities. It is believed that Xi may groom Chen as his ultimate successor, though it is too early to say after the removal of the presidential terms limits.

## Conclusion

Striking hard on corruption has been used by various Chinese leaders to boost their public image. Bo Xilai's campaign 'singing red songs and striking hard on criminals' was no different and was endorsed by Zhou Yongkang during his Chongqing visit in 2010. It was also Zhou who told Bo how to deal with Wang Lijun's defection to the US Consulate, as revealed by Bo during his trial in August 2013. 'Leaking state secrets' by Zhou was that he warned Bo Xilai in 2012 that Bo was about to be ousted. The scandal not only halted Bo's campaign as a credible contender to CPC's top post but also opened up a pandora's box, which now implicated his patron Zhou Yongkang. It is also clear that irrespective of your affiliation to a particular faction there is a startling degree of widespread corruption and abuse of power among high-ranking leaders, more so at the bureau and provincial levels as various studies show. Nepotism and cronyism remains entrenched. A recent *weibo* post that has been deleted within hours since it surfaced, for violating China's law, makes just this point. The post titled 'Political conmen of a County' by Peng Junqi, a Ph.D researcher at China's prestigious university reveals that in Xinye county in Henan, of 2018 cadres he investigated at section and director level posts, without exception hailed from 161 political families. It has continued generation after generation, and it was impossible for an outsider to join the bureaucratic ranks in this county.

Unlike Zhou Yongkang and Bo Xilai, Xi Jinping has no solid power base. Nonetheless, he has proved that he has handled the statecraft with a master strategy. Xi has neither aligned himself to the reformers nor the conservatives, for he is aware that both the reformers and conservatives are very strong in China; siding with anyone will invite trouble. Conversely, he has unfolded the agenda that has forced both the camps to lend their support to Xi. For example his pet project China Dream is not his creation as generally attributed, rather it was a PLA colonel Liu Mingfu who wrote a book titled *China Dream: Great Power Thinking and Strategic Posture in the Post American Era* in 2009, and expounded the notion. The book is typical of Maoist and Sino-centric ideology; it was written to denounce the 'peaceful development of China' by the reformists. It may be remembered that the word 'peaceful rise' was replaced with 'peaceful development' in a white paper by the Chinese government in 2006. Colonel Liu rather advocates military rise of China and believes that China should surpass the US as number one military power of the world. No wonder the book was so popular and Hu Jintao had to ban the reprinting of the book. Under Xi, reprint of the book has been allowed. In the same vein, Xi took the notion of 'Silk Road Economic Belt and 21$^{st}$ Century Maritime Silk Road' an idea of the reformists that is been increasingly seen as a game changer as far as geo-economics and geopolitics across continents is concerned.

Furthermore, in order to diminish the influence of Zhou Yongkang in China's security apparatus, in an unprecedented move Xi created a National Security Commission, which controls the police, intelligence and judicial apparatuses and became its Chairman. In order to keep the reformists under his command, he created Central Leading Group for Comprehensibly Deepening Reforms and became its head. In order to take ultimate control of the People's Liberation Army, he reorganised previous seven military regions into five theatre commands, and assumed the title of Commander in Chief of the PLA. Xi, therefore, has displayed enormous wisdom, patience and ultimate art of statecraft, and has emerged as the strongest leaders of the CPC since Mao Zedong. All this was in evident through the proceedings of the 19$^{th}$ National Congress of the CPC. Nevertheless, the debate on corruption and factionalism as well as the fight against these will be continued and intensified.

## NOTES

1. Lord Acton wrote three letters to Bishop Creighton in 1887; this is a quote from the first letter written on April 5, 1887.
2. The party fights corruption and abuses of power mainly through the central and local discipline inspection commissions Disciplinary inspection was institutionalised in 1929 when the Central Supervision Commission was created. In 1978, the party reinstated the Central Discipline Inspection Commission (CDIC) A branch of CDIC was established in each province, prefecture, county, and township.
3. 十九大后打虎路线图:还有10高官落马未公布 *shijiu da hou hu luxian tu: Hai you 10 gaoguan luoma wei gongbu* [Roadmap for catching the tigers after 19$^{th}$ Party Congress:

There are 10 more whose names are being withheld], *Vision Times*, https://www.secretchina.com/news/gb/2017/10/20/838822.html (accessed on 26 October 2017).

## REFERENCES


Action, Lord. 1887. '*Acton-Creighton Correspondence* (1887)' available at http://oll.libertyfund.org/titles/2254

Bao, Tong. 2015. 鲍彤纪念六四，兼谈邓小平与中国的腐败'，纽约时报中文版，*Bao Tong jinian liusi, jiantan Deng Xiaoping yu Zhongguo de fubai, The New York Times* (Chinese),3 June, It was translated into English by the same paper titled ["How Deng Xiaoping Helped Create a Corrupt China]." https://cn.nytimes.com/opinion/20150603/cc03bao/

Deepak, B R. 2016. *India and China: Foreign Policy Approaches and Responses*. New Delhi: Vij Books.

Gu Ren. 2015. '党内还有多少帮派和山头?' *dang nei hai you duoshao bangpai he Shantou?* [How many factions and mountain tops are still there in the party?] 5 January, 中国共产党新闻网 *People's Daily Online*, http://cpc.people.com.cn/pinglun/n/2015/0105/c241220-26327893.html (accessed on 5 June 2017).

Li Hui. 2017. 'Mapping Corruption in China: What are the distinctions between bribery and graft, and which officials are most likely to stray to each side?', *Sixth Tone*, November 20, 2017. http://www.sixthtone.com/news/1000960/mapping-corruption-in-china

Miller, Alice. 2017. 'The Trouble with Factions', *China Leadership Monitor*, Vol. 46 http://www.hoover.org/sites/default/files/research/docs/clm46am-2.pdf

*My Old Times.com*. 2017. '清理"军队经商"的来龙去脉： 幸亏被习总制止， 否则自毁长城!', *qingji jundui jingshang de lailong gumai: xingkui bei xi zong zhizhi fouze zi hui changcheng!* (The ins and outs of clearing up the 'military business': thanks to the total stop put up by president Xi, otherwise the Great Wall would have collapsed!) http://www.myoldtime.com/a/shidai/zatan/2017/1115/11308.html (accessed on 16 December 2017).

*News QQ.com*. 2014. '20年立案 / 落马官员数据图' *20 nian li'an/luoma guanyuan shuju tu*, [Graphical depiction of people investigated and punished in the last 20 years], available at http://news.qq.com/zt2014/20ffdata/index.htm (accessed on 27 July 2017).

*Sina News Centre [SNC]*. 2017. '重庆日报：薄熙来搞独立王国孙政才消极应付中央' *Chongqing Ribao: Bo Xilai gao duli wangguo Sun Zhengcai xiaoji yingfu zhongyang* (*Chongqing Daily*: Bo Xilai created an independent kingdom and Sun Zhengcai negatively responded to the Central Government) http://news.sina.com.cn/c/nd/2017-11-20/doc-ifynwnty5574830.shtml (accessed on 21 November 2017).

Tai, Ming Cheung. 2001. *China's Entrepreneurial Army*. Oxford: Oxford University Press.

The Supreme People Court [SPC] of the People's Republic of China. 2015. '最高法发布法院工作年度报告' *zuigao fa fabu fayuan gongzuo niandu baogao* (2014) "白皮书 (Annual Work Report of the Supreme People's Court (2014) (White Paper))" available at http://www.court.gov.cn/zixun-xiangqing-13842.html (a ccessed on 21 March 2018).

Transparency International. 2016. 'Corruption Perception Index 2016,' https://www.transparency.org/news/feature/corruption_perceptions_index_2016 (accessed on 27 February 2018).

Vile, M.J.C. 1998. *Constitutionalism and the Separation of Powers. (2nd ed.)* Indianapolis, Liberty Fund 1998. Available at http://oll.libertyfund.org/titles/vile-constitutionalism-and-the-separation-of-powers

Wedeman, Andrew. 2012. 'Growth and Corruption in China', https://www.chinacenter.net/2012/china_currents/11-2/growth-and-corruption-in-china/ (accessed on 27 July 2017).

Xi Jinping. 2017. "Secure a decisive victory in building a moderately prosperous society in all aspects and strive for the great success of Socialism with Chinese Characteristics for a New Era." Speech delivered at the 19th National Congress of the Communist Party of China on October 18, 2017 (English Version) released by Xinhua News Agency on November 3, 2017

*Xinhua*. 2014. "中共中央政治局：党内决不容忍搞团团伙伙、结党营私、拉帮结派" *zhonggong zhongyang zhengfu ju: dangnei jue bu rongren gao tuantuan huohuo, jiedang yingsi, labang jiepai*, (CPC Political Bureau: Banding together in gangs, forming cliques for private ends, or forming factions is not permitted within the party), 29 December, http://news.xinhuanet.com/politics/2014-12/29/c_1113818162.htm (accessed on 11 July 2017).

*Xinhua*. 2015. "反腐打掉的那些 '团团伙伙'" *fanfu da diao naxie tuantuan huo huo* (Those 'gangs' that anti-corruption has taken down), 3 January, http://news.xinhuanet.com/politics/2015-01/03/c_1113856708.htm (accessed on 16 August 2017).

# 7

# Corruption and the CPC under Xi Jinping:
## The Purge Within

*Raviprasad Narayanan*

As the old Latin saying goes... *Corruptio optimi pessima est* (The corruption of the best is the worst). This holds true with regard to the existential problem faced by the Communist Party of China (CPC) when faced with corruption.

The 19th Party Congress held in October 2017 did flag the issue of corruption more forcefully than before as a challenge to be addressed without delay. Since assuming the mantle of the Party and State, and being the 'core leader', Xi Jinping, has clamped down on corruption reaffirming the CPC's foundational roots and legitimising itself further by identifying corruption as having the potential to disrupt established political order challenging the state and its legitimacy. This article will explain the institutional capacity of the party-state in addressing this issue and the leitmotif it provides to the Party to renew itself before celebrating a century in existence in 2021. The role of the Central Commission for Discipline Inspection (CCDI) together with the State Supervision Commission created in 2018 provides insights into the institutional processes adopted by the CPC in addressing and highlighting corruption as an existential issue with strong overtones of ensuring the continuity of the party as the central vector of China's political and economic future.

The biggest challenge CPC confrontsisthat of corruption. The leadership of the Party recognises the potential posed by graft to the system it has fostered in the political and economic realms with both these spheres morphing into a process where institutional checks and balances in an intra-party setting are given short shrift in the pursuit of a *xiaokang* society, where the CPC envisages a 'moderately well-off' economy by 2020, to celebrate the centenary of the Party that in very many ways epitomises the trials and tribulations faced by a nation in the past century – political, economic and societal.

This essay situates the CPC led by Xi Jinping as identifying the elimination of corruption as the primary agenda shaping the earnestness of purpose of a leadership wanting to further economic reform without yielding space to new political actors. Divided into four sections, this paper teases out the consistencies and inconsistencies in the challenges faced by the CPC in its existential battle against corruption.

## The Sisyphean Battle against Corruption

> 'A country's national self-image reflects not only its basic political values and ideals but also its responses to how others perceive it.'[1]

At the recently concluded 19th Party Congress in October 2017, CPC General Secretary and President Xi Jinping waxed eloquent on the success the CPC has had in stemming corruption. He stated:

> We have taken firm action to 'take out tigers,' 'swat flies,' and 'hunt down foxes'. The goal of creating a deterrent against corruption has been initially attained; the cage of institutions that prevents corruption has been strengthened; and moral defenses against corruption are in the making. The anti-corruption campaign has built into a crushing tide, and is being consolidated and developed (Xi 2017: 7).

Xi Jinping's crusade against corruption afflicting the CPC began earlier in his first term. On 4 December 2012, the Communist Party of China announced the 'Eight-point Regulation' providing a clear guidance for party and government officials to eliminate corruption. Xi's leadership and the issuance of the 'Eight-point Regulation' are generally regarded as the start of the anti-corruption campaign in China (*Xinhua* 2012).[2]

Corruption in the CPC has further exacerbated a sense of deprivation felt in certain sections of society that are yet to benefit from the reforms and the largesse it has bestowed, sadly, accumulating more in the direction of the decision makers – the CPC. Such grievances have clearly motivated an increasingly large number of 'petitioners' comprising the elderly and those who were dispossessed of their meagre land holdings to make way for prestige projects – to mount collective action (Xi 2012: 54-55). The obloquy raised by sections of society who have gone through decades of political upheaval followed by economic reforms where the elderly in particular feel left out is a blot on the carefully cultivated image of the CPC.

The CPC in essence lords over a system it has created for several reasons. First is the absolute monopoly (or hegemony) of the CPC on legitimate political organisation in China. Second, is the 'residual value' of the Party based on indigenous origin and a uniqueness of identity spelt out in its revolutionary fervour. Third, the CPC, through political campaigns in the past and an exclusively economic agenda in the reform period post 1979 has been constantly evolving and renewing its roots as a 'patronage machine.' Fourth, its accommodation of the reality and adoption of a pragmatic course has symbolised the Party's response to the needs of the day. Fifth, the CPC no longer harps about class struggle and is polemically and institutionally in favour of economic modernisation. Sixth, its continued mobilisation skills and political reliability and centrality have coincided with its evolving from a doctrinaire cadre to a technocratic and legalist cadre. The higher echelons of the CPC are dominated by a highly educated professional cadre. Seventh, it is creating new institutions (social organisations like chambers of commerce, professional associations, sports and hobby clubs) linking the state to society and openness in co-opting new elites has in many ways co-opted limited dissent and potential alternatives from emerging.

In effect, the CPC appears to have realised that a more effective manner in which it can 'legitimate' itself is by 'institutionalising' itself for a clean transparent government. Ideological campaigns seem to have a 'shelf life' while a process of institutional reforms would rejuvenate the Party. A process of auto immunisation motivates the CPC to take a stand on combating corruption that is seen as a 'virus' eating the very vitals of the system in political and economic terms. As J. Hillis Miller has said:

> 'Any community, such as a nation state, has a built-in "unconscious", and inscrutable destiny to destroy itself, in a suicidal act that Derrida calls 'auto-co-immunity'. Just as the body may turn its immune system against its own organs, so any community or state, in its attempt to protect its borders, to achieve its homeland security, and to make itself safe and sound inevitably turn sits self-protective mechanisms against itself. This makes things worse rather than better. It can lead to the auto-destruction of the community or state.'[3]

## The CPC: Governing Society with Chinese Characteristics

Xi Jinping, China's current leader, has described fighting corruption as a 'key task' of the CPC and reiterated that enforcement of anti-corruption comprises the raison d'ètat of the CPC that must be conducted 'regularly' into the foreseeable future. Xi Jinping has committed the CPC under his stewardship, to eliminating corruption by targeting both 'tigers' and 'flies', referring to the censuring, identifying and jailing of senior political figures from within the Party as well as low-level perpetrators (Zhuo and Peng 2017: 13). Staying the course on clamping down hard on corruption, Xi Jinping at his address at the 19th Party Congress stated:

> Currently, the fight against corruption remains grave and complex; we must remain as firm as a rock in our resolve to build on the overwhelming momentum and secure a sweeping victory. We will continue to see that there are no no-go zones, no ground is left unturned, and no tolerance is shown for corruption. We will impose tight constraints, maintain a tough stance and a long-term deterrence, punish both those who take bribes and those who offer them, and prevent interest groups from arising within the Party (Xi 2017: 61).

What this reveals are the existence and worryingly enough, erstwhile condoning of corruption at extremely high levels in the CPC. This drift in tackling a serious issue has been recognised by the current leadership as a challenge needing to be addressed if it has to remain at the vanguard of 'socialist modernisation with Chinese characteristics' (Wang 2008: 51–59). The privatisation, exploitation, inequality, and corruption that have emerged in the wake of continued economic reform have shaken people's faith in socialist ideology (Xi 2012: 80). It is an accepted fact in China that rampant official corruption involves senior party leaders and their relatives which reflects an especially 'decadent form of crony capitalism' (Li 2013: 42) with the Party being used by the 'entrepreneurial' within, to lavishly feather their nests! The casualty in this 'entrepreneurial zeal' of self-aggrandisement is the CPC and the haloed ideology it has created for itself as being at the vanguard of the people, especially the peasants, urban workers and the elderly – considered the 'forgotten' in China's reform period since 1979 (Thogersen 2003: 207). Staying the course in his address to the 19th Party Congress, Xi Jinping made it clear:

> Disciplinary inspections have cut like a blade through corruption and misconduct; they have covered every Party committee in all departments at the central and provincial levels (Xi 2017: 7).

Interestingly, perhaps owing to the inadequacy of the legal system to strike an independent path, or the 'learning curve' being adopted in constructing a legal framework as society modernises. Political contributions are beyond the purview of corrupt practices or illegal contributions as existing laws are silent on this very vital aspect, that in many ways operates in systems where ambiguity permits the entry of 'donations' that lubricate the political system with shadowy entrepreneurs and the right connections (关系 *guanxi*) willing to do so. With 109 Chinese entities – mostly state owned – in the Fortune 500 list of 2016, the reticence on identifying and isolating corporate links to corruption is imperative in the case of China.

Early this year saw a landmark legislation designed to challenge and defeat graft in China. The National Supervision Law was adopted by China's national legislature on 20 March 2018, formalising a legal approach to tackle graft by empowering an anti-graft network. The National Supervision Law was adopted at the first session of the 13th National People's Congress (NPC) through a vote after three readings of the draft law. This session presided over the selection of Yang Xiaodu as elected director of the national supervisory commission, that administratively creates local commissions at provincial, city and county levels. '[W]ith the new law, the country will pool supervisory powers that used to be divided, and form a centralised, unified and efficient state supervisory system,' said Professor Ma Huaide, vice president of the China University of Political Science and Law.[4]

## The Central Commission for Discipline Inspection (CCDI)

The CCDI is the CPC's most powerful anti-corruption organ with a presence across the spectrum of the Party from central to local levels. Led by Wang Qishan until the 19th Party Congress, the CCDI is now headed by Zhao Leji, a recently inducted Politburo Standing Committee member. The CCDI as an institution has established itself along with local discipline inspection commissions at various administrative levels along with Party committees investigating violations of discipline and personal aggrandisement.

Xi Jinping's campaign against corruption after assuming the mantle of leading the CPC had by early 2015 hollowed out the Central Committee of the CPC with thirteen members and alternate members facing charges of corruption and violation of Party discipline. The corruption charges against Zhou Yongkang,[5] former Politburo Standing Committee member, sentenced to life imprisonment and his associates was an indicator of the seriousness displayed by Xi Jinping to target corruption at the highest levels and initiate a trickle-down effect. To ordinary Chinese, the Zhou Yongkang case revealed the truism inherent in the saying, 'power corrupts and absolute power corrupts absolutely.' By reiterating his stance on clamping down on corruption Xi Jinping stated:

> We must develop a positive and healthy political culture in the Party and improve the Party's political ecosystem, resolutely correct misconduct in all its forms, and show zero tolerance for corruption (Xi 2017: 23).

Three features mark out the institutionalisation of the CCDI. First, disciplinary power concentrated in the executive bodies of Party committees; second, disciplinary powers being concentrated with the Party centre, and, third, investigation and punishment of corruption being a disciplinary tool to consolidate power within the Party. The third aspect bears greater attention with the consolidation of powers taking place with Xi Jinping at the helm of the CPC and considered the 'core leader.'

Laying out the charter for the CCDI is Article 43 of the CPC. 'The Party's Central Commission for Discipline Inspection functions under the leadership of the Central Committee of the Party' (*Xinhua* 2013). The discipline inspection commissions at all levels in the party come under a dual leadership of party committees at a corresponding level with the immediate higher level commission for discipline inspection. Empowered by the Party Charter (amended 1982), the Central Disciplinary Inspection mechanisms have three main tasks as specified by Article 44. These are 'preserving [the authority of] the Party Charter and other important party regulations'; assisting Party committees in rectifying 'Party style; and, inspecting the implementation of the line, principles, policies, and decisions of the Party.'

To cite Article 44 of the CPC: 'The main tasks of the Party's commissions for discipline inspection at all levels are as follows: to uphold the Constitution and other statutes of the Party, to check up on the implementation of the line, principles, policies and resolutions of the Party and to assist the respective Party committees in improving the Party's style of work and in organising and coordinating the work against corruption' (*Xinhua* 2013).

Denoting the seriousness of the issue at hand and the sacrosanct nature of in-built processes, the CPC has to satisfactorily address the complex issue of 'corruption within.' Article 43 of the Party Charter (1982) stipulated that the CCDI has to be headed by one amongst the Politburo Standing Committee – the highest decision making body of the CPC. The flexibility of the CCDI and its local level authorities comes from their being not only enforcement agencies but also a supervisory mechanism overseeing disciplinary action at intermediate and subordinate levels. The CCDI also has the power to conduct investigations.

Acknowledging a vast audience more familiar with electronic forms of communication and the power of the visual medium and In trying to be in sync with the times, the CCDI announced its pro-active war against corruption by airing an anti-corruption documentary titled 永远在路上 (*yongyuan zai lu shang*) (Always on the Road) on CCTV-1 featuring a dozen indicted officials confessing to their crimes (Mulvenon 2017). This aspect of the CCDI reveals a 'populist' agenda being crafted, inherent in the clamping down on corruption and the shaming of individuals to send the message across that graft is accompanied by a very public naming process through the visual medium, apart from the judicial process a guilty individual has to go through.

There are three features in the CPC's efforts to institutionalise the disciplinary mechanism enforcing anti-corruption initiatives. First is the 'concentration of disciplinary power in the executive bodies of Party committees – the Politburo and its Standing Committee for the Central Committee and local Party standing committees for local Party organisations.' Second, is 'the centralisation of disciplinary power vertically from local CDIs all the way up to the CCDI.' The third feature is that 'the party has gone through a significant policy shift since 1989, whereby corruption has replaced political offenses and become, perhaps, the only legitimate cause to expel Party members' (Li 2016).

## Analysing challenges posed by corruption to the CPC

The people resent corruption most; and corruption is the greatest threat our Party faces (Xi 2017: 60). Xi's address undoubtedly caters to an audience beyond the party faithful. The challenge faced by Xi Jinping, is to make the war he has unleashed against graft a rational-legal process and not stamped with strong shades of 'rule of man' over 'rule of law.' It could be argued, that the CPC has transitioned from its 'revolutionary' roots with strong political overtones, to a trajectory where it evolves into a 'guardian' of economic progress. This transition in political terms has been overshadowed by economic dictates of the day where a vacuum emerges with shortfalls in ideological moorings being compensated by excesses in rent-seeking. It is precisely this conundrum that faces the CPC – how to eliminate graft and bring a political correctness without strong shades of ideological excess. Put succinctly, a tight rope walk is what the leadership faces without any relaxation in opening-up political space.

As indicated by Bao Tong, a senior architect of China's reforms until 1989, when he opposed the crackdown in Tiananmen Square, 'China's economy and society have grown too complex to be directed even by a modernising Party' (Zhao 2006: 55). An apposite statement, if any. Suisheng Zhao says that the CPC has to completely separate the Party step by step from the state and from economic activities, open its ranks to critical discussion, and allow the local grassroots electoral process to percolate to the top (Zhao 2006: 57). A radical proposition if any.

A couple of salient characteristics flowing from the above bear mention. First, the CPC as the leading (and only) centrifugal force in China's politics is witness to, and presiding over a phase where its political strength has changed vastly. Its revolutionary history of being the sole representative of the working class has transformed into becoming a 'political stakeholder', albeit the sole such one, caring most about its own interests (commercial and political) and the stability of its regime. This is because a large part of its members have gained immensely from economic reforms and development, and they have become and consider themselves, a new social stratum, superior economically and politically to other social stratums who comprised the bedrock of the rank and file that made the Party an expression of popular will.

Second, the political structure and institutions complementing the political edifice created intermittently, are the main barriers hindering anti-corruption efforts. Indeed, a string of Chinese leaders have railed against widespread corruption undermining the legitimacy of the Party, but none have been willing to suggest structural reforms, especially inner Party reforms, that would help tackle it (Dai 2016). Worryingly, the levels of corruption in the Party require an intervention that may just be beyond the Party's ability and all measures undertaken to eliminate corruption end up in 'flies' getting caught and not many 'tigers'![6] If the clamp down on corruption is akin to folderol, the worst-case scenario will be an implosion of the CPC if measures against corruption fail to succeed.

David Shambaugh had hinted as much in an opinion piece titled 'The coming Chinese crackup', where he notes that crackdown on corruption strengthens Xi Jinping's personal power, and 'his despotism is severely stressing China's system and society – and bringing it closer to a breaking point' (Shambaugh 2015). For an astute observer of China and a scholar of the eminence of David Shambaugh to state this is either being prescient or being way off the mark.

Third, leaders in China have always stressed the necessity of rule of law. However, while rules, laws and regulations have been initiated too many loopholes and weaknesses compounded by a legal system not independent have permitted the hoodwinking of the law by the powerful and entrenched. For a long lasting and perhaps permanent imprint of anti-corruption measures to succeed, the rule of law needs to be enshrined through a legal debate involving a wider spectrum of opinion not restricted to party forums and the independence of a judiciary that upholds the law and not beholden by considerations of the central and only political actor.

Corruption is not a new phenomenon in Chinese politics, and has existed from ancient times to the present. The collapse of every dynasty in imperial Chinese history from the first unified dynasty, the Qin, to the last dynasty, the Qing, a commonality to be inferred is, every dynasty's collapse was preceded by high levels of government corruption, although every dynasty and political regime had other short comings in addition to corruption. The Revolution of 1911 benefited from the Qing government's corruption, but the nationalist government could not avoid the same mistake. The Kuomintang (KMT) of Chiang Kai-shek, lost the civil war to the CPC not only militarily but also due to economic reasons with hyperinflation, corruption and wartime profiteering alienating the citizenry – rural and urban alike (Bramall 2009: 45–7).

The CPC is no dynasty, yet levels of corruption have encouraged arguments linking the rise of corruption to a point where a regime faces political extinction.

A charitable view would be that the system does not produce corruption but has tolerated 'rent seeking' by officials who use their absolute and unbridled power to enrich themselves using the monopoly on political power and economic allocations the CPC has (Zhou 2016).

## Conclusion

Corruption and anti-corruption measures undertaken pose an existential challenge to the Party and the regime in China. In its long history, China developed its own tradition, culture, ethics, political heritages, administrative norms rather different from those of the rest of the world. Regarding this, China must find its own political conviction to cope with mounting corruption. Three and half decades of economic reform in China has created 'independent sources of wealth, power and influence' that the CPC feels should be co-opted, lest independent political ideas germinate beyond the reach of the Party, hollowing out the very edifice that fostered this exponential economic growth. The battle against corruption also seeks to address the emergence of any political alternatives that would erode the existing compact, and hence visible measures against an 'evil' that has embedded within it seeds that could overthrow the existing political arrangement. It also has to be said that the norms and values required to transform China's political culture have to emerge from the CPC itself.

Is the CPC under Xi Jinping up to the challenge or will the current dispensation prefer a status quo where the system will coalesce around a 'paramount leader' willing to put the 'individual' over the 'process' and the 'institution' gravitating outwards from a centralising tendency beyond scrutiny and accountability? And, what can India make of the anti-corruption crusade launched and represented by Xi Jinping in China?

Since the 18th National Congress of the Communist Party of China (CPC) in 2012, and the recently concluded 19th National Congress, the CPC has made efforts – polemical and institutional – to implement Xi Jinping's blueprint for achieving the 'China Dream' (中国梦 *zhongguo meng*). The on-going anti-corruption campaign is part of the road map towards the 'China Dream'. Interestingly, Xi Jinping's crusade against corruption might no longer remain a domestic issue and could involve the 'rendition' of the corrupt back home to face justice. To quote from Xi's address:

> Wherever offenders may flee, they will be brought back and brought to justice. We will work for the adoption of national anti-corruption legislation and create a corruption reporting platform that covers both disciplinary inspection commissions and supervision agencies (Xi 2017: 61).

An explanation for corruption in the reform era with its tentacles spreading from the Party outwards, is that corruption is the concomitant result of an imperfect market emerging from the lack of de-politicisation in avenues of economic production where the state holds sway. The challenge faced by the CPC goes beyond corruption. It has to do with the gradual transition of a single Party system into a 'ruling party' guided by the very ethos of a civilisation where 'virtue' determines legitimacy. The CPC also acknowledges expectations of a people and society transformed by a prosperity where the material subsumes the 'virtuous.' If the whole 'crusade' against corruption displays smarmy, it is the CPC that gets further eroded.

The Chinese government on its part is in no hurry to transform itself to combat corruption mimicking western processes and methodologies where the constitution plays an important role. To Beijing there is no hurry to copy western methodologies to combat corruption when there are innate methods to combat and confront graft with the CPC emerging as a signpost of society. Political stability is what motivates the CPC especially since it looks towards a century of its existence in 2021 and Xi Jinping will be at the very core at that time with political stability, economic growth, a visible improvement in the standard of living and a unified CPC at the political helm being primary non-negotiable caveats in China.

In China's political culture, the 'institution' has more importance over the 'individual' (Zeng 2016: 11). The essential timbre of the state prevails over the whims of an individual at the helm. The 'state' as an institution dominates, anchoring itself in a political culture where the state is not an abstract concept. The 'state' in China, has displayed its tangible strengths in galvanising people over issues, campaigns and forging a common identity which resonates with calls to maintain social cohesion and stability as the primary task before the instruments of the state. The war against corruption is increasingly the leitmotif of the Xi Jinping epoch. Succeeding in emerging triumphant in this existential battle is the challenge facing the CPC and the 'China Dream.' An assumption to conclude this paper is whether the crusade against corruption in China launched by Xi Jinping will last his tenure in office and his successors will continue the crackdown or go slow on what Xi has imprinted his tenure on.

## NOTES

1. Lucian W. Pye, 'China's Self-Image as Projected in World Affairs', Chapter 9 in Gerrit W. Wong and Bih Jaw Lin, *Sino-American Relations at a Time of Change.* (CSIS-Washington and IIR-Taipei, 1994, p.157.
2. The eight-point regulation (in simplified Chinese 八项规定 *baxiang guiding*) was a document adopted in a meeting of the Political Bureau of the Communist Party of China (CPC) Central Committee, the country's top-ruling body, on Tuesday, Dec 4, 2012. The document made explicit requirements on how Political Bureau members should improve their work style in eight aspects, focusing on rejecting extravagance and reducing bureaucratic visits, meetings and empty talk. See 'Eight Point Regulation', *Xinhua*, 5

December 2012, http://cpcchina.chinadaily.com.cn/2012-12/05/ content_15992256.htm (accessed on 23 July 2017).

3. Miller, J. Hillis. 2009. *For Derrida*. New York: Fordham University Press, p. 238.
4. Lu Hui. 'China Focus: Supervision law gives legal teeth to China's graft-busting agency', *Xinhua* (Beijing) 20 March 2018, http://www.xinhuanet.com/english/2018-03/20/c_137053224.htm (accessed on 3 September 2018).
5. The corruption cases against Zhou Yongkang, former Politburo Standing Committee member and internal security chief is an instance of how the Xi Jinping administration is conducting an all-out war on graft with strong political overtones since Zhou Yongkang was very closely allied to Bo Xilai, the controversial 'princeling' who lost the power struggle within the CPC with his murky dealings reflecting in many ways what the party has become.
6. Xi Jinping's speech to the top party discipline body, the Central Committee for Discipline Inspection, had mentioned 老虎苍蝇一起打 *(laohu cangying yiqi da)* 'strike tigers and flies together,' referring to high level officials and low level cadres as 'tigers' and 'flies'.

## REFERENCES

19th National Congress of the Communist Party of China October 18, 2017. *Xinhua*, 19th CPC National Congress, 3 November, http://www.xinhuanet.com/ english/ special/19cpcnc/ index.htm (accessed on 12 November 2017).

Article 44. 'Full Text of the Constitution of the Communist Party of China', *Xinhua,* 29 March 2013, http://english.cpc.people.com.cn/206972/206981/8188098.html (accessed on 2 August 2017).

Bramall, Chris. 2009. *Chinese Economic Development*. Abingdon: Routledge, 45–47.

Dai, Changzheng. 2013. "Corruption and Anti-corruption in China: Challenges and Countermeasures," in Stephan Rothlin and Parsiisa Haghirian (eds.) *Dimensions of Teaching Business Ethics in Asia.* Amsterdam: Springer, 61-76.

Hui, Lu. 2-18. 'China Focus: Supervision law gives legal teeth to China's graft-busting agency', *Xinhua* (Beijing) 20 March, http://www.xinhuanet.com/english/2018-03/20/c_1370532 24. htm (Retrieved on 3 September 2018).

Li, Cheng. January 2013. 'China at the Tipping Point? Top-Level Reform or Bottom-Up Revolution, ' *Journal of Democracy.* Volume 24, Number 1, p.42.

Li, Ling. 2016. 'The Rise of the Discipline and Inspection Commission, 1927–2012: Anticorruption Investigation and Decision-Making in the Chinese Communist Party,' *Modern China,* Vol. 42(5), 2, pp. 447–482.

Liu, Xiaobo. 2006. 'Reform in China: The Role of Civil Society,' *Social Research*, Vol.73, No.1, p.123.

Miller, J. Hillis. 2009. *For Derrida*. New York: Fordham University Press.

Mulvenon, James. 2017. 'Scraping Poison Off the Bone' (刮骨疗毒): An Examination of the Campaign to "Eliminate the Baneful Influence of Guo Boxiong and Xu Caihou" *China Leadership Monitor*, No.52, http://www.hoover.org/research/scraping-poison-bone-examination-campaign-eliminate-baneful-influence-guo-boxiong-and-xu (accessed on 12 August 2017).

Munro, Susan. 2015. 'China,' Chapter 2, in Mark F. Mendelsohn, *The Anti-Bribery and Anti-Corruption Review.* (Fourth edition), London: Law Business Research, p.29.

Paul van Els and Elisa Sabattini. 2012. 'Introduction: Political Rhetoric in Early China' in Extrême-Orient Extrême-Occident, No. 34, pp. 5-14 and Baogang Guo, 'Political Legitimacy in China's Transition Toward a Market Economy,' in Lowell Dittmer and

Guoli Liu (eds.) 2006. *China's Deep Reform – Domestic Politics in Transition.* Lanham: Rowman & Littlefield), pp.147–76.

Pye, Lucian W. 1994. 'China's Self-Image as Projected in World Affairs'. Chapter 9 in Gerrit W. Wong and Bih Jaw Lin, *Sino-American Relations at a Time of Change*, CSIS-Washington and IIR-Taipei

Shambaugh, David. 2015. 'The Coming Chinese Crackup', *Wall Street Journal*, (New York) 6 March, https://www.wsj.com/articles/the-coming-chinese-crack-up-1425659198 (accessed on 12 August 2017).

Thogersen, Stig. 2003. 'Parasites or Civilisers: The Legitimacy of the Chinese Communist Party in Rural Areas', *China: An International Journal* 1, 2, pp. 200–223.

Wang, Shaoguang. 2008. 'The Great Transformation: The Double Movement in China', *Boundary 2*, Vol 35. No.2, pp. 15–47.

Xi Jinping, 2017. 'Secure a Decisive Victory in Building a Moderately Prosperous Society in All Respects and Strive for the Great Success of Socialism with Chinese Characteristics for a New Era,' p. 61.

Xi, Chen. 2012. *Social Protest and Contentious Authoritarianism in China.* New York; Cambridge University Press, pp.54–80.

Zeng, Jinghan. 2016. *The Chinese Communist Party's Capacity to Rule Ideology, Legitimacy and Party Cohesion.* New York: Palgrave Macmillan, p. 11.

Zhao, Suisheng. (ed.) 2006. *Debating Political Reform in China – Rule of Law vs. Democratization.* M.E. Sharpe: Armonk, New York, p.55.

Zhou, Jinghao. 2016. 'Will the Communist Party of China Be Able to Win the Anticorruption Battle?',*Contemporary Chinese Political Economy and Strategic Relations: An International Journal*, Vol. 2, No. 3, pp. 1007–1048.

Zhuo, Jing-Schmidt and Xinjia Peng. 2017. 'Winds and tigers: metaphor choice in China's anti-corruption discourse',*Lingua Sinica*, Vol. 3, No. 2, p. 13. Springer Open Access Journal/ Creative Commons Attribution.

# 8

# Legal Reforms under Xi Jinping:
## The Curious Case of the Anti-Corruption Law

*Santosh Pai*

The Chinese legal system has been in a state of creative flux since the end of the Cultural Revolution. Legal reforms had been undertaken in the Qing era and during the Republic of China (ROC) era too, but it was Mao's decimation of the legal system that gave the Communist Party of China (CPC) a veritable institutional blank slate. Since 1976, there has been a legal renaissance, which was an integral part of the larger 'reform and opening up' (*gaige kaifang*) agenda. This is borne out by several key milestones in the pre-Xi Jinping era such as the Third Plenum of the Eleventh Central Committee in 1978 when a need to adopt, implement and enforce laws was first proclaimed, key slogans under Jiang Zemin which included 'ruling the country by law' (*yifa zhiguo*) and 'building a Socialist rule of law state' (*jianshe shehui zhuyi fazhi guojia*) and Hu Jintao's 'terming of the constitution as a 'fundamental' (*genben dafa*) and inviolable law to be implemented by all State and private entities, accompanied by a record number of references to the constitution in his report to the Communist Party's 17th National Congress in 2007 (De Lisle 2017).

### A New Discourse on Rule of Law

Xi Jinping first emphasised role of law at the 30th anniversary of the 1982 constitution, by declaring that China 'must firmly establish throughout society the authority of the constitution and the law'. The Communique and the 60 Points policy document issued at the 18th Central Committee's Third Plenum in November 2013, made pledges to 'promote and construct rule of law in China' (*tuijin fazhi zhongguo jianshe*), 'strengthen rule of law guarantees' (*jiaqiang fazhi baozhang*), 'safeguard the authority of the constitution and the laws' (*weihu xianfa falu quanwei*) and 'constrain power within a cage of institutions' (*ba quanli guan jinzhi du longzi*). The Fourth Plenum declared the rule of law to be a guiding and driving force in pursuing the Party's major tasks (including economic development, political modernisation and realisation of Xi's 'China Dream'), and adopted sweeping plans for legal change. Xi included 'governing the country according to law' (*yifa zhiguo*) among his 'four comprehensives' (*sige quanmian*), which included other goals that law has been expected to advance: deepening reform, building prosperity and limiting party misbehavior. The Fifth Plenum reaffirmed commitments to 'persist in governing the country according to law' (*jianchi yifa zhiguo*) and 'strengthen consciousness about the rule of law' (*zengqiang....fazhi yishi*) (DeLisle 2016). It is fair to suggest that the idea of rule of law reform has been supported at the highest levels of the Chinese political system (Heuser 2004) with the twin aims of avoiding the lawlessness of the Cultural Revolution, and to advance economic development (Szto 2016).

President Xi has continued rhetorical support to legal reforms throughout the first five years of his Presidency. In November 2015, rule of law was included in the 'Four Comprehensives', which is a statement of Xi Jinping Thought. The agenda for rule of law reforms was specified in a number of documents – the Third Plenum decision (2013), the Fourth Plenum decision (2014), and in Xi's Report to the 19th Party Congress (2017). These documents provide a theoretical understanding of what it means to 'comprehensively govern the nation according to law' (*BBC* 2015). They also lay out the detailed roadmap by which a 'Socialist system of law with Chinese characteristics' is to be achieved (*Xinhua* 2017).

There is clarity that the rule of law reform is not an end in itself; it is not rule of law for the sake of rule of law, but reflects the need to deepen reform to shift the market from a 'basic to a decisive role' (CPC 2013). A dependable guarantee by rule of law is necessary to create a moderately prosperous society (Subba 2014). The 18th Party Congress, for the first time, and later the 19th Party Congress, recognised that the heart of 'law based governance' is the supremacy of the constitution. The Fourth Plenum decision laid out the detailed measures through which this law based governance was to be achieved.

Xi Jinping's first term has seen the implementation of a comprehensive set of reforms which includes both the hardware of legal infrastructure, and the software of legal culture (Perenboom 2002). There have been several areas in which Xi Jinping's initiatives have made lasting contributions to rule of law reforms in China. Notably these include – recognition of constitutional supremacy and steps towards constitutional interpretation and supervision (Garrick 2016), issuance of the first White Paper on judicial reform (*China Daily* 2017), establishment of circuit courts to deal with problems of local protectionism (Garrick 2016), and professionalism of the judiciary (Li 2016).

The 19th Party Congress indicates that legal reforms would continue beyond the achievement of a 'moderately prosperous society' in 2020. The aim would be to have a system by 2035 in which the 'rights of the people to participate and develop as equals is adequately protected; and the rule of law for the country, people and society is basically in place' (*China Daily* 2017). An idea of the direction of these reforms is found in the section on 'Improving the system of institutions through which the people run the country and developing Socialist democracy'. It includes the following – democratic elections, legal protection of human rights in accordance with the law, law-based decision making, public oversight, people's exercise of state power through people's congress, consultative democracy through the Chinese People's Political Consultative Conference (CPPCC), impartial administration of justice, setting up of a central leading group for advancing law based governance, public awareness of the principle that no individual or organisation has the power to overstep the constitution, delegation of power to government bodies at Provincial and below levels, and development of the united front.

However, the 19th Party Congress also reaffirmed that these reforms have to be based on the reality of China's national circumstances, and not a copy or imitation of other countries' models. The fundamental principle that is the basis of China's unique national circumstance is that the Party leadership is the fundamental guarantee for ensuring that governance in China is law-based (Perenboom 2002). Thus, the kind of legal system which is envisaged in these Socialist legal reforms is fundamentally different from a Western liberal democratic system of law. In the former, 'the superiority of the law' *(fada)* is constrained by 'the superiority of the Party' *(dang da)*, whereas in the later the law stands above the people and the rulers. This difference has led to the critique that, like previous attempts at rule of law reforms in China, these reforms are also not 'rule *of* law' *(fazhi)*, but 'rule *of* man' or 'rule *by* law' *(renzhi)* (Trevaskes 2017).

## The Anti-Corruption Campaign

The discussion around Xi's anti-corruption campaign encapsulate this debate. Is the anti-corruption campaign a purge to consolidate his power (a power grab theory), or a genuine attempt at systemic reform (a genuine reform theory)? (Wedeman 2017).

There are many ways in which the anti-corruption campaign may be seen as an arbitrary power grab, which undermines the rule of law. Paradoxically, the campaign suffered due to its extensive focus on high profile cases of public officials (Guo 2008). Like previous anti-corruption campaigns, Xi Jinping began at the top with cases of the 'tigers', to drum up public support for the campaign against the 'flies' (lower ranking officials) (*Nikkei Asian Review* 2017). The prosecution of high prolife potential challengers to Xi, like Bo Xilai, Zhou Yongkang and Sun Zhengcai, led to the criticism that the anti-corruption campaign was more a purge (Lynch 2017).

The fact that the anti-corruption campaign has relied mostly on the CCDI machinery and the *shuanggui* (double designation) system (Article 20 of the Administrative Supervision Law) which falls within the internal disciplinary procedures of the Communist Party of China, but outside the mainstream legal system, is also problematic. Anti-corruption laws in China are currently in the Criminal Code. A criminal prosecution is triggered when the People's Procuratorates place on record evidence of corruption among State functionaries (Article 18(2) of the Criminal Procedure Law). The People's Procuratorates are made up of three distinct departments, those responsible for investigation, supervision of investigation and prosecution. There is also an anti-corruption and bribery bureau, under the People's Procuratorate, which is responsible for investigating and initiating certain specified charges (Qiuhong 2011). However, the system was found to be inadequate on account of several reasons, such as inability to act on tip-offs, easy withdrawal of confessions, lack of cooperation from government departments where the corruption was committed, etc. (Qiuhong 2011). Conducting anti-corruption procedures through the Central Commission for Discipline Inspection (CCDI) is seen as a more effective option (*China Economic Review* 2015), but that made the campaign appear to lack institutional autonomy. The mechanism was also opaque, and without institutional safeguards such as judicial review, access to legal counsel, etc.

There is an alternate school of thought that believes the current anti-corruption campaign has been coupled with administrative reform and disciplinary regulation, to bring about a fundamental shift in China's political culture (Keliher and Wu 2016). For instance, the use of online tip offs and whistleblowers increase public participation in the campaign; as also placing the power of appointments of local Commissions for Discipline Inspection (CDIs) with the CCDI. Formalising administrative regulations for inspection procedures and disciplinary action; standardising salaries, which brings in transparency and departmental anti-corruption education are all aimed at reducing corruption. (Keliher and Wu 2016). In the lead upto the 19$^{th}$ Party Congress, there was widespread debate among legal academics (Sun and Yuan, 2017) whether this process would continue through the institutionalisation of a 'supervision law', which would be based on pilot programmes for reforming the anti-corruption supervision systems launched in November 2016, in three Provinces – Beijing, Shanxi and Zhejiang (*Xinhua* 2016). The details of these pilot programmes are not publicly available.

## Towards a National Supervision Law

Soon after the 19th Party Congress, a draft of the supervision law was released for public consultation on November 6, 2017 (*Xinhua* 2017). The draft law aims to create a national level body called the National Supervision Commission that will operate at the same level as Cabinet, Legislature and Supreme Court under the direct supervision of the National People's Congress (Mai 2016). The draft National Supervision Law is largely based on *liuzhi* (retention in custody), an adaptation of the CCDI's *shuanggui* system with certain safeguards such as stricter internal procedures; detentions with time limits – three months, and, upon approval, another three months; families to be notified within 24 hours; prohibition of mistreatment and videotaping of interrogations (Human Rights Watch 2017). Apart from these procedural safeguards, the revolutionary impact of the proposed legislation is the merging of the State and the Party in a system of 'one entity with two names' (Wang 2017). This led to two major types of concerns about the legislation. One, the procedural concern that the new system will institutionalise *shuangguai*, with only a few cosmetic changes. The second is the constitutionality of the law itself, owing to these measures falling outside the purview and safeguards of mainstream criminal law provisions (Walsh 2017). The National Supervision Law was subsequently adopted at the first session of the 13th National People's Congress and its scope extended to staff of Party organs, legislatures, governments, courts, procuratorates, political advisory bodies, as well as their own staff, executives of state-owned enterprises, staff of public institutions and mass organisations, among others, in public office. It even covers contractors engaged in government contracts. (*China Daily* 2018)

The anti-corruption law is thus a paradox that seeks to further rule of law (with Chinese characteristics), by sidestepping commonly accepted constitutional safeguards. This corresponds to a debate between the 'thick' and 'thin' ideas of the rule of law, which can be understood as a distinction between the minimum standards of law, versus higher, aspirational standards (Rijpkema 2013). The thin or minimum standards means that government has be carried out within a framework of laws which have positive qualities like generality, clarity, publicity, stability, and prospectively (Waldron 2016). The thick idea of law is based on the principle that the specifics of the rule of law have to conform to a normative system, which transcends the rules themselves. For the purposes of this discussion, the focus is on the school which believes that there has to be a normative basis, and critiques the Chinese developments of rule on law on the basis of lack of the normative basis. In the Western tradition, this 'thick' or aspirational rule of law is associated with ideas of liberal democracy most notably that the supreme political authority has to be bound by the laws of the land. The historical roots of this understanding have been traced to the *Magna Carta* which was the first written document constraining the rights of the King through substantive commitments to individual liberties and the notion of limited government (Fernandez-Villaverde 2015).

One line of argument is that since the Chinese system does not believe in the supremacy of individual liberties, so the rule of law lacks the normative aspect and is merely instrumental or 'thin'. There is a long history of analysis both in the West and in China, which holds the view that the substantive rule is incompatible with China's system (Turner 1992). However, such an approach overlooks the legal and intellectual history of China, which has a distinct conception about the relationship between law and the political authority. The historical idea of law in China is based on Confucian and Legalism beliefs that placed the ruler above the law, and valued the judgement of moral men more than that of legal institutions. The state, exemplified by a few morally superior individuals, bore a fiduciary relationship to the people. This idea is similar to an authoritarian government, but not one that sanctioned an arbitrary, lawless abuse of power (Turner 1992).

## Normative or Instrumental in Character?

Thus, structure of the legal system is not based on an instrumental idea, but rather a normative system based on an 'inner morality of the law.' This is the basis on which the legal reforms and anti-corruption campaign enjoy public legitimacy. That is why, unlike in most other jurisdictions where the anti-corruption legal reforms are focused on prescribing penalties for defined offences and on the due process of law to be followed once a suspect is apprehended, throughout China's long history of anti-corruption legal reforms, the supervision system that prevents corruption in the first place, has received more attention than the due process of law. This is because the success of anti-corruption measures in China depends to a greater degree on their social acceptance, which increases legitimacy, than on the will of legislators or institutional design (Ling 2011).

This is the intellectual heritage that is carried forward in the idea of a 'disinterested government', that is, that CPC's top leadership eschews rent-seeking behavior and differentiated interests in society in favour of a disciplined commitment to economic development (Mazur 2017). The proposed Supervision Commission should be seen in this jurisprudential background. It is not a unique concept. Similar systems have been put in place earlier in Singapore and Hong Kong. The Corrupt Practices Investigation Bureau (CPIB) in Singapore and the Independent Commission Against Corruption (ICAC) in Hong Kong was set up by the British authorities in 1952 and 1974 respectively, both of which are independent agencies, responsible directly to the supreme British political authority.

Determining the rule of law and implications of the proposed anti-corruption mechanism has significance beyond domestic reform and politics in China. The anti-corruption campaign of Xi has some novel features which had never been attempted in the past, brings an international dimension to the evolving laws (Wedeman 2017). First, Chinese prosecutors have started prosecuting foreign companies that paid bribes (Robinson 2016). As was demonstrated during the GlaxoSmithKline case, this could have grave implications for international businesses. Secondly investigators stepped up efforts to bring fugitive officials back to China and to crackdown on what are known as 'naked officials' (Wedeman 2017). Operations Foxhunt and Skynet were launched to bring back economic fugitives and to recover stolen assets. Anti-corruption cooperation has now become a component of bilateral cooperation, particularly with OECD countries.

However, of greater interest is China's agenda of international norm setting in anti-corruption. The current international regime of anti-corruption emerged from the agenda of rule of law promotion which was adopted by international organisations like the United Nations, World Bank, and IMF (Carothers 1998). Notable international conventions are the 1997 OECD Convention on Bribery of Foreign Public Officials in International Business Transactions, and the UN's Convention against Corruption. Anti-corruption is one of the seven areas that was identified by Xi Jinping as 'rising fields' of international rule setting (Ng 2017). China's emphasis has been on shifting the focus in anti-corruption cooperation away from institutional reforms to punitive measures like stringent extradition treaties (Lang 2017).

For India, this specific case is of relevance to understand the manner in which China is trying to become a norm generator and norm shaper in the international system. Notably, in India, the legal system is geared towards the liberal democratic rule of law. The debate between positive and normative concepts of law was most notably carried out in the context of the positivist phrase 'procedure established by law' included in Article 21 of the Constitution of India. The Supreme Court of India, in the case of *Maneka Gandhi* v. *Union of India* (1978) held that there was an implied requirement of substantive ideals of liberty. As China becomes more prominent as a norm generator and norm shaper in the international legal system, the concept of rule of law can certainly be a productive area for engagement and debate.

## REFERENCES

2017. 'China issues white paper on judicial reform of Chinese courts[1]' – *Chinadaily.com.cn*. 27 February, http://www.chinadaily.com.cn/china/2017-02/27/content_28361584.htm (accessed on 30 May 2018).

2017. 'China: Revise Draft National Supervision Law', *Human Rights Watch*, 10 November, https://www.hrw.org/news/2017/11/10/china-revise-draft-national-supervision-law (accessed on 30 May 2018).

2016. Annual Report, Congressional-Executive Commission on China. https://www.cecc.gov/publications/annual-reports/2016-annual-report (accessed on 30 May 2018).

2015. Exclusive: Monthly data detail China's often soft-handed anti-corruption campaign, 23 December, https://chinaeconomicreview.com/exclusive-monthly-data-detail-chinas-often-soft-handed-anti-corruption-campaign/ (accessed on 30 May 2018).

2014. 'Communiqué of the Third Plenary Session of the 18th Central Committee of the Communist Party of China', *China.org.cn.* 15 January, http://www.china.org.cn/china/third_plenary_session/2014/01/15/content_31203056.htm (accessed on 30 May 2018).

*BBC News*. 2015. 'China's Xi unveils latest slogan', 25 February, http://www.bbc.com/news/world-asia-china-31622571 (accessed on 21 Feb. 2018).

Carothers, T. 1998. 'The Rule of Law Revival', *Foreign Affairs*, (March/April 1998). https://www.foreignaffairs.com/articles/1998-03-01/rule-law-revival (accessed on 21 May 2018).

deLisle, J. 2016. 'Law in the China Model 2.0: Legality, Developmentalism and Leninism under Xi Jinping', *Journal of Contemporary China*, Volume 26, Issue 103, 68–84.

Explanation of the 'CCP Central Committee Decision Regarding Some Major Questions in Comprehensively Promoting Governance According to Law', https://www. chinalawtranslate.com/explanationof4thplen/?lang=en (accessed on 30 May 2018).

Fernandez-Villaverde, Jesus. 2015. 'Magna Carta, the Rule of Law and the Limits on Government', *MPRA Paper*, University Library of Munich, Germany, https://EconPapers.repec.org/RePEc:pra:mprapa:69862. (accessed on 25 May 2018).

Garrick, J. (Ed.), Bennett, Y. (ed.) 2016. *China's Socialist Rule of Law Reforms Under Xi Jinping.* London: Routledge.

Guo, Y. 2008. 'Corruption in Transitional China: An Empirical Analysis', *The China Quarterly, 194*, 349–64.

Heuser, R. 2004. 'What is 'rule of law'? The traditional Chinese concept of good governance and the challenges of the 21st Century', http://www.zaoerv.de/64_2004/64_2004_3_a_723_734.pdf. (accessed on 30 May 2018).

Hsiao, Kung-Chuan. 2015. *History of Chinese Political Thought: From the Beginnings to the Sixth Century A.D. Volume 1.* Translated by Mote, F. W., New Jersey: Princeton University Press. https://muse.jhu.edu/book/39643 (accessed on 24 May 2018).

'Is China Committed to Rule of Law?', Council on Foreign Relations. (n.d.) https://www.cfr.org/interview/china-committed-rule-law (accessed on 30 May 2018).

Keliher, M. Wu, H. 2016. 'Corruption, Anticorruption, and the Transformation of Political Culture in Contemporary China', *Journal of Asian Studies*. 75 (1), 1–14.

Lang, B. 2017. 'China's anti-graft campaign and international anti-corruption norms: Towards a "new international anti-corruption order"?', *Crime, Law and Social Change*. 10.1007/s10611-017-9742-y.

Li, A. 2016. 'Centralisation of Power in the Pursuit of Law-based Governance', *China Perspectives*, http://journals.openedition.org/chinaperspectives/6995 (accessed on 29 May 2018).

Ling, S. 2011. 'Construction of Anti-corruption Institutions and Culture in Traditional China and Its Implications for Modern China', *Social Sciences in China*, 32:4, 162–175.

Lynch, E. 2017. Rule of Law at China's 19th Party Congress – Oh no Xi didn't, *China Law and Policy, 16* October, http://chinalawandpolicy.com/2017/10/16/rule-of-law-at-the-chinas-19th-party-congress-oh-no-xi-didnt/ (accessed on 30 May 2018).

Mai, J. 2016. 'China to set up new anti-corruption body to oversee all public servants as it intensifies battle against graft', *South China Morning Post*, 8 November, http://www.

scmp.com/news/china/policies-politics/article/2044014/china-set-new-anti-corruption-body-oversee-all-public (accessed on 30 May 2018).

Mazur, J., & Ursu, A. 2017. 'China's Disinterested Government and the Rule of Law', *Asia & the Pacific Policy Studies*, 4(2), 376–382. https://doi.org/10.1002/app5.176 (accessed on 21 April 2018).

Ng, T. 2017. '7 things you need to know about Xi Jinping's vision of a 'new era' for China', *South China Morning Post,* 18 October, http://www.scmp.com/news/china/policies-politics/article/2115858/key-points-xis-speech-chinas-communist-party-congress (accessed on 30 May 2018).

Oki, Nagai. 2017. Xi's corruption crackdown nets hundreds of party 'tigers'. *Nikkei Asian Review,* 11 October, https://asia.nikkei.com/Politics-Economy/Policy-Politics/Xi-s-corruption-crackdown-nets-hundreds-of-party-tigers (accessed on 30 May 2018).

Peerenboom, R. 2002. *China's Long March towards Rule of the Law.* Cambridge: Cambridge University Press.

Qiuhong, X. 2011. 'China's Anti-Corruption Strategies from the Viewpoint of Criminal Justice', *Social Sciences in China, 32*(4), 176–91.

Rijpkema, P. 2013. 'The Rule of Law beyond Thick and Thin', *Law and Philosophy,* Vol 32, No, 6.

Robinson, M. 2016. 'Glaxo to Pay $20 Million SEC Fine Over Bribery in China', *Bloomberg,* 30 September, https://www.bloomberg.com/news/articles/2016-09-30/glaxo-to-pay-20-million-sec-fine-over-bribing-chinese-officials (accessed on 30 May 2018).

Subba, B. 2014. '18th CPC Central Committee Fourth Plenum: Rule of Law with Chinese Characteristics', *ICS Analysis.* No. 22.

Sun, Y. and Yuan, B. 2017. 'Does Xi Jinping's Anti-Corruption Campaign improve regime legitimacy?', *Modern China Studies,* Vol 24, Issue 2.

Szto, M. 2016. 'Chinese Gift-Giving, Anti-Corruption Law, and the Rule of Law and Virtue', *Fordham International Law Journal, 39*(3), 591.

Trevaskes, S. 2017. 'China's party led rule of law regime, *East Asia Forum,* http://www.eastasiaforum.org/2017/10/02/chinas-party-led-rule-of-law-regime/ (accessed on 30 May 2018).

Turner, K. 1992. 'Rule of Law ideals in Early China', *Journal of Chinese Law,* Vol. 6, No. 1, 1992.

Waldron, J. 2016. 'The Rule of Law', in E.N. Zalta (ed.) *The Stanford Encyclopedia of Philosophy* (Fall 2016). Metaphysics Research Lab, Stanford University. https://plato.stanford.edu/archives/fall2016/entries/rule-of-law/ (accessed on 25 May 2018).

Walsh, M. 2017. 'China Invites Public Feedback on New Anti-Corruption System', *Sixth Tone,* 9 November, https://www.sixthtone.com/news/1001144/china-invites-public-feedback-on-new-anti-corruption-system (accessed on 30 May 2018).

Wang, Z. J. 2017. China's new anti-corruption body raises worrying questions about the rule of law', *The Conversation,* 17 May, http://theconversation.com/chinas-new-anti-corruption-body-raises-worrying-questions-about-the-rule-of-law-77001 (accessed on 30 May 2018)

Wedeman, A. 2017. 'Xi Jinping's Tiger Hunt: Anti-Corruption Campaign or Factional Purge?', *Modern China Studies,* Vol 24, Issue 2.

Xi Jinping. 2017. 'Full text of Xi Jinping's report at 19th CPC National Congress', *Xinhua,* 3 November, English.news.cn. http://www.xinhuanet.com/english/special/2017-11/03/c_136725942.htm (accessed on 30 May 2018).

*Xinhua.* 2016. 'Xinhua Insight: China starts supervision efficiency pilot schemes', English.news.cn. 11 November, http://www.xinhuanet.com/english/2016-11/11/c_135822667.htm (accessed on 30 May 2018).

*Xinhua*. 2017. 'China Focus: China publishes draft supervision law to solicit public opinion' English.news.cn. 8 November, http://www.xinhuanet.com/english/2017-11/08/c_136735002.htm (accessed on 30 May 2018).

*Xinhua*. 2018. 'Supervision law gives legal teeth to China's graft-busting agency', *China Daily*, 20 March, http://www.chinadaily.com.cn/a/201803/20/WS5ab1172da3106e7dcc143eef.html (accessed on 22 July 2018).

# 9

# The Party's Online Media during the 19th Congress

*Tilak Jha*

The 19th National Congress of the Communist Party of China (CPC) once again demonstrated that the most evident indicator of a crucial political event in the Chinese Party-State is: its impact, positive or negative, on the media. The 19th Congress in October 2017 was crucial as it marked the emergence of Chinese President and CPC General Secretary Xi Jinping as the Party's 'core' (*hexin*) and China's most powerful leader in decades. Hence, the Party-State deployed every available means to use both the traditional and the new media to build a rhetoric of order and harmony.

Before jumping on to how media actually worked during and around the historic 19th Party Congress and what Xi signalled about it in his crucial speech, it would be relevant to highlight the context before it. There are two key aspects that we will take into account to understand the context: media as a mouthpiece of the Party and Chinese media morality.

At the outset, it has to be conceded that despite all the privatisation and commercialisation, Chinese media *de facto,* yet caters to its role as a mouthpiece (*houshe*) of the CPC. The shoots of a media ecosystem differing from this traditional role has existed off and on, mainly in the Chinese cyber domain. Over the last decade or so, since internet arrived in China, this space existed despite the Party-State being conscious about it. However, Xi's speeches point out his determination to bring it in line with the Party's objectives. On more than one occasion, including in a key speech in 2016 in Beijing, Xi specifically pointed out the challenge of new media and called for promoting 'integrated development' (*yiti fazhan*) of traditional and emerging media as a 'strategic deployment' (*zhanlue bushu*). Xi talked about the 'unprecedented change' brought in media by internet and the challenge of managing it. The Chinese leader underscored the need to adapt to the new situation and called for 'occupying the commanding heights of information dissemination' (*zhanling xinxi chuanbo zhi gao dian*) by 'strengthening internet thought' (*qianghua hulianwang siwei*), among others (Xi 2017a).

Given the above line adopted with respect to new media, traditional media, particularly the Chinese newspapers were entirely expected to shed their 'individualities' in terms of carrying similar headlines and displaying little difference in their coverage of the Congress. Traditional media is also relatively easy to monitor, as its structure is primarily top to bottom, and the Party has been used to controlling it as a tool of propaganda for decades. Still, the 19th Congress went far beyond in putting effective curbs on the much more democratic and decentralised new and social media, which was increasingly sheltering dissents and views critical of the Party.

In the 2016 speech, Xi had also called for 'creating a clean and righteous environment' in the cyberspace as it was in the interest of the people (*fuhe renmin liyi*). Xi attached 'highest priority' (*zhongzhong zhizhong*) to wage a persistent ideological struggle (*yishi xingtai lingyu douzheng*) to overcome the challenges in the cyber domain (Xi 2017a).

Despite heavy censorship on any sensitive subject, the only noticeable resistance was occasionally visible in the online domain. However, by gradually making anonymity online trackable by putting the onus on administrators, individuals and service providers, the Xi leadership literally marked the death knell for the uncensored world online. As we will discuss later, this gradually expanded to cover live streaming of events and foreign programmes, and online community platforms as well.

Another key to understand Xi's framing of new media in the larger ideological work of the Party is that media professionalism and morality in the Chinese Party-State does not involve questioning the Party's authority. Unlike media's watchdog and often anti-establishment nature which is upheld in the liberal-western set up, the discussion on media ethics in China is remarkably limited to daily morality. Rather, even in case of a moral dilemma about the Party itself or its policies, media is to take a cue from the Party's policies and the instruction given by its leaders. However, these cues and instructions themselves can often be in conflict with morality and, also inconsistent and unreliable (*BBC Chinese* 2016). The market forces have further complicated this dilemma (Hu 2017). Since assuming office, Xi also gave a whole set of directions calling for encouraging high morale (*guwu shiqi*), and spread public morality (*cheng fenghua ren*), among others, but it is difficult to argue if that has helped much (Bandurski 2016).

The arguments regarding media in China suggest that the Party-State clearly sees a political incentive in continuing with the policy of keeping all forms of media including new media under its watch. Thus, during the run up to arguably the most prominent political event in decades, unsurprisingly, Chinese new media platforms had to shed their identities and imitate official traditional media's reports and stories. They all were thus highlighting how many and who would attend the Congress from which Province, and how happy they were to do so. The most 'critical' stories were about anti-corruption campaign and how imperfect most other political set ups were compared to China's. The online media therefore prioritised the Congress related news by placing them atop their news sections and home pages – a trend that seems here to stay. Learning from the closures of several popular TV shows, and 'controversial' media platform[1] and accounts on social media, online media followed the lead provided by the traditional official media organs at the top, namely *Xinhua*, CCTV (China Central TV) and *Renmin Ribao*.

## Xi's Work Report and Online Media

Xi Jinping re-asserted the need for new media to follow the Party line in his Political Report to the 19[th] Congress. Predictably, the conception of new media for the CPC, as the report shows, is entirely in line with the way print or other traditional media have been for the Party. Thus, his only direct reference about 'media' in his entire three-and-half hours speech was while talking about culture. Speaking on the theme of 'Building stronger culture confidence and helping socialist culture to flourish', he said:

> 'We will maintain the right tone in public communication, give priority to improving means of communication and to creating new ones, and strengthen the penetration, guidance, influence, and credibility of the media. We will provide more and better online content and put in place a system for integrated internet management to ensure a clean cyberspace. We will implement the system of responsibility for ideological work, and further consolidate our positions and improve management in this field. We will distinguish between matters of political principle, issues of understanding and thinking, and academic viewpoints, but we must oppose and resist various erroneous views with a clear stand' (Xi 2017b).

Xi's speech points to the fact that like traditional media, the Party has no reason to see the new media any differently. Thus, Xi kept his focus upon ideological work to ensure the Party and its leadership's sway over political affairs and social rhetoric. He also clearly steered away from giving any different institutional or theoretical recognition to the online media. Rather, the Chinese leader vowed to make sure the management of online content remains in line with the ideological objectives of the Party and any view that could be a potentially deviating one is effectively countered.

Giving an account of the achievements over the past years in the ideological domain, Xi said: 'We have strengthened Party leadership over ideological work and explored new ground in advancing Party related theories'. Ideological work came again when he talked about building a community with a shared future for mankind and while talking about upholding socialism.

A crucial theme of Xi's speech was on the existential threat that corruption posed to the Party in winning people and how 'a sweeping victory against corruption' was inevitable for 'long-term stability of the Party and the country'. However, he did not accord any *de jure* recognition to the *de facto* oversight role that social media in particular has been assigned by China's corruption watchdog in recent years (*Xinhua* 2015). Xi mentioned about oversight mechanism to ensure 'that power is exercised under public oversight' and 'oversight through public opinion' but the stress appears to be more on top-down approach than bottom-up.

Xi's recipe to 'improve and strengthen ideological and political work' also does not reside on the idealism or enlightenment of its citizens but on the *initiative of the Party* and its ability to improve the governance of China. He called for keeping 'a firm hold on the initiative' in the Party's work so that it can manage risks, or – better still – pre-empt them before they arise. For Xi, it is the study of 'Marxism-Leninism, Mao Zedong Thought, Deng Xiaoping Theory, the Theory of Three Represents and the Scientific Outlook on Development' that has created free minds in the Party. The President said that the Chinese socialist democracy's purpose was to 'give full expression to the will of the people, protect their rights and interests, spark their creativity, and provide systemic and institutional guarantee to ensure the people run the country'.

However, in place of giving media an independent role, Xi called for legal guarantee for people's rights and freedom, and their right to be informed – all under the leadership of the Party. For example, he called for improving the credibility of environmental assessment by making mandatory release of related information. Information and internet, according to Xi, are critical to improve governance.

In the same spirit, Xi's mention of internet was in purely technical terms mostly talking about its role in governance and entrepreneurship, and about the need and importance to avoid its misuse. He also talked about the need to maintain the sanctity and security of cyberspace, and the need to enhance China's strength in this and other technological domains such as artificial intelligence, which could be used in media sector sooner rather than later (Schmidt 2018).

## Online Media and 19th Congress

The online coverage of the 19th National Congress of the CPC was a reinforcement of Party propaganda in the traditional media at a scale far exceeding the capacity of online media on its own. The nature of online media the world over has been not to follow the print and the TV media, but to set the trend for them.[2] However, the build-up to determine the media coverage before the 19th Congress showed that in China, the Party-State was determined to make sure that the online media adhere to the priorities underlined by the Party on one hand, and to take the lead from traditional media, on the other. This, it was expected to use to propagate the Party among Chinese netizens. To ensure this, the CPC not only mobilised new media to push its version of news and propaganda to the national and international audiences, but it also took steps to censor information and divert people's attention from the big event.

### *Momentum Online*

Given the trend in favour of online media, the stress on this relatively new form of media seems entirely justified (Fig. 1).

**Fig. 1: Media reach in China in 2015**

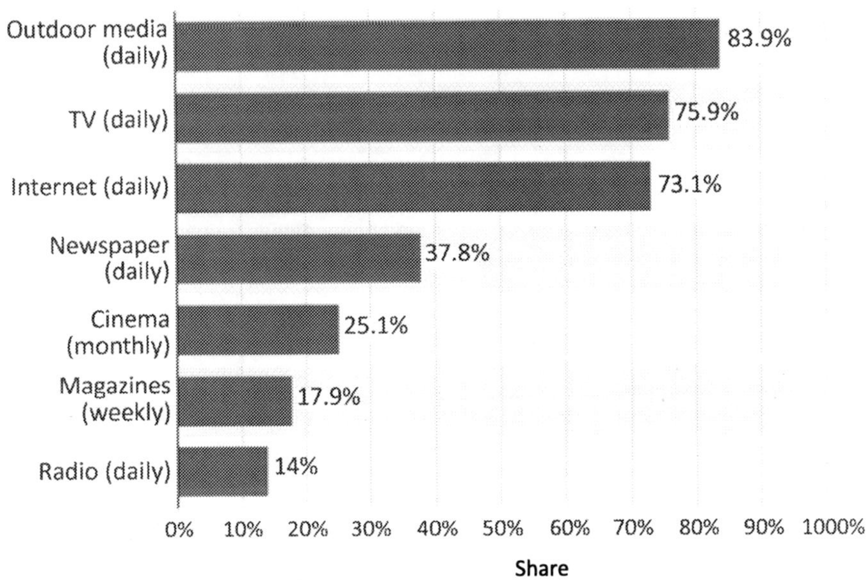


(Figure 1 provides the reach of different forms of media in percentage terms)
*Source:* Statista (2017)

As the statistics shows, TV remains one of the most engaging sources of media consumption in China reaching daily to over 75 percent of the audience in 2015. Newspapers, cinema and radio reach a relatively smaller audience though internet was close to TV in 2015 itself. Recent statistics point to further consolidation of the audience momentum in favour of internet and mobile. This trend is accompanied by a constantly declining share of audience time over traditional media forms namely radio, TV, print and even basic voice phone. Between 2012 and 2017, all these media witnessed consistent decline while the time spent by users on smartphone and tablet grew many-fold.

Figure 2 shows that between 2012 and 2017, the average time spent by adults with all the major media grew from an average of 5.14 hrs a day to 6.13 hrs. Out of this, the share of digital media grew from around 40 percent in 2012 to above 50 percent in 2016. While TV and radio, more or less maintained the time users spent on them, their share in audience media consumption still took a hit.

**Fig. 2: Average time spent per day with major media by adults in China, 2012–17**

| | 2012 | 2013 | 2014 | 2015 | 2016 | 2017 |
|---|---|---|---|---|---|---|
| **Digital** | **2:07** | **2:33** | **2:49** | **2:57** | **3:05** | **3:14** |
| Mobile (nonvoice) | 1:06 | 1:30 | 1:45 | 1:56 | 2:04 | 2:13 |
| –Smartphone | 0:39 | 0:54 | 1:03 | 1:11 | 1:18 | 1:26 |
| –Tablet | 0:11 | 0:22 | 0:30 | 0:33 | 0:36 | 0:38 |
| –Feature phone | 0:16 | 0:14 | 0:13 | 0:12 | 0:11 | 0:10 |
| –Desktop/laptop* | 1:01 | 1:03 | 1:04 | 1:02 | 1:01 | 2:38 |
| **TV**** | **2:42** | **2:42** | **2:41** | **2:40** | **2:39** | **2:38** |
| **Radio**** | **0:11** | **0:11** | **0:11** | **0:11** | **0:11** | **0:11** |
| **Print**** | **0:14** | **0:12** | **0:11** | **0:10** | **0:10** | **0:10** |
| –Newspapers | 0:12 | 0:11 | 0:10 | 0:09 | 0:09 | 0:09 |
| –Magazines | 0:01 | 0:01 | 0:01 | 0:01 | 0:01 | 0:01 |
| **Total** | **5:14** | **5:38** | **5:53** | **6:00** | **6:06** | **6:13** |

Figure 2 explains the time spent with each medium regardless of multitasking among users of age group 18 and above.
*Source*: eMarketer (2016)

The concern of the government arises from the fact that social media has become big enough in China. How big is the Chinese social media can be imagined from the fact that on 18 October 2017 – the day Xi delivered his work report to the 19th Congress, *Sina Weibo* trending topics related to the congress, together attracted over 1.8 billion views, according to Weibo's trend ranking index. Not unsurprisingly, Ruan notes that 'CPC increasingly sees the internet as the core battleground for ideological control and its very own survival' (Ruan 2017).

## *Regulatory Curbs*

The willingness of the Party to replicate its traditional dominance over TV and print in the domain of internet and social media has replicated in stricter surveillance and censorship over the years, particularly during this Congress. The fast growth of internet, its popularity among the younger generations, and the many exits it offers to access all sorts of contents the Party considers sensitive, has been a matter of great concern for it. With these things in mind, a series of curbs have been put in force on the media in general and online media in particular beginning several months before the Congress.

China's State Administration of Radio, Film and Television (SARFT) had begun to target entertainment and foreign TV shows well before the October Congress as early as since April and May of 2017. The agency issued guidelines to do away with major TV dramas to ensure proper welcome of the 19$^{th}$ Congress. At least nine popular TV programmes of various TV stations (other than the Phoenix), were either stopped or put on hold on various counts such as vulgarity, spreading false information, inching on privacy, or discussing too sensitive topics (Toutiao 2017).

The shutting of the highly rated talk show *Qian Qian San Ren Xing*, however, did not go down well with the netizens. After it was taken down, searching it on Weibo showed no results implying it was being censored. Censorship monitoring platforms noted that several netizens expressed their disappointment and commented that all being shown in those shows was the truth (RFA 2017).

There was no backing down due to such protests online. Rather, in early June 2017, the SARFT went a step further and mandated that no 'uncut' version of TV programmes be shared on any platform including internet either. SARFT in yet another notice issued in June 2017 asked telecom companies to stop illegal Internet Protocol Television (IPTV) services (SARFT 2017a). SARFT also ordered in late June to stop broadcasting of several illegal and disguised ads, mostly health products, for violating regulations related to duration of advertisement (SARFT 2017b).

Bilibili, a video website with more than 150 million users – mostly born after 1990 (*jiushihou*) – had to remove several of its popular American, British and Thai TV shows such as *Yes Minister* and *The IT Crowd* mainly to 'clean up' internet from foreign contents. Of course, there has also been a consistent effort to weed out the Virtual Private Network (VPN) services which allowed circumventing the censor by moving the server. These steps faced backlash online and followed by deleting or censoring of related key phrases (Li 2017).

All the above curbs still seemed temporary until the new provisions to erase anonymity online, the proverbial last nail in the coffin, were announced in late August and early September. The Office of the Central Leading Group of Cyberspace Affairs published Regulations on the Management of Internet Forum Community Services (*Hulianwang luntan shequ fuwu guanli guiding*) on 25 August (Cyberspace Administration of China 2017a) and Regulations on the Information Service of Internet Groups (*Hulianwang qunzu xinxi fuwu guanli guiding*) on 7 September (Cyberspace Administration of China 2017b) primarily holding web service providers and individuals responsible for any controversial online content deemed sensitive, offensive or causing rumour. The regulations came in effect beginning 1 October and 8 October 2017 respectively.

The main target of this notification happened to be the online communities such as Tianya and those who run such community services. Several such platforms have been considered to be one of the last vestiges offering significant space for free discussions. This notice sought to put the onus on service providers to maintain a database of identity and identity proofs of all its users and a track of who writes what. With these regulations and subsequent cleaning of the online community forums such as Tianya, the mission was complete.

### *Dedicated Online Platforms and Social Media*

Before the Congress, the Party's propaganda managers took several steps online that would attract different constituencies. One such thing was the *People's Daily* publishing a *Xuexi Cidian* in September 2017, basically a dictionary with a total of 110 terms related to the Party's new thinking, concepts and strategies that cadres must know (Wang 2017).

On 10 October 2017, *Renmin wang* (*People's Daily* Chinese version) launched an exclusive video '*Shi jiu da yao kai la*' about the convening of the 19$^{th}$ Congress. The 2 minute 50 seconds animated video explains what the Party was and what amendments were made to the Party constitution.

The Congress organisers set up a dedicated press centre and a website *19thcpcnews.cn* releasing updates in an orderly and organised fashion, even if mostly from *Xinhua*. The press centre indeed took a good care of the several affairs from information and technical support, increase in media desks and information rooms, expansion of network bandwidth, and 'giving all journalists more convenience and pleasing experience' (Press Centre of the 19$^{th}$ CPC 2017). The 19$^{th}$ CPC also had a dedicated bilingual WeChat account on which enquiries about the services provided could be made (*Xinhua* 2017b). Few of the Congress participants gave interviews and still fewer of them came from the top.

The press centre was basically only distributing official news media, primarily Xinhua's reports on the Congress. But the way it was promoted, everyone looked towards this platform than looking elsewhere.

China's official party-affiliated Xinhua News Agency, whose releases are widely distributed by the online media even otherwise, maintained a dedicated webpage with its entire coverage of the CPC Congress. *Xinhua* was also quite active on *WeChat*. Its Chinese *WeChat* account *xinhuashefabu*1 published a video on 12 October on 96 years of CPC history. However, the 6 minutes 52 second video produced by Diyi Gongzuo Shi ('Xinhua All-Media Service') mentioned only Mao Zedong and Xi Jinping. *Xinhua* produced a series of small length videos entitled 'Our self-confidence (*women zixin*)' before the Congress. On the eve of the 19th Congress, the news agency published another video lauding Xi the 'navigator (*ling hang*)' (*Xinhua* 2017c).

On the other hand, the day before the Congress was to begin, Chinese mainland social media users got a 60-character notification from their service providers such as *WeChat, QQ* and *Weibo* that they will not be able to change their profile pictures, usernames or personal details until November due to 'system maintenance'. Because of similar reasons, such freezes rarely went beyond a couple of hours earlier. This time, however, the freer and more open the platform, the bigger the restrictions. So, while the relatively closed group kind of social media platform *WeChat* with nearly 900 million users stayed with only these changes, *Weibo* – one of China's most popular social media platforms with more than 360 million active users and with a system of publicly visible post unlike *Weixin*, also stopped overseas registration for new members till 30 October 2017 (*Weixin* 2017). Earlier, online short-term rental companies such as Airbnb cancelled all their central Beijing bookings. Special attention to the youth reflected in universities being required to submit daily cybersecurity reports between 8–27 October 2017 (Shen 2017).

One of China's most popular live-streaming platforms Wuhan-based *Duoyu.com* set up a 'celebrity Party branch' on 30 June 2017. It hired CPC members as anchors to live-stream celebrity party members and their party activities online. They also focused on activities such as singing patriotic songs and red-tourism.

This trend extended to China's media-technology giants Baidu, Alibaba and Tencent as well. The three biggest Chinese tech companies have also reported CPC members working with them. Tencent has reportedly more than 3000 CPC members working for it, while Alibaba and Baidu staff more than 2000 and 2500 party members respectively (*Beijing Review* 2017).

Some of the keywords censored during the key political event included 'Beijing subways', 'security checks' pointing to long queues due to increasing security checks which users were seen clicking photos and sharing online. 'Microblog system maintenance' was the other key phrase that got censor's notice as it drew attention to the temporary profile freeze on social media sites. 'Xiamen TV' got censored as it drew attention being one channel showing a cartoon in place of live coverage of the congress. The key phrase pointing to Jiang Zemin's participation in the Congress – 'The Elder' – was also among the censored ones.

In brief, without all the tools that the Party applied to determine the Chinese media's coverage of the 19th Congress, it could have looked much different than it did.

### *A timeline of build-up towards regulated online coverage of 19th Congress*

Much before the 19th Congress was held, the tightening of the internet was underlined at the highest level by the entire leadership (Xi's we have already discussed). On 27 December 2016, Wang Xiujun, the Deputy Director of State Internet Information office, said releasing China's National Cyberspace Security Strategy that while cyberspace was 'comprehensively changing people's way of production and living but security issues are not to be neglected' (Wang 2016). The strategy followed approval from Central Leading Group for Cybersecurity and Informatisation which underlined nine related tasks including cyber sovereignty, preventing cyber-crime and cyber violations, strengthening cyber security and cyber space protection (*Xinhua* 2017a).

In January 2017, head of the Central Propaganda Department (CPD), Liu Qibao wrote an article in organ newspaper *Remin Ribao* citing the 18th CPC Central Committee's 'Guiding opinions regarding how to promote the integrated development of the traditional media and the emerging media'. He also underlined Xi Jinping's stress in the direction and said that it was necessary to integrate traditional and new media outlets (Liu Qibao 2017). The campaign continued. In February 2017, Li Yanyan of the School of Marxism Studies at the University of Science and Technology, Beijing wrote in CPC's leading theory journal *Qiushi* that 'the internet was the biggest arena for airing public opinions in China and yet it was also where rumours of all kinds, abusive language and verbal violence occurred most frequently'. Thus, Li called for supervision, particularly of online opinion leader through a scoring system (Li Yanyan 2017). Several other leaders gave similar statements at various levels.

As the period of the 19th Congress came close, these indirect signals reflected in more concrete actions. For example, on 3 August, China's Twitter-like social media platform *Weibo* reported that it will 'rectify vulgar information and accounts over the week'. Under this, more than 20,000 'vulgar video clips' and another 72 vulgar accounts were either removed or shut down. *Sina Weibo* also said that the action was to continue till the end of August 2017 and netizens were invited to report of any vulgar materials or accounts (*Hong Kong Xinbao* 2017a).

Few days later, on 5 August, fictional character *Winnie the Pooh* got censored on Chinese social media after a YouTube user with a similar nickname forwarded several clips by controversial Chinese businessman Guo Wengui about the corrupt lifestyle of many high-ranking Chinese officials. Guo Wengui facing a blanket block on Chinese internet and social media platforms, also resulted in to a *de facto* ban on *Winnie the Pooh*. Many Chinese *Weibo* users who shared either of the nearly 120 video clips relating to Guo from *Winnie the Pooh*, had their account shut down (*Hong Kong Xinbao 2017b*).

Entertainment content followed. The target this time was not only *Sina Weibo* but also *WeChat.* Twenty-five famous *WeChat* public accounts faced shutdown. Government figures showed a jump of more than 40 percent in censoring of illegal and unhealthy internet content (*Sing Tao Ribao* 2017).

Such clean-up also included an effective filtering out of keywords associated with Nobel prize winner Liu Xiaobo. Anything related such 'Xiaobo', 'Xiaobo+Liu', 'Teacher Liu' and 'Liu Xia+housearrest', all remained inaccessible. Around Liu's death, photo sharing either on *WeChat* groups, *WeChat* moments or one-to-one *WeChat* messaging were all disabled. The censor was extremely sophisticated and images of empty chair or candles could either be not sent, according to Joseph Chan Man of the Chinese University of Hong Kong (Man 2017).

Beyond tightening of censorship and restrictions on the one hand, China's propaganda managers also had support from online private enterprise. For example, *Zhihu*, a popular Chinese platform like *Quora*, set up a CPC branch and convened a meeting on 22 August. At the meeting, the CPC branch's Secretary called for adhering to the principle of 'party rules the media' (*Hong Kong Xinbao* 2017c).

There was also a clear spike in the level and manner of engagement with the online public as the Congress came closer. As on 11 September 2017, there were reports of the CPC website setting a new database for Xi's important speeches on *Wechat* with the id: *xuexixiaozu* (*Weixin* 2017).

Beijing organised a National Cybersecurity Propaganda Week in mid-September 2017, where the Deputy head of the Central Leading Group on Cybersecurity and Informatisation, Liu Yunshan said that China needs to be a cyber powerhouse in line with Xi's vision. Liu also clearly linked the goals of the Party with the Congress when he called 'to build good cyber environment for a victorious convocation of the Party's 19th National Congress' (Liu Yunshan 2017).

Just a day before, the Theoretical Studies Centre Group of the Cyberspace Administration of China wrote an article which said that public opinion work online was increasingly the most important task of propaganda and ideological work. It also said that keeping it under control was inevitable and the Party's voice in the cyberspace must always be the strongest. The article talked about Xi's 'Four Principles' and 'Five Propositions' (*si xiang yuanze, wu dian zhuzhang*) for internet governance and cyberspace regulation which the Chinese president mentioned at a December 2015 speech. The article also declared, as on previous occasions: 'If the Party could not overcome the hurdle presented by the internet, it cannot traverse the hurdle of remaining in power for long' (Theoretical Studies Centre Group of Cyberspace Administration of China 2017).

Somehow, there appeared to be all argument being given in the Chinese media about why it was good if the Party controlled the internet. In a report by Jiang Lin of *Nanfang Dushi Bao*, several online platforms in China had renewed their privacy terms according to the norms of Cyberspace Administration of China (CAC). These platforms included *Weixin, Weibo, Taobao, Jingdong, Alipay, Gaode maps, Baidu maps, Didi, Umetrip* and *Ctrip*. The report claimed that leave eight platforms operated by Tencent, Alibaba, Netease and Baidu who had relatively higher level of transparency, most others protected information inadequately. The argument clearly seemed to be aimed at convincing the readers about the inevitability of the Party over cyberspace (Lin 2017).

On 19 September 2017, *Hong Kong Ming Bao* newspaper reported that not only the CPC banned unauthorised media campaign for Xi before the Congress but it required web portals including *Sina, Tencent, NetEase* and *Sohu* to place news reports and articles related to Xi Jinping at the top of their news sections (*Hong Kong Mingbao* 2017). CAC also wanted these articles to be read, resulting in some web portals misreporting the click rate data. Chinese authorities also arrested several social media users for all sorts of purposes such as live streaming 'illegal speeches' (*Hong Kong Xinbao* 2017d).

Chinese objective of controlling online propaganda was not limited to the mainland alone as was evident when Facebook closed the account of political fugitive Guo Wengui who was posting sensitive rumours about Chinese leaders (*Hong Kong Xinbao* 2017e).

### *Impact on online coverage*

All the above actions helped the Party push its 19th Congress propaganda by all count. Other than the fact that every next online media platform including their social media sites were awash with $19^{th}$ Congress related live and active coverage, the related topics trended pointing to the success of the Party's propaganda objectives.

As of 1300 hours China time on 18 October, three of the top six trends on *Sina Weibo* (Fig 3) related to the $19^{th}$ Party Congress. The top trend on Weibo at the time was a *People's Daily* story headlined '*Ni zuiniu de beijingshi jintian de zhongguoren*' meaning 'Most awesome thing about you is that you are Chinese'. Most of the visible comments on the trend were positive. Other top trends related to the party congress on Weibo at the time were '*Zhibo Shijiu Da*' (Live Nineteen), '*Shijiu da kaimu*' and 'Grand Nineteenth Opening'.

**Fig. 3: Screenshot of Weibo trend page on 18 October 1300 hours, China local time**

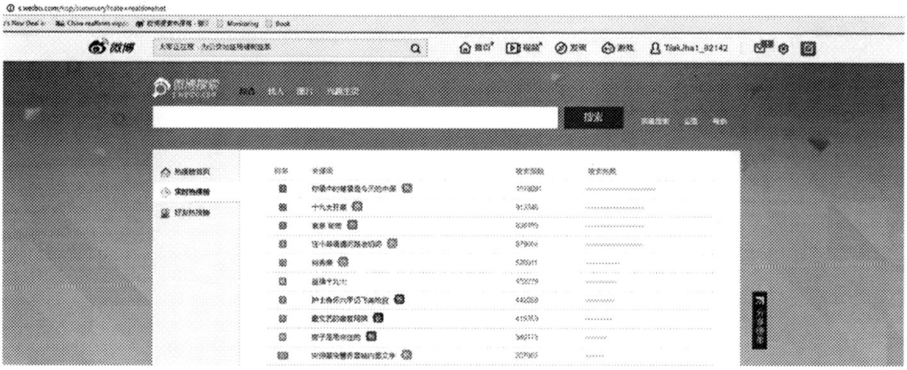

*Source*: Self-monitoring.

On 19 October, as of 1.30 pm China time, the top trend on *Sina Weibo* was again party related key words. After a slowdown in the subsequent days, on 24 October 2017, the day of the closing of the congress, the closing ceremony itself was amongst top trends on *Weibo* as of 1.15 pm China time with nearly 500,000 people following the Chinese term for the concluding ceremony – '*Shijiu Da Bimu Hui*'. Many Chinese media sites also posted updates related to the Party Congress while several posts, mostly positive, with the key word *Shi Jiu Da* ($19^{th}$ Party Congress) were posted on *Weibo.* One user wrote: 'Look forward to the great rejuvenation of the Chinese nation and quick realisation of the Chinese dream'.

Overall, in between 17–25 October, the $19^{th}$ Congress was on top of *Weibo* users on the first couple of days before subsiding. Nevertheless, the fact that it remained among the top trends and invited hundreds of thousands of comments, likes and shares points to the success of the Party's intended agenda. Indeed, as the subsequent discussions regarding online media point out, China under Xi wants to take the campaign of online propaganda further. In line with this, the

Central Committee of the CPC issued a document on 2 November 2017 about its decision on how to implement the 19th Congress spirit. The release quoted:

**Fig. 4: Screenshot of Weibo trend for the period 17–25 October.**

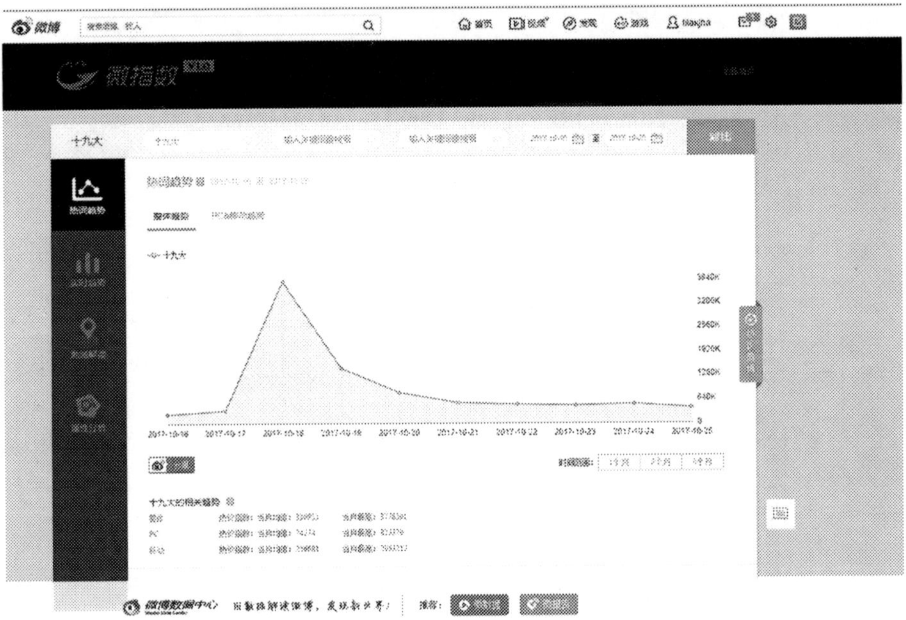

*Source*: Self-monitoring.

> 'We should actively initiate Internet propaganda as well as make good use of new technology and new applications, such as 'Weibo, WeChat and Mobile News' to fully mobilise the enthusiasm of the netizens for participation and enhance the effectiveness and influence of Internet propaganda.... We should make full use of new technology and new applications to create new media dissemination methods and continuously enhance the practical effects of propaganda' (*Xinhua* 2017a).

In brief, the 19th Party Congress is over but its spirit is going to keep making the Chinese cyberspace, the Party's cyberspace, beyond the Congress as well. In any case, even after the Congress, the most crucial curbs on new media platforms which initially appeared to be a temporary measure, remains in force. Ironically, months after the Congress, every next political news story in China continues to talk about upholding the message of the 19th Congress. At least for now, nowhere does it seem more relevant than in the 'clean' cyberspace which the Chinese Party-State seems determined to maintain.

## NOTES

1. The TV campaigns offensive was also accompanied by shutting down of several popular TV programmes such as the Hong Kong based Phoenix TV's 19-year-old popular celebrity talk show *Behind Headline with Wen Tao* (*qiang qiang san renxing*) on 12 September. The show was known for focusing upon sensitive political issues. Two other TV shows namely *Peter Qiu's Talk (zhen hai ting feng lu)* and *Current Affairs Debate* (*shishi bianlun hui*) were also shut down (Global Times 2017). Such shows were replaced by seven series of 'special topic programmes' (*zhuantipian*) highlighting China's and particularly Xi's achievements in the field of political reforms, economy, governance, diplomacy, law, military and anti-corruption.
2. China's party-affiliated newspaper the *Renmin Ribao* (*People's Daily Chinese*) published a *Guangming Ribao* article as early as in 2006 which said that the emergence of new media has changed the rules of the game for traditional media due to its three special features: real-time, interactivity and multi-medium format (print, audio, video all combined in one) (*Guangming Ribao* 2006). However, another article published in the *People's Daily* in 2014 said that the classical agenda setting had its limitations in the new media environment which has made everyone a media producer and, means and types of media consumption have changed. But the article does concede that traditional media's agenda setting role remains under question as their mass media role is no more the way it used to be. Globally as well, whether social media by an individual does actually set the wider agenda is a matter of great debate. Nonetheless, there is no denying that social media has started playing a crucial role in what would feature on the next day's front page of a newspaper.

## REFERENCES


Bandurski, David. 2016. 'How Xi Jinping views the news' *China Media Project*, 3 March. https://medium.com/china-media-project/how-the-president-views-the-news-2bee482e1d48 (accessed on 9 June 2018).

*BBC Chinese*. 2016. '*Zhengzhi he daode chongtu de zhongguo meiti* [Political and moral conflict of Chinese media]', 11 January, http://www.bbc.com/zhongwen/trad/china/2016/01/160111_cr_china_media (accessed on 30 May 2018).

*Beijing Review*. 2017. 19 October, https://monitoring.bbc.co.uk/product/c1dmtkhw (accessed on 23 November 2017).

Cyberspace Administration of China. 2017a. '*Hulianwang luntan shequ fuwu guanli guiding* [Provisions on the Management of Internet Forum Community Services]', 7 September, http://www.cac.gov.cn/2017-08/25/c_1121541921.htm (accessed on 16 November 2017).

Cyberspace Administration of China. 2017b. '*Hulianwang qunzu xinxi fuwu guanli guiding* [Internet Group Information Service Management Provisions]', 7 September, http://www.cac.gov.cn/2017-09/07/c_1121623889.htm (accessed on 23 November 2017).

*eMarketer*. 2016. 'Average time spent per day with major media by adults in China, 2012–17', April, https://www.emarketer.com/Chart/Average-Time-Spent-per-Day-with-Major-Media-by-Adults-China-2012-2017-hrsmins/189275 (accessed on 13 November 2017).

*Global Times*. 2017. 'Phoenix TV cancels popular talk show', 13 September, http://www.globaltimes.cn/content/1066324.shtml (accessed on 19 November 2017).

*Guangming Daily*. 2006. '*Hulianwang yingxiang xia de meiti yicheng shezhi* [Media agenda setting under the influence of internet]'. *People's Daily*. 12 January, http://theory.people.com.cn/GB/49154/49156/4020146.html (accessed on 25 June 2018).

*Hong Kong Mingbao*. 2017. '*Zhong xuanbu jintoubu xuanchuan Xi sixiang* [CPC Propaganda Department bans unauthorised media propaganda about Xi's though]', 19 September, https://news.mingpao.com/pns/dailynews/web_tc/article/20170919/s00013/1505758171653 (accessed on 30 January 2018).

*Hong Kong Xinbao*. 2017a. '*Xinlang Weibo qing 2 wan tian disu zixun* [Sina Weibo clears 20,000 vulgar messages]', 3 August, http://www1.hkej.com/dailynews/cntw/article/1622949/新浪微博清2萬條低俗資訊 (accessed on 11 January 2018).

____ . 2017b. '*Weinibeijinshi yin zhuan Guo baoliao* [Censorship of Winnie the Pooh linked to Guo Wengui]', 5 August, https://news.mingpao.com/pns/dailynews/web_tc/article/20170805/s00013/1501869432303 (accessed on 21 December 2017).

____ . 2017c. '*Shejiao pingtai Zhihu dang guan* [Party and social media platform Zhihu]', 25 August, http://www1.hkej.com/dailynews/cntw/article/1640725/社交平台知乎「黨管」 (accessed on 30 December 2017).

____. 2017d. '*Liang Weixin hu fayanbu dang zaojuliu* [Two WeChat account holders detained for illegal speeches]'. 20 September, http://www1.hkej.com/dailynews/cntw/article/ 1661044/兩微信戶發言不當遭拘留 (accessed on 24 January 2018).

____. 2017e. '*Go Wengui FB tuizao fengsuo* [Closure of Guo Wengui's FB account]', 3 October, http://www1.hkej.com/dailynews/articlePrint/id/1670501 (accessed on 18 January 2018).

Hu, Yong. 2017. '*Xin meiti shidai hongguo xinwe lunli de liangnan kunju* [Two ethical dilemmas of Chinese journalism in the new media era]'. *Caixin*. 1 November, http://huyong.blog.caixin.com/archives/170865 (accessed 12 June 2018).

Jiang Lin. 2017. '*Gebie pingtai shejiao gongneng zengqiang yinsi baohu wei genshang* [Majority of China's social media platforms do not have enough privacy protection]',

Li, Eva. 2017. 'TV fans angry after foreign shows suddenly pulled from popular Chinese video-sharing sites' *South China Morning Post*, 13 July, http://www.scmp.com/news/china/society/article/2102509/tv-fans-angry-after-foreign-shows-suddenly-pulled-popular-chinese (accessed on 23 November 2017).

Liu Qibao. 2017. '*Tuijin meiti shendu ronghe dazao xinxing zhuliu meiti* [To push deep integration of media to create new type of mainstream media]', http://paper.people.com.cn/rmrb/html/2017-01/11/nw.D110000renmrb_20170111_1-06.htm (accessed on 18 December 2017).

Li Yanyan. 2017. '*Guan meichang jiaqiang jianguan wangluo yijian lingxiu* [Government to reinforce supervision of online opinion leaders]' *Hong Kong Xinbao*, 7 February, http://www1.hkej.com/dailynews/articlePrint/id/1486786(accessed on 7 January 2018).

Liu Yunshan. 2017. '*Wei dang de shijiuda shengli zhaokai yingzao lianghao wangluo huanjing* [Build a good cyber environment for victorious convocation of the 19th National Congress]'. *Xinhua*. 16 September, http://www.xinhuanet.com/politics/2017-09/16/c_1121674897.htm (accessed on 22 January 2018).

Man, Joseph Chan. 2017. '*Cong Liu Xiaobo sixun kandalu shejiao meiti de guankong* [Chinese social media control after Liu Xiaobo's death]' *Hong Kong Mingbao*. 10 August, https://news.mingpao.com/pns/dailynews/web_tc/article/20170810/s00012/1502300940933 (accessed on 27 December 2017).

Press Centre of the 19th CPC. 2017. 'The Press Centre of the 19th NCCPC Opens', 11 October, http://19th.cpcnews.cn/english/n100/2017/1011/c159-596.html (accessed on 23 November 2017).

Renming Wang. 2017. '*Xuexi cidian: Dang de shiba da yiliai dang yuan ganbu bi zhi de xinci lanmushang xixan* [New words that Party cadres must know]', 18 September, http://theory.people.com.cn/n1/2017/0918/c40531-29541538.html (accessed on 23 November 2017).

RFA. 2017. '*Fenghuang Weishi "Qiang Qiang San Renxin" deng san shiping jiemuzao ting bochuan beijing leiling zhenggai* [Three programs of Phoenix TV including San San Ren Xing stopped by Beijing]', 12 September, http://www.rfa.org/mandarin/Xinwen/4-09122017133148.html (accessed on 14 November 2017).

Ruan, Lotus. 2017. 'Internet censorship: how China does it' *The Strategist*, 9 October, https://www.aspistrategist.org.au/internet-censorship-how-china-does-it/ (accessed on 23 November 2017).

SARFT. 2017a. *'Guangdian Zongju: Bude zairen heping taishang chuanbo suowei "Wei shanjian ban" jiemu* [SARFT calls for preventing distribution of uncut version on any platform]', 2 June, http://china.huanqiu.com/article/2017-06/10781830.html (accessed on 17 November 2017).

SARFT. 2017b. '*Guangdian Zongju: Zeling zhongguo liantong, zhongguo yidong tingzhi weigui* IPTV yewu [SARFT orders China Unicom, China Mobile to stop illegal IPTV services]', 9 June, http://www.thepaper.cn/newsDetail_forward_1705147 (accessed on 21 November 2017)

SARFT. 2017c. *'Guojia xinwen chuban guangdianzong jubangong ting guanyu lijiting zhibo chu "Miao Xian Hai Chuan Fang" deng 40 tiaoweigui guanggao de tongzhi* [SARFT asks to immediately stop "Miao xian kechuan fang" and 40 other illegal ads]', 23 June, http://www.sapprft.gov.cn/sapprft/contents/6588/338194.shtml (accessed on 22 November 2017).

Schmidt, Christine. 2018. 'China's news agency is reinventing itself with AI' *Niemanlab*, 10 January, http://www.niemanlab.org/2018/01/chinas-news-agency-is-reinventing-itself-with-ai/ (accessed on 29 January 2018).

Shen, Alice. 2017. 'China in cyber lockdown as WeChat, QQ and Weibo ban changes to users' profiles' *South China Morning Post*, 18 October, http://www.scmp.com/news/china/society/article/2115913/china-cyber-lockdown-wechat-qq-and-weibo-ban-changes-users (accessed on 23 November 2017).

*Sing Tao Ribao*. 2017. *'Wangluo da saochuyu wuluan cheng xiaoxianrou* [Do not implore the new round of internet clean up targeting teen idols]', 7 August, http://std.stheadline.com/daily/news-content.php?id=1644519&target=2 (accessed on 17 December 2017).

Statisa. 2017. 'Media reach in China', https://www.statista.com/statistics/272517/media-reach-in-china/ (accessed on 13 November 2017).

Theoretical Studies Centre Group of Cyberspace Administration of China. 2017. '*Shenru guanche Xi Jinping zongshuji wangluo qiangguo zhanlue sixiang zhashui tuijin wangluo anquan he xinxihua gongzuo* [Deepening the implementation of General Secretary Xi Jinping's strategic thinking on building China into a cyber superpower and steadily advancing cyber security and informatisation work]', 15 September, http://www.qstheory.cn/dukan/qs/2017-09/15/c_1121647633.htm (accessed on 17 January 2018).

Toutiao. 2017. '*Hunan wishi "Baike Quan Shuo" deng 9 da zongyi bei guangdian mingling jinbo* [9 programs including Hunan TV's Encyclopaedia asked to stop airing]', 24 April, http://news.china.com/socialgd/10000169/20170424/30453760_all.html#page_2 (accessed on 15 November 2017).

Xi Jinping. 2017a. 'Rang hulianwang genghao zaofu renming [Let the internet serve the people better]' *Xinhua*. 18 April, http://www.xinhuanet.com/politics/2017-04/18/c_1120833088.htm (accessed 28 May 2018).

____ . 2017b. 'Secure a Decisive Victory in Building a Moderately Prosperous Society in All Respects and Strive for the Great Success of Socialism with Chinese Characteristics for a New Era', 19th National Congress of the Communist Party of China. *Xinhua*. 18 October, http://www.xinhuanet.com/english/download/Xi_Jinping's_report_at_19th_CPC_National_Congress.pdf. (accessed on 31 January 2018).

*Xinhua*. 2015. 'Social media encouraging corruption whistleblowing', 9 May, http://www.chinadaily.com.cn/china/2015-05/09/content_20665420.htm (accessed on 10 January 2018).

*Xinhua*. 2017a. 'Authorised release: Decision of the Central Committee of the Communist Party of China [CPC] in conscientiously study, propagate, and implement the spirit of the 19th CPC National Congress', 2 November, translated and published by BBC Monitoring, 12 November, https://monitoring.bbc.co.uk/product/c1dnczz4.

*Xinhua*. 2017b. '19th CPC National Congress website, WeChat account to open on Oct. 11', 9 October, http://news.xinhuanet.com/english/2017-10/09/c_136667310.htm (accessed on 23 November 2017).

*Xinhua*. 2017c. '*Xinhua she zhenhan dapian: Linghang* [Xinhua agency amazing video: The navigator]', 17 October, http://news.xinhuanet.com/video/2017-10/17/c_129721329.htm (accessed on 23 November 2017).

Wang Xiujun. 2016. '*Guojia wangxin fabu (guojia wangluokong anquan zhanlue) tichuhan wei wangluo kongjianzhu quandeng renwu* [State Internet Information Office releases National Cyberspace Security Strategy, setting tasks such as defending cyberspace sovereignty]'. *Xinhua*. 28 December, http://www.xinhuanet.com/mil/2016-12/28/c_129423081.htm (accessed on 13 December 2018).

*Weixin*. 2017. 'Xuexi liqi! *Guanyu Xi Jinping de suoyou ziliao douzai zheshu juku li la* [Outstanding study: All the information related to Xi Jinping are in this database]', 11 September.

# II. THE GLOBAL PERSPECTIVE

# 10

# Xi Jinping's Diplomatic Strategy

*Kishan S Rana*

The key foreign policy theme of Xi Jinping's opening speech at the 19th Congress of the Chinese Communist Party was restoration of 'China's rightful place at the centre of the world'. First, recent Chinese foreign policy statements speak of 'great power diplomacy with Chinese characteristics' (*The Economist* 2017).[1] That great power status is a dominant preoccupation is demonstrated by Xi's use of the term 'great power' or 'strong power' some 26 times in his opening speech: 'China will continue to play its part as a major and responsible country', he asserted. This was a departure from the past when leaders in Beijing depicted their country as a poor, modest player abroad, in line with Deng Xiaoping's 1989 doctrine that China should 'hide its capacities, bide it time and never take the lead'. This posture evidently corresponds to both China's expanded capacity and the global environment, but the strident urgency is new. Second, few had anticipated the incorporation of 'One Belt, One Road' (OBOR), also called the 'Belt and Road Initiative (BRI), into the Party Constitution. It establishes OBOR's centrality to China's foreign and economic policy, albeit at the cost of flexibility. Third, moving further from the 'peaceful rise' doctrine of the mid-2000s, China now stresses its first class military capability: the PLA is 'built to fight'. How will China's neighbours take crude assertion of power? Overall, China places itself at equality with the US, i.e. a superpower in effect, even if that term is not its self-description. Four, a novel assertion: China's development presents a new choice for other countries; Xi spoke of 'blazing a trail for other developing countries...Chinese wisdom and a Chinese approach to solving problems' (Xi 2017). Is that the start of a 'Beijing consensus'? Finally, gone is Deng's notion of collective leadership, flowing from experience with Mao's dictatorship. Deng found place in the Party Constitution only after his death; Xi, raised to that status, is now given singular authority, and by inference, lifelong leadership. Of course, the March 2018 National People's Congress (NPC) confirmed this.

Consider also what is missing. One of these is the notion of multipolarity. Asserting 'centre stage' role in world affairs, China no longer speaks of a consortium of global powers (Kantha 2017a). Those that have discussed Asian affairs with Chinese scholars confirm this; they have little interest in notions of a multi-power future for Asia. This has profound implications for Asia and the world. First, it throws a gauntlet, declaring Beijing's a putative primacy. That ill-suits the Asian reality, where Asian region powers, Australia, India, Indonesia, Japan, South Korea and Vietnam, jostle for their place in the sun, with the US and Russia playing the Asia game by right, as it were. Second, China simply fails to understand that the grand connectivity-plus-infrastructure project OBOR creates 'global public goods' which are of legitimate concern to many different states, even those not contributors or direct participants. Collegial consultation is the best assurance of full value from the OBOR investments, from Beijing's own perspective. Will China understand what its hubristic mindset portends? Third, globalisation, with all its flaws and caveats, has created an eco-political frame that runs counter to redox of pre-1990 two-power domination. Each superpower, actual or putative, confronts other contesting entities, especially when chains of alliances have weakened.

## The Chinese System

The opacity of the Chinese system, combined with the rapid transformation produced through the 1979 reforms, sometimes gives the country an aura of omniscience, i.e. its policy and actions are imbedded in a master schema that unrolls with precision. True, China has long applied strategic planning in foreign affairs. Its overarching Party system also endows it with a *unified decision system,* plus a *comprehensive policy implementation capacity* that is truly Leninist, more centralised perhaps than in any other country (Jakobson and Knox 2010). At the very apex of its national system, both these processes work well, but some – and often a great deal – of that unified force is dissipated by the time it reaches the nooks and crannies of the Provinces, counties and the sub-units. Ministries and agencies pull in different directions, especially on matters of detail. Another reality is that within the international system, China remains a normal country, subject to the same pressures and limitations as any other, even if its style and some actions reflect special characteristics. It is thus an error to endow China with a deeper governance capacity, or capabilities to produce outcomes radically different from what other states can accomplish.

In foreign affairs, as elsewhere, China's apex policy-making straddles two entities: the government system (headed by the State Council and Ministries), and the Communist Party of China (CPC) Central Office. The Politburo, especially its seven-member Standing Committee, commands both. When it comes to international relations, the core agency is the 'Foreign Affairs Leading Small Group'. Similar 'Leading Small Groups' (LSGs) deal with a multitude of different subjects, including the one established in 2014 to deal with national security; another deals with Taiwan affairs, and perhaps Hong Kong and Macao as well. Neither their membership nor modes of functioning are public. We also do not know how an overlap between foreign policy and national security is handled. Small bits of information trickle out on occasion.[2] That adds to mystique.

Following the March 2018 NPC important changes have taken place. A new unification of foreign aid execution now comes through a new 'Department for Overseas Relations', under the joint control of the State Council and the Party, headed by State Councillor Yang Jiechi, now a Politburo member; this department takes charge of foreign aid, through the 'International Development Cooperation Agency', with the Ministries of Commerce and of Foreign Affairs harnessed into it.[3] Foreign Minister Wang Yi also rises in rank as State Councillor (*SCMP* 2018).

## Key Issues

Consider the likely impact of the 19th CPC on China's foreign affairs.

**First, what role is OBOR likely to play in China's relations with neighbouring countries and regions, and in its policy in Asia, Africa and Europe?**

An amendment to the Party Constitution now reads: 'The Congress agrees to include into the Party Constitution the following statements....[F]ollow the principle of achieving shared growth through discussion and collaboration; and pursue the Belt and Road Initiative' (*Xinhuanet* 2017). Despite its blandness, this is unique. In his 18 October 2017 speech at the opening session of the Congress, President Xi said:

> We should pursue the Belt and Road Initiative as a priority, give equal emphasis to 'bringing in' and 'going global', follow the principle of achieving shared growth through discussion and collaboration, and increase openness and cooperation in building innovation capacity. With these efforts, we hope to make new ground in opening China further through links running eastward and westward, across land and over sea...China will actively promote international cooperation through the Belt and Road Initiative. In doing so, we hope to achieve policy, infrastructure, trade, financial, and people-to-people connectivity and thus build a new platform for international cooperation to create new drivers of shared development (Xi 2017).

OBOR is long on declaratory statements, principally from Chinese sources that furnish partial, fragmentary information. But OBOR activities at the ground level are short on data and details that might permit sustained analysis (Rana 2017a). For example, past experience has been that China's announced lines of credit and loans to foreign countries do not all translate into action; this happens with most aid providers, but with China the gaps are larger. Whether the eventual global figure of OBOR projects reaches $900 billion or $1.3 trillion (as per different guesstimates), or even half of such figures, it is a vast, multi-dimensional collection of projects that will take a decade and more to implement. Some have likened it to a new 'Marshall Plan', but it is too mercantile for that comparison. Sharp questions persist over the debts it will leave behind for China's partner countries, given the long gestation and very gradual profitability of all infrastructure investments. In 2017 Sri Lanka, converted 70 percent of its debt into a part-sale of Colombo port to a Chinese company. Will such actions be more palatable for the recipients than a debt overhang? OBOR is intended to be Xi's lasting legacy for China, but it can become a millstone.

OBOR will create a web of obligations and dependencies on China for the countries receiving loans and grants for infrastructure and other investments (Jacob 2017). That is to China's benefit. But the downside is the hard loan repayment obligations, on which most information is not in the public domain, though some bits seep out. For example, published information on the China-Pakistan Economic Corridor (CPEC), a centrepiece of OBOR, shows that loans carry an onerous return-on-investment commitment of 17 percent (rising to 25 percent if the concessions given to China are factored in), and payable in US dollars, as a former governor of the State Bank of Pakistan wrote recently (Kardar 2017). Have some leaders of the borrowing countries made these long-term commitments anticipating that they may not be around when payback is to be made to Beijing? Can China show flexibility when it faces a demand for loan write-offs or for easing of repayments? This has the potential of becoming a messy situation for China, the more so with its domestic public increasingly alert in demanding financial accountability. In the next five years, more Sri Lanka type of situations will arise, and China will confront borrower demands. Of course, some investments will become productive, enhancing China's image and influence.

There is another avenue for OBOR. Many projects will create 'global public goods', i.e. connectivity and other infrastructure usable by third countries, including ports, roads, rail-lines, and industrial estates. On 8 January 2018, French President Macron told an audience in Xi'an: 'The ancient Silk Roads were never only Chinese. By definition these roads can only be shared. If there are roads, they cannot be one way' (*Reuters* 2018). This is just one instance of countries cautioning Beijing on the need for better transparency and openness towards putative OBOR beneficiaries (Rana 2017b).

Might China engage in wider 'OBOR Plus' consultation with third countries who, along with international financial institutions, can become potential investors? This seems unlikely at a time when China comes across as assertively autonomous in its management of OBOR actions, as we saw at the May 2017 OBOR Forum where the participating countries were cast in an applauding role, with no real consultation. But the possibility should not be excluded, especially if China really wants other agencies to finance some projects. Even the AIIB, based in Beijing (and the BRICS-run NDB), will seek participatory roles if they are to fund OBOR projects.

In the coming five years, before the 20th CPC in 2022, OBOR may show successes and failures; an overall achievement rate of 50 percent may qualify for success. Such an outcome might make China a better partner in the international community. Or, domestic discord might tempt Beijing to use the foreign theatre to shore up its domestic image. Both possibilities need to be considered.

## Second, how might China handle transition to the status of a global power? What are the likely trends?

Graham Allison's book, *Destined for War: Can America and China Escape Thucydides's Trap* (2017), has made it fashionable to speak of a Thucydides Trap, where an entrenched power lashes out against a competing, rising power. Arthur Waldron noted in an incisive review of this book that the dilemma is captured in one sentence of Thucydides's text: 'What made war inevitable was the growth of Athenian Power and the fear which this caused in Sparta.' Waldron argues:

> Allison seems to have been impressed above all by Chinese numbers…if that sentence from Thucydides is correct, then China is clearly a rising power that will want her 'place in the sun' – which will lead ineluctably to a collision between rising China (Athens) instigated by the presumably setting U.S. (Sparta), which will see military pre-emption as the only recourse to avert a loss of power and a Chinese-dominated world. To escape this trap, Allison demands that we must find a way to give China what she wants and forget the lessons of so many previous wars….The reality, however, is that Allison's recipe is actually a recipe for war. Appeasement of aggressors is far more dangerous than measured confrontation….When it comes to China, we might want to be more mindful of the 'Chamberlain Trap' after the peace-loving prime minister of England, one of the authors of the disastrous 1938 Munich agreement that sought to avoid war by concessions, which in fact taught Hitler that the British were easily fooled. That is the trap we are in urgent need of avoiding…. [China's] slightly delusional view of her claims, first made explicit in ASEAN's winter meeting of 2010 in Hanoi, was that

> 'small' countries would all bow respectfully to China's new pre-eminence. This has failed to occur. All of China's neighbours are now building up strong military capabilities. Japanese and South Korean nuclear weapons are even a possibility. Over relying on their traditional concept of awesomeness (威 *wei*), the Chinese expected a cakewalk. They have got instead an arms race with neighbours including Japan and other American allies and India, too. With so much firepower now in place, the danger of accident, pilot error, faulty command and control, etc. must be considered. But I'd wager that the Chinese would smother an unintended conflict (2017).

The Doklam confrontation at the Bhutan-China-India border trijunction suddenly emerged on 16 June 2017. What did it show? China manufactured a crisis by building a road right up to that trijunction. India's robust response, sending troops and blocking construction activities, was followed by limited mutual ratcheting up of tension in this and other border areas. On 28 August the two sides announced, separately and with differing emphasis, an end to that crisis. Climbing down is always harder than the first push, but we also witnessed caution in actions – not in words – that has been a Chinese hallmark. One is reminded of the crosschecking Beijing carried out in mid-1962 with the US via the Warsaw channel (to gauge Taiwan's posture) before its hard military strike against India in October 1962 (Kissinger 2011).

Is China still a 'partial' or incomplete global power? China's positives, in military power, economic achievement, technological progress, and comprehensive new foreign policy engagement via OBOR, were trumpeted at the 19th CPC. But consider the negative side of the balance: First, a persisting, overriding concern over the long-term survival of the CPC, sharpened under the Xi regime. Witness also a sense of threat over foreign culture infusions, producing ever-tightening control over the internet and the media. Second, economic vulnerability persists, despite 30 years of rocketing GDP growth, the highest that the world has witnessed, giving China the status of the world's second largest economy. China depends on market access abroad, and harbours a domestic debt burden that approaches 300 percent of GDP, well over the recognised danger mark. Third, societal challenges persist, ranging from sharpening income inequalities, endemic corruption, eco-social industrial and agricultural labour unrest, and resistance from the Tibet and Xinjiang communities. Xi's anti-corruption campaign addresses political opponents, but not quite the system that engenders this pervasive corruption. Stronger authoritarianism in the near future, if it comes to pass, will accentuate these challenges (Shambaugh 2015).

Russia is a special enigma in world affairs. With its own relationship with the US and the EU having deteriorated in recent years, it is closer to China than before, but both remain wary. Their friction points, especially Beijing's increasingly strong presence in Russian Siberia and OBOR's threat to Russia's position in Central Asia, have not gone away. The EU, focused mainly on its burgeoning economic relationship with China, seems to awake from time to time to the political challenge, but it is the US and the Asian states that must cope with this rising power.

For the next five years an ambitious set of leaders in Beijing are well entrenched in their positions – the 10-year leadership norm was discarded in March 2018. They can face domestic challenge through an economy that does not automatically deliver near-10 percent annual growth, and face societal resentment, of different kinds, from the bottom and the upper echelons, pushing them to greater authoritarianism, which may evoke deeper domestic resentment.

## Third, how does China's neighbourhood and Asia policy support its power projection objectives?

China wants acceptance as the dominant Asian and global power. Past rhetoric about never becoming a superpower is forgotten, or is framed in sophistry – 'they' have behaved in domineering fashion, but that is not China's way. The major catch is that, unlike the Americas where the US implemented a Monroe doctrine unchallenged by any 'local' power, Asia is home to other large powers that do not accept Beijing's hegemony. This rubs China continually against putative challengers – Australia, India, Indonesia, Japan, South Korea, Russia and Vietnam in particular – even while none of these states is not overtly anti-China, and frames its policy in a manner that allows it to work with China as much as is feasible, i.e. each practicing its own version of 'contestation, to coexist and cooperate' (might we call it 'C2CC'?). And let us not leave out of account ASEAN, a collective with a will of its own. China has its ASEAN proxy, in the shape of Cambodia; none of the other 'new' ASEAN members is a pushover.

Asia will witness stronger Chinese assertiveness, as in the South China Seas confrontation, and a pushy policy towards the entire region. It is this interplay of forces, interests and mutual C2CC activity, as also shifting arrangements resembling a three-dimension chess game, that make today's Asia Game volatile, unpredictable, complex and ambiguous – a metaphor for our 'VUCA world'.[4] Let us attempt some risky prognostication on what might emerge when China asserts itself further as a dominant Asian power, seeking to impose its will on the others.

A. Replay of the 2014-16 South China Seas power grab? That occurred in a special situation, using a kind of window of opportunity that no one anticipated. Within two years Beijing created three permanent air-and-sea bases that bristle with firepower, to a point where China has gained de facto near-archipelago status, though this is denied to it under

UNCLOS. Only Japan acted with foresight, acquiring formal ownership of the Senkaku/Diaoyutai islands in 2012, swiftly incorporating them into Japanese territory. No similar opportunity is now visible.

**B.** Might China marshal economic prowess to push Asian states to its will? This has happened earlier with Australia, which bent over backwards, treating China as a special, permanent customer for its minerals, based on locational advantage. Japan and South Korea are too astute to let the China market circumscribe their political options. Rather, we see from Tokyo robust mobilisation of its own levers of influence, in ASEAN, and across the region, and especially in the priority that Japan has given to expanding the eco-political relationship with India. Right up to the mid-1990s, Japan used to say that for it Asia ended at Myanmar: 'South Asia is too complicated for us'.[5] Today we witness an eco-political partnership moving to real actions.

C. A putative, loose political coalition of states that will stand up to China is emerging, extending to Australia, India, Japan plus the US, possibly widening to Indonesia and Vietnam. ASEAN will surely sympathise with this. Will Beijing be adroit enough to block its emergence? India has joined Australia, Japan and the US in a new quadrilateral, blessed by the leaders of these countries at the November 2017 Manila EAS summit. Australia and India will strive to avoid overt positions against China, but it was a clear warning to China.

D. The 'other' Asian power, the US, will play its cards partly openly and to a large extent behind the scene. What we witness goes beyond naval exercises and war games, i.e. political convergence and synchronisation.

China can opt for a softer, velvety posture in Asia. That is entirely feasible, but hubris, predicated on recent achievements may come in the way. A small example is the way China deals with its Mekong basin river partners. As an upper riparian, it acknowledges no limits on its own conduct, assuming a tough attitude in the sub-regional group, GMS. (Might we see this in the Brahmaputra basin too, as some predict?). This merits closer study. This owes to geography. China is not a major lower riparian to any country.

In Asia, China's near-superpower status produces neither subservience nor deep admiration – unlike, say, in Africa and Latin America; those at a distance are more captivated by its rise. But OBOR and its onerous financial terms are also hinting at pushback and disenchantment. Might that make China more unpredictable, or conversely, produce a course correction?

## Fourth, what trends are we likely to see in China's response to global issues, including trade and other economic flows, and its multilateral policy?

Xi told the 19th CPC: '…[T]here has been a clear shift away from the tendency to neglect ecological and environmental protection….Taking a driving seat in international cooperation to respond to climate change, China has become an important participant, contributor, and torchbearer in the global endeavour for ecological civilisation' (Xi 2017). China raised support to the Paris Accord after President Trump's withdrawal.

> As awareness of global warming and climate change prompted growing international criticism of China's activities, Beijing's initial reaction was a defensive one. The government…felt singled out. Chinese spokespersons routinely (and correctly) cited the fact that the per capita rate of emissions was still much lower than the U.S. and most European countries….This [realisation of their own environmental problems] prompted the most impressive reversal of environmental policy the world has yet witnessed (Fendos 2017).

China is also driven by its remarkable progress in developing environment technology, making it a long-term element in its economic policy.

> President Xi told the Party Congress: China now leads the world in trade, outbound investment, and foreign exchange reserves…We will expand foreign trade, develop new models and new forms of trade, and turn China into a trader of quality. We will adopt policies to promote high-standard liberalisation and facilitation of trade and investment (Xi 2017).
>
> But is not an easy ride. At WTO, China confronts a US-led blockage against the 'market economy status': The onus remains on China to prove that it is a 'market economy'. Indeed, the fact that China has been simply running out the clock on Article 15 could be taken as evidence in itself for the fact that China is not a 'market economy'…. Australia, for example, recognised China as 'market economy' as long ago as 2006, yet still applied anti-dumping measures on Chinese steel earlier this year' (Bulloch 2016).

India is publicly non-committal, but evidently unwilling to support market status. Interestingly, China does not openly campaign its case. Is this to avoid publicising an issue when it would lose face domestically, or does it prefer the tag that some give it, of a country that mostly plays by international rules?

Globally, China is a huge investor, even leaving out all the OBOR projects. China's acquisition of companies in the West, including Japan, under the rubric of M&A (merger and acquisition) activities, now runs at over $200 billion per year, which is more than double the inflow of FDI. These figures need deflation, to eliminate the sums illegally taken out by super wealthy Chinese, i.e., representing capital flight, but what remains is still impressive.[6] What might be the outcome in terms of international economic arrangements over the next five years? Some experts are of the view that OBOR will reframe global supply chains in a radical manner.[7] Assuming that China may not gain market economy status at WTO for now, this will not greatly deter it when it is already the world's leading trading nation, with the clout to negotiate side deals and facilities. Its trump card is the attraction of its market, for the West, including Japan. That limits President Trump's cards, for all his social media fulminations. This assumes that the Chinese economy will continue to power ahead, without any stumble or setback. Is this over-optimistic?

## Fifth, are China's diplomatic structures and methods adequate for its quest for world status, and the management of complexity in bilateral, regional and global challenges?

In *Asian Diplomacy*, I examined the structure and working of the Chinese Foreign Ministry; the final three chapters of the book compared the foreign ministries of China, India, Japan, Singapore and Thailand (Rana 2007: 17–45, 161–222). Updated, the following emerges: In 2016, China had the third largest diplomatic network (Embassies, Permanent Missions and Consulates), at 258; the US had 270, and France, 267 (Lowy Institute 2017).[8] Its diplomatic style is more confident and assertive than before, at all levels. But initiative by embassies is still relatively stunted, owing to risk-aversion mindsets. What is new is strong defense of the diaspora.[9] In multilateral diplomacy, China is active, showing flexible pragmatism, seldom taking a high profile, but demanding on issues considered vital to its interests. It is active at the UNSC, while conservative in the use of the veto. Its ambassadors mainly come from the career track.[10] With training being a key feature of China's Party system, this also means career-long professional diplomatic training.[11]

In net terms, Chinese diplomatic machinery is fit for purpose. But it is probably not as supple in its actions as it might be. In Central Asia, Myanmar, Pakistan and elsewhere, the scale of OBOR investments will now compel China's involvement in those countries' domestic politics to protect its interests. How adroitly it manages this is an open question.[12]

## Sixth, how might these 19th CPC events impact on India-China relations?

Can a putative Athens (India) adroitly manage its relationship with a Sparta-that-is-also-Athens (China), in the midst of the latter's other, larger global ambitions, repeatedly evoked in Xi's speech and other documents, vis-à-vis the 'real' Sparta, the US? How should India deal with this centre-of-world-stage China?

Let us consider possible future trajectories for India. First, the option of deeper proximity to the US, e.g. a virtual 'alliance', ill-suits an India that has nailed its flag to the mast of strategic autonomy, i.e. judging issues on merits. That also holds for the 'quad' that is now in play. That is a useful hedging choice, but India is no way on par with the three allied states, the US, Japan and Australia. None is likely to really support India in a crisis. Second, Modi's 'Neighbourhood First' doctrine is especially apt for dealing with the long neglected smaller countries of our region. But its success hinges on rapid, efficacious execution of projects and bilateral commitments, a persistent Indian weakness (Rana 2017a, 2017c). Third, Japan (as also Indonesia, South Korea, and Vietnam, plus ASEAN), merit special attention from New Delhi. They widen India's options, bringing economic and other benefits; especially welcome was the January 2018 dictum for ASEAN – 'Commerce, connectivity, culture'.[13] Beyond this, laser-like focus on domestic stability and socio-economic growth remains the key to India's future, and for revitalising foreign policy actions.

The Modi-Xi Wuhan two-day 'informal summit' of April 2018 has been a game-changer. Without over-anticipating an outcome that is still under development, it marks a shift in the New Delhi-Beijing engagement, predicated on a reassessment by both sides of their potential for better direct cooperation, and need for mutual confidence building.[14]

India has long engaged in adroit policy management and agile diplomatic tactics. To implement this optimally, it needs stronger investment in its diplomatic system, across the board, in material and human resources, including training. That will not of itself resolve problems, but widens options and enables better foreign policy execution (Rana 2017b).

The political management of its China relationship is India's key international challenge. That subsumes and is shaped by all the principal connections, with the US, Pakistan, Japan and Russia, among others. Consider the complex India-China backdrop: a legacy border problem that is on-backburner-but-not-dormant; contested domestic politics in which the opposition traditionally frames foreign policy in the optic of short-term political advantage; a combative media, especially the 150-plus Indian news channels that project external issues through daily confrontational on-screen dramatisation, supported by a large cast of fractious talking heads. Just 26 percent of Indians hold a favourable view of China, one of the lowest figures in Asia (Japan, 13 percent; Vietnam, 10 percent) (Pew Research Center 2017). These factors shrink the space for New Delhi's calculated, strategic actions. It remains a paradox that non-adversarial historic and cultural connections between these two civilisational states have not translated into real proximity (Bhoothalingam 2017; Sen 2017). But the potential is alluring.

How might Beijing handle a rising India? 'The footprints of the two re-emergent countries will increasingly overlap' (Kantha 2017b). The Modi-Xi meeting on the margins of the September 2017 Xiamen summit showed a desire for mutual engagement; some positives are now visible (Luo 2017a).[15] But India knows that China, and the world, respect only its solid achievements, not premature assertions of Indian capabilities, as some Indians proclaim from time to time. Yet, even in the midst of sharp contestation, the logic of congruence persists; pragmatism demands that such opportunities not be neglected. The Chinese Ambassador to India recently described the two countries as 'neighbours that cannot be moved away. We live under the same sky'. He described Modi's New India initiative and Xi's Chinese Dream as 'closely connected' and potentially 'synergised as well' (Luo 2017b). Beijing's interest in India as a 'swing' state is undiminished.

Chinese investments in India have grown since 2014 when the two sides spoke of taking the total to US$20 billion or more. The reality is modest, but holds promise. In 2011, the inflow of Chinese investments into India was $102 million. In 2016, it rose to US$1 billion. (Figures reported by the two sides usually vary, but the trend is clear). Some investments come *via* Hong Kong or other places. The Chinese Vice-Minister for finance, Shi Yaobin, was quoted as saying that 'China has cumulatively invested $4.07 billion in India, and India has invested $650 million in China' (*Hindustan Times* 2017). India is one of the few stable destinations that can absorb very sizable FDI, and give profitable returns. This exemplifies the possible.

India needs to work to this vision – alert in safeguarding its interests, not swayed by worst-case scenarios, confidently focused on realising its own potential. This also entails exerting itself through strategic and tactical actions, to proactively shape favourable outcomes, finding ways to deal with Xi's China.

## NOTES

1. In Xi's CPC opening speech the term 'great power' or a 'strong power' was used 26 times, a departure from the past when leaders in Beijing depicted their country as a poor, modest player abroad. 'China will continue to play its part as a major and responsible country', he asserted.
2. A few years back I learnt *via* a chance remark by a Chinese interlocutor that the heads of the major official think-tanks have a monthly meeting with the Foreign Affairs LSG (or its alternate persona, the LSG dealing with security affairs).
3. In 2013 the Indian Ministry of External Affairs (MEA( created its 'Development Partnership Administration' presaging China's action, but the comparison ends there. MEA's action was delayed by two years as the Finance Ministry would not sanction additional posts for this unit, until it carried out internal adjustment to set up this agency. Whole of government actions remain a problem in India. See: Rana, India's Aid Diplomacy', *Business Standard*, 12 May 2013.
4. An acronym of the words 'volatile, unpredictable, complex and ambiguous'.

5. Both these comments came from an unusually candid Japanese diplomat who knew India well. It is notable that in 1998–2000 Japan had funded several academic institutions to undertake a three year, interdisciplinary study of the politics, economics and social conditions of South. India's nuclear tests of 1998 produced a brief freeze, but within four years a strategic partnership was established. Under the post-2014 Modi government, this has been taken to an entirely new level.
6. The percentage that represents capital flight can only be guessed, but figures of property purchase in Western cities across the world show a high proportion of Chinese private buyers that snap up high value real estate. Chinese language billboards in Australian and Canadian cities advertising new top end housing projects tell the same story.
7. This was the broad conclusion of a discussion meeting on China's role in the WTO, held at the India International Centre, New Delhi, on 5 September 2017.
8. As with communist states in the Cold War era, China still does not appoint honorary consuls, but it has receives such appointments since the 2000s. Russia and other former socialist states now have their own honorary consuls.
9. See the *Reuters* report of 29 September 2015, 'China Defends Envoy to Malaysia after Comments on Racism'. The report said: 'China on Monday defended the actions of its ambassador to Malaysia after he was summoned to clarify his remarks criticising extremism and racism ahead of a planned pro-Malay rally in the capital, Kuala Lumpur' (*Reuters* 2015).
10. The only exceptions are some appointments from the heads of province level foreign affairs offices, sent to minor embassies and consulates; they are typically also appointed to the MFA at Beijing.
11. Example: each year 140 persons, at first secretary rank, after keenly contested selection go to major world universities for a year's sabbatical. No other country offers comparable mid-career training.
12. Foreign Minister Wang Yi's three-stage proposal, announced in November 2017 to help resolve the Rohingya issue in Myanmar while also invoking the help of Bangladesh, is a rare new instance of regional activism.
13. This regional diplomacy slogan is also a first for India.
14. This essay is written in mid-May 2018.
15. It appears, going by information available in June 2018, that the new Chinese representative at these talks is Foreign Minister Wang Yi (who also holds the rank of State Councillor), and that the talks are due to take place in Delhi shortly. It also appears that the long suspended foreign ministry level consultations are to go ahead.

## REFERENCES

Bhoothalingam, Ravi. 2017. 'Why India and China Matter to Each Other', 30 October, http://spsindia.in/2017/10/31/changing-asia-series-on-why-india-and-china-matter-to-each-other-by-ravi-bhoothalingam-on-october-30-2017/ (accessed on 31 March 2018).

Bulloch, Douglas. 2016. 'China Doesn't Deserve Its 'Market Economy' Status By WTO', *Forbes*, 12 December, https://www.forbes.com/sites/douglasbulloch/ 2016/12/12/china-doesnt-deserve-its-market-economy-status-by-wto/#285ccbc6b 937 (accessed on 15 August 2017).

*The Economist*. 2017. 'God's Gift', 16 September.

Fendos, Justin. 2017. 'Why China is Already the World's Leader on Climate Change', *Morning Consult*, 21 July, https://morningconsult.com/opinions/china-already-worlds-leader-climat e-change/ (accessed on 16 August 2017).

*Indian Express*. 2017 'Nirmala Sitharaman Talks Trade Deficit with Chinese Counterpart', 2 August, http://indianexpress.com/article/business/economy/nirmala-sitharaman-talks-trade -deficit-with-chinese-counterpart-zhong-shan-4778090/ (accessed on 4 September 2017).

Garver, John. 2001. *Protracted Contest.* Seattle: University of Washington.

*Hindustan Times.* 2017. 'More Chinese Companies Investing in India but Political Thaws, Barriers Remain', 10 April, http://www.hindustantimes.com/business-news/more-chinese-companies-investing-in-india-but-political-relations-barriers-remain/story-MABF9zw9hBAFqUy6LasFSP.html (accessed on 18 September 2017).

Jacob, Jabin T. 2017. 'What does India Think of China's 'Belt and Road' Initiative?' Occasional Paper No. 19, Institute of Chinese Studies, http://www.icsin.org/uploads/2017/ 12/18/8664fcac0850b0af2c40791465301e17.pdf (accessed on 21 October 2017).

Jakobson, Linda, and Dean Knox. 2010. *New Foreign Policy Actors in China,* SIPRI Policy Paper No. 26. Stockholm Peace Research Institute, September, https://www.sipri.org/publications/2010/sipri-policy-papers/new-foreign-policy-actors-china (accessed on 27 April 2018).

Kantha, Ashok K. 2017a. 'China Congress – a Multipolar World goes out of the Window', *South China Morning Post,* 29 October, http://www.scmp.com/week-asia/opinion/article/2117368/opinion-china-congress-multipolar-world-goes-out-window?utm_source=Direct (accessed on 30 October 2017).

——. 2017b. 'The Rise and Rise of Xi Jinping', *The Hindu,* 4 November, http://www.thehindu.com/opinion/lead/the-rise-and-rise-of-xi-jinping/article19977457.ece (accessed on 5 November 2017).

Kardar, Shahid. 2017. 'Understanding CPEC', *Dawn,* 17 July, https://www.dawn.com/ news/1345741( accessed on 25 September 2017).

Kissinger, Henry. 2011. *On China.* London: Allen Lane.

Lowy Institute. 2017. 'Global Diplomacy Index', https://globaldiplomacyindex. lowyinstitute.org/country_rank.html (accessed on 8 April 2018).

Luo Zhaohui. 2017a. 'The Xi Path to Prosperity', *Indian Express,* 4 November, http://indianexpress.com/article/opinion/columns/the-xi-jinping-path-to-prosperity-china-communist-Party-4921557/ (accessed on 6 November 2017).

——. 2017b. 'Speech at Seminar on China-India Relations', New Delhi, 6 November 2017.

Pew Research Center 2017. 'Global Indicators Database, Opinion of China', August, http://www.pewglobal.org/database/indicator/24/ (accessed on 29 November 2017).

Rana, Kishan S, *Asian Diplomacy: The Foreign Ministries of China, India, Japan, Singapore and Thailand* DiploFoundation, Malta and Geneva, (2007).

——. 2013. 'India's Aid Diplomacy', *Business Standard,* 12 May.

——. 2017a. Guest Editor's Introduction', *China Report,* Vol. 53, No. 2, 99-103.

——. 2017b. 'China's Belt and Road Initiative (BRI): Impact on India and its China Diplomacy', *ICS Occasional Paper* 16 (September), http://www.icsin.org/publications/chinas-belt-and-road-initiative-OBOR-implications-prospects-consequences-impact-on-indian-its-china-diplomacy (accessed on 29 August 2017).

——. 2017c. 'Will Shashi Tharoor's Recommendations Reform the MEA for the Better?' *The Wire,* 25 October, https://thewire.in/190617/will-shashi-tharoors-recommendations-reform-mea-better/ (accessed on 27 October 2017).

*Reuters.* 2015. 'China Defends Envoy to Malaysia after Comments on Racism', 28 September, http://uk.reuters.com/article/uk-china-malaysia-idUKKCN0RS0V120150928 (accessed on 15 October 2017).

*Reuters.* 2018. 'China's New Silk Road Cannot be One-way', 8 January, https://www.reuters.com/article/us-china-france-silk-road/chinas-new-silk-road-cannot-be-one-way-frances-macron-says-idUSKBN1EX0FS (accessed on 9 January 2018).

Saran, Shyam. 2017. 'Is A China-Centric World Order Inevitable?' ICS-IIC Lecture, 20 July, http://www.icsin.org/newsletter/show/reminder-ics-lecture-series-is-a-china-centric-world-order-inevitable-by-amb-shyam-saran-20-july-6pm-seminar-hall-kamaladevi-complex-india-international-centre-iic (accessed on 27 July 2017).

Sen, Tansen. 2017. *India, China and the World: A Connected History*. Delhi: Oxford University Press.

Shambaugh, David, 2015. *China's Future*. London: Polity.

*South China Morning Post* (*SCMP*). 2018. 'China to Restructure Foreign Affairs Team in Push for Greater Role on World Stage, Source Says', 10 March, http://www.scmp.com/news/china/diplomacy-defence/article/2136651/china-restructure-foreign-affairs-team-push-greater (accessed on 12 March 2018).

*The Hindu*. 2017. 'Sri Lanka, China Sign $1.1 billion Hambantota Port Deal', 29 July, http://www.thehindu.com/news/international/sri-lanka-china-sign-11-bn-hambantota-port-deal/article19385932.ece (accessed on 2 August 2017).

Waldron, Arthur. 2017. *Supchina Newsletter*, 10 June, http://supchina.com/2017/06/12/no-thucydides-trap/ (accessed on 16 August 2017)

Xi Jinping. 2017. 'Secure a Decisive Victory in Building a Moderately Prosperous Society in All Respects and Strive for the Great Success of Socialism with Chinese Characteristics for a New Era', Speech delivered at the 19th National Congress of the Communist Party of China, October 18, 2017, http://www.xinhuanet.com/english/ download/Xi_Jinping's_report_at_19th_CPC_National_Congress.pdf

*Xinhuanet*. 2017. 'Full Text of Resolution on Amendment to CPC Constitution', 24 October, http://www.xinhuanet.com/english/2017-10/24/c_136702726.htm (accessed on 26 October 2017).

# 11

# Bridging the Domestic and the Global: Deconstructing Xi Jinping's Perspective

*Alka Acharya*

Since the disintegration of the Soviet Union and the collapse of the bipolar world order, there is probably no other subject, which has so occupied International Relations theorists as well as area studies experts, particularly over the past two decades, than a rising China and what to make of it. At the macro-level of global politics, contextualising a rising China in world historical experience has led many to conclude that the consequences are more likely to be disruptive than beneficial and poses the greatest potential challenge for the existing world order and the current hegemon, the United States.[1] The power-preponderance theory in the western realist discourse, which has many proponents, posits that war invariably results in the confrontation between a rising power and a hegemon on the decline. Some recent works speak of an inevitable direct strategic confrontation between the US and this rising China. From theoreticians and scholars who grapple with concepts such as world order, power transition and globalisation, to policy and decision makers who are adjusting their tactics and strategies *vis-a-vis* this rising power, to security and strategic communities who ponder over the PRC's capabilities and intentions, to the business and commercial sectors around the globe, whose fortunes have been – and continue to be – shaped by their dealings with China, the interest and concern is palpable.

The Chinese – officials and scholars – have naturally countered these arguments in various, and interesting, ways. Some have responded by taking the 'process approach' inspired by the Chinese philosophical thought and traditions (Qin 2010) while others have variously pointed out that the US is 'still far ahead of China in terms of politics, military strength and international influence' (Sha as cited in *Global Times* 2013). The point is made that 'China has enjoyed superpower status several times' and its decline was a historical mistake 'which they should correct.' Since this essentially involves regaining lost status, it is equated with 'restoration of fairness' not with acquiring advantage. Secondly, the Chinese writings have been strongly and consistently stressing that the rise of China is and will be peaceful (Kaufman 2010). There is also a major ongoing debate within China, whether the PRC could – or may not – dominate the 21st century.

## Prelude to the Congress

Since mid-2017, few domestic events in a foreign country have been as much debated and dissected across the world, as the 19th Party Congress of the Communist Party of China, which met in Beijing from 18-24 October 2017. This is a profound testament to the transformative impact of the rise of China on the international system, on the regional orders, and even on the domestic calculations of a large number of countries over the last three decades. Much of the interest centered on the 19th Party Congress was essentially about the consolidation of President Xi Jinping's power and control over the Party and State – arguably commanding the same degree of authoritativeness as Mao Zedong. While Xi has been steadily acquiring extensive powers and centralising control domestically, his growing stature as a global leader is directly linked to the range of initiatives – both at the regional and global level – that he has undertaken since 2012, when he took charge as Party General Secretary. His first term was widely – though not entirely accurately – assessed as marking a shift in the 'consensual' or 'collective' model of leadership that had come to characterise Chinese politics since the reforms ushered in by Deng Xiaoping. Indeed, the focus on the personality cult of Xi Jinping – (both within and outside China) – while not unexpected, was often not very useful, since the accompanying question invariably was limited to how Xi Jinping and the PRC under his leadership would change the world.[2]

But it must be recalled that Xi had taken charge after more than a decade of some significant advances in the external realm under his predecessors, Jiang Zemin and Hu Jintao. Since the end of the 1990s in fact, China's economic power expanded steadily, along with its self-confidence and 'talks of 'revitalising the Chinese nation, (*zhenxing zhonghua*) became prevalent inside China.' (Zhu 2010: 1) Since the turn of the century, in the economic realm, China advanced from the 7th to the 3rd position in the world economy, negotiated the teething troubles of the WTO entry, crossed the hurdle of the global financial crisis and pulled off a technologically spectacular show at the 2008 Beijing Olympics (McGregor 2017). Internationally *daguo waijiao* (great power diplomacy) was actually inaugurated under Jiang Zemin with the objective of playing a bigger role in the Asia Pacific region. This was actively promoted with a strong stress on multipolarity, along with 'good-neighborly' policy to secure a 'harmonious environment' for economic growth, 'building solid relationships with key countries in Africa and Latin America' and pursuing energy security (Lam 2006: 160–61). Above all, it was during this period that the PRC took the initiative to host the Six-Party Talks, to defuse the North Korean nuclear crisis.[3] The Hu Jintao-Wen Jiabao team has been credited with taking a more 'comprehensive approach…(and) paying a lot of attention to the foreign policy implication of trade, economic cooperation, technology, and energy' (Lam 2006: 161).

China now has 'multi-layered interests and manifold purposes in each of the regions where it has conducted active diplomacy,' (Zhu 2010: 4) commensurate with its interests as an emerging world power. It may also be mentioned here that it was in 2000, at the 16th Party Congress that a comprehensive analysis of the 'new century in the new stage' was undertaken, which sought to contextualise China's global strategy in light of the then prevalent domestic and international 'trends and contradictions.' This 'major strategic assessment' undertaken by the 16th Congress, designated the next two decades as a 'period of strategic opportunity' during which the PRC's 'comprehensive national power, international competitiveness and influence were expected to rise as a result of favorable domestic and international factors' (*Xinhua* 17 November 2002, in Heath 2015: 13). Finally, it must also be recalled that the 'China Threat' discourse had already begun to do the rounds since the turn of the century. There has always been an 'assertiveness' in so far as its core interests were concerned, even before Xi Jinping.[4] During the Hu Jintao period, *heping jueqi* (peaceful rise) was conceptualised to counter this and it underscored the fact that China would never seek *baquan* (hegemony) and that far from hurting or threatening it, China's emergence would actually be beneficial for the world (Zheng 2004; Wang 2014).[5] It is now a fundamental plank of China's foreign policy. *The 'strategic assessment' undertaken at the 19th Congress thus sought to take the discourse further.*

It is therefore important to situate the 19th Congress of the Communist Party in the context of the developments over the last decade and properly historicise the Xi Jinping period – *the PRC, under the CPC had begun to change many things in the world even before Xi took charge.* China's global strategy has been in the making over the past two decades – in tandem with its economic rise. There is a critical inter-relation between China's domestic transition to a developed country status and its global stature – in fact the former may be seen as the precondition for the latter. It is truism that foreign policy is invariably an extension of domestic politics and ever since the reforms initiated by Deng Xiaoping in 1978, the PRC's foreign policy has been unmistakably development-oriented. But it is also necessary to examine how the domestic economic reforms have shaped

China's unprecedented integration and enmeshing with the world system, which in turn has then conditioned China's domestic and international politics. In his study on China's quest for international status, Yong Deng has summed up this aspect well: 'China's reformers at levels from the centre to the factory have capitalised on economic globalisation and substantive integration into the world mainstream to lock in and deepen key policy reforms, market transitions, and institution-building. In this way, the dominant interests in Chinese society are closely tied to the world market, to major international institutions, to the advanced economies, and to neighbouring regions in Asia and other parts of the developing world' (Deng 2008: 66). In that context therefore, the Congress did not merely extend a second term to Xi Jinping, but fully endorsed the further advances made by the PRC under his leadership during his first term (i.e. 2012 – 2017) and therefore it would be useful to bear in mind the continuities along with the changes.

## The 'Rise' of Xi Jinping

The 19th Party Congress is a turning point in that sense and it was therefore keenly scrutinised for the specific manner in which it would endorse Xi Jinping's second term in office. At a preparatory meeting with the Party delegates in Beijing in July 2017, Xi Jinping described his first term in office as 'extraordinary' for China and that the country had reached a historic turning point. He went on to say that '[O]ver the five years, the Party's central leadership…solved many challenging problems [the party] wanted to solve for a long time but couldn't, and achieved many things it wanted to achieve in the past but didn't manage to achieve….the Chinese nation…has achieved the historic leap of rising to our feet, getting rich and getting powerful.' (As reported in Gan 2017).

As mentioned earlier, a critical element in shoring up the domestic legitimacy of the CPC, in addition to delivery on the economic front, is making China respected as a strong power in the world. The CPC leaders have therefore sought to create a favorable international environment for their growth and modernisation on the one hand and equally pushed for carving China's niche, as a power in its own right, in a western (US)-dominated world order. In most assessments, it was under Xi Jinping's stewardship during the last five years that the linkage between China's domestic imperatives and priorities and its foreign and global initiatives, have been unmistakably accompanied with an 'assertive' trend in China's external stance and behavior. There has also been a high degree of confidence and assurance displayed by Xi Jinping at all the regional and global platforms and in initiating the establishment of new institutions, chiefly the Asian Infrastructure Investment Bank (AIIB).

A quick look at some of these initiatives shows the range and extent of China's global role: The notion of *'Community of Common Destiny'* ('the foundation of sustainable development serves the common and long term interests of all the people', outlined in his speech at the Boao Forum for Asia in April 2013); the One Belt One Road (September 2013, Kazakhstan) Concept of Responsible Nuclear Security (March 2014, The Hague); Harmonious Coexistence of all Civilisations (March 2104, UNESCO); New Asian Security Concept (Asia Summit Meeting, May 2014) and the Asia-Pacific Dream (November 2014).

Above all, it is the launching of the grand strategy with global implications, that bears Xi Jinping's personal imprimatur, the Belt and Road in 2013, one of the most ambitious strategies for Eurasian – and global – connectivity, which has major transformative potential. In the short to medium term, it would certainly alter the Eurasian landscape, bringing about a vast swathe of countries into the Chinese sphere of strategic and commercial influence. Finally, vis-à-vis its chief strategic competitor, the United States, the PRC has shown great adroitness in utilising the strategic opening during the last year of the Obama administration and the commencement of the Trump administration in the US. Xi Jinping was able to demonstrate China's reach and capability, as the PRC not only decisively pushed its territorial and maritime claims in the South China and East China Sea, but also spread its influence with sure-footed and nimble diplomacy, using its enormous material and human capacity with aplomb. And now, by donning the mantle of the new champion and upholder of economic globalisation, as the Trump-led US appears to retreat from its commitments to a globalised economy, Xi Jinping has taken a step further in underscoring the global profile of the PRC. In his speech at the World Economic Forum in Davos in 2017, he said, '[W]hether you like it or not, the global economy is the big ocean that you cannot escape from. Any attempt to cut off the flow of capital, technologies, products, industries and people between economies, and channel the waters in the ocean back into isolated lakes and creeks is simply not possible. Indeed, it runs counter to the historical trend.'

## Deconstructing Xi Jinping's Report

Xi's Report at the 19th Congress was widely seen as putting forward game-changing ideas, heralding China's determination to rule the world. A couple of caveats are in order. First, the Report is primarily a document for the Party, of the Party and by the Party leader. Its purpose is a reassertion of the role, relevance and centrality of the CPC, and it seeks to convey a unified message to the people. It sets out China's achievements – both domestic and international – (given that they constitute important bases of the legitimacy of the CPC) and lays out the important tasks for the road ahead. Thus the comparison of Xi

Jinping with Mao acquires a special resonance for the Party and the people; the flavor of this comparison is entirely different for those outside this frame. Take for instance the use of the term 'Contradiction.' Xi said that '[A]s socialism with Chinese Characteristics has entered a new era, the principal contradiction facing Chinese society has evolved. What we now face is the contradiction between unbalanced and inadequate development and the people's ever-growing needs for a better life' (Xi 2017). This is of relevance only in the domestic context – the extrapolation of this term for external implications is therefore entirely misleading. There would thus be no question of a 'United Front' in the realm of foreign policy. It may be pertinent to recall that it was in June 2017, that Xi Jinping had made a major speech about his intention to wage an all-out campaign on poverty, detailing the policies which would be adopted for 'meeting the basic needs of all of the country's rural poor in three years,' in tandem with a systematic push for building the Party's grassroots apparatus. 'The official goal is to eliminate poverty, defined as annual income of less than 2,300 yuan (HK$2,728), and build an 'all-round well-off society' by 2020 with all resources available.' (Lau 2017).

However, as scholars have pointed out that, '[A]lthough party congresses normally do not address Chinese foreign policy in any detail, they nevertheless have invariably provided assessments of the external environment, descriptions of China's developmental goals and a summary of broad initiatives and priorities relating to foreign and defense policy….' (Swaine 2017). It would be worthwhile to bear these aspects in mind as we analyse the Report.

The most widely held assessment of this Report is that it decisively – and finally – signals the end of *tao guang yang hui*, the 'hide and bide' tenet of Chinese foreign policy that had been laid down by Deng Xiaoping. It is seen as the most authoritative assertion of having finally *arrived* – a declaration of intent, as it were, to create a 'new type of International Relations'. As has been mentioned earlier, we need to see this assertion in a longer time frame. In the following section there is a brief sketch of how the Report prioritises the issues, enumerates the features of China's 'new' global role and sets forth its vision for the new order. This would also enable an assessment of the domestic-global linkage and China's emerging global role under Xi Jinping.

Xi begins[6] by laying out the empirical data regarding China's new stature in terms of its 'leading' role among the major economies, in trade, outbound investment and foreign exchange reserves. Additionally, there is an exhaustive listing of developmental achievements for the people to take pride in, since they clearly underscore the growth and modernising dimensions of China's rise. Advances in 'socialist consultative democracy', 'institution-building' and 'law-based governance' have contributed to all round progress and development, and hence 'Chinese cultural soft power and the international influence of Chinese culture have increased significantly.' This leads him to conclude that China's international stature has risen as never before.

In this context, Xi raises the issue of environmental governance and ecological civilisation – foregrounding the arena where the PRC would like to be taken on the role of a world leader. He says: 'Taking a driving seat in international cooperation to respond to climate change, China has become an important participant, contributor, and torchbearer in the global endeavor for ecological civilisation.'

There is a glowing section on China's achievements in the diplomatic field, viz, the Asian Infrastructure Investment Bank, the Silk Road Fund, the successful hosting of the Asia-Pacific Economic Community Meeting, the BRICS Summit and the 4th Summit on Confidence Building Measures in Asia through the course of 2016–17. It may be useful to remind ourselves that China has also already taken a lead in shaping the agenda insofar as creating a security community is concerned. All these achievements Xi concludes, '[H]ave seen a further rise in China's international influence, ability to inspire, and power to shape; and China has made great new contributions to global peace and development.' China's external posture will therefore be marked by a continuous opening up to the world, the Belt and Road will be pursued as a priority, China would significantly ease market access and equal treatment will be meted out to all businesses registered in China.

The next element pertains to the section on the achievements of the Party in the domestic socio-economic context – which concludes with suggesting that the Chinese model of development has '[blazed] a new trail for other developing countries to achieve modernisation.' This has been interpreted largely as the PRC's attempt to project the 'Beijing consensus' and another departure from Deng Xiaoping, for whom there was no question of China being a model – (Deng's emphasis was on learning from others, though Mao and Khrushchev had sparred over the relevance of the China's 'revolutionary model' for Asia, Africa and Latin America.) But it is important to note Xi Jinping's inflection as he talks about the relevance of the Chinese model: He stresses the significance of this model as 'offer[ing] a new option for other countries and nations who want to speed up their development *while preserving their independence*; it offers Chinese wisdom and a Chinese approach to solving the problems facing mankind.' – *in other words, a way that would allow nation-states to protect their sovereignty* (emphasis added).

But this assertion is leavened by sobering reality: '[T]he basic dimension of the Chinese context – that our country is still and will long remain in the primary stage of socialism – has not changed. China's international status as the world's largest developing country has not changed' – and which would, in a sense continue to underpin the PRC's global strategy. National rejuvenation, the realisation of the China Dream and the tasks for the PRC as a whole to achieve socialism with Chinese characteristics in the new era – is elaborated at great length as the primary domestic objective before the Party and the people. Given the enormity of these tasks, 'China [will] continue its efforts to safeguard world peace, contribute to global development, and uphold international order.'

Xi Jinping then sets out a *timeline* for China to attain its goals: from 'now' to 2020 (which period 'would be decisive in finishing the building of a moderately prosperous society in all respects';) thereafter there would be two stages: In the first, from 2020 to 2035, China would 'build on the foundation to see that socialist modernisation is basically realised'. Here, for the first time there is a definitive and specific mention of China as a *global leader,* and this is in the context of 'innovation'. Innovation is a vital part of the first stage – and this is the only element singled out in terms of global leadership. In the second stage from 2035 to the middle of the 21$^{st}$ century, having basically achieved modernisation, China would work hard for a further 15 years and develop China into 'a great modern socialist country that is prosperous, strong, democratic, culturally advanced, harmonious and beautiful.'

This identification of stages, interlinked with one leading to the other, would *prima facie*, imply a defensive orientation and it may not be entirely off the mark to suggest that China would avoid any major and overt conflict in this period. However, there is also a section on strengthening and revitalising the armed forces, by 'adapt[ing] to the trend of a new global military revolution and to national security needs....(we) will make it our mission to see that by 2035, the modernisation of our national defense and our forces is basically completed; and that by the mid-21$^{st}$ century our people's armed forces have been fully transformed into world class forces.' The nationalist message also rings out loud and clear. 'We stand firm in safeguarding China's sovereignty and territorial integrity and will never allow the historical tragedy of national division to repeat itself. Any separatist activity is certain to meet with the resolute opposition of the Chinese people.'

The last section is wholly devoted to 'Following a Path of Peaceful Development and Working to Build a Community with a Shared Future for Mankind'. This is the section in which China's view of the world, the dominant trend of the times [Peace and Development], the characteristic features – Globalisation, Multipolarity/ Economic Globalisation – i.e., increasing inter-dependence and interconnectedness; the changes in the global governance system and international order are expounded. There is also a statement to the effect that the 'Relative international forces are becoming more balanced' – which has been taken to mean – probably rightly a relative (and continuing) decline of US power (Swaine 2017). The characteristic features of Chinese foreign policy reflect the continuities, viz, 'peaceful pursuit', 'cooperation', 'win-win', 'support for the UN', etc; and *cumulatively and effectively, they point to a China irreversibly engaged with the world.* Finally, the theme of the Chinese dream, Xi stresses, is closely connected with the dreams of the peoples of other countries; the Chinese Dream can be realised only in a peaceful international environment and under a stable international order. 'We must keep in mind both our internal and international imperatives, stay on the path of peaceful development, and continue to pursue a mutually beneficial strategy of opening up.'

## Conclusion

The discourse that emerges from Xi Jinping's report to the 19th Party Congress is thus the discourse of a 'rising' power – with the largest economy; the largest number of trading partners for which it is the principal trade partner; a rising technological giant pushing the frontiers of the most advanced technologies, and commanding human resources geared to strengthening its reach. It therefore claims the right to play a larger global role – even as it attempts to moderate this desire with assurances of correcting erroneous trends. As Yong Deng has pertinently observed,

> '[S]ince the late 1990s, China's multipolar vision of the world has shown greater concern over how the US 'hegemony' is managed, than the power configuration itself, with policy geared toward restraining US unilateralism and reducing western dominance in the name of promoting 'democratisation', 'pluralisation,' and 'harmony' in international relations.... The PRC clearly prefers a more democratic, pluralistic world where one set of values does not become the sole standard; the western political system is not the only legitimate form of government; and no single power center dictates world affairs' (Deng 2008: 44-5).

What does seem fairly certain is that China does not appear to have any fundamental contradictions with the world or with the existing world order – there is however a degree of palpable dissatisfaction with the manner in which this order continues to operate. In that sense, the specific change that we observe in the PRC's behavior over the last five years in particular, is the determination to promote and push for such changes in the global political and economic architecture that would be required to undercut the dominance of the US on the one hand and ensure that China's development and modernisation maintain their momentum.

Since the onset of its growth and economic liberalisation, China has increasingly relinquished a whole range of 'systemic' obligations. In this sense, China has moved from a systemic approach in its global strategy, to the more obvious, relational level. It started its quest for its place and share in the world distribution of power and appears to have reached the point where it has donned more of a managerial role and has shown itself as capable of playing the power game, replete with the politics of rejection and exclusion. Indeed it is a new China – in some ways, it is a power that is really not hard to comprehend – indeed, it is no 'supervillain' – (Glaser 2016) but may not necessarily be easy to deal with.

The 21$^{st}$ century we are told, will witness the emergence of a multipolar world. The current trend toward multilateralism is certainly highly pronounced – though as yet an unfolding one – it is still characterised by elements of both competition and cooperation. The confrontations have so far sought to be avoided, but whether it would lead to genuine multipolarity – is not yet certain. Newer dynamics have entered into this debate – with a 'new' discourse on the Indo-Pacific, the inevitable competitiveness of the rising powers of Asia, the return of 'geopolitics', etc. What is certain is that all these issues are indicative of certain preferences for a particular kind of order. What kind of alliances would one build and with whom – are once again becoming vital issues of the day. China's rise has certainly complicated the task enormously. These are issues that are also being debated intensely within China – and it is important to study them carefully. A major series of publications around the time China was getting ready to host the Olympics, put forward an interesting thesis by the Chinese historian Zhang Baijia, who 'suggested that China should try to influence the world by changing China itself first. Reforming its own behavior is the main source of strength for China and its foreign policy.' It was described as 'perhaps a Chinese version of the constructivist perspective to look at the relationship between China and the outside world' (As cited in Zhu 2010: 217).

At a time when all nations are engaged in the task of building a modern industrialised state, it is also important to ask ourselves the questions that are necessary and critical to the future of Asia – as also of the world. Questions that focus on the choices we are making – and why? Clearly, the responsibilities of those powers being identified as the potential shapers of the coming century – in terms of the creation of the ideas and political movements of the future – will be critical.

## NOTES

1. For a range of the most recent works on the debate whether China's rise is likely to be beneficial or disruptive, see, David M. Edelstein, *Over The Horizon: Time, Uncertainty, and the Rise of Great Powers* (Cornell University Press, 2017); Graham Allison, *Destined for War: Can America and China Escape Thucydides's Trap?* (Boston and New York, Houghton Mifflin Harcourt, 2017); Michael R. Auslin, *The End of the Asian Century: War, Stagnation, and the Risks to the World's Most Dynamic Region* (Yale University Press, 2017); Oliver Stuenkel, *Post-Western World: How Emerging Powers Are Remaking Global Order* Polity, 2017); Alastair Iain Johnston (2013) 'How New and Assertive is China's New

Assertiveness?' *International Security*, Vol 37, No.4 (Spring), pp. 7-48; Zhu, Zhiqun (2010) *China's New Diplomacy: Rationale, Strategies and Significance* (Ashgate, Surrey).

2. See for instance Camilla T.N. Sørensen. 2015. 'The Significance of Xi Jinping's 'Chinese Dream' for Chinese Foreign and Security Policy: From 'Tao Guang Yang Hui' to 'Fen Fa You Wei'', *Journal of China and International Relations*, Vol. 3, No. 1, pp. 53–73.
3. The six parties were the United States, Russia, Japan, South Korea, North Korea and China and China's role in bringing them together on one platform undoubtedly added to its stature as a major power in the region.
4. For an objective and critical analysis of this argument see Alastair Iain Johnston. 2013. 'How New and Assertive is China's New Assertiveness,' *International Security*, Vol. 37, No. 4, pp. 7-48.
5. Later, this was refined to the more soothing *heping fazhan* (peaceful development). At the Boao Forum for Asia in 2004, President Hu had used this term.
6. Xi Jinping. 2017. Secure a Decisive Victory in Building a Moderately Prosperous Society in All Respects and Strive for the Great Success of Socialism with Chinese Characteristics for the New Era,' Delivered at the 19th National Congress of the Communist Party of China, http://www.xinhuanet.com/english/download/Xi_Jinping's_report_at_19th_CPC_National_Congress.pdf (accessed on 3 November 2017).

## REFERENCES


All selections have been taken from Xi, Jinping (2017), Secure a Decisive Victory in Building a Moderately Prosperous Society in All Respects and Strive for the Great Success of Socialism with Chinese Characteristics for the New Era,' Delivered at the 19th National Congress of the Communist Party of China., http://www.xinhuanet.com/ english/ download/Xi_ Jinping's_ report_at_19th_CPC_National_Congress.pdf (accessed on 3 November 2017).

Deng, Yong. 2008. *China's Struggle for Status: The Realignment of International Relations.* Cambridge: Cambridge University Press.

Gan, Nectar. 2017. 'China Has Reached a Turning Point in its History, Xi Says,' *South China Morning Post,* 27 July, http://www.scmp.com/news/china/policies-politics/article/2104406/ china-has-reached-turning-point-its-history-xi-says (accessed on 27 November 2017).

Glaser, Bonnie S. and Mathew Funaiole. 2016. '5 Common Myths about China's Power: Beijing's no supervillain', *National Interest,* 16 June, http://nationalinterest.org/feature/5-common-myths-about-chinas-power-16623 (accessed on 18 June 2016).

Heath, Timothy. 2015. 'Xi's Bold Foreign Policy Agenda: Beijing's Pursuit of Global Influence and the Growing Risk of Sino-US Rivalry', *China Brief,* Vol. XV, Issue 6, March 15, pp. 12-16.

Kaufman, Alison A. 2011. 'The 'Century of Humiliation' and China's National Narratives,' Testimony before the U.S.-China Economic and Security Review Commission, March 10. www.uscc.gov/sites/default/files/3.10.11Kaufman.pdf (accessed on 24 July 2012).

Lam, Willy Wo-Lap. 2006. *Chinese Politics in the Hu Jintao Era: New Leaders, New Challenges.* New York: ME Sharpe, Armonk.

Lau, Mimi. 2017. 'We must send our best to the front line: Xi Jinping goes all out to rid China of poverty in three years', *South China Morning Post,* 1 September, http://www.scmp.com/author/mimi-lau (accessed on 29 September 2017).

McGregor, Richard. 2017. 'Xi Jinping's Moment', 6 October, https://www.lowyinstitute.org/publications/xi-jinping-moment (accessed on 11 October 2017).

Qin, Yaqing. 2010. 'International Society as a Process: Institutions, Identities, and China's Peaceful Rise', *The Chinese Journal of International Politics*, Vol. 3, pp. 129-153.

Sha, Zukang. 2013. Cited in 'China Must be Open-minded to Deal with Changing Geopolitics,' *Global Times* (Beijing), 19 December 2013

Swaine, Michael D. 2017. 'The 19th Party Congress and Chinese Foreign Policy', Carnegie Endowment for International Peace, 16 October, http://carnegieendowment.org/ 2017.10.16/ 19th-party-congress-and-chinese-foreign-policy-pub-73432 (accessed on 15 November 2017)

Wang, Zheng. 2014. 'The Chinese Dream: Concept and Context', *Journal of Chinese Political Science*, 19, 1, 1–13.

Xi Jinping. 2013. Speech at the Conference on the Diplomatic Work with Neighboring Countries, Ministry of Foreign Affairs of the PRC, 25 October, online: www.fmprc. gov.cn/mfa _ eng/wjb_663304/wjbz_663308/activities_663312/t1093870.shtml (accessed on 28 April 2016).

Zheng, Bijian. 2004. 'China's Peaceful Rise and Opportunities for the Asia-Pacific Region', presentation at Boao Asia Forum, Hainan, April, www.csis.org/isp/us_China_sd/0404_ zheng.pdf

Zhu, Zhiqun. 2010. *China's New Diplomacy: Rationale, Strategies and Significance.* Surrey: Ashgate Publishing Limited, Surrey.

# 12

# PLA's Reorganisation towards Joint War

*Atul Kumar*

On 18 October 2017, China's President Xi Jinping delivered his Political Report to the 19th Party Congress (Xi 2017). The Report dealt comprehensively with his agenda for China's defence forces. Xi declared that China will reorganise its troops towards efficient conduct of joint operations and outlined contours of his higher command reorganisation which established new theatre commands and brought forth a refined chain of combat command. Xi further pronounced that the PLA will achieve complete mechanisation by the year 2020 and modernise across the board, in terms of theory, organisational structure, service personnel and weaponry by the year 2035. As per Xi, the PLA would become a world-class force by 2050.

Xi's main emphasis on the PLA's joint operational development in his Report has become a clarion call. Chinese forces intend to substantially improve their combat capabilities for joint operations, based on networked information system, through their ability to fight under multi-dimensional conditions. Xi also mentioned that China will strengthen the unified leadership in the PLA, ensure top-level design, reform and innovation while expediting implementation of major projects. China will deepen reform of defence related science, technology and industry, achieve greater military-civilian integration and build integrated national strategies and strategic capabilities. The President's Report made it clear to all China watchers that the PLA will sharpen its focus on joint war strategy and integrate its capabilities in a network-centric environment. The leadership was not ready to tolerate any ambivalence on this crucial military doctrine any further.

## The Context

The Joint Warfare Doctrine (JWD) is a method of war that promotes the fundamental and beneficial effects of teamwork, unity of command, synergy from integration and the synchronisation of military operations, in time, space and purpose (Joint Pub 3-0-2001: II-1). It refers to military operations and command structure in which, two or more armed services of a nation integrate their individual strengths and conduct joint operations under a joint force commander (JFC) to accomplish a strategic, operational or tactical objective. An armed force is required to streamline its organisational structure, acquire necessary hardware and develop skills to achieve a better level of efficiency in conducting joint operations.

The JWD is the pre-eminent military doctrine for the American (US) forces and the doctrine has maintained its predominance in the US defence discourse and its national defence strategy, since the Second World War. The doctrine's centrality was reinforced through the passage of the Goldwater-Nichols Act in 1986. This act has played a critical role in shaping and advancing the American ability to conduct expeditionary warfare and long-range power projection, evident through successive conflicts in Kuwait, Kosovo, Afghanistan and Iraq.

The PLA has keenly observed this military doctrine's emergence on the global stage, since the conduct of British-Argentinean conflict in the Falklands Islands in 1982, as well as American military engagements in the Persian Gulf, Kosovo and Afghanistan. The lessons learnt during these conflicts were internalised in military training and in shaping the nature and scope of the military modernisation that began in the PLA in 1980s. While following the joint doctrine's principles, Chinese political leadership has made an effort to reduce the PLA Army's pre-eminence. Its sister services such as the PLA Air Force and the PLA Navy have achieved near-parity. Additionally, in a major restructuring exercise, seven military regions (commands) have given way to five theatre commands and the PLA has shed about 300,000 troops in a demobilisation drive. The anti-corruption campaign has further taken down 13,000 officers, including 100 of general rank (Huang 2017; Nathan 2018).

The PLA's drive to integrate its forces and implement jointness and interoperability is crucial for its conduct of military operations and long-range power projection. However, due to enormous size of the PLA, any structural reform's success depends upon multiple factors. The political guidance, quality of higher command appointments, investments in the development of critical military technologies and formulations of military regulations and training objectives are some of the crucial components. Predominantly, the political guidance to the PLA in the 19$^{th}$ Party Congress, regarding its future area of responsibility and expected capability developments are essential to the PLA's joint operational proficiency.

## JWD Implementation in the PLA before 2007

The issue of JWD has been systemically and intensively researched, discussed and debated inside China's defence policy-making community (Zhang and Li 1997). China has strived to imitate American concepts on joint operations, although there has been an effort to give it a Chinese name and character. Therefore, interoperability has become synergetic harmony; joint support relationships have become pattern relationships; while dispersed deployments, concentrated attacks on targets, simultaneity and synchronous attributes of joint operations are borrowed without any sinification.

Although the integration drive in the PLA had begun in 2004, its features became visible only by 2010–12, especially during Fan Changlong's tenure as the Vice-Chairman of the CMC. As Fan turned 70, and retired at the 19$^{th}$ Party Congress, his successor such as Li Zuocheng would be crucial to the further intensification of integration and interoperability initiative.

During its Tenth Five Year Plan (2001–2006), the PLA assigned the National Defense University (NDU) to conduct a major revision of PLA's strategic theoretical framework with special emphasis on campaign planning and cross-service strategy (Xue, Ding, An and Shi 2009: 3). This effort dealt with two aspects of joint operations: joint operational missions and joint force creation. The study found out that there were roughly three phases of doctrinal shifts, facilitating JWD's progress, namely, combined-arms operations (CO) period, elementary joint operations (EJO) period and integrated joint operations (IJO) period.

The first period was dominated by combined-arms operations, which continued even after the Gulf War and remained prevalent through the early 2000s (Wang 2007: 59). By early 2004, intensive discussions and research over joint operational concepts began in the PLA as the PLA high command realised that combined operations were not enough and jointness was necessary (Xue, Ding, An and Shi 2009: 3). The high command therefore sought to address four questions: what will joint operations achieve for China? Where do they fit in Chinese military doctrine? How will China implement joint operations? Who is qualified for being a joint operations commander? These questions drove the second phase of Elementary Joint Operations (EJO) till 2008 and thereafter, the onset of Outline of Military Training Evaluation (OMTE) guidelines in 2008 launched the final era of Integrated Joint Operations (IJO).

The first comprehensive theoretical definition and framework of JWD was enunciated in China by Fan Changlong, the then Jinan MR Commander and former Vice-Chairman of the CMC in 2004. He argued that an accurate definition of joint operations was not yet clear and the army was studying it. In his understanding, 'informatised warfare was a system confrontation on the basis of overall integration of individual operational units and elements, and integrated joint operations by the various service arms.' He believed that the Chinese military was moving ahead from coordinated joint operations to integrated joint operations. He argued that operations, development and training were three key phases to develop the IJO. The first step for him was to test integration on a smaller level and then expand outwards in the military (*Military Art Journal* 2004: 42).

The theoretical understanding of joint operations also emerged in other statements by senior PLA officials such as Zhang Bing, Lu Dengming, Chen Shijun and others. The JWD implementation further garnered strong support from single service integration advocates. One branch of these advocates argued that the Navy, merchant fleet and fishing fleet, all could play important parts together during a conflict (Zhou 2004: 57). Another branch called for a unified command in Space (Feng & Cui 2004: 51–4). Since space operations are of a strategic nature, this was considered necessary for effective coordination, reducing the possibility of contradiction among predetermined targets and avoiding unnecessary internal frictions (Feng & Cui 2004: 51–4). Air-Land Battle was another promoted feature in this process (Zhu 2007). The PLA General Departments, taking the lead in 2004, focused on a top down approach which ensured that the JWD theory development preceded its experimentation at a small scale (Xiao, Wang, Pang 2004: 1).

## Naysayers

However, not everyone agreed with the move and differing reports argued that China had neither the firm foundations nor conditions to conduct integrated military training in 2004 (Jing and Zhang 2004). The lack of a comprehensive integrated information system as a prerequisite condition was another issue (Feng and Zhao 2004: 2). The services expressed hostility to the idea of joint operations through the appraisal of one service's importance against others (Liu 2005: 12–6).

Additionally, all through their history, Chinese troops have fought battles on the spirit of competitiveness among units, which makes the issue of jointness seriously problematic. Those units which had traditionally excelled in a certain area or had latest weapons would not let other units surpass them, even in an unrelated domain (Yuan, Zhang, Li, Tang 2008: 1). This problem recurred after Xi decided to re-designate all military units nationwide. Old units with immense amount of pride in their history refused to concede to the central order (*Asia*

*Times* 2018). Generals of Jinan and Lanzhou military regions continued their silent protest against elimination of their military region and smaller units, merged with larger ones, delayed the merger procedure.

Moreover, during the 2004-08, the PLA was confused on the format of the training and commanding authority (Yuan, Zhang, Li, Tang 2008: 2). Often, one service would try to monopolise an exercise by formulating a phony joint training plan. The communication between units was another problem. In addition, the priority of joint training exercises was low against individual service exercises so scheduling and coordination remained a big problem (Yuan, Zhang, Li, Tang 2008: 2). Many units even faked joint exercises and the drive to develop a joint logistics and support system, launched before 2004, was incomplete even in 2014 (*PLA Daily* 2014). In fact, till 2008, the lack of authoritative manuals and guidelines in the PLA on joint operational development was a major obstacle. The first OMTE to categorically focus on joint operations and training appeared only in 2008 (*OSC Analysis* 2008).

## Post 2007-08 Period: Hu Jintao's Political Report and the OMTE

At the 17$^{th}$ Party Congress in 2007, Hu Jintao presented his Political Report (Hu 2007). He declared that local war under IT conditions was a confrontation between systems and its basic form of operations was integrated joint operations. Hu's drive, for a PLA that was more revolutionary, modernised and standardised in an integrated manner, provided a strong impetus to the joint operational development. In addition, his reinforced emphasis on promoting innovation in military theory, organisation and management, which would adjust the structure, staffing and institutions of the PLA to gradually develop a scientific mode of organisation, aimed to promote further integration. Hu later specified the military doctrine of China as 'local Wars under joint warfare conditions' (Editor 2007: 4). His report was widely discussed in all military regions and units and the discourse in the PLA on JWD implementation became quite nuanced.

Additionally, a big push towards jointness in the PLA came through the CMC promulgation of the Outline for Military Training and Evaluation (OMTE) in 2008 (*OSC Analysis* 2008). The OMTE ruled categorically in favour of joint training and implementation of JWD, which then became compulsory for all services and arms. The OMTE advised services to follow the innovative thinking of 'three-phase military training' through individual training, overall training and combat-realistic training. These regulations led to the PLA modernisation programme's increased focus upon integrated joint operations (IJO) capability development.

The emphasis upon the development of simultaneous, synchronous and real time operational capability, leading to autonomous and interactive methods of attacking targets became crucial (Zhan 2007: 11–21). In IJO, the requirement was a 'comprehensive supremacy', the target was the 'system destruction' of adversary and the methods were 'precision strikes' (Xue, Ding, An, Shi 2009: 3). During the IJO, the PLA strived to enhance its interconnection, intercommunication and real time information dissemination capabilities for efficient conduct of joint operations.

## Consistent Implementation of Joint Principles (since 2008): Four Areas

The PLA has remained resolute to implement jointness among its ranks during 2008–17. Four of China's military regions, namely, Jinan, Guangzhou, Nanjing and Shenyang remained at the forefront of implementing joint training systems. In addition, numerous conferences were conducted to improve the joint training programmes across uniformed services. The number of joint military exercises, whether effective or not, has skyrocketed, and every military region has been conducting joint training and military exercises every year. In four main areas, efforts were made to carefully implement concepts of the JWD in the PLA. These are as follows:

### *Joint Training*

If there is one area where the PLA has focused substantially for implementing the JWD concepts, it is in the realm of joint training. Starting in 2005, scenario simulation, issue awareness, case studies, foreign press interaction skills, exposure to foreign affairs and international relations were introduced even in lower level military academies (Wang, Huang and Peng 2005: 1-3). Multi service training and joint operations knowledge were gradually introduced in lower command colleges (Wang, Huang and Peng 2005: 3).

Joint courses and joint institutions have proliferated across China over the last two decades (Ayuso and Henley 2014: 176–82). The National Defense University has emerged into a multidiscipline joint command university (Wang 2009). A Joint Military Training Coordination Zone (MTCZ) has been established in every erstwhile MR/Theatre Command. This establishment is aimed to improve the mutual understanding among forces and increase the frequency of coordinated confrontation exercises. The faculty expertise level in these schools is growing gradually, even though the faculty members' lack of experience, of actual joint operational combat, remains a concern.

### *Joint Information Systems*

The second area where substantial implementation of the JWD concepts has taken place is in the development of joint information systems. These 'integrated command platforms (ICPs)' for assessing real time battlefield situations, C4ISR data and command decisions are crucial for joint operations (Ayuso and Henley 2014: 176–84). The ICPs have proliferated and are a constant feature of almost all military exercises in military regions, MTCZs and joint exercises with international force contingents (Xiong and Luo 2008).

However, there are some crucial problems which these systems are facing. The PLA personnel proficiency level to operate these systems remains low. In addition, the lack of standardisation due to different manufacturers of these systems remains a major handicap. Nevertheless, the proficiency of the PLA in the use of ICPs has been growing considerably and is poised for further growth once old soldiers retire and a new tech-savvy generation are recruited.

### *Joint Logistics System*

The third area where PLA has been pushing jointness is in the logistics and support domain. Jinan MR Theatre started experimenting with a joint logistics system as a tactical level test case in 2005 (Liu and Liu 2005: 1). In the older logistics supply system, general supplies were shared by everyone while dedicated supplies were handled by each service branch's logistics systems. In the new joint system in Jinan, a multi-lateral cooperative type of logistics supply system was introduced where all service branches could manage it. So, from 'two channels and two parallel lines of operations', the logistics system moved to 'one channel and one line of operation' for simplification. The Jinan MR proved to be a suitable test bed for tactical joint logistics (Liu and Liu 2005: 1).

On the back of success in this test case for three years, another larger logistics system at the campaign level was established in Jinan MR in 2007 (Zhao and Fan 2007: 1). The Jinan model would be later expanded for a comprehensive joint logistic system for the entire PLA. Similar to the Jinan MR joint logistics system, many others have proliferated throughout other military regions and services (Cao and Yu 2007:2; Huang et al. 2007: 3).

### *Joint Officer Corps*

Finally, the fourth area where the jointness has emerged in the PLA is in the domain of the selection and development of joint commanding officers. The emergence of a professional joint officer corps is absolutely critical for the implementation of jointness and interoperability in an armed force. The 'Talents Building Guidance Commission (TBGC)', under the Vice-Political Commissar, and the 'Talents Building Research Commission (TBRC)' were two nodal agencies under the erstwhile MR which had the mandate to train joint officers. TBGC was the coordinating agency that performed liaison with the Central Authorities and guided MR level authorities. TBRC started conducting conferences for building Joint Officers Training Curriculum since 2007 with the help of its eight members who were drawn from the NDU, the CPC Central Committee Organisation Department and the Academy of Military Science (AMS) (Xue et al. 2009: 3).

These conferences dwelled on the quality structure of joint officer corps as well as the focus, models, policies and mechanisms to train them. Cross-College Training and Cross-Services/Arms Internship/positions were two methods amongst others promoted for imparting jointness in officers. All uniformed services joined these efforts and the PLA Navy began training its officers for joint duties by posting them in sister training academies (Yu et al 2008: 3). The cadre promotion procedure was revised as well. Earlier during the cadre selection, the person with the longer service record was preferred but now the person with the largest number of inter-service deployment experience is preferred (Zhong et al. 2009).

In addition, through the 'Training Different Commanders in Colleges of Multiple Arms' scheme, 30 commanders at division and regiment levels in the Ground Forces were sent to Naval Command College, Air Force Command College and the Second Artillery Corps Command College to study for one month. In these cross-service trainings, knowledge of the different arms' technologies was especially emphasised. The officers were evaluated on five qualitative and quantitative description tests for joint operations commanders, namely, command, science and technology, theories, studies, and physical quality. Moreover, efficiency in joint operations command, mastering and utilisation of modern science and technology, understanding of basic theories for operations and training, perception and studies of major military issues, and creative development and stratagem for military trainings were prominent evaluation criteria (Ma 2009: 2).

## Xi's Emphasis on Jointness and Major Higher Command Re-organisation

President Xi Jinping further reinforced the PLA's drive towards jointness at the 19$^{th}$ CPC Congress, through his reassertion of support for joint war principles. Xi stated in his political report that historic breakthroughs were made in reforming the PLA with a new military structure, where the CMC exercised overall leadership, the theatre commands were responsible for military operations while the services focused upon developing capabilities (Xi 2017). Xi further mentioned that as per the demands of the day, a strong China needed a strong military and towards that the PLA must develop strong and efficient joint operations commanding institutions for theatre commands, and create a modern combat system with distinctive Chinese characteristics. In addition, Xi put a target of 2020 as the year when mechanisation in the PLA would be complete and by the year 2035, the PLA will modernise across the board in terms of theory, organisational structure, service personnel and weaponry. Xi offered his vision of converting the PLA into a world class force by the mid-21st century (Xi 2007).

Xi's strong emphasis on joint operations, his drive for clarity in terms of chain of combat command in the PLA and focus upon higher command reforms, provided a defining impetus towards joint war in the PLA. Apart from his reiteration of support to jointness in his Political Report, Xi has been visiting military institutions and stations to reinforce the message frequently. Everywhere, he has emphasised upon the development of joint capabilities and combat readiness. Starting from his inspection tour of Guangzhou armed forces in December 2012, Xi mentioned this concept in a commentary in the *PLA Daily* in May 2016 and in his speech in the NDU in 2016 (*Xinhua* 2016a). In addition, during his tour to the Joint Battle Command Centre in April 2016, he asked officers to 'change their ideas, innovate and tackle difficulties, in a bid to build the joint battle command system capable of winning wars' (*Xinhua* 2016b). He reinforced the concept again in July 2016. In another tour to the centre in November 2017, Xi 'demanded progress in joint operation command systems, especially at regional theatre command level' (Dong 2017). His strong support and demand for accountability has remained a big factor pushing the implementation of jointness in the PLA.

The implementation of JWD picked up pace after major reorganisation of its higher command in late 2015 and early 2016 (Liu 2016; Clove 2016). It is at present demobilising 300,000 soldiers and simultaneously, the ground force is being brought down at the same level as the Air Force, Navy and other services. The major changes include elimination of four general departments and establishment of 15 offices under the direct control of the Central Military Commission (CMC). All military regions have undergone restructuring and only five theatre commands are left. Most importantly, all senior officials of these theatre commands have been transferred out of their comfort zones (*People's Daily* 2017). Their longer tenures in their erstwhile military regions had led to closer links with local authorities. Their increased scope for patronage and unit-linked parochialism, were leading invariably to corruption, especially in logistical acquisition and officer promotions. Therefore, the transfers were a major jolt to entrenched higher command officers.

In addition, the reorganisation and reform has led to, for the first time, officers from the navy and air force becoming theatre commanders. The CMC, elected by 13th National People's Congress in 2018, looks less dominated by the PLA Army, which is now a defined and distinct service in the PLA (*Xinhua* 2018). Most of these changes remain under process and their effects on China's joint operational capability will be visible only after 2020, if not 2025, because higher command reforms take a substantial time period to settle.

Moreover, the Central Commission on Discipline Investigation (CCDI) is investigating hundreds of senior military officers and has punished more than 242 officers for graft (Blasko 2015). The receptivity to jointness and higher command reforms has proven to be a crucial factor in these investigations (Cheng 2018). Initially, a measure of dissent and difference was allowed and the reforms were launched after widespread discussions and negotiations inside the PLA. As per one account, more than 860 seminars and forums were organised to solicit suggestions (Zhao 2015). In addition, a survey of nearly 700 PLA units and government departments and more than 900 high ranking officers were conducted to fine-tune the joint doctrine according to Chinese requirements. However, once the contours of reorganisation towards jointness was formalised, Xi has either removed or punished all those holdovers from the previous era, which could resist these military reforms on political and patronage terms.

All suspected future obstacles, to the PLA's drive towards jointness and to some extent, Xi's complete control over the PLA, have undergone these internal PLA investigations. A number of top PLA officials, close to previous rulers, have undergone investigation and purge and some have even committed suicide (Chan 2017). Not surprisingly, the demobilisation has not gone down well and the PLA veterans have organised multiple protest demonstrations and marches for better pay and facilities (*Reuters* 2017). Therefore, the utmost priority of the Chinese President Xi Jinping is to maintain stability and order in the PLA and ensure its loyalty to the party. This explains the quick promotion of Li Zuocheng and other Xi loyalists in the PLA.

Li Zuocheng, the current head of the Joint Staff Department under the CMC, has experienced an eventful career. A veteran of China-Vietnam War, Li was honoured by the CMC as a 'war hero' and awarded the 'First Class Merit' (*South China Morning Post* 2017). Subsequently at the 12$^{th}$ Party Congress in 1982, Li served on the presidium of the Congress and was the youngest PLA representative. He was widely considered then as a rising star in the PLA Officer Corps. Further, Li led his troops through major disaster-relief campaigns such as the Yangtze 'grand floods' in 1998, the Sichuan Wenchuan earthquake in 2008, the Sichuan Lushan earthquake in 2013 and Yunnan Ludian earthquake in 2014 (Dai 2016). Although sidelined by Jiang Zemin, Li maintained his loyalty during Bo Xilai's fall in 2013 and impressed President Xi. This attribute, coupled with his combat experience and a general honest reputation raised his profile in President Xi's Administration. Thereafter, he has achieved faster promotions and was appointed as the head of the Joint Staff Department at the 19$^{th}$ Party Congress.

Li will provide stability and improve Xi's anti-graft image in the PLA. He is also a poster boy for meritorious promotion and can be counted upon to suppress those officers who still maintain covert loyalties to the Jiang faction. Li is popular and respected in the PLA so will be valuable in maintaining morale of troops during the undergoing military reforms and consequent upheaval while ensuring the impression of Xi being in charge. His appointment focuses upon improvement of joint capabilities and interoperability in the PLA and therefore, he would stress upon improving PLA's combat readiness. In this regard, Li can count upon the support of Xu Qiliang and Zhang Youxia from the CMC as well. Both senior-most officials of the CMC have offered full support to the process and led to innovative steps in the process.

## Conclusion

The reorganised CMC, after the 19th Party Congress, remains a shaky structure which may undergo further revisions in the near future. The awareness and theoretical understanding of the PLA on the JWD is fairly adequate. The discourse on jointness that began in 1990s has now transformed into a drive to develop joint operational capabilities. Hence, the focus is not only on structural modifications but suitable material inductions are also in the pipeline to provide base to joint operations. It is evident that during 1991–2004, the drive to implement jointness in the PLA achieved considerably less than expected. Consequently, a sustained push has been in place since 2004, to turn the JWD principles into practice and develop a standard joint operational capability. In this regard, one can find fair progress in terms of joint operational training, development of joint information systems, joint logistics systems and the emergence of a joint officer corps. The drive towards jointness has become urgent during 2012-17, owing to various technological and geopolitical reasons. The higher command restructuring since 2015 and the considerable push by President Xi in the 19th Party Congress and the 13th NPC will further improve China's joint operational capability and interoperability among its services.

### REFERENCES

2008. 'Revised PRC Military Training Guidance Codifies Joint Operations,' *OSC Analysis,* 8 September, at [OSC CPF20080908538001].

Ayuso, Wanda & Lonnie Henley. 2014. 'Aspiring to jointness: PLA training, exercises and doctrine 2008-2012', in Roy Kamphausen, et al. (eds.), *Assessing the People's Liberation Army in the Hu Jintao Era,* Carlisle, PA: Strategic Studies Institute, pp. 171-206.

Blasko, Dennis. 2015. 'Corruption in China's military: One of many problems', *War on the Rocks,* 16 February, https://warontherocks.com/2015/02/corruption-in-chinas-military-one-of-many-problems/ (accessed on 26 February 2018).

Chan, Minnie. 2017. 'Top Chinese General in graft probe commits suicide in Beijing', *South China Morning Post,* 28 November, http://www.scmp.com/news/china/diplomacy-defence/article/ 2121892/disgraced-chinese-general-commits-suicide (accessed on 29 March 2018).

Clover, Charles. 2016. 'Xi's China: Command and Control', *Financial Times,* 26 July, https://www.ft.com/content/dde0af68-4db2-11e6-88c5-db83e98a590a (accessed on 1 August 2016).

Dai Zhong. 2016. '李作成火箭上升 江时"弃将"获习重用' *Li Zuocheng huojian shangsheng jiangshi "qi jiang" huoxi zhongyong,* [Xi Jinping promtes Li Zuocheng as general, a rising star who was sidelined during Jiang Zemin's term], *DWNEWS.COM,* 4 April, http://news.dwnews.com/china/news/2016-01-04/59707956.html (accessed on 26 June 2018).

Dong Zhaohui. 2017. 'Xi instructs army to improve its readiness for war', *Xinhuan*et, 3 November, http://english.chinamil.com.cn/view/2017-11/03/content_7812091.htm (accessed on 21 November 2017).

Qian Jin Bao. 2007. 'Paying attention to exploration and practice of Joint Training,' 24 December, accessed from Open Source Center on 20 April 2011 at [OSC CPP2008020 64 78005], p. 4.

Feng, Jinghai & Zhao, Shaoxian. 2004. 'Information System: The Foundation Platform of Integrated Training,' *Zhanqi Bao,* 16 April, [OSC CPP20040616000157], p. 2.(accessed 17 April 2018).

Feng, Shuxing & Cui, Yang. 2004. 'A Study of the problem of Space Operational Command System,' *Zhuang bei Zhihui Jishu Xueyuan Xuebao* [Translated], 2 February, at [OSC CPP20080606572003], pp. 51–54.

Huang, Cary. 2017. 'Why Xi's anti-corruption drive in China's military needs a long-term solution', http://www.scmp.com/comment/insight-opinion/article/2122930/xis-sweeping-anti-corruption-drive-chinas-military-may-prove (accessed on 5 December 2017).

Hu, Jintao. 2007. 'Hold High the Great Banner of Socialism with Chinese Characteristics and Strive for New Victories in Building a Moderately Prosperous Society in all', 17th National Congress of the Communist Party of China, *Xinhua,* 15 October, http://www.china.org.cn/english/congress/229611.htm (accessed on 27 September 2017).

Joint Publication 3-0, 2001. Doctrine for Joint Operations, Washington DC: US Government Printing Office, https://www.fs.fed.us/fire/doctrine/genesis_and_evolution/source_materials/dod_ joint_ops_doctrine.pdf (accessed on 2 April 2018).

Jing, Yu & Zhang Weijia. 2004. 'Establish integrated training dominance', *Jiefangjun Bao,* 27 July, http://www.pladaily.com.cn/gb/pladaily/2004/07/27/20040727001080.html (accessed on 10 July 2010).

Liu Dingping. 2005. 'Thinking about Anti-Air Raid Operations in the Future,' *Junshi Wenzhi* [Translated], 1 May, at [OSC CPP20040526000250], pp. 12-16.

Liu, Wei & Liu Mingxue. 2005. 'Reform of joint logistics achieves initial success in Jinan theatre', *Jiefangjun Bao* [Translated], 20 July, in FBIS, p.1.

Liu, Zhen. 2016. 'Chinese military launches two new wings for space and cyber age', *South China Morning Post,* 1 January, http://www.scmp.com/news/china/diplomacy-defence/article/1897356/chinese-military-launches-two-new-wings-space-and-cyber (accessed on 10 January 2016).

Ma Sancheng. 2009. 'Lanzhou MR Combined Tactical Training Base's Efforts To Temper 'Blue Team' for Confrontation Training Exercises,' *Jiefangjun Bao Online,* 2 January, at [OSC CPP20090102702001], p. 2.

*Military Art Journal.* 2004. 'Actively exploring new theories of integrated joint operations and training during test-bed practice', *Junshi Xueshu* [Translated], 1 May in FBIS, 25 October 2007, p. 42.

Nathan, Andrew J. 2018. 'China: Back to the future', *The New York Review*, 10 May, http://www.chinafile.com/library/nyrb-china-archive/china-back-future (accessed on 11 May 2018).

*People's Daily*. 2017. 'PLA Stresses combat readiness, reassigns officers based on battle requirements', 11 December, http://en.people.cn/n3/2017/1211/c90000-9302606.html (accessed on 12 December 2017).

*Reuters*. 2017. 'Hundreds of veterans stage fresh protests over pensions', 23 February, http://www.scmp.com/news/china/diplomacy-defence/article/2073400/hundreds-chinese-military-veterans-stage-fresh-protests (accessed 27 July 2017).

*South China Morning Post*. 2017. 'Decorated Chinese war veteran to take up top job at heart of Xi's military reform drive', 27 August, http://www.scmp.com/news/china/diplomacy-defence/article/2108441/decorated-chinese-war-veteran-take-top-job-heart-xis (accessed on 13 March 2018).

Wang, Chengqing. 2007. 'Basic principles that must be established in enforcing Joint Blockade Operations', *Junshi Xueshu* [Translated], 4 April, at [OSC CPP20071025325006], p. 59.

Wang Guangjin, Huang Quan& Peng Lihua. 2005. 'Surfers Stand on Top of Waves-Report on Overall Transformation of Military Region's Comprehensive Training Base in Preparation for Military Struggle,' *Zhanshi Bao* [Translated], 21 November, at [OSC CPP20060131318001], pp. 1–3.

Wang Xibin. 2009. 'Personal Experience of the Strategic Transformation of High-Ranking Commanding Officer Training of Our Army', *Jiefangjun Bao* [Translated], 31 January, at [OSC CPP20100908090003].

Xiao, Zhongwen, Wang Quan& Pang Lihua. 2004. 'One network links, trains and tests three arms online', *Zhanshi Bao* [Translated], 4 June in FBIS, 12 July 2004, p. 1.

Xi, Jinping. 2017. 'Secure a Decisive Victory in Building a Moderately Prosperous Society in All Respects and Strive for the Great Success of Socialism with Chinese Characteristics for a New Era', 19th National Congress of the Communist Party of China, Xinhua, 18 October, http://www.xinhuanet.com/english/download/Xi_Jinping's_report_at_19th_CPC_National_Congress.pdf (accessed on 27 December 2017).

*Xinhua*. 2016a. 'China headlines: Xi brings strength, integrity to Chinese armed forces', 30 July, http://www.xinhuanet.com/english/2016-07/30/c_135551433.htm (accessed on 26 April 2018).

*Xinhua*. 2016b. 'Xi stresses joint battle command for military reform', 20 April, http://www.xinhuanet.com/english/2016-04/20/c_135297662.htm (accessed on 26 April 2018).

*Xinhua*. 2018. 'Xu Qiliang, Zhang Youxia endorsed as vice chairman of Central Military Commission of PRC', 18 March, http://www.npc.gov.cn/englishnpc/Special_13_1/2018-03/18/content_2051096.htm (accessed on 12 June 2018).

Xiong Yongjun & Luo Liyan. 2008. 'Group Army Turns Old and New Armaments into Overall Combat Capabilities', *Jiefangjun Bao*, 8 January, [OSC CPP20080108702001] (accessed on 20 April 2011).

Xue Ren, Ding Haiming, An Dongjun & Shi Jingzhong. 2009. 'Who Is Going to Command Next War: Interviews and Reports on the Joint Operations Command Talents Nurturing Coordination Zone in Shenyang Theater,' *Jiefangjun Bao Online* [Translated], 2 March, at [OSC CPP20090202710007], p.3.

Yu Zifu, Dong Xiaopo, Zhan Kejia & Li Yibao. 2008. 'Tempering All-around Commanders for Future Naval Warfare – The Record of East Sea Fleet Cultivating Joint Operations Command Personnel by Centering on Missions and Tasks', *Renmin Haijun* [Translated], 8 December, at [OSC CPP20090120478001], p3.

Yuan Zhenjun, Zhang Xinxin, Li Taowei and Tang Zhongping. 2008. 'Why are two out of three commands left in Neutral Gear? Joint Command Calls for Joint Mechanism', – Part 2 of

Series Report by *Renmin Haijun* Reporters on Tour of Theatres,' *Renmin Haijun* [Translated], 29 October, at [OSC CPP20081210478004], p. 2.

Zhang, Qinsheng and Li Bingyan. 1997. 'Series of Talks on the 'Two Basic Transformations' Understanding Gained From Studying CMC Strategic Thinking on the 'Two Basic Transformations', *Liberation Army Daily,* 14 January.

Zhao, Jianwei & Fan Juwei. 2007. 'CMC Member and PLA General Logistics Department Director Liao Xilong 14 February Calls for Deepening the Joint Logistics Reform in the PLA at a Teleconference on the Conclusion of the Jinan Theater's Experiments with the Joint Logistics Reform,' *Jiefangjun Bao* [Translated], 15 February at [OSC CPP20070215 710005], p. 1.

Zhao Lei. 2005. 'More power will go to lower levels under reform', *China Daily,* 28 November, http://www.chinadaily.com.cn/china/2015-11/28/content_22525493.htm (accessed on 26 July 2018).

Zhong Youguo, Li Huamin, Zhang Kejin & Yan Deyong. 2009. 'Build a Joint Training Big Special Zone-Analysis of Guangzhou Theatres Exploration of Joint Operations and Joint Training Process of its Three Branches,' *Jiefangjun Bao Online* [Translated], 2 March, at [OSC CPP20090303707002].

Zhou, Xiaoping. 2004. 'Consider Points of Emphasis in the Building of Our Merchant Ships from the Successful Experience of Building Merchant Ships in the World,' *Junshi Xueshu* [Translated], 1 January at [OSC CPP20071025325002], p. 57.

Zhu, Xiaodong. 2007. 'Actively promote integrated training of Army and Air force units according to law of integrated training of ground and air forces', *Junshi Xueshu* [Translated], 1 August, in FBIS, 14 December 2007.

# III. ECONOMIC AND SOCIAL DEVELOPMENT: NEW INITIATIVES?

# 13

# Can China become a Global Leader in Innovation?

*Ravi Bhoothalingam*

## Political Governance in China and the Role of Innovation

When China's former President Hu Jintao delivered his Political Report at the 18th Party Congress in 2012, several sections of that document were devoted to the progress made in 'making China an innovative country' (Hu Jintao 2012).[1] In the following years, President Xi Jinping made innovation a critical part – indeed, the cornerstone (Xi Jinping 2016)[2] – of the re-balancing and transformation of China's economy, and a major driver of 'the rejuvenation of China' itself. At the 19th Congress of the Communist Party of China held in October 2017, Xi's Report contains many specific references to innovation, including a whole chapter devoted to the place of innovation in achieving the two 'centenary goals' for China: i.e. 'achieving a moderate level of prosperity' by 2021, and becoming 'a strong, modern socialist country' by 2049 (Xi Jinping 2017).[3]

It is important to define 'innovation' for this essay. We can state it simply: an innovation is a creative idea that has gone through at least a rudimentary process of reality testing and emerges from that process as a promising new approach to solve a hitherto intractable problem. How high or how low one sets the bar for reality testing determines both the number of 'innovations' as well as their redemptive power. Innovations can range all the way from a fundamental discovery which alters the basic scientific paradigm, to a technological tweak that marginally reduces the cost or improves the quality or performance of a product or service. Innovations are not limited to the scientific or technological sphere: they include developing 'workforce(s) of higher quality.... strategy of innovation-driven development...innovation in management...' (Hu Jintao 2012)[4] and new ways to rearrange or even re-conceptualise economic, social, cultural and psychological relations, particularly with the advent of digital technology.

Xi Jinping's own views (Xi Jinping 2014) on the crucial role for innovation 'to make dreams come true' were set out early, starting with his speech on October 21, 2013,[5] where he waxed eloquent/poetic on innovation as 'the soul of a nation's progress, the inexhaustible force driving a country's prosperity…' He went on to link innovation with continuous learning, a modern and scientific outlook, openness to ideas from whatever be the source, and willingness to reform one's ways. The language may be flowery, but such words cannot be dismissed as mere political rhetoric.

The reason for such strong emphasis on innovation in China is not difficult to fathom. Chinas' problems are manifold and multi-dimensional, and they need to be tackled all together – delayed resolution can result in catastrophic setbacks. Soil degradation, chemical and air pollution, desertification, water scarcity, sex ratio, population profile, disease burden, pension liabilities, job creation, regional and income disparities, cyber-security, privacy...the list is legion. Such issues are difficult to solve with traditional methods. If China is to emerge unscathed out of this modern version of the labours of Hercules, the quality of innovation and governance will be the two instruments that will lead to its salvation. (The same can be said of India).

Moreover, the Communist Party of China (CPC) derives its legitimacy primarily on its performance record, with the definition of 'performance' changing with the times, and in tune with the needs and aspirations of the people. Indeed, in his Political Report, Xi Jinping spelt out how this definition is to be determined – it is by identifying the 'principal contradiction' facing the people. For the forthcoming two decades, Xi identifies this contradiction as: 'between unbalanced and inadequate development and the people's ever-growing needs for a better life'.[6] Since the Party has no safety valve of an electoral or other public process to act as a fall-back position in case of failure, any sustained period of poor performance in resolving this contradiction has a risk of evoking unforeseen – and unpleasant – consequences. Hence the pervading fear of *luan* (chaos) in the Chinese polity over the years – both in the Imperial and the modern era. And to maintain performance in increasingly challenging times requires the willingness to adopt innovatory approaches in many dimensions, including that of governance.

Therefore, the inclusion of innovation in a discourse about governance – which is what the Party Congresses are (supposedly) all about – is not only appropriate but necessary. This is particularly so since the traditional methods of any entrenched bureaucracy (including that of the CPC) need wholesale revision if they are to create a climate that nurtures innovation. Therefore, it is not surprising for innovation to have been portrayed in the 19th Party Congress as a necessary and crucial ingredient to achieve the goals set out by the Party for the country and indeed for the revitalisation of the CPC.

The Political Report presented at the Party Congress is also important in that it provides *inter alia* the guidelines for the Five-Year Plans which operationalise the Party goals. China's record of achieving its stated Five-Year Plan goals has been creditable: doubling its 1980 GDP by the target year 2000, and doubling that again by 2010, as planned. As of today, China is on course to double its 2010 GDP once again by 2020, to reach the 'moderate level of prosperity' that is the 'centenary goal' for the year 2021.

## The Historical Background of Innovation in China

What sort of soil has China provided over the years to the practice of discovery, invention and innovation? The master-reference here can be none other than the prodigious *tour de force* of the scientist and Sinologist Joseph Needham (Needham 1954-2004)[7] whose magisterial 27-volume history of Chinese science *inter alia* painstakingly documents every single invention made in China over the last 3000 years. As Simon Winchester says in his biography of Joseph Needham, '...considering only the most intellectually fertile phase of China's history, between the Han and Ming dynasties, Needham pointed out that in every century the Chinese dreamed up nearly fifteen new scientific ideas – a pace of inventiveness unmatched by the world's other great ancient civilisations – including the Greeks. The nature of the inventions was remarkable enough, Needham wrote, but the rate at which they came was like nowhere else on earth, and like no other time in history' (Winchester 2008).[8] Apart from the familiar examples of paper, printing, gunpowder and the compass, these inventions included the axial rudder, urinary steroids, the rain gauge and the wheelbarrow.

Let us look at three aspects that Needham uncovered in the course of his research. These relate to: (i) the nature of Chinese innovation and the driving forces behind it, and (ii) the suitability of Mandarin as a scientific language. In addition, we shall also look briefly at (iii) the background of intellectual property protection in China.

(i) What Needham found was that the course of Chinese innovation took a very different route from that of Europe. European innovation was largely driven by an aristocratic elite and scientists in the university system. A supportive eco-system of merchants, traders and financiers facilitated their interaction within and between Europe and other parts of the world. A class of craftsmen also emerged who produced scientific instrumentation such as microscopes, electrical meters, measuring instruments etc., involving precision work such as lens-grinding that required years of apprenticeship. This triangular combination of scientists, craftsmen and financiers/traders created a mutually beneficial eco-system that sustained a high level of innovative activity.

In the Chinese case, however, the motive force for innovation was much more empirical. Here, the principal actors were the practitioners – the lens-grinders, instrument-makers, blacksmiths, and doctors trained in traditional Chinese medicine. They were not just 'doers' but experimenters in their own right, sometimes by design and sometimes by chance, in their search for a better method or product, or just the pursuit of a 'what-if' whimsy. This integration of 'thinking-cum-doing' produced a more rapid rate of innovation, but not always accompanied with a coherent and complete theoretical construct or an organised scientific process of reasoning. For example, trigonometry and geometrical proof in China were nowhere near the high levels reached by the Greeks. Even then, as Angus Maddison has pointed out, China generated about a third of the world's GDP (Maddison 2001) by 1820.[9]

(ii) The second finding from the Needham enquiry concerns the capability of the Chinese language as an effective vehicle for scientific and technological discourse. Volume VII.2 of Needham's series contains the detailed expositions[10] of how classical Chinese fares in terms of precision, efficiency, classification, comparison, measurement and mathematics – all of importance for a language to function as an effective vehicle for the production, recording and transmission of scientific information. Needham's work (and the supporting references) show that Mandarin performed this task as well if not better than Latin, before vernacular languages gradually replaced Latin in Europe after 1700. More recent evidence[11] has shown that the Chinese language is eminently suited for the digital world and for communication across the Internet; in fact, in many ways, characters already compress information content in a natural way, and thus lend themselves to digital transcription and the efficient conduct of communication in cyber-space. (Typically, Chinese language texts are about 30 percent shorter in length, compared with English translations).

(iii) The history of intellectual property (IP) protection in China throws some interesting light on its contribution to inventions and innovations in China through the ages. The Chinese introduced the practice of protecting intellectual rights well before the guild monopolies of Europe were established in the 16th century. Since then, Chinese IP law has had a better balance between protecting IP property owners and the users of intellectual works (Ke 2006).[12] This enabled China to develop its educational and technological sectors and indeed its economy so much so that it was the world leader in these spheres for three centuries before 1820 (Maddison 2001).

In 16th century China, trademarks and proprietary methods were family secrets of craftsmen, and were hard to duplicate. Also, the State played a leading role in promoting 'useful' innovations. Since there was a greater flow of inventions in China as compared to Europe (as Needham has noted), there was no need for a strong patent law either to stimulate inventions, nor to attract them from other countries. Indeed, Chinese guilds had less monopoly power than the London book-sellers' guild in the early 18th century.

This experience should make developing countries pause and think before rushing to adopt the 'standard' IP law prescribed by the developed world. A fair IP regime is one where all nations can grow through the development and export of their own creativity.

## Resources and Environment for Innovation in China Today

Now, we turn to a brief examination of the state of innovation in China today, the resources available to foster innovation, the nature of its supportive eco-system, and draw some inferences as to China's capability to be amongst the global leaders of innovation by 2035.

### *(i) Talent and Education*

In the early years of the People's Republic of China, Mao made public health and public education top priorities of Government policy. As a result, China today has an enrolment ratio of 99 percent in primary education and 94 percent in secondary education. China turns out 30,000 Ph.Ds in science and engineering (*The Mckinsey Quarterly* October 2015)[13] each year. Since 2008, a concerted drive has been launched to persuade leading and very highly specialised scientific personnel in the Chinese overseas diaspora to return home, with promises of interesting work, and good working conditions. More than 5208 such returnees – popularly known as 'sea turtles' – have been confirmed in the year 2015 (WEF 2016).[14]

Further, with the launch of China's National Medium and Long-Term Talent Development Plan 2010-2020, which aims at increasing the number of 'highly skilled' workers from 114 million (2010) to 180 million by 2020, and the simultaneous increase of Human Resource Development (HRD) expenditure from 10.75 of GDP to 15 percent of GDP in the same period, the organisation and investment base to enlarge the talent pool for innovation is well under way

(Wang, 2010).[15] A caution, however, is sounded by the Mckinsey study[16] that the rote-learning system is a drag on the creative abilities of Chinese education, and to that extent, these large numbers need to be treated with caution.

### *(ii) Market and Eco-system*

With more than 618 million Internet users (WEF 2016),[17] 500 million mobile users and 301 million internet shoppers amongst its population of 1.3 billion, China presents a massive market. This market size is a huge incentive for the growth of companies – particularly small and medium enterprises (SMEs). Government policy encourages the development of high-tech parks to house many of these companies – there are presently 130 such parks which account for 40 percent of the total investment in R&D. Such parks foster cross-fertilisation of ideas and can even lead to cutting edge innovation: an example is *Zhongguancun* in Beijing which has incubated globally leading work in artificial intelligence, bio-medical sciences and genomics. Good transport and energy infrastructure is provided for these parks on even better terms than for industrial clusters.

### *(iii) Research, Development and Intellectual Property*

China invests US$ 200 billion each year in R&D (*Mckinsey* 2015) – the second-highest in the world after the USA. As a result, 820,000 patents were filed in China in 2013: Huawei filed 10 percent of these, while Sinopec – a State owned enterprise – filed 2844. Although the standard of the patents – as indeed the overall quality of China's 'modern' IP regime – is still somewhat less than robust, the sheer numbers indicate a strong upsurge in inventive activity. Governments – central, provincial and local – support research institutes and encourage both the State-owned sector and local SME's to interact with research bodies and Universities. As a result, over 65 percent of patents emerge from SMEs (WEF 2016). No wonder that the World Economic Forum describes China as a 'game-changing world player when it comes to innovation' (WEF 2016).

Nevertheless, the IP scene in China is changing by the day. One recent account[18] has this surprising observation: 'In addition to filing twice as many patents as the US, China is increasingly being selected as a key venue for patent litigation between non-Chinese companies'. Why? The answer is another surprise: fair treatment. 65 foreign concerns won 81 percent of the cases they fought to protect their IP, the same ratio as that for domestic companies. This evolution should not raise any eyebrows – China is following much the same path as the United States, Europe or developed Asia did over the past two centuries.

Prof. Doron Ben-Atar of Fordham University, New York City, makes this pungent observation about how the United States acquired intellectual property in the early days of its industrial rise: 'Officially, the young republic pioneered a new criterion of intellectual property that set the highest possible standards for such claims – worldwide originality and novelty. At the same time, through a variety of measures, the government endorsed and supported the violation of intellectual property of European states and individuals. The United States emerged as the world's industrial leader by illicitly appropriating mechanical and scientific innovations from Europe' (Ben-Atar 2004).[19]

### *(iv) Technology Transfer and Bargaining Power*

China, too, has been no laggard in this area. In fact, its Government as well as its legal system have enabled – if not encouraged – such naked appropriation. But this stage is nearing its end, as Chinese ownership of, and investment in, its own self-generated IP has increased. Rather, China now acquires IP more through the sheer bargaining power conferred by its huge market. This is where the Chinese government's ability to 'coordinate' even the actions of its private players (let alone State-owned enterprises) makes its mark. By placing large and consolidated orders on a foreign supplier, or by creating a consortium of interests on the Chinese side, China is enabled to wield enormous power to extract terms from foreign companies that others find difficult, and these terms usually include transfer of technology over an agreed period of time.

In an editorial piece,[20] *The Economist* asks whether Chinese competition is illegal, intense and unfair. It concludes that the illegal part (pure theft, hacking etc) has reduced markedly after an agreement with America in 2015. Yes, Chinese competition is intense, but largely legal. As for being unfair, *The Economist* describes it as 'sharp practice that breaks no global rules'. For India – facing the brunt of U.S. pressure to dilute its policies on food security as well as inexpensive medicines, both of which are hugely consequential for India's poor population – it might be worth carefully studying the Chinese practice.

### *(v) Frontiers of Fundamental Discovery*

What about China's capability to generate its own high-technology and breach the frontiers of scientific discovery? The innovations listed in Xi's Political Report[21] give us an indication that China's major achievements are still in technology adaptation followed (in that order) by high technology development, and the rapid growth of pure science. This finding is relevant when we assess the probable and potential levels of innovation that China might achieve in the future.

The Mckinsey study concludes that China is currently able to drive about 25 percent of its GDP growth through innovation, and sets a target of 50 percent for China to qualify as a true leader in innovation. Is that attainable? Mckinsey notes that the obstacles to such achievement are mostly inefficient government processes, weaknesses in the IP system, and the gaps (earlier mentioned) in the quality of the talent pool. But it remains reasonably confident that the target is within China's reach, given its present capabilities as well as limitations. That brings us to a key question: can China's governance system foster – and even more, live in peace with – creativity and innovation of increasingly higher levels?

## Authoritarian Creativity – An Oxymoron?

China's governance system can certainly be described as 'authoritarian'. It does not have the classical features of a Euro-American democratic state (universal suffrage, strict separation of powers, rule of law and a code of human rights based on constitutional safeguards etc). One doubts whether the highest echelons of the Communist Party of China could be prosecuted and removed from office under law through due process, as would be the case if impeachment proceedings succeeded against a sitting U.S. President. But neither is China a crude dictatorship. The nature of the governance system erected and followed by the Communist Party of China over the last seventy years draws heavily on China's own historical and cultural heritage, including Confucian philosophy and the development of China's mandarinate over two thousand years. (For a detailed argument and description of China's governance (Bhoothalingam 2010).[22]

Can a Leninist-Confucian bureaucracy – even an adaptive, highly trained and continuously learning organisation as the CPC – foster and also cope with continuous creativity and innovation? Let us look at the historical record globally first, and then focus on the Chinese case over the last seventy years.

The last four hundred years since the Enlightenment and the scientific revolution were a period of mostly non-democratic rule[23] for at least three-fourths of that period – even in Europe and North America. Creativity, discovery and innovation thrived in the sciences, medicine and engineering at that time. Authoritarian states – Fascist as well as Communist – seem to have worked out a formula whereby scientific and technological innovation was relatively left unscathed, though innovations in the arts and social sciences came under greater ideological scrutiny. Still, the sciences did not get away entirely scot-free. In the Soviet Union, Trofim Lysenko ruined an entire generation of Soviet geneticists by his anti-Mendelian and unscientific insistence on the 'inheritance of acquired characteristics'. And by its rabid anti-Jewish policies, the Nazi regime lost valuable scientific talent in Germany and Austria to foreign exile (Einstein and Freud being just two examples). But by and large, we can conclude that scientific and technological discovery flourished in many countries even when their governance was far from being a model of democracy.

In recent times, the Chinese state focused – correctly – on land reforms and human and social development in the early years after 1949. The rapid progress in these areas led to China's human capital being well-positioned to take advantage of Deng Xiaoping's 'reform and opening up' after 1978. China's embrace of the low-cost manufacturing space in the years 1980-2010 enabled a massive increase in employment and a concomitant reduction in Chinese poverty, giving the State the capability to weather the global financial crisis of 2008. Since then, China has been engaged in an attempt to rebalance its growth model to move towards greater consumption and imports, and less reliance on investment fuelled through debt. These changes have been propelled, *inter alia*, by a series of innovations – scientific, social and structural – and sustained by a well-nurtured long-term planning and monitoring process which remains the core strength of the 'China model'.

China has also managed to escape what could have been the hugely disruptive consequences of global developments in social innovation. In 2011, the 'Arab Spring' – popular ferment against the despots in the Middle East – destabilised governments from Tunisia to Yemen. These movements were both generated and accelerated through the newly-discovered power of social media – Facebook, Twitter and the like. There was a strong feeling that China would be next, and that a 'Jasmine Summer' would shake up the CPC if not in Beijing, at least in Hong Kong. Nothing of the sort transpired. On the other hand, the Chinese state apparatus understood the *modus operandi* of social media very quickly, and was soon able to bend it for its own ends, through a combination of cooperation, co-option, and coercion.. Today, Google and Facebook are standing at the gates of the Middle Kingdom, hat in hand, to do business there. The indications are that they will concede more than the CPC in whatever bargain is struck eventually. In the meantime, Chinese internet unicorns – near-trillion dollar companies – with global influence, have taken firm root in China, and are spreading their wings across the world.

However, the downside of the China model is that mistakes by the CPC – when they happen – are likely to be huge, and to have serious after-effects. The lack of adequate countervailing checks and balances, media challenge, and a vibrant and legally empowered civil society, have combined in the past to allow a blindsided leadership stumble into costly errors such as the 'Great Leap Forward', the Great Proletarian Cultural Revolution, and the one-child policy. These are all examples of disastrous errors in Chinese governance, and the people of China have paid a grievous human cost for these mistakes.

## Conclusion

So, will China become a global leader in innovation? On the form and evidence presented so far, it is a 'Yes'. Between 2035 and 2050, China is likely to enter that small group of nations who will enjoy per capita income levels at the upper end of the middle-income scale and possess the capability to drive further growth largely through innovation. For India, this conclusion has some important implications. And so too for China, though for very different reasons.

### *Implications for India*

China decided over a decade ago that innovation was vital to overcome its existential problems and to achieve its 'rejuvenation'. This realisation is even more pertinent for India today – trailing much behind as it is on most development indicators. Two points stand out. First, it means that the factors that support innovation – education and talent development, investment in science and technology, an open eco-system that fosters creativity through collaborations with both domestic and foreign players, a social climate and work culture based on rationality and scientific temper – need implementation at once, strongly and consistently. If not, India risks falling further behind, since the rewards of innovation in today's globalised economy flow disproportionately to the innovator.

Second, India needs to re-evaluate its ambivalence in engaging with China, especially on the economic front. As economic – and innovative – power shifts East, India should move imaginatively and confidently to capture the benefits that full-throated engagement with China can bring for our population. Though India lags China in development parameters as stated earlier, as a polity and a nation we have complementary strengths that can add value, perhaps in areas where China has vulnerabilities.

### *Implications for China*

For China, caveats arise out of its success. Principally, there are two.

One derives from the very nature of the scientific challenges. Technologies such as artificial intelligence, robotics, genetic manipulation, disease eradication and the delay or elimination of aging, will greatly increase human welfare. They also pose very serious – even existential – risks, and some fundamental ethical problems. Mistakes in addressing these issues can lead to consequences much worse than those listed in the previous section. Such matters can only be solved by a robust governance system that is both competent in applied science, and capable of drawing on strong historically-rooted ethical traditions, and willing to engage in public reasoning before implementing policy decisions. This 'triple competence' implies virtuous governance of a sort most closely approximated (in human imagination) by the idealised rule of a 'philosopher-king', *shi-wang* or *dharmaraja*[24] under the ancient Greek, ancient Chinese and ancient Indian traditions, respectively. An evolutionary challenge thus faces the CPC.

The second caveat arises from the earlier-quoted 'principal contradiction' identified by Xi Jinping himself: 'the people's ever-growing needs for a better life...' What might that 'better life' be in 2050? With greater global communication and travel, will there be greater global convergence of values and ideas, even of governance systems? Will the Chinese people demand more social and cultural choices? Or even spiritual offerings? The last-named would certainly tax the CPC to its limits, since that is a frontier the Party has never wished to explore.

China may well reach both its centennial goals by 2050. But before that date, the CPC will confront the twin challenges of virtue and ethical humanism. Here lies the ultimate test for future congresses of the CPC. If China can find answers to these questions, *tianxia datong* (Tan Chung, 2015)[25] would be within reach for everyone on earth, and mankind's eternal quest for the meaning of life would have come to an end.

## NOTES

1. Hu Jintao. 2012. 'Full Text of Hu Jintao's Report at 18th Party Congress,' *Xinhua,* 17 November http://news.xinhuanet.com/english/special/18cpcnc/2012–11/17/c_131981259.htm (accessed on 26 July 2017).
2. 2016. Chinese Communist Party Central Document Research Office, ed., Excerpted Comments of Xi Jinping on *Science & Technology Innovation,* Beijing: Central Document Press.
3. Xi Jinping. 2017. Full text of Xi Jinping's report at 19th CPC National Congress, http://www.xinhuanet.com/english/download/Xi_Jinping's_report_at_19th_CPC_National_Congress.pdf (accessed on 21 January 2018).
4. Hu Jintao. 2012. op.cit.
5. Xi Jinping. 2014. *The Governance of China,* Beijing: Foreign Languages Press, pp.63–68,
6. Xi Jinping. 2017. op. cit.
7. Needham, J., Wang, L. and Lu, G.D., 1963. *Science and Civilisation in China.* (27 Volumes). Cambridge: Cambridge University Press.
8. Winchester, Simon. 2008. *The Man Who Loved China,* HarperCollins, New York, 2008, (page 188). In addition, 292 original Chinese inventions in total between 1500 B.C. and 1700 A.D. are listed in Appendix I, pp. 267-277.
9. Maddison, Angus. 2001. *The World Economy – A Millennial Perspective.* OECD, 2001.
10. Needham, Joseph. op.cit, *Science and Civilisation in China* Vol. VII.2, Chapter 50(e).
11. Mullaney, Thomas S. 2017. *The Chinese Typewriter: A History,* MIT Press, 2017.
12. Ke Shao. 2006. 'What May Validate Intellectual Property in a Traditional Chinese Mind? Queen Mary Intellectual Property Research Institute, University of London: in the *Journal of Information, Law and Technology* JILT 2006 (1).
13. 2016. 'Gauging the strength of Chinese innovation,' October 2015, *The Mckinsey Quarterly,* https://www.mckinsey.com/business-functions/strategy-and-corporate-finance/our-insights/gauging-the-strength-of-chinese-innovation (accessed on 12 November 2017).
14. World Economic Forum (WEF): China's Innovation Ecosystem, www.weforum.org, 2016.

15. Wang, Huiyao. 2010. 'China's Talent Plan: Where will it lead to?' The Brookings Institution, 20 September, https://www.brookings.edu/wp-content/uploads/2012/04/0920_china_powerpoint.pdf (accessed on 23 November 2017).
16. 2016. 'Gauging the strength of Chinese innovation,' October 2015, op.cit.
17. WEF op.cit.
18. 'China as an IP Powerhouse'–www.slash.org, April 13, 2017.
19. Ben-Atar, Doron. 2008. *Trade Secrets: Intellectual Piracy and the Origins of American Industrial Power,* Yale: Yale University Press.
20. *The Economist*, 2017. Does China Play Fair? 23 September.
21. Quote from Xi Jinping's Political Report (op.cit): 'We have seen much accomplished toward making China a country of innovators, with major advances made in science and technology, including the successful launch of Tiangong-2 space lab, the commissioning of the deep-sea manned submersible Jiaolong and of the five-hundred-meter aperture spherical telescope (FAST) Tianyan, the launch of the dark matter probe satellite Wukong and the quantum science satellite Mozi, and the test flight of the airliner C919.'
22. Bhoothalingam, Ravi. 2010. *China 2020: A Confucian Democracy*? The Observer Research Foundation, Mumbai, July 20, 2010. www.orfonline.org
23. Factors considered in making this assertion include: lack of universal suffrage, no laws prohibiting discrimination on the basis of gender or race, religion etc, and no minority protections under Constitutional provisions.
24. Plato's Republic and other works expound on virtuous rule being possible only when philosophers become kings; *shi-wang* translates roughly as 'sage-king' and *dharmaraja* is similar.
25. Tan, Chung. 2015. *Himalaya Calling: The Origins of China and India*, New Jersey, USA: World Century Publishing Corporation. In Tan Chung's usage, the term *'Tianxia datong'* translates as 'Grand harmony of all under Heaven' and is akin to the Indian concept of *'Vasudhaiva Kutumbakam'*.

# 14

# Economic Reforms, the 19th Party Congress and Beyond

*Aravind Yelery*

Reform and opening-up are the most distinctive features of contemporary China. The Party and the State have used them to design the way China looks at itself inward and outward. The Chinese Socialist market economy, byproduct of these forces, was rationalised to broaden Party's agenda to make it more inclusive. Through Party Congresses,[1] continuous measures were adopted to let market forces play a decisive role in economic affairs without undermining the Party-based rule of law or seriously impending development of the capital market in China. The 19th Congress of the Communist Party of China (CPC) makes it clear that it is necessary to deepen the reform of the financial system, enhance the financial sector's ability to provide real economy, increase the proportion of direct financing and promote development of a multi-level capital market. The National Financial Work Conference (NFWC) which was held prior to the 19th Party Congress in July (2017) focused on a new set of issues for debate including an overhaul of the financial regulatory regime, financial security and opening up of the financial markets.[2] It was for the first time, since the NFWC was set up in 1997, the need for bold reforms were brought into discussions. The 19th Congress' role is crucial to gauge the path of Chinese economic policy making and its foundations.

## Why Party Congresses are Critical?

The Party Congress in China is the key step in a top-down process of leadership's role in leveraging from economic development and at the same time carefully deleveraging from the risks involved. It is also a drill for politicians providing oversight of economics portfolios. It is evident from the past Party

Congresses that they play a critical role in putting forward the politically appropriate assumptions and calculations to lessen the impact of misguided policies. It was this policy framework, delicately meshed in theoretical outline which would guide the new initiatives. Party Congress, specifically until 17th Party Congress, acknowledged China's economic accomplishments and moderately touch the hurdles ahead. Thus, the role of Party Congress was two edged, on the one hand, it ratified and generalised the pilot policy initiatives carried by leaders or institutions and on the other hand, it theorised to make the decisions popular. However, since 17th Party Congress, these meetings repeatedly demonstrated an urgency to surmount existential challenges.

The determination to bring more institutional reforms became the core of Party Congress since 2007, the year Chinese model of growth underwent a reality check. While 14th, 15th and 16th Party Congresses were determined to provide Chinese economy the much-needed ecosystem to grow, the 17th and 18th Congresses were quite different if one looks at the set of challenges.[3] The two previous Party Congresses were steered to look inward and follow diligent policy making to correct the economy. The room to rectify the policies were narrowing much faster than expected. The regulators, to be very specific, had run out of space to innovate and risk the already slowing economy. The policy corrections were expected to come from the leadership by bringing in more institutional readjustments and these adjustments meant more disruption in traditional inter-institutional, inter-Party tensions, and Provincial power dynamics. The State-Owned Enterprises (SOE) reforms were one of the early examples when the Party had to do a lot of political heavy lifting. The risk was to balance the interests between regulators (Banking, Insurance, SASAC – The State-Owned Assets Supervision and Administration Commission of the State Council etc.) and at the same time, countering the agitation from Provincial Party leaders who had to deal with the layoffs. The fiscal reforms in mid-90s and property bubble tested Party's will to manage these differences.

In recent years (since 2007), the slowing economic growth exposed a lot of gaps in Chinese economy and also implied that functional remedies were not sufficient to resolve the core problems. Given the high risk involved in poorly managed reforms and continued slowing down of economic growth, the Party Congresses in the past 10 years or so (the period covering 17th and 18th Party Congresses) focused on realigning Party's central role in China's economic policy making. To bring the fundamental changes in the economy, Party needs to come clean in terms of defining and ending the opaque policies being implemented and patronised by institutions across sectors of the economy with operational and institutional liabilities. This was evident during the 17th and 18th Party Congresses but the pressure kept mounting and at times, Party lost it to mid-term adhocism. Either loose rule or the over concentration of powers and functions can best explain this adhocism. During last 11 years (post-17th Party Congress and peak point of China's export driven economy) the growth and development parameters, amplified political, legal and economic indices set by the Communist Party of China. In simple language, during these years, the economic challenges had direct impact on the functioning of the CPC and Party Congresses were left to coding a new set of rules and laws. The State being the paramount regulator and the Party being the sole facilitator, law and rules mattered in the Party proceedings. In the past as well, the laws and rules were brought in to institutionalise and generalise the adhoc policies for economic reforms. This was clearly evident in case of minor non-regulatory reforms, be it land reforms or those related to the banking system. The 19th Party Congress had a major challenge of laying the foundation of laws which would define how the reforms would be carried out to oversee the behaviour of regulators, allowing them to firm stands and help achieve the 'Chinese dream'.

## Moving from the 18th to the 19th Party Congress

The Communist economies in other parts of the world are not new to the element of direct authority being exercised but the Chinese economy has evolved through the tension between political control and the capitalist behavior of the economic structures for past couple of decades. The political control exercised by the Party remained in line with growth trajectories. Instead of unleashing control over the economic forces, the Communist Party used its intervention to make the reforms look politically correct. In that context, areas and sectors which the CPC overlooked threatened the Chinese state in the last couple of years, stock market crash is one recent case. Especially when the cases of economic volatilities occur at regular intervals, the political intervention deepens. That has been on display since the 18th Party Congress. For example, in the recent past, General Secretary Xi Jinping attempted a fresh approach by allowing political authorities wielding control through supervisions, appointments, scrutiny of assets and putting a check on outward capital movements.[4] President Xi's control and use of power was not only limited to picking new members to deliver at the top post but making the new appointments of Party Secretaries and Governors across the federal landscape. With political correctives in place, economic pressure mounting, major official communication and decision are cautious and demand increasing role for 'Mr. Dependables'. Dozens of committees (dealing with economic affairs), directly under the leadership of Xi, exercise control over economic policy making. Political control is increasingly used as one of the overriding tools to regulate reforms and decision regarding economy and advance leaders' own authority.

In his Report at the 19th National Congress of the Communist Party of China on 18 October 2017, Xi Jinping as the General Secretary of the Party, connected three important dots namely – centrality of theory, overcoming institutional ailments and innovation. In his speech, Xi reiterated that "only with reform and opening can we develop China, develop Socialism, and develop Marxism".[5] And to deepen the reforms, Xi Jinping has aformidable task to get it pass through political pressure points. Indicating where the reforms need to be focused, Xi in his Political Report also declared that the leadership must have the determination to get rid of all outdated thinking and ideas and all institutional ailments, and break through the blockades of vested interests."[6] The Report was subtle in underpinning the need for bold reforms to get rid of ill practices in the economy, for example – shadow banking, regulatory irresponsibility, non-performance, debt among others. It is noteworthy that the Political Report highly praised the role of new economic frontiers which the government need to braise. The report then indicated that the new Party Congress should take a pro-active approach towards making government's role deeper and better, and adopt new industrialisation, IT application, urbanisation, and agricultural modernisation. Although the 18th Political Report did emphasise on innovation it was not as emphatic as the 14th Party Congress which was more emphatic. The Political Report of the 14th Party Congress had declared that an ideological innovation for reform should not be constrained by the abstract question of whether such innovation was Capitalist or Socialist. Xi wants to keep the new reforms within reach and fit them in a stencil of periodic goals and deliverables. As described in the Political Report and deliberated much in detail, Xi inherited two lofty economic targets set by the Party's previous leadership together known as 'two centennial goals'. The first centennial goal is to build a 'moderately prosperous society' by wiping out poverty by 2021, the 100th anniversary of the Party's founding. The second and more challenging goal is to turn China into a 'fully developed nation' by 2049, the 100th anniversary of the founding of the People's Republic.[7] The two goals lays down broader and ambitious framework for economic reforms.

With speeches related to globalisation, internationalisation of trade and investments, the belt and road, connectivity in the neighbourhood, supply chain reforms, poverty alleviation, Xi Jinping looks like a 'master' reformer and is cognisant of structural nuances of the economy. Examples indicate that political intervention bring casualties to the national economy, but it is also apparent that in case of China, political intervention to end the Party induced 'incentivisation' may prove to be the turning point.

## 19th National Congress and the Usual Suspects

Keeping the above discussion at the centre, Xi had no option but to line-up reforms intended to deliver on two fronts – not letting the growth slip below a decent rate of 6.5 percent and carry out institutional reforms without causing any conflicts. For any political economy, non-performance leads to subsequent decline in political control and culminates in the rise of adversaries which further block reforms. The recent revelations regarding non-profitable overseas investments by public and private enterprises delayed reforms in regulatory bodies. The reforms did not come out of nowhere and it would be wrong to ignore the challenges posed by the prevailing situation.

The collapse of the stock market and the over concentration of authority in hands of a few regulators caused extensive damage to the Chinese economy, the better regulatory mechanism were seen fundamental to rectify these critical issues. The 19th Party Congress strategically deployed the comprehensive plan to deepen reform in the new era. The China Securities Regulatory Commission (CSRC) system and the securities and futures industry will be the first in line to comply stricter guidelines.

As a result, one of the most important institutional reforms that caught the attention of economic analysts was the scraping of the China Banking Regulatory Commission (CBRC) and the China Insurance Regulatory Commission (CIRC) to form the China Banking and Insurance Regulatory Commission (CBIRC) leading to a merger of rule-making and macro prudential powers.[8] CIRC is seen as being stricter than its banking counterpart in approving financial product.[9] After combining, it is expected that the supervision for insurance sales and commercial banking related insurance business will be tightened.

However the securities regulator, CSRC remained untouched (People's Bank of China – PBoC – coming out as a winner from the financial institution reshuffle). Guo Shuqing (郭树清) would be leading the newly created CBIRC. According to *The New York Times*,[10] he is known as 'whirlwind Guo' on account of his 17-month stint as head of China's securities regulator from 2011 to 2013, when he issued approximately 80 policy directives to crack down on insider trading and market manipulation. He is generally considered as a reform minded policy maker who is willing to take aggressive steps. The greatest challenge for him would be to control the shadow banking sector in China, which he tried to streamline in his previous role at CBRC. Guo has also previously served as the Governor of Shandong Province.

Another key development, post-19th Party Congress, is related to the State International Development Cooperation Agency, which is expected to end the rivalry that existed between Ministry of Commerce and Ministry of Foreign

Affairs regarding control of Chinese foreign aid. The Chinese aid system is complex and consists of 33 government agencies. In an article[11] published by *People's Daily* on 12 March 2018, Ding Xuexiang, Director of the General Office of the CPC Central Committee said the cabinet restructuring was intended to address problems plaguing government agencies, such as organisational overlap, ambiguity of authority and responsibility, and low efficiency. This Ministry is expected to play a key role in the expansion of Belt and Road Initiative and other projects in South Asia, Southeast Asia, Central Asia and Latin America.

In addition, as China is gearing up to become the key player in global capital market, the 19th Party Congress decided to focus on the capital market. As the economy shifted from a period of rapid growth to a phase of high-quality development, the capital market in China has been unable to balance the financial system vis-à-vis the multi-level and diversified financing needs generated by the rapid development of the real economy. The decisions to further open up China's capital market to boost reform and development, especially those geared to better serve the real economy, increase the proportion of direct financing and cultivate the healthy development of multi-layered capital markets were significant. This was later confirmed by Politburo Member and Vice-Premier Liu He at his speech in Davos 2018, where he spoke about the imminent announcement of new market access measures and greater protection for intellectual property.[12] President Xi underlined the same during his inaugural speech at the Boao Forum in April 2018 (Table 1).[13]

If supply-side structural reform became a target for industries, enhancing the quality and efficiency of the capital market in serving the real economy is essential. The capital market and the real economy are symbiotic. While the capital market in China is curated under strict control by raising the proportion of direct financing, continuing to steadily push forward the reform of the stock issuance system, and expanding the multi-level, diversified and complementary equity financing channels, will help China to attract national technology companies to list or relist domestically. It will also help internationalisation of the Chinese capital markets. The systematic transformation of China's capital market has the potential to culminate in China's ascendancy as a global financial powerhouse.

One also needs not to overlook the fact that a massive bureaucratic reorganisation plan was unfolded during the first session of the 13th National People's Congress that called for new analyses of the political economy of Chinese bureaucratic administration.[14] The new players and latest institutions tasked with new roles and responsibilities in the massive overhaul, calling for greater attention to the mandates granted to each of these with a greater scrutiny.

## Conclusion

The reforms and readjustment announced during the 19th Party Congress may need time to push the economy in the right direction (See Table 1). The structural reform would take considerable time to sync. There is also the danger of the policy reforms accidently triggering an inertia leading to unintended results. In line with the 19th Party Congress and the State Council directives since 2018, the People's Bank of China (the Central bank of China) slightly adjusted the previous financial deleveraging strategy, and gradually promoted financial liquidity.[15] So far, the Central Bank has continuously promoted financial liquidity by opening market operations, and at the same time carried out the targeted RRR cuts thrice.[16] However, the released liquidity did not bring the desired results on China's credit market. The obvious explanations could be – one, the insufficient bank capital fund restrained the credit expansion to a certain degree and second – the harsh and uncertain supervision rules hit banks' lending ability.[17] The pressure on economy can be best avoided by pursuing some of the bitter policy initiatives and while doing so, the growth rate may fluctuate causing alarm. Still this policy has to stay on course. As the country continues to deepen its reforms, it aspires to exploit newer frontiers of growth and consolidate its leadership in global finance, innovation and technologies.

**Table 1: Major Policy Announcements since 19th Party Congress**[18]

| *Date* | *Leader/entity* | *Description of reforms and policy revision* |
|---|---|---|
| 19 Sept. 2018 | Li Keqiang | Li Keqiang: China will never rely on the depreciation of the renminbi to stimulate exports. |
| 19 Sept. 2018 | Li Keqiang | Li Keqiang: The Chinese government is studying a policy to significantly reduce the burden of corporate taxes and fees. |
| 19 Sept. 2018 | Li Keqiang | Li Keqiang reiterated that China will unswervingly adhere to the 'two unshakable', further implement and improve the policies and measures to support the development of the private economy, resolutely eliminate all kinds of unreasonable obstacles that hinder the development of the private economy, and relax the commitment of the government to relax private enterprises. In to the field, we must increase efforts to promote progress. |
| 19 Sept. 2018 | Li Keqiang | Li Keqiang: All localities will keep their existing social security policies unchanged. |
| 18 Sept. 2018 | Li Keqiang | Li Keqiang presided over the State Council executive meeting and demanded that the established tax reduction and fee reduction measures be put in place to ensure the stability of the current social security premium collection policy. |
| 15 Sept. 2018 | Xi Jinping | Xi Jinping's speech at the Eastern Economic Forum: 'China advocates' to activate the Northeast Asian economic circle |
| 12 Sept. 2018 | Li Keqiang | Li Keqiang presided over the convening of the State Council executive meeting, deployed in the country to promote the 'separation of licenses' reforms in an orderly manner, and continued to solve the problem of 'access is not allowed to camp' |

| *Date* | *Leader/entity* | *Description of reforms and policy revision* |
|---|---|---|
| 25 May 2018 | Li Keqiang | He hosted the plenary session of the State Council: to ensure that the economic operation is in a reasonable range and deepen the reform of personal income tax. |
| 16 May 2018 | Li Keqiang | He hosted the State Council executive meeting and determined measures to further reduce the logistics cost of the real economy. |
| 2 May 2018 | Li Keqiang | He presided over the State Council executive meeting and took measures to reduce the time for approval of enterprise start-ups and construction projects by more than half. |
| 27 April 2018 | Li Keqiang | He pointed out at the first clean government work meeting of the State Council on April 27 that the government should minimise the direct allocation of market resources. |
| 25 April 2018 | Li Keqiang | He presided over the State Council executive meeting and decided to introduce seven tax reduction measures to support entrepreneurial innovation and the development of small and micro enterprises. |
| 13 April 2018 | Xi Jinping | He announced at the 30th anniversary of the establishment of the provincial special economic zone in Hainan that the central government supports the construction of a free trade zone in Hainan Island and the construction of a free trade port to support Hainan's establishment of international energy, shipping, bulk commodities and other trading venues. |
| 11 April 2018 | Xi Jinping | He spoke with representatives of Chinese and foreign entrepreneurs attending the 2018 Annual Meeting of the Boao Forum for Asia and said that China is promoting the development of the blueprint for the East Asian Economic Community and promoting the construction of the Asia-Pacific Free Trade Area. |
| 10 April 2018 | Xi Jinping | He said in a keynote speech at the opening ceremony of the 2018 Annual Meeting of the Boao Forum for Asia on April 10 that China will greatly relax market access. He proposed to launch several landmark initiatives. "(1) In the service industry, especially the financial industry, the major measures announced at the end of last year to relax the restrictions on foreign-funded shares in the banking, securities and insurance industries should be ensured, and the opening process of the insurance industry should be accelerated, and restrictions on the establishment of foreign-funded financial institutions should be relaxed. The scope of foreign-funded financial institutions in China; (2) China to create a more attractive investment environment. In the first half of this year, China will complete the revision of the negative list of foreign investment and fully implement the pre-entry national treatment plus negative list management system. (3) China will not aim at pursuing a trade surplus, and will attempt to expand imports and promote the balance of current account balance. In 2018, China will reduce the import tariffs on automobiles by a considerable margin, while reducing the import tariffs of some other products, and strive to increase the import of special advantage products with relatively concentrated needs of the |

| *Date* | *Leader/entity* | *Description of reforms and policy revision* |
|---|---|---|
| | | people and accelerate the process of joining the World Trade Organisation's 'Government Procurement Agreement'." |
| 10 April 2018 | Xi Jinping | He met with the President of the International Monetary Fund, Lagarde, and conveyed that China will continue to support free trade, trade and investment liberalisation and facilitation, and is willing to continue to strengthen cooperation with the International Monetary Fund. |
| 28 March 2018 | Li Keqiang | At the State Council executive meeting, it was determined to deepen the VAT reform measures, unify the VAT small-scale taxpayer standards, and allow more enterprises to enjoy the preferential tax rate according to the lower levy rate; decided to set up a national financing guarantee fund to promote the mitigation of small and micro enterprises, and solve financing problems such as 'three rural issues'. |
| 28 March 2018 | Xi Jinping | He presided over the first meeting of the Deepening Reform Committee, deliberated and approved the establishment of the Shanghai Financial Court, deepened the reform and opening up plan of the Guangdong, Tianjin and Fujian Free Trade Zones, and adopted the guidance on regulating the asset management business of financial institutions. |
| 21 March 2018 | Li Keqiang | He presided over the executive meeting of the State Council. The meeting called for speeding up the implementation of the 'six-one' key tasks and tax reduction and fee reduction measures, such as reducing the start-up time of enterprises and reducing the number of business operations, and improving the business environment for market participants. |
| 20 March 2018 | Li Keqiang | He answered questions from reporters at the two sessions: China will further expand its opening up and relax service industry access; it must ensure more adequate employment through various efforts; Guangdong, Hong Kong, Macao and Dawan District will be built into a world-class, planning outline is under development; further expand opening up and relax service industry access. In 2018, China to raise the financial subsidy for basic medical insurance; the relevant departments have been required to improve the domestic listing rules, and Internet companies will be welcome to return to the territory; the pension to be guaranteed to be paid in full and on time. |
| 2 Feb. 2018 | Li Keqiang | He presided over the State Council executive meeting and deployed further measures such as market-oriented debt-to-equity swaps to reduce corporate leverage, promote risk prevention and control, and improve development quality. |
| 4 Feb. 2018 | Document No. 1 of the Central Government | Start to fully deploy and implement the rural revitalisation strategy. |
| 1 Feb. 2018 | Li Keqiang | The government to continue to optimise the entry and approval procedures for foreign companies entering the Chinese market. |

| *Date* | *Leader/entity* | *Description of reforms and policy revision* |
|---|---|---|
| 11 Jan. 2018 | Li Keqiang | "With the continuous deepening of cooperation, we must keep pace with the times and expand cooperation in the fields of digital economy, environmental protection, health, customs, youth, etc. on the basis of consolidating the '3+5 cooperation framework' and gradually form '3+5+'." |
| 23 Nov. 2017 | | Put forward opinions on promoting the in-depth development of military and civilian integration in national defence science and technology industry |
| 20 Nov. 2017 | | Municipalities and sub-provincial cities and prefecture-level cities that meet certain conditions may apply to create a 'Made in China 2025' demonstration zone. Cities with similar distances and high industrial relevance may jointly apply for the creation of demonstration zones. |
| 19 Nov. 2017 | | Abolition of the Provisional Regulations on the Business Tax of the People's Republic of China |
| 19 Nov. 2017 | | Proposing to deepen the 'Internet + advanced manufacturing' development of the industrial Internet |
| 14 Nov. 2017 | Li Keqiang | Vigorously promote trade liberalisation and facilitation, and gradually move toward a single market. |

## NOTES

1. The Party Congress, also referred as the National Congress of the Communist Party of China (NCCPC), is held every five years.
2. *Xinhua News Agency*. 2017. 'China Focus: Financial reform plans unveiled to serve real economy in sustainable manner', 16 July, http://www.xinhuanet.com/english/2017-07/16/c_136446619.htm (accessed on 10 September 2018).
3. The 14th, 15th, 16th, 17th, and 18th party congresses were held in the years 1992, 1997, 2002, 2007, 2012, and 2017 respectively.
4. *China Daily*. 2018. 'All-round supervision of outbound capital to include comprehensive law', 23 October, http://www.chinadaily.com.cn/a/201712/23/WS5a3d81c7a31008cf16da2fca.html (accessed on 14 September 2018); U.S. Department of State. 2017. 'China: 2017 Investment Climate Statements', 29 June, https://www.state.gov/e/eb/rls/othr/ics/2017/eap/269807.htm (accessed on 14 September 2018).
5. *China Daily*. 2017. 'Full text of Xi Jinping's report at the 19th CPC National Congress', 04 November, http://www.chinadaily.com.cn/china/19thcpcnationalcongress/2017-11/04/content_34115212.htm (accessed on 12 September 2018).
6. *Xinhua News Agency*. 2017. 'Full Text of Xi Jingping's report at the 19th CPC National Congress', 03 November, http://www.xinhuanet.com/english/special/2017-11/03/c_136725942.htm (accessed on 12 September 2017).
7. *Xinhua News Agency*. 2017. 'CPC Q&A: What are China's two centennial goals and why do they matter?', 17 October, http://www.xinhuanet.com/english/2017-10/17/c_136686770.htm (accessed on 12 September 2018).
8. *China Banking News*. 2018. 'China banking and Insurance Regulatory Commission', 21 April, http://www.chinabankingnews.com/wiki/china-banking-insurance-regulatory-commission/ (accessed on 15 September 2018).
9. *Reuters*. 2018. 'Exclusive: Regulator shopping in vogue as China's shadow banks evade Beijing's grip', 19 March, https://www.reuters.com/article/us-china-financial-risk-crackdown-exclus/exclusive-regulator-shopping-in-vogue-as-chinas-shadow-banks-evade-beijings-grip-idUSKBN1GV018 (accessed on 15 September 2018).

10. *The New York Times.* 2018. 'China Names GuoShuqing, a Rapid-Fire Regulator, to Oversee Troubled Banks', 24 February, https://www.nytimes.com/2017/02/24/business/china-banks-guo-shuqing.html?_r=0 (accessed on 15 September 2018).
11. *People's Daily.* 2018. '深化党和国家机构改革是推进国家治理体系和治理能力现代化的必然要求 (Deepening the reform of Party and state institutions is an inevitable requirement for advancing the modernisation of the national governance system and capacity)', 12 March, http://paper.people.com.cn/rmrb/html/2018-03/12/nw.D110000renmrb_ 2018 0312_1-06.htm (accessed on 15 September 2018)
12. World Economic Forum. 2018. ;3 Critical battles China is preparing to fight', 24 January, https://www.weforum.org/agenda/2018/01/pursue-high-quality-development-work-together-for-global-economic-prosperity-and-stability/ (accessed on 13 September 2018).
13. US-China Perception Monitor. 2018. 'Transcript: President addresses the 2018 BOAO Forum for Asia in Hainan', 11 April, https://www.uscnpm.org/ blog/2018/04/11/transcript-president-xi-addresses-2018-boao-forum-asia-hainan (accessed on 13 September 2018).
14. Wong, Chun Han. 2018. 'China unveils overhaul of government bureaucracy', *The Wall Street Journal,* 13 March, https://www.wsj.com/articles/china-unveils-overhaul-of-government-bureaucracy-1520905490 (accessed on 11 September 2018).
15. *Bloomberg.* 2018. 'China unveils new measures to aid growth amid trade uncertainty', 23 July, https://www.bloomberg.com/news/articles/2018-07-23/china-says-monetary-policy-will-balance-easing-and-tightening (accessed on 11 September 2018).
16. *China Daily.* 2018. 'China stands firm on monetary stance, fine-tunes policies', 25 June, http://www.chinadaily.com.cn/a/201806/25/WS5b30d229a3103349141deab3.html (accessed on 11 September 2018).
17. *Bloomberg.* 2018. 'China faces problem in getting its banks to lend more money', 13 August, https://www.bloomberg.com/news/articles/2018-08-12/china-faces-problem-in-getting-its-banks-to-lend-more-money (accessed on 11 September 2018).
18. Author collated data from various sources.

# 15

# The 'Regional' Approach in Xi Jinping's Governance Strategy

*Jabin T Jacob*

It has always been widely understood that despite its identity as a unitary state under single-party rule, China has always in reality tended towards a great degree of decentralisation, federalism even. This has been so even in imperial times and during the Republican era both in times of central government weakness when Beijing could not always bring its authority to bear in far-flung provinces and regions and in times of strength when Beijing realised that efficient administration required a fair degree of autonomy and freedom of action at the sub-national level. Indeed, it is inevitable that any polity the size and population of China will require a fair degree of decentralisation in order to have the government work and move at some reasonable pace.

That said, China has always undergone cycles of centralisation and decentralisation in its history and under Xi Jinping today as General Secretary of the Communist Party of China (CPC), it would appear that the country is in a phase of recentralisation of power in Beijing. This paper looks at how the 'regional' was reflected in Xi's Report to the 19$^{th}$ National Congress of the CPC delivered on 18 October 2017 and titled, 'Secure a Decisive Victory in Building a Moderately Prosperous Society in All Respects and Strive for the Great Success of Socialism with Chinese Characteristics for a New Era' (Xi 2017). The chapter also uses Chinese Premier Li Keqiang's Work Report at the 13$^{th}$ National People's Congress in March 2018, to provide additional support to the arguments made here (Li 2017).

The 'region' here is defined as any spatial approach that in the Chinese domestic context crosses provincial boundaries but remains at the sub-national level and at the international level crosses the national boundary. It must be noted that in the domestic context, the Chinese text as several versions of what in English is simply translated as 'region' or 'regional – 区域 (*quyu*, 'regional') as in 区域发展 (*quyu fazhan*, 'regional development') or 区域发展差距 (*quyu fazhan chaju*, 'regional development disparities'); 带 (*dai*) or 'belt' as in 经济带, (*jingji dai*) or 'economic belt'; 部 (*bu*) or 'part' as in 中西部 (*zhong-xi bu*, 'central and western regions'); 地区 (*diqu*) or 'area'/'region' for 港澳地区 (*Gang-Aodiqu*, Hong Kong and Macao Special Administrative Regions); 省级 (*shengji*) for the provincial government level as in 中央和省级党委 (*zhongyang he shengji dangwei*, central and provincial Party committee levels); and, 边疆 (*bianjiang*, border area) (Xi 2017).

## 19th CPC Report: Multiple Levels of the 'Region'

The 'region' is an important framework for policymakers in China. There is a specific sub-section 'Implementing the coordinated regional development strategy' in Xi Jinping's report under Section V. 'Applying a New Vision of Development and Developing a Modernized Economy' (pp. 28–29). He opens with a promise to

> '... devote more energy to speeding up the development of old revolutionary base areas, areas with large ethnic minority populations, border areas, and poor areas. We will strengthen measures to reach a new stage in the large-scale development of the western region; deepen reform to accelerate the revitalization of old industrial bases in the northeast and other parts of the country; help the central region rise by tapping into local strengths; and support the eastern region in taking the lead in pursuing optimal development through innovation' (p. 28).

Li uses practically similar language in his Work Report,

> 'We have unveiled a whole series of reforms and innovative measures to see the western region develop, northeast China revitalized, the central region rise, and the eastern region spearhead development. We have stepped up support for old revolutionary base areas, areas with large ethnic minority populations, border areas, and poor areas, and strengthened work to support Tibet, Xinjiang, and Qinghai' (Li 2018).

It is obvious that China's rulers have a clear conception from both political and economic perspectives of why and how policies need to be targeted. The old revolutionary base areas and ethnic minority areas in China's interior are a traditional political concern for China's rulers but especially so under a newly ideological China under Xi. The industrial decline of China's northeastern provinces has been a matter of some political concern for well over a decade but it is really the broad divisions of eastern, central and western China that convey in the simplest and yet starkest terms the nature of regional divisions and inequalities in China today. And Chinese leaders' prescriptions for each also reflect very real limitations in the state's capabilities to micro-manage and support balanced or 'coordinated' regional development. Thus, it is the eastern region that as the leader of economic growth in China is also marked out for leadership in China's new growth strategy based on 'innovation', while the central and western regions must still manage on the basis of their local advantages.

In his Work Report, Li is more candid saying that 'some regions still face considerable downward economic pressure' and goes on to add later in the Report that 'The central government will increase general transfer payments to local governments by 10.9 percent, to strengthen local finances, *especially* (emphasis mine) in the central and western regions'. Elsewhere, he also states that 'central and western regions should continue to be the priority for major infrastructure construction' and that the government 'should encourage processing trade to shift to the central and western regions' (Li 2018).

### *Economic Development*

Xi starts early with the use of a regional approach in the first section of his speech 'The Past Five Years: Our Work and Historic Change', where he declares that China has 'made major achievements in economic development' (p.1) and as part of which he states that 'Regional development has become more balanced (also see p.24); the Belt and Road Initiative, the coordinated development of the Beijing-Tianjin-Hebei region, and the development of the Yangtze Economic Belt have all made notable progress' (p.2).

This statement packs in several aspects of both China's concerns and its plans and choices for development. For one, 'more balanced' indicates both that there is/was a problem of regional disparities and that there is still more that needs to be done to resolve the problem. Indeed, in the first stage, from 2020 to 2035, in the two-stage development plan for 2020 to the middle of the century, it is expected that 'Disparities in urban-rural development, in development between regions, and in living standards are significantly reduced' (p.24).

Here, Li's Work Report goes into a little more detail about what constitutes these disparities when he refers to

> 'The vast majority of cities in China have eased restrictions on permanent residency. A residence card system has been put into effect nationwide, and basic urban public services now cover all permanent residents. Development between urban and rural areas and between regions has become better coordinated' (Li 2018).

In other words, there is an acknowledgement that the cities have worked to protect their advantages through a discriminatory *hukou* (户口) system.

Regional concerns are also evident in the call to 'expedite the creation of a modern public finance system, and establish a fiscal relationship between the central and local governments built upon clearly defined powers and responsibilities, appropriate financial resource allocation, and greater balance between regions' (p.30). In one sentence is captured the fault-lines of centre-province conflict and inter-provincial competition in China on the one hand and the consequences thereof in terms of unbalanced regional growth on the other.[1] Indeed, fiscal issues have long plagued centre-province relations and despite the big reform of 1994, it would appear there is much that remains to be done according to Xi and this is evident when he says China 'will deepen reform of the taxation system, and improve the local tax system' (p. 30). Indeed, the manner and nature of implementation of tax reforms will likely also have consequences at the provincial and regional level in either widening or narrowing disparities between them.

### *Growth Areas*

'Securing a Decisive Victory in Building a Moderately Prosperous Society in All Respects and Embarking on a Journey to Fully Build a Modern Socialist China' will require a 'coordinated regional development strategy' (p. 23). However, the specific mention of the Beijing-Tianjin-Hebei region and the Yangtze Economic Belt (Yangtze River Delta region) in Xi's opening remarks as well as in Li's Work Report suggests that 'coordinated' is a euphemism for 'targeted'. China's domestic economic strengths still lie in its developed coastal regions and that the Chinese leadership will continue to rely on these regions to pull up the rest of China as economic growth slows and to actually take the lead in making China a 'country of innovators' (p. 2).

Xi Jinping's first visit outside of Beijing after taking over as General Secretary in 2012 was an inspection tour of Guangdong that was billed as his equivalent of Deng Xiaoping's *nanxun* (南巡) or 'southern tour' of 1992 (Chen 2012). Guangdong – China's top province in GDP terms (*China Internet Watch* 2017) – finds mention but only in the context of Hong Kong and Macao. Xi's reference to 'the development of the Guangdong-Hong Kong-Macao Greater Bay Area, cooperation between Guangdong, Hong Kong, and Macao, and regional cooperation in the pan-Pearl River Delta' (p. 50; see also Li 2018), appears to be intended in a more political context of ensuring that the Special Administrative Regions are tied in ever more closely to the mainland Chinese economy.

But one must also wonder if as part of Xi's tendency towards political centralisation, involves bringing Guangdong – with its long history of often acting as if 'Beijing is far away' – to heel. Such an approach would involve not just propping up or encouraging competing regional growth areas but also giving rather more onerous responsibilities. Dealing with Hong Kong's current political climate and weakening economic climate (Economic Analysis and Business Facilitation Unit 2016; Sun 2017; *HKTDC Research* 2018) might be just such a responsibility.

By contrast, Li's Report refers several times specifically to Shanghai as a center for 'scientific and technological innovation' (alongside Beijing), the site of a pilot free trade zone (along with other cities and provinces), as part of the Shanghai-Hong Kong Stock Connect (a trans-boundary investment channel).

Further, Xi's specific plan to 'create networks of cities and towns based on city clusters, enabling the coordinated development of cities of different sizes and small towns' appears to confirm a trend in Chinese political economy of the central government seeking to undercut provincial identity and potential competition by encouraging the growth of urban agglomerations – often cutting across provincial boundaries such as the YRD or the PRD, for example – and city-based frames of reference.[2] The plans to 'relieve Beijing of functions nonessential to its role as the capital' and to develop the Xiong'an New Area (p.29, also Li 2018) are part of this effort. And Li's Work Report follows up also with an apparent explanation of what 'coordinated' means – that it should prevent disparities from emerging – by stating that the government has 'implemented plans for developing major city clusters, and pursued more balanced development of small, medium, and large cities, and small towns'.

### *Social Development*

The concept of the 'region' is evident in several social sectors. Xi's statement on education states, 'All-round progress has been made in the development of education, with remarkable advances made in the central and western regions and in rural areas' (p.4) while on poverty alleviation he says, 'We will strengthen collaboration on poverty alleviation between the eastern and western regions (p.43). The division of the country broadly into western, central and eastern, reflects also the basic divisions of income and opportunity in China today. This is nothing new and this particular division has solidified in the decades since the economic reforms began in the late 1970s.

It is evident that the 'region' is an important level of analysis in the CPC's assessment of its achievements or the lack thereof when Xi says, 'There are still large disparities in development between rural and urban areas, between regions, and in income distribution' (城乡区域发展和收入分配差距依然较大, *cheng-xiang quyu fazhan he shouru fenpei chaju yiran jiaoda*) (p.8, see also p.24 and Li 2018).

What is also interesting is how the richer, better off coastal regions in the east are expected to support their poorer counterparts in China's interior. Indeed, it has been in practice for quite some time that the better-off provinces help the poorer provinces especially minority-provinces such as Tibet and Xinjiang with both financial and human resources such as for example, through the Aid Tibet programme in the Tibet Autonomous Region or any number of development programmes in Xinjiang. In his Report, Li talking in the context of poverty alleviation, also highlights the need to 'shore up weak links in infrastructure and public services, strengthen collaboration on poverty alleviation and paired assistance between the eastern and western regions…'.[3]

The questions that arise here, however, are of hierarchy and agency – do the giving provinces demand and receive preferential treatment in these poorer provinces? What agency exactly exists with the receiving province?

Again these are not new questions but it is worth examining if and how these trends have evolved under Xi Jinping. There has been a new wave of Han Chinese migrants to Tibet and Xinjiang since the Western Development Strategy got underway in the 1980s. In his Work Report, Li gives added support to this migration when he suggests that the government 'improve the wage and subsidy system for the employees of government offices and public institutions, and weight the system *toward regions where conditions are harsh* [emphasis added] and toward special posts'.

Meanwhile, at least in Xinjiang, if not also in other minority provinces, there has been an element of conflict between the older generation of Han migrants and their offspring who are considered more invested in the progress and development of their 'new' provincial home than the later migrants who are seen as coming in with little ideological or political commitment to the development of a 'new China' and essentially as coming in because of the financial and career incentives available to them for service in difficult areas that they can then parlay into faster career progression back in their home provinces.

Indeed, many Aid Tibet cadre are sent on short-term assignments from the aid-giving provinces to specifically keep track of their investments and to have a say in decisions involving such financial commitments. These officials take on official administrative positions while many simultaneously also hold positions back in their home provinces (Ranade 2018).

### *Territorial Integrity*

The other use of the term 'region' is, of course, in reference to the Special Administrative Regions (SARs) of Hong Kong and Macao and perhaps also to Taiwan – there is a whole section devoted to the three entities – No. XI titled,

'Upholding 'One Country, Two Systems' and Moving toward National Reunification' (pp.49–51). With respect to Hong Kong and Macao, there is reference to 'the central government's overall jurisdiction' over the two areas while ensuring also 'a high degree of autonomy' for them (p.21). Xi makes clear that 'The development of Hong Kong and Macao is closely tied up with that of the mainland. We will continue to support Hong Kong and Macao in integrating their own development into the overall development of the country' (p.50). There cannot be a more clearer reiteration of the sidelining of the 'one country, two systems' concept as originally understood in Hong Kong and outside of China's borders than this that the two SARs are seen primarily as carrying out the role of meeting the demand and interests of the rest of China, including 'the historic responsibility of national rejuvenation'. And yet, the distinction maintained between 'the mainland' and 'the two regions' suggests that integration is not complete and there is a distance yet to be covered.

With respect to Taiwan, however, the 'mainland' continues to seek the breaking down of barriers to closer cross-Straits relations. The use of the expression 'blood is thicker than water' is used as a way of exercising control, even if of the imagination, over the concept and nature of the region. Taiwanese independence would be an explicit rejection of this concept of the region advocated by the Chinese. Instead, Xi by his repeated references to 'the great rejuvenation of the Chinese nation', seeks to underline a fundamental unity of China that overcomes its regional divisions.

Li also refers to the need to ensure 'that celebrations to mark the 60$^{th}$ anniversaries of the founding of Guangxi Zhuang Autonomous Region and Ningxia Hui Autonomous Region are a great success'. This statement it must be noted comes immediately after the Chinese Premier states,

> 'The Chinese nation is a big family in which we live together in peace, unity, and amity. We need to uphold and improve the system of regional ethnic autonomy and fully implement the Party's policies on ethnic groups' (Li 2018).

### *Border Areas*

Of a piece with 'regional autonomy', is 'regional ethnic autonomy' (民族区域自治制度, *minzu quyu zizhi zhidu*) (p.19). Xi has generally kept up an extensive travel schedule to provinces or military units as part of his targeting corruption and seeking military reforms. By that token he has visited Xinjiang only once in his first term as General Secretary (Buckley 2014) and not visited Tibet at all.[4] This will likely change in the second term but it might also have to do with external reasons such as the Dalai Lama, relations with India and so on. Similarly, while Xi specifically promises in his report, to 'accelerate development in the border areas', he also immediately adds another promise to 'ensure their stability and security' (p.29). Taken together, these developments indicate that his primary concern as General Secretary of the CPC remains political stability in China's restive west.

Still, it must be remembered that Xi chose to announce the first leg of his grand 'one belt, one road' or 'belt and road' initiative (BRI) – the Silk Road Economic Belt (SREB) – in Kazakhstan opposite Xinjiang. Despite its political instability and China's highlighting of threats from apparent terrorism in Xinjiang, it is very clear that the western province is at the forefront of the outreach to Central Asia both through older forums such as the China-Central Asia Expo or the newer BRI. As implied above, even Tibet is now slowly gaining an important role under the BRI in outreach towards Nepal, for example. These trends in turn suggest a continued adherence by the CPC to the belief that economic development is the panacea to ethnic disaffection and political instability.

Thus, Xi has called for 'open[ing] the western region wider' and it is a good bet that the pilot free trade zones and opening of free trade ports that he mentions alongside the call to 'develop new ways of making outbound investments, promote international cooperation on production capacity, form globally-oriented networks of trade, investment and financing, production, and services, and build up our strengths for international economic cooperation and competition' (p.30) will all happen in China's border regions, including in TAR at an increased scale.

## Moving the Regional Approach from the Domestic to the External

Right at the outset, Xi refers to 'frequent outbreaks of regional conflicts and disturbances, and intensifying global issues' outside China's borders (p.1). In Chinese, the 'regional' here is 局部 (*jubu*) and is distinct from the many forms of 'region' or 'regional' used so far in China's domestic context. Indeed, it is notable that the international has such a large space devoted it in Xi's political report.

Both China's vaulting global ambitions and the reference to the BRI in Xi's report to the 19th CPC suggests that China's concept of the 'regional' is not or will not remain limited to only within its borders. The history of China's economic reforms and opening up to the outside world in the post-Mao era shows how closely linked the country's economic growth was to economies across its boundaries. Today, those linkages have gained China considerable advantages in its abilities to influence politics and strategic choices in its near neighbourhood. As the larger economy by several times compared to most of its neighbours, it might be to China's political and economic advantage to meld its concept and practice of the 'regional' at the domestic level to encompass neighbouring economies. This would perform much the same function as regional free trading agreements but also reflect a modern version of China's past economic and political dominance in Asia.

Li confirms that Xi's call to 'open the western region wider' also has an international dimension. In the Work Report he states,

> 'We should expand opening up in the western region, inland areas, and border areas and enhance development in border and cross-border economic cooperation areas, creating new opportunities for China's opening up and cooperation with other countries' (Li 2018).

### *The Belt and Road Initiative*

The BRI, of course, is a tool for such opening up. The mention of the BRI also reflects another aspect of how the CPC defines its concerns and its plans and choices for development. The BRI is seen as an important vehicle to redress regional imbalances in China but while the BRI is sold as a major *national* foreign policy initiative, it can also be justified domestically as a way of shifting excess domestic industrial and infrastructure capacity out of China.

That China's state-owned enterprises (SOEs) are at the forefront of the BRI push abroad is easily observed but equally important to note is that many of these SOEs are provincial-level SOEs and that the BRI has set off an intense competition between Chinese provinces to position themselves at the lead of the project, as possessing some unique characteristics or identity that supports the BRI best.

The BRI appears to have something for every province or region in China. It helps underdeveloped regions in the interior to both receive excess capacity from their better-off counterparts on the coast and to build their ties and capacities vis-à-vis China's neighbours. At the same time, the more developed provinces in the east can take advantage of their own position at the forefront of economic development in China to further strengthen their comparative advantages vis-à-vis other Chinese provinces by leading the Chinese state's charge on new technologies and innovation, and global acquisitions.

Despite the development targeted at border areas highlighted in the previous section, what this then suggests is that the central government in Beijing probably gives greater weightage to the BRI as a 'national' project of promoting Chinese influence in its neighbourhood and globally rather than one that is designed to overcome regional differences within the country. China's border provinces while poorer than their counterparts in the interior and coastal regions are nevertheless by and large economically better off than their neighbours across international boundaries in most cases. Thus, the SREB might help provinces like Xinjiang strengthen existing linkages with Central Asia and create new linkages with the Pakistani economy but it is also quite possible that these links might exacerbate regional disparities within China itself given the lack of economic rationale to many BRI projects including the China-Pakistan Economic Corridor where Xinjiang is at the forefront for China. Similarly, there is an increasingly active role that the Tibet Autonomous Region is being placed in vis-à-vis connectivity with Nepal. Here again, it is not yet clear just how economically feasible proposed rail links between Lhasa and Nepal will be from the point of view of the transfer of industrial merchandise or even tourists.

The BRI's role in the development of provincial and regional economies in China might not be in question, but it might be too soon to say that it will contribute to easing regional inequalities within the country. It might be useful to reiterate at this juncture the connection Xi makes between 'development in the border areas' and 'ensur[ing] their stability and security' (p.29).

### *International Regional Security*

Legitimate questions can therefore be asked if there is more to the BRI's role in the region than just economic development. Xi's linking 'development in the border areas' and 'ensur[ing] their stability and security' (p.29), can be extended to an interest in the factors that affect these emanating from outside China's borders. In many ways, the Chinese formulation of a 'community of common destiny' either confirms or is supportive of the 'regional' approach crossing Chinese borders to incorporate or bring under sway in some form or the other, other neighbouring economies and polities. Xi's statement, 'We should cherish our cultural roots, draw on other cultures, and be forward-thinking. We should do more to foster a Chinese spirit, Chinese values, and Chinese strength to provide a source of cultural and moral guidance for our people' (p.20) has a strong cross-international border element. The statement is interesting for subsuming the foreign – 'other cultures' – into the Chinese or towards China's interests and 'values' and possibly also gives an idea of where China might go with its cross-international border initiatives and approaches.

## Maritime Dimension

It is also somewhat interesting that Xi should mention, China's pursuit of a 'coordinated land and marine development, and step[ped] up efforts to build China into a strong maritime country (海洋强国 *haiyang qiangguo*)' (p.29) in the section on coordinated regional development strategy. While no doubt, the blue economy concept has gained increasing traction as a economic development concept around the world, including in China and India and also supports the 21$^{st}$ Century Maritime Silk Road (MSR), which is part of the BRI.

Under the MSR framework, coordinated land and maritime development towards China's goal of becoming 'a strong maritime country' will be about drawing in the economies of China's neighbours into an ever closer embrace with China. Already many Southeast Asian economies are heavily dependent on China and this has considerably weakened their abilities to resist Chinese pressure on territorial disputes in the South China Sea, for example.

## Military Restructuring

China's military restructuring and reforms at the end of 2015 also resulted in the reorganisation of its previous seven Military Regions into five Theatre Commands and set off in India, at least, considerable confusion on what it meant in terms of China's threat perception of India. The reduction in numbers from seven to five, effectively meant that where two Military Regions existed in China's west, they have now been combined into a single theatre command with responsibility for all of Central Asia, including parts of Russia and all of South Asia. Hitherto, the borders with India had been a divided responsibility with the Western Sector of the boundary dispute mostly falling under the purview of the Lanzhou Military Region while the Chengdu Military Region took care of the rest. From the Indian point of view, a single Theatre Command covering such a wide swathe of geography with significant variety in terrain, political conditions and strengths of neighbouring militaries it had to deal with, appeared to suggest that China did not foresee a serious military threat emanating from its west, including from India.

In other words, just as the United States State Department's and Defence Department's division of the world into various blocs for ease of analysis or of military planning as the case might be has had consequences for the countries that fell into these categories created by one of the world's preeminent economic and military powers, so too might China's plans or approaches along similar lines for its neighbours. At the core here, will be the questions of why and how China chooses to link its domestic regional development approaches to its neighbourhood.

## Conclusion

Xi's Report at the 19$^{th}$ Congress of the CPC suggests that even as he seeks what appears to be a centralising ideal of the 'great rejuvenation of the Chinese nation' (p. 51), he will, like leaders before him, have to contend with the sheer diversity of the country and employ a variety of approaches to achieve economic development and/or political control over different parts of China. The 'regional' approach will, therefore, always be an important framework for analysis of China as is inevitable for any country with the size and internal diversity of geographies, populations, cultures, and economies as China has. Alongside, China's growing economic integration with the outside world will also have implications for the governance of China, including questions of centre-local relations and balanced regional development.

## NOTES

1. For more on these aspects of conflict and competition, see Jacob (2008).
2. See Jabin T. Jacob, 'China's Cities: New Centres of Political Power and Economic Growth', paper presented at the *3rd All India Conference of China Studies*, Jadavpur University, Kolkata, 20 December 2010.
3. The Chinese original does not however, refer specifically to 'eastern and western region', saying more generally 激发脱贫内生动力 (*jifa tuopin neisheng dongli*) or 'stimulate internal impetus for poverty alleviation', suggesting perhaps that there is resistance to such transfers from east to west.
4. The last occasion Xi visited Tibet was during his tenure in the 17th PBSC (*People's Daily Online* 2011).

## REFERENCES

Buckley, Chris. 2014. 'In Xinjiang, Xi Pushes Vision of Uighur Integration', *The New York Times*, 29 April, https://sinosphere.blogs.nytimes.com/2014/04/29/in-xinjiang-xi-pushes-vision-of-uighur-integration/ (accessed on 18 November 2017).

Chen Zhuang. 2012. 'The symbolism of Xi Jinping's trip south', *BBC News*, 10 December, http://www.bbc.com/news/world-asia-china-20662947 (accessed on 16 November 2017).

*China Internet Watch*. 2017. 'Top China Provinces/Municipalities by GDP in 2016', 21 February, https://www.chinainternetwatch.com/19810/top-cities-gdp-2016/ (accessed on September 2017).

Economic Analysis and Business Facilitation Unit, Financial Secretary's Office, Legislative Council of the Hong Kong Special Administrative Region of the People's Republic of China. 2016. 'Hong Kong's Recent Economic Situation and Near-term Outlook', 13 May, http://www.legco.gov.hk/yr15-16/english/panels/fa/papers/fa20160606cb1-987-3-e.pdf (accessed on 18 September 2017).

*HKTDC Research*. 2018. 'Economic and trade Information on Hong Kong'. 14 June, http://hong-kong-economy-research.hktdc.com/business-news/article/Market-Environment/Economic-and-Trade-Information-on-Hong-Kong/etihk/en/1/1X000000/1X09OVUL.htm (accessed on 15 June 2018).

Jacob, Jabin T. 2008. *The Provinces in China: Provincialism, Regionalism and Transnational Linkages since the 1990s*, Unpublished Ph.D. Thesis, Jawaharlal Nehru University, New Delhi.

Li Keqiang. 2018. 'Full Text: Report on the Work of the Government', delivered at the First Session of the 13th National People's Congress of the People's Republic of China on March 5, 2018, *People's Daily*, 3 April, http://en.people.cn/n3/2018/0403/c90000-9445262.html (accessed on 26 April 2018).

*People's Daily Online*. 2011. 'China's Xi vows to speed up Tibet's development while fighting separatism', 19 July, http://en.people.cn/90001/90776/90785/7444645.html (accessed on 18 August 2018).

Ranade, Jayadeva. 2018. *Cadres of Tibet*. New Delhi: Knowledge World Publishers.

Sun, Nikki. 2017. 'Hong Kong economy set for tough year in 2017, economists warn', *South China Morning Post*, 4 January, http://www.scmp.com/news/hong-kong/economy/article/2059331/hong-kong-economy-set-tough-year-2017-economists-warn (accessed on 1 October 2017).

Xi Jinping. 2017. 'Secure a Decisive Victory in Building a Moderately Prosperous Society in All Respects and Strive for the Great Success of Socialism with Chinese Characteristics for a New Era', delivered at the 19th National Congress of the Communist Party of China, *Xinhua*, 18 October, http://news.xinhuanet.com/politics/19cpcnc/2017-10/27/c_1121867529. htm (accessed on 24 November 2017).

# 16

# Management of Labour and Social Security by the Chinese Party-State*

*P K Anand*

'...we will build an educated, skilled, and innovative workforce, foster respect for model workers, promote quality workmanship, and see that taking pride in labour becomes a social norm and seeking excellence is valued as a good work ethic' (Xi 2017: 26-27).

The above lines figure under the sub-heading, 'Furthering supply-side structural reform', in the Political Report of Xi Jinping delivered at the 19th Congress of the Communist Party of China (CPC). Providing a glimpse of the workforce envisaged by him for the country's advancement into a 'New Era', the report, while laying out his long-term vision and plan of action for the country, also brings into focus, the various challenges that confronted the country in the road ahead. Among these, the arena of labour presents a significant challenge for the Party-State. Contained within his articulation of the principal contradiction in Socialism with Chinese Characteristics for a New Era, that is 'between unbalanced and inadequate development and the people's ever-growing needs for a better life' – thus marking a shift from the earlier pronouncement of 'the ever-growing material and cultural needs of the people and backward social production' – is the underlining of challenges posed by income inequality in the country's workforce. In the week preceding the beginning of the 19th Party Congress of the Communist Party of China (CPC), state-run media trumpeted the increase in minimum wage levels in 17 regions and cities in China in 2017 (*China News* 12 October 2017). Out of these, four major cities namely, Beijing,

---

* An abridged version of this paper was published as a research blog post in icsdelhiblogs.wordpress.com on 7 November 2017

Shanghai, Shenzhen and Tianjin, have set the minimum wage levels at 2,000 RMB per month. The increase in the minimum wage levels does not carry a linear narrative, however; some provinces have expressed reluctance to implement minimum wages. Further, they are also not commensurate with rising house rents, increasing costs of travel from home to the workplace, etc. (*China Labour Bulletin* 17 October 2017). On the other hand, the increase in wages also results in the rise of labour costs for investors and enterprise managements by manifolds, thus making them either to look for alternative locations like India or South-east Asia or move into inland China, from the coasts (Koty and Zhou 2017). In this scenario, the Party-state has the task of striking a fine balance between maintaining economic growth and encouraging investments, while also increasing the material wealth and ensuring the well-being of the workforce. Therefore, Xi Jinping's Political Report to the 19$^{th}$ Party Congress is reflective of the apprehensions and disquiet of the Party-state in the need to undertake this balancing act. The section on industrial overcapacity and deleveraging in Premier Li Keqiang's Work Report delivered at the First Session of the 13$^{th}$ National People's Congress in March 2018, highlights the tensions and challenges confronting the Xi administration in this balancing – labour's predicament vis-à-vis industrial reforms:

> '...we have cut steel production capacity by more than 170 million metric tons and coal production capacity by 800 million metri tons, and over 1.1 million affected employees have been assisted' (p. 6).

With a projection of creating 'over 11 million new urban jobs' and reducing the 'unemployment rate within 5.5 percent', the Chinese Party-State's tactical balancing of growth with improvement of living standards gets further underlined (Li 2018: 20).

Notwithstanding the intertwined relationship of labour relations and employment-based welfare, to better understand both the vectors and to analyse the gamut of issues surrounding them and their location in the 19$^{th}$ Congress, it is desirable to focus them separately. Having discussed both these issues at some length, in the conclusion, I would move to discuss the changing nature of the Chinese state and its implications on labour and social security.

## LABOUR RELATIONS

### Issues in the Report

Within Xi's report, two main talking points can be identified having direct implication and relevance for labour. The first one falls under the domain of advancement of law-based governance, pertaining to the promotion of rule of law.

### *Law-based Governance and Labour Relations*

...'we will build a rule of law government, promote law-based government administration, and see that law is enforced in a strict, procedure-based, impartial and non-abusive way' (2017: 34).

Beginning from the Hu Jintao-Wen Jiabao era, China has taken the route of legislations for addressing challenges posed in the labour arena. In addition to the deft use of the 'left' – wage, welfare and other related concessions – and 'right' hands – use of repressive measures to end labour protests, arrest leaders/activists and censor NGOs – by the Party-state,[1] introduction of laws like the Labour Contract Law, Law of Labour Dispute Mediation and Arbitration, and Law of Employment Promotion (promulgated in 2008), along with the Law on Social Security in 2011, were rules-based responses to provide employment and welfare rights as well as to channelise grievances and settle disputes 'amicably'. 'Due to China's reliance on Foreign Direct Investment (FDI), the role of law is particularly important in China's restructuring of the economy and its gradual integration with the global economy' (Gallagher 2005a: 103-4). Further, 'these laws were instrumental in chaneling disputes and conflicts toward officially sanctioned resolution processes, so in this sense they contributed to the state's ability to maintain control over workers despite rapid economic and social change'; the Party-state's calls for the workers to 'use law as a weapon' thereby providing avenues for grievance redressal and disputes settlement for the workers (Gallagher 2005a: 103; Gallagher 2005b: 54-83). In this context, Xi's emphasis on law-based governance signifies the Party-state's determination to pave the way for a regime of rule of law, aimed at ensuring 'peaceful', 'conflict-free' workplaces. A closer reading of the law-based approach – which falls within the domain of 'Rightful Resistance'[2] – also offers the other side of the argument: the 'legal absorption of absorption of the labour conflicts' *individualizes* workers' demands and concerns, thereby discouraging the emergence of *collective*, class-based solidarities (Leung and So 2013: 136). A point of reference in this regard is the gradual marginalisation of Collective Bargaining, an important negotiating instrument between the employers and a representative group of the workers in an enterprise, with the aim of concluding agreements for enhanced payments and improved working conditions. Over time, in order to find a 'harmonious' middle ground, which suits both the employee and employer, 'Collective Consultation' *(jiti xieshang)* gradually replaced 'Collective Bargaining' *(jiti tanpan)*, aimed at bringing about 'win-win' agreements without serious contention, work stoppages, strikes and other such disruptive actions. Thus, 'aggressive' bargaining reminiscent of western-style trade unions, could potentially be discouraged and/or avoided (Pringle 2009: 223). The renewed emphasis on law-based governance does hint at further *individualisation* of the grievance redressal and dispute settlement.

### *Growth of Innovation, But Retreat of Workers?*

The second talking point is related to the aim of making China, 'a country of innovators'. Opening the frontiers of scientific research and fostering a culture of innovation has been emphasised by Xi in his report. As part of the Made in China 2025 initiative, robotics has become a focal point – plans are in place to produce 100,000 industrial robots a year and having 150 robots in operation for every 10,000 employees by 2020, a figure known as robot density (Merchant 24 October 2016). To offset labour costs, industrial centres in south China have already started experimenting with robots on the assembly lines. While advanced production with cutting-edge technology and less dependence on human labour might be the stated intentions, the adoption of automation changes the dynamics of labour relations and has cast prophecies about 'displacement of workers' to manage wage and employment costs (*Bloomberg News* 3 July 2017; Whelan and Fung 16 August 2016). However, such obsession with automation also leaves behind unanswered questions for workers – will there be complete shunting of the workers or will some human element still be retained in the manufacturing sector? Will human capacities be completely lost? How are workers retrenched in the process of automation going to be rehabilitated? The Party-State has not been able to answer these questions in concrete terms.

### *Industrial Accidents – Time for Close Attention*

Another area identified for improvement with regard to workers in the report is augmenting the responsibility system for workplace safety. Workplace accidents have been a common feature in the country, with estimates putting the average rate of accidents at 135 per day and 75 deaths each day (*China Labour Bulletin* 9 August 2016). The explosion caused by hazardous chemicals in a warehouse in Tianjin in 2015, apart from resulting in the loss of over 170 lives had also laid bare the lackadaisical attitudes, as well as unscientific and lack of professional systems at workplaces in the country. To overcome the dents and blight caused, the Party-State has identified the need for adoption of proper safety measures, with adequate supervision, in addition to professional training being imparted to the workers.

## ...And Issues not in the Report

However, there are areas of relevance in the labour arena which remains in the background and have not necessarily been covered in Xi Jinping's Report.

### *Precarious Employment and Students – Workers*

There has been significant transformation of labour relations, with the emergence of new forms of casual and informal work arrangements thus making the relations of labour, fluid and dynamic. At times, outside regulatory frameworks – and often conveniently ignored – these forms of employment while casualise production relations and make workers precarious entities. One prime illustration for such non-regular workers is Student Interns and Student Workers. In the Mao period, a Work-Study *(gongxue jiehe)* model combining school-based education with on-the-job training in factories through apprenticeships in Vocational and Technical Education, was promoted to train skilled workers for China's rapid industrialisation (Ye and Meng 2008, cited in Zhang 2015: 58). However, with the deepening of market reform in 1990s, cut in funding by central government and promotion of marketisation, many of the vocational schools have been crippled for the want of teachers, outdated textbooks, and quality resources, thus forcing many of them to collaborate with enterprises and send the students for full time work under internships, in exchange for funding and other resources (ibid). Often treated as 'cheap, temporary manual labourers', very often working overtime, unprotected by labour laws, and without contracts, thereby being 'ineligible to receive social insurance benefits and to join labour unions', they are 'vulnerable to exploitation and workplace abuse' (Zhang, 2015: 58-59); in many cases, even local governments, have been found to be involved in facilitating such arrangements from vocational schools, to meet investors' demand for large number of cheap and flexible workers (Pun and Chan 2012). Instances of forced internships have been largely found in automobile and electronics manufacturing factories (Zhang 2015; Zhuang 21 July 2017; Hodal and Bengsten 6 October 2017; Yang 21 November 2017).

### *Labour Dispatch*

Labour Dispatch *(laowu paiqian)*, or temporary agency work is a growing phenomenon of non-regular employment, whereby, dispatch agencies provide workers to enterprise managements according to the latter's needs and demands. Though these temporary workers work under the enterprise managements, they are counted as employees of the particular dispatch agency, thus lessening the wage costs of enterprise managements, bringing down social security entitlements and also circumventing labour law provisions. In fact, some of the managements resorted to laying-off workers and then went on to re-employ them through the labour dispatch arrangement with the same purpose in mind. In this manner, the managements are able to stave off their responsibilities of being the primary employer and thus, look towards outsourcing the wages as well as social security entitlements to the dispatch agency. Despite provisions in the Labour Contract Law of 2008 providing protection for workers employed through labour dispatch, they continue to remain vulnerable without adequate support mechanisms.

### *Burgeoning Service Sector – New Site of Labour Conflicts*

The diversification of the economy and growing urbanisation have led to the growth of a burgeoning service sector in China, and the creation of an informal labour class. Delivery workers, sanitation staff, taxi and bus drivers, etc. are some of the representatives of this labour class, without any representative agency to espouse their cause and genuine demands. The rise in the labour protests from the segments of this class in different urban centres in the country has not been adequately configured by the Party-state.

## Social Security

While 'Social Welfare *(shehui fuli)* is broadly referred to as assistance and services to the vulnerable sections of the society', the Chinese prefer the usage 'Social Security *(shehui baozhang)* as an inclusive concept to cover all types of social arrangements for social care and support' (Wong 1998: 9). In the main, social security is the total system of comprehensive protection of life for all members of society under socialism. Social insurance, social welfare and social relief are instruments of its implementation. They are indispensable parts of the social security system (Lu 1986: 90, as quoted in Wong 1998: 9; Emphasis added by Wong). Employment-based welfare system lies at the heart of the social security system in the country, and it contains five pillars, namely Old-Age Pension Insurance, Medical Insurance, Unemployment Insurance, Workplace Injury Insurance and Maternity Insurance. The employment-based welfare is disseminated as social insurance, through the Pay-as-You-Go (PAYGO) model, comprising contributions by employer, and employee, with the state contributing a small portion, if necessary; it involves the social pooling of funds. The social security system is given legal basis through the Social Insurance Law (SIL) promulgated on 28 October 2010; it took seventeen years to make the law and bring it into force. The SIL sets out the basic framework, principles and schemes of the social insurance system, including the five mandatory insurance schemes: basic pension, basic medical, unemployment, work-related injury and maternity; the law covered all employers within China along with all full time and part-time employees, as well as self-employed individuals working within the PRC. In terms of the administration of the social insurance system in the country, the responsibility for coordinating as well as formulating various policies and standards regarding social insurance, lies with the Ministry of Human Resources and Social Security (MOHRSS). The MOHRSS and Ministry of Finance work jointly to strengthen the supervision of nationwide social insurance funds, with the Department of Human Resources and Social Security (DOHRSS) at provincial and sub-provincial levels. (Ministry of Human Resources and Social Security, 2008, as quoted in Casale and Zhu 2013: 84).

Housing, considered a vital element along with the other five pillars of social security finds a special mention in Xi's report. In emphasising that 'housing is for living in, not for speculation', there is a political cognition that property bubbles and rising prices in the cities, could serve as breeding ground for disillusionment, leading to loss of support and legitimacy for the Party-state among the salaried, urban middle class.

While the report discusses the need 'to develop a sustainable multi-tiered social security system that covers the entire population in both urban and rural areas', 'bring pension schemes under a unified management' at the national level and reiterates the need to improve all components of the five insurances, these issues have continued to remain as vexed as they have in the past. The stratification and segmentation of the labour force in the country over decades, has meant that the 'core of the state-sector workforce remains protected under the preferential welfare programmes run by SOEs' (Frazier 2011: 78). It leaves those employed in private, non-state enterprises with a skewed amount of coverage. Even though the central government issues guidelines and imparts a 'benevolent' cognition, it is the local governments who bear the responsibility of implementation as well as financing; they turn seek to transfer the insurance burdens to the enterprise managements, thereby making them firm-specific, limited to an interface between the employer and employee. Similarly, inadequate social insurance coverage among migrant workers is another ill plaguing the system. The absence of a unified national framework leads to impediments in terms of portability – in the absence of coordination between departments, maintenance of 'contributory continuity' is difficult as 'migrant workers move from one job/jurisdiction to another'. 'In less developed regions where they maintained their household relations, rural social security systems were often incomplete or non-existent. So, those of them who returned to their households, found it difficult to transfer their personal social security account to their place of origin' (Wang 2011: 180). Further, while the social security policy allowed migrant workers 'to cash in their social security account when they move to another city and work for a different employer', they could only 'recover the contributions paid into their personal social security account – their contributions to the social pool are effectively lost' (Wang 2011: 181). Furthermore, lack of formal employment contracts for migrants and shortfalls in fund accumulation with regard to benefit payment obligations continue to plague the system. Poor awareness and information asymmetries have also served as deterrents to workers' participation in social security mechanisms; they are further dissuaded by the complexity in policy designs and other impending concern. The prevalence of relative flexibility and autonomy for enterprise and workplace managements in implementing social security, coupled with lack of resources by the local government for supervision and monitoring, often results in partial payments/contributions.

## Representation, Primary Trade Union, Workers' Agency

Statistics of the delegates who attended the 19th Congress revealed that 'a total of 771 delegates, or 33.7 percent of the total delegates, were from frontline production and manufacturing, an increase of 3.2 percentage points compared with the 18th Congress five years ago; among them, 198 were workers or migrant workers and 283 are professional technical personnel (*Xinhua* 2017). While the marginal increase in the representation of workers is positive, the occasion is also apt to look at the positioning and role of the primary trade union – All-China Federation of Trade Unions (ACFTU) – in the dynamic and fluid landscape of Chinese labour relations. From that of a 'Transmission Belt'[3] under state socialism, the ACFTU today is an organisation with an ambiguous identity and struggling for legitimacy in the aftermath of market oriented economic reforms. 'From an institutional perspective, the Party needed the unions for two important reasons: first, to keep the workers loyal to its overall authority and prevent any unrest or organised opposition, and second, to smoothen the path to economic reform by mediating between policy-makers and workers' (White 1996: 441).

The challenges and dilemmas confronting the trade unions were largely twofold: first, ambiguity regarding the sections that the trade unions actually represented, and second, lack of clarity on the modalities of representing a differentiated and diffused workforce. The market reforms highlighted a 'double identity' (or, double responsibility) for the trade unions. While on the one hand, they had to promote the national interest, on the other, they had to protect workers' rights and interests. This meant, 'the ACFTU could be viewed as an organisation that is situated in both the state and society, and had a double institutional identity of being a state instrument and a labour organisation in new industrial relations' (Feng 2003: 1007). With the infusion of market reforms and retreat of the state from a paternalistic role, the state-labour relations were transformed and eventually became highly contradictory, as workers' interests came into conflict with the remodeling of the economic activities. The dilemma and ambiguity induced by the 'double identity' phenomenon, made the ACFTU's positioning very complex, as they had to be very cautious in negotiations activities and even giving views. The 'gnawing tension of this dilemma' highlights the challenge 'confronting the ACFTU, namely maintaining its legitimacy' (Howell 2003: 4). The issue of legitimacy acquired a greater importance in the context of the rise in the number of spontaneous protests by the workers in various parts of the country, thus, attempting to come up with alternate ways of mobilisations and organisation rather than being limited to the conventional control mechanisms of the ACFTU. Essentially, there exists a greater inclination among the workers to find newer associations and networks rather than rest their hopes on the primary trade union.[4] The alarm and apprehensions sounded by the workers towards the trade union and trade union officials is also illustrated through the subordination of the trade unions to the enterprise managements, and the close-knit relationship between the trade union officials and the managements. The trade union leaders were largely drawn from the ranks of the management, with a full-time trade union president being paid by the employer and this responsibility was often considered equivalent to that of a deputy director-general of the company. The personal careers and interests of the union leadership thus aligned closely with that of the management. Such 'close integration' of the two entities indicated a 'consensual' approach by the trade unions and there was no attempt, at a 'reconciliation of differences of interest; thereby not challenging the prevalent asymmetrical power relations. (Clarke et al. 2004: 244).

The operation of Labour NGOs, albeit under surveillance, and other similar collectives in south China (Pearl River Delta) – the country's industrial heartland – providing legal aid, provisioning simple vocational skills, and training, is directly related to the lack of tools and strategies for timely and effective responses to worker's initiatives.

## Conclusion

The diversification of the labour system in China, through *informalisation, casualisation* and *flexibilisation* of employment relations and work arrangements and the developing of a labour market, has led to a gradual shift towards *Destatification,* or a redefinition and reduction of the direct regulatory role of state agencies. The withdrawal of the state from a tripartite relationship with the workers and enterprise managements, for wage and rights bargaining, lies in parallel with the legal channelling of labour conflicts – through laws, mediation, arbitration and adjudication procedures – thus indvidualising workers and discouraging the emergence of any collective, consciousness-wise or mobilisation-wise. Even though labour thus ends up as an autonomised entity, it also creates space with possibilities for newer, creative and differential forms of associations. In the same breath, for the Party-state to meet the challenges of rising labour conflicts and actions, it needs to be more sophisticated and accommodative – a more peaceful and harmonious workplace in China can materialise only by providing at least a modicum of operative and representative space for workers in a collective setting.

The emergence of 'new interests' and the CPC's support for them is indicative of the changing social base of the Party-State – and the need to grasp the 'new realities'. The 'new interests' in China are the burgeoning nouveau rich and upwardly mobile middle class, beneficiaries of the high consumer growth under the market economy.[5] The privileging of the middle class' interests has not only led to the Party-state becoming largely urban-centric, but also made it more of a 'managerial' entity, rather than an instrument of change. Governance is increasingly about 'skillfully' managing and/or controlling conflicts and glossing over the apparant cracks/challenges. This transformation of the State in China and rising social contradictions, tensions and conflicts – especially in the area of labour – only serves to reinforce the widening gulf between the state and the working classes. The state is no longer the provider and patron of welfare, having withdrawn from its responsibility as the chief sponsor to take up a more of a facilitation role.

Much of the official and academic discourse around the nature of Party-state in China and its prioritisation of economic growth and development in the decades following the economic reforms posits it as a logical evolution and a necessary fallout of the gradual retreat of the state from the social arena. Despite its formal description of being a socialist system, the party-state and its interface with labour in contemporary China, displays contradictory characteristics; in fact, these are not entirely different from the experiences prevalent in the 'capitalist' world. This character of the Chinese Party-State portends to the development of a possible Market State, where the state in alliance with big enterprise attempts to secure power, through a broadening or widening of opportunities for the market even while retaining some elements of protectionism and welfare.

## NOTES

1. The analogy of the left and right hands of the state has been borrowed from the reference used by French sociologist Pierre Bourdieu. For more, see: http://www.variant.org.uk/32texts/bourdieu32.html
2. 'Rightful Resistance' is a concept wherein aggrieved citizens, while accepting the legitimacy of the laws, values and policies of the state, use institutional means and mechanisms as provided within the system to protest, if they feel the state has not fulfilled its promises or mandates – they thus resort to using petitions, legal systems and government's own directives to highlight their cause. This resistance – falls within the permissible ambit allowed by the state – has been explained in detail by Kevin O'Brien in 'Rightful Resistance', *World Politics*, Vol. 49, No.1 (1996): 31-55.
3. V.I. Lenin, had likened trade unions to a transmission belt, which connected the party and the masses, as the transmission belt did with the motor and the machine. So, while the trade unions transmitted the party's policies downwards to workers, they transmitted the workers' concerns upwards to the party leadership for its references in making policies and improving work.
4. Instances of such associations have been provided in the following works: Perry, Elizabeth (1995), "Labour's Battle for Political Space: The Role of Worker Associations in Contemporary China", in D.S. Davis, Richard Kraus, Barry Naughton and Elizabeth Perry (eds.) *Urban Spaces in Contemporary China*, Cambridge: Cambridge University Press;

Wilson, J.L. 1990. "The Polish Lesson: China and Poland 1980-1990", *Studies in Comparative Communism*, Vol. 23, No. 3-4: 259-279.

5. According to the 2015 edition of the Forbes China Rich List, there are 335 billionaires in Mainland China. The minimum fortune to make the list was $830 million. Mainland China stands behind the USA in the Forbes Billionaire List (Russell, Flannery (2015), "Inside The 2015 Forbes List Of China's 400 Richest: Facts And Figures About China's Wealthiest", *Forbes*, 28 October 2015, [Online: web] Accessed 14 July 2016, URL: http://www.forbes.com/sites/russellflannery/2015/10/28/inside-the-2015-forbes-china-400-facts-and-figures-on-chinas-richest/#69d7a6254b7f

## REFERENCES

*Bloomberg News*. 2017. 'China Robots Displace Workers as Wage Spiral Pressures Profits', 3 July, https://www.bloomberg.com/news/articles/2017-07-02/china-robots-displace-workers-as-wage-spiral-pressures-profits (accessed 12 November 2017).

*China Labour Bulletin*. 2017. 'China Trumpets Minimum Wage Increases prior to Party Congress', 17 October. http://www.clb.org.hk/content/china-trumpets-minimum-wage-increases-prior-party-congress (accessed on 7 November 2017).

______. 2016. 'The Grim and Mundane Reality of Work Accidents in China', 9 August, http://www.clb.org.hk/content/grim-and-mundane-reality-work-accidents-china (accessed on 12 November 2017).

*China News*. 2017. 今年已有17地区提高最低工资这四地≥ 2000 元, *jinnianyi you 17 diqutigao-zuidigongzizhesi de ≥ 2000 yuan*, [Among the 17 regions which raised minimum wages, 4 regions have raised higher than or equal to 2000 yuan], 12 October, http://www.chinanews.com/cj/2017/10-12/8350416.shtml (accessed on 9 November 2017).

Clarke, Simon, Chang-Hee Lee and QiLi. 2004. 'Collective Consultation and Industrial Relations in China', *British Journal of Industrial Relations*, Vol.42, No. 2, June, 235-254.

Frazier, Mark. 2011. 'Social Policy and Public Opinion in an Age of Insecurity', in Sarosh Kuruvilla, Ching Kwan Lee and Mary Elizabeth Gallagher (eds.), *From Iron Rice Bowl to Informalization: Markets, Workers and the State in Changing China*, Ithaca and London: ILR Press.

Feng, Chen. 2003. 'Between the State and Labour: The Conflict of Chinese Trade Unions' Double Identity in Market Reform', *China Quarterly*, No. 176, December: 1006-1028.

Gallagher, Mary Elizabeth. 2005a. *Contagious Capitalism: Globalization and the Politics of Labor in China*, Princeton, NJ and Oxford: Princeton University Press.

____ . 2005b. "'Use the Law as Your Weapon!': Institutional Change and Legal Mobilization in China", in N. Diamant, S.Lubman and Kevin O'Brien (eds.), *Engaging the Law in China: State, Society and Possibilities for Justice*, Stanford, CA: Stanford University Press.

Hodal, Kate and Peter Bengsten. 2017. 'Chinese Factory Supplying Major Laptop Brands Accused of Student Labour Abuses', *The Guardian*, 6 October, https://www.theguardian.com/global-development/2017/oct/06/laptop-firms-accused-of-labour-abuses-against-chinese-students-sony-hp-acer (accessed on 17 October 2017).

Howell, Jude. 2003. 'Trade Unionism in China: Sinking or Swimming?', *Journal of Communist Studies and Transition Politics*, Vol. 19, Issue 1: 1-15.

Koty, Alexander Chipman and Zhou Qian. 2017. 'A Complete Guide to 2017 Minimum Wage Levels Across China', 15 October, http://www.china-briefing.com/news/2017/11/15/complete-guide-2017-minimum-wage-levels-across-china.html (accessed on 9 November 2017).

Leung, Parry and Alvin Y. So. 2013. 'The New Labor Contract Law in 2008: China's Legal Absorption of Labor Unrest', *Journal of Studies in Social Sciences*, Vol. 4, No. 1: 131-160.

Li, Keqiang. 2018. 'Report on the Work of the Government', delivered at the First Session of the 13th National People's Congress of the People's Republic of China. *People's* Daily. 5 March, http://www.http://en.people.cn/n3/2018/0403/c90000-9445262.html (accessed on 18 August 2018).

Lu, Mouhua. 1986. *Shehui Gongzuo He Shehui Fuli* (Social Work and Social Welfare), Beijing: Zhongguo Shehuixue Hanshou Daxue (Chinese Source). Cited in Linda Wong. 1998. *Marginalization and Social Welfare in China*, New York: Routledge.

Merchant, Nomaan. 2016. 'Robots at Center of China's Strategy to Leapfrog Rivals', *Associated Press*, 24 October, https://apnews.com/ef47138e581d443aa0a530267cc6c47c/robots-center-chinas-strategy-leapfrog-rivals, (accessed on 29 October 2017).

Ministry of Human Resources and Social Security. 2008. *Functions and Organization of the MOHRSS*, Beijing: China Labour and Social Security Publishing House (Chinese Source). Cited in Giuseppe Casale and Zhu Changyou. 2013. *Labour Administration Reforms in China*, Geneva: International Labour Office.

Pringle, Tim Edward. 2009. *The All China Federation of Trade Unions: The Challenge of Labour Unrest*, Ph.D. Thesis, University of Warwick.

Pun, Ngai and Jenny Chan. 2012. 'Global Capital, the State and Chinese Workers: The Foxconn Experience', *Modern China*, Vol. 38, No.4: 383-410.

Whelan, Robbie and Esther Fung. 2016. 'China's Factories Count on Robots as Workforce Shrinks', *Wall Street Journal*, 16 August, https://www.wsj.com/articles/chinas-factories-count-on-robots-as-workforce-shrinks-1471339805 (accessed 12 November 2017).

Wang, Zhikai. 2011. 'Social Security for China's Migrant Workers', *International Labour Review*, Vol. 150, No. 1-2: 177-187.

White, Gordon. 1996.'Chinese Trade Unions in the Transition from Socialism: Towards Corporatism or Civil Society?', *British Journal of Industrial Relations*, Vol. 34, No. 3, September: 433-457.

Wong, Linda. 1998. *Marginalization and Social Welfare in China*, New York: Routledge.

Xi, Jinping. 2017. 'Secure a Decisive Victory in Building a Moderately Prosperous Society in All Respects and Strive for the Great Success of Socialism with Chinese Characteristics for a New Era', report delivered at the 19th National Congress of the Communist Party of China (CPC). *Xinhua*. 18 October, http://www.xinhuanet.com/english/download/Xi_Jinping's_report_at_19th_CPC_National_Congress.pdf (accessed on 7 November 2017).

*Xinhua*. 2017. 'China Focus: 19th CPC National Congress Delegates Feature More Workers, Women', 30 September, http://news.xinhuanet.com/english/2017-09/30/c_136651533.htm (accessed on 21 October 2017).

Yang Yuan. 2017. 'Apple's iPhone X Assembled by Illegal Student Labour', 21 November, https://www.ft.com/content/7cb56786-cda1-11e7-b781-794ce08b24dc (accessed on 23 November 2017).

Ye, Hua and Jing Meng. 2008. '*Gongxuejiehezhiyejiaoyumoshi de tantao*' [Discussions on the work-study model], *China Electric Power Education* 104: 48-49. Cited in Zhang Lu. 2015. *Inside China's Automobile Factories: The Politics of Labor and Worker Resistance*, Cambridge: Cambridge University Press.

Zhang Lu. 2015. *Inside China's Automobile Factories: The Politics of Labor and Worker Resistance*. Cambridge: Cambridge University Press.

Zhuang Pinghui. 2017. 'University in China Apologises After Students Forced to Do Internships at Foxconn', *South China Morning Post*, 21 July, http://www.scmp.com/news/china/society/article/2103529/university-china-apologises-after-students-forced-do-internships, (accessed on 15 October 2017).

# 17

# The New Turn in China's Urban Question

*T G Suresh*

Agrarian China and its modern destinies were the epochal themes of most of the CPC national Congresses held since its inception. China remained essentially a society of peasant farmers and rural artisans during most part of the socialist era. But as China completes four decades of reforms and opening-up, the agrarian character and socialism appear as distant history with which the nation's contemporary age share barely any resemblance. China has entered a new age which is pervasively urban, increasingly post-industrial, technology dominated and consumption driven. On the eve of the 19th Congress, the paramount social and economic questions that needed novel state responses were closely linked to and arise out of China's endless urbanisation.

The CPC leadership since Deng Xiaoping has continuously regarded urbanisation as a pivotal element of China's development. Over the last four decades, China has been on the path of rapid urbanisation without any interruptions. By the time the CPC convened for the 19th Congress, these processes have already acquired certain definite characteristic, propensity and momentum. Urbanisation is irrefutably the most dominating factor in China's economic growth story for which there are scarcely any parallel elsewhere. While Xi Jinping's leadership has introduced decisive shift in certain policy arenas, urbanisation still looks interminable as the Congress has yet again reiterated the enduring vision. This paper examines why China's urbanisation still remains a long-term economic trend. It seeks to offer a broad framework of analysis to understand the nature of China's urbanisation to explain why the new CPC leadership continues to lend strong policy commitment.

Aspects of the urban question has been elaborated in six brief sections. In the first section, I have identified China's urban system as a structural configuration to place it in perspective. The social and institutional actors involved in urban process and what makes their exchanges mutually gainful is elaborated in the second section. How does the urbanisation become an enduring vision in the CPC's overall development plan is outlined in the third section.

The following section reflects on why regime inheritance can impose historical restrictions on Xi Jinping's policy autonomies. But still he introduces a semblance of novelty in the plan for Xiong'an with a call for a new technological paradigm. The two following sections examine these aspects. Last section explores the scope of China's new official environmentalism for inhibiting the pace of urbanisation.

## China's Urban System in Perspective

Nearly seven decades after the agrarian revolution, China's physical geography looks like an extended city that has dispersed, though unevenly, across the Yellow river and Yangtze, and from Yan'an in north to Hainan in the down south. China today is an urban society, a thorough metamorphosis from the rural past where it has been estimated that about 56 percent of the Chinese population is urban. They live in 12 megapolis, 22 large cities and hundreds of district level cities. This figure is still far short of any closer approximation of the actual urban population, as it only covers people with urban *hukou*. If we include the people who are living and working in the cities without being formally classified as urban population, it will add up at least 150 million people more. This urban explosion goes well beyond population figures. In physical terms, vast megapolis have engulfed region size territories up north, in the plains of the upper and middle Yangtze, along the banks of Huangpu and swallowed up much of the undulated Pearl river delta in Southeast.

I characterise China's urban system as a structural configuration, the fundamental determinant on which the national economy is anchored. It propels the economy towards a certain direction in certain ways. China's economy is the measure of its urban system which provides the momentum for growth and creates the scale and magnitude of economic activities. The projection that China's has become the second largest economy in the world is based on, in part, the output and consumption in the cities, so is the case with the story of the 6.7 percent growth rate. The urban system supersedes all other spheres of economic and social life as the rest of the spheres are heavily depended on the cities for their survival. As a structural formation, the urban system does possess certain amount of relative autonomy even from the state in as much as the economic rationalities are concerned. Because these economic rationalities provide the basic propulsion for the Chinese economy.

The cities in China perform vital role in China's economic globalisation. The cities like Dongguan, Shenzhen, Chengdu, Shanghai Pudong, Beijing, Tianjin and Hong Kong are the key nodes through which China intersects itself with the global economic flows. They are the vibrant sites where global production networks connects China's firms, market, households and labour with the global economy. In the global urban hierarchy, the Chinese cities form an Asian regional network where the infrastructures of capitalist accumulation are greatly concentrated in terms of producer services, production networks, banking, finance, factories and plants, innovations and research. Within China the metropolis marks the ascendance of new spatial sites and prominence thus receding the geographical relevance of agrarian China. Essentially, the Chinese economy is anchored in her megapolis and cities. China's extraordinary economic growth draws its sustenance and dynamism from her cities. In other words, without the urban China there is no Chinese economy, nor its growth.

## Urbanisation in Times of State Capitalism

This paper examines how the preponderance of the urban sector over other spheres of economy has created new structural conditions for China's economic growth. This question seems to dominate the policy planning debates within the Communist Party of China (CPC) and sway over it's development agenda for the future. Much of the CPC's new social contract ideas including the promise of prosperity and well-being in return for political monopoly derive from the premise of sustained generation of economic surplus. Nearly four long decades of unbridled urbanisation has thus far been an inexhaustible source for wealth creation as well as for the absorption of the rural surplus labour and their incorporation into the general processes of China's capitalist economic transformations. Since the reforms the economic development was planned in terms of urban sectors and the general process of urbanisation was seen as synonymous to development. In other words, if the land reforms and rural collectivisation were the defining features of the Mao era socialism, urbanisation and city construction are the characteristics of the post-reform era. The CPC's successive leadership since Deng Xiaoping have been the chief patron of this urbanisation driven development which is now Xi Jinping's regime inheritance.

China's urban processes have completed a long period of continuous development. Some of the early mode of urbanisation such as the conversion of agricultural land for commercial use and land privatisation in general seem to have lost their steam. Secondly the Chinese model of urbanisation where the government not only debt financed the commercial projects but also transferred its monopoly over land ownership to the developers for a rentier fee thus making the government capital to circumnavigate between the Chinese central banks, state owned companies and the local governments has already created problems of over production, market distortions and possible asset bubble. These factors weigh heavily upon the central leadership as they search for new instruments for stabilisation and even perhaps course corrections. Are there any evidence in that direction in the national leadership meetings including the NPC – CPPCC conference in March 2017 and 19$^{th}$ National Congress of the CPC in October?

None of these meetings have left behind a definite policy document formulating a coherent response to these complex questions on urban process. But there are clearer indications and implicit propositions that reveal much about the CPC's approach to urban question.

## Urbanisation and Economic Growth: An Enduring Vision

This paper presents a set of propositions gleaned from the two work reports and other important announcements pertaining to urbanisation. Although this topic was not given any particular significance nor focused treatment such as economic growth, innovation or new technologies, there are clearer indications in the form of overt commitments, implicit suggestions and restrictive caveats that elaborate much of the CPC's current thinking on the subject. We can identify three aspects that provide a broad framework for the future of China's urbanisation. The first is a renewed affirmation about the direction in which the Chinese economic growth is progressing and a long-term commitment to sustain it. This clearly signals continued urban process without which aggregate growth is difficult to achieve. The Work Report lists the increase in the level of urbanisation at an annual 1.28 percentage points and 80 million people from the rural areas gaining permanent urban residency as one of the historical achievements. While the continued scope for urbanisation has been indicated, what is not clear is the nature of the future urbanisation, whether urbanisation continued to be that of capital construction creating vast built environment for the mass consumption needs such as residential apartments, retail offices, shopping malls etc. or will it be more of demographic change where an increasing proportion of the population becoming formal urban residents. There are hints and inclination for the second aspect. Some of the other concerns taken up seriously in the Report inhibiting conditions for the further creation of vast physical assets. The new accent seems to be on the qualitative shift brought about through innovations, aesthetics and new technologies.

Signs of a new departure in urbanisation is well revealed in the Political Report. The implications for the broader shifts indicated earlier is that Xi Jinping is calling for an end to the low road in urbanisation based on labour intensive construction, mass production of standardised physical assets and heavily supply oriented. What he proposes then is a new model, the urban clusters where capital, technologies, innovations, human resources and production can be concentrated. Clustering as such is not any novel economic idea. China has already pioneered and perfected industrial clusters to some extent. The 2014 national urbanisation plan has already unveiled the cluster idea. But the suggestion in the Work Report has two novel aspects. Firstly, the new urban clusters are seen as catalysts to induce economic growth in less developed regions thus addressing problems of regional inequalities. Northeastern region, Hebei province and up north, a hinterland area which does not offer much locational advantage is identified as destination for new urban clusters. The development of Beijing-Tianjin-Hebei region has been a recurring theme in Xi Jinping's earlier speeches. The city clusters inevitably create mega urban regions capable of diffusing economic growth to the outlaying areas. But whether the new cluster model is designed to or intended for replicating diffusion that happened in Guangdong province and elsewhere is still not clear.

Why go North East? Is it that Hebei offer greater scope of urbanisation where the accumulated capacities in steel, cement and engineering can be disposed of to stabilise some of the behemoth state owned companies? Will it be an antidote to the rural surplus absorption problem as Hebei and Jilin already have substantial number of outward labour migrants? The early indications do not provide anything to confirm these hypotheses. Because if the plan is to use regional inequality as an excuse to dispose construction inventories or a bait to bring in Northeast as the focus area of the supply-side reforms, it will lead to the same low road to urbanisation. The CPC leadership is clearly bringing about changes there.

## Regime Inheritance and their Burdens

Regime inheritance can, sometimes, overwhelm the new incumbent with the burdens of the predecessor that sometimes renders policy orientations without alternatives. The reason why Xi Jinping's political ascent did not accompany parallel departures in economic policy sums up these limits imposed by preceding regime practices. His complicated inheritances were manifested in cumulative industrial capacity, currency surplus and rent appropriating habits rampant among cadre level and above. The industrial capacity in steel and cement had already created serious glut in the market and induced building and construction activities at a rate only large-scale urbanisation could absorb. By that time Xi Jinping took over, the Chinese economy was fueled by urbanisation process where a portion of the overcapacities in steel and cement could find absorption. The industrial overcapacity was portent with general economic disruptions causing panic run deep among ordinary investors as well as speculators. These burdens of legacies were so formidable, that it forced Xi Jinping to spent most part of his early years in Zhongnanhai grappling with and search for policy responses to the problem of the plenty.

The crafting of what has been called the supply-side reforms is one of the responses to the problems of overcapacity. This new policy calls for and broadly prescribe a set of measures to regulate and make necessary corrections that could control industrial capacity, reduce inventory, etc. The supply side reforms have now become part of the core theme in Xi Jinping's ideas. Interestingly it appears that the overcapacity has prompted two parallel policy responses; supply side reforms at home and a hyped corollary abroad, the OBOR. Over the last decade many of China's leading state owned companies in key industrial sectors have accumulated production capacities and inventories far surpassing the market demands. This has resulted in the distortions in the economy in the form of glut in market, falling prices and artificial demand creation through local government. Urbanisation and building construction was one of the outlets through which the local government agencies usually find temporary fixes to the problem of overcapacity. The question arises here is whether Xi Jinping's much touted supply – side reforms can rein in and introduce a semblance of regulation and balance in the otherwise anarchical production tendencies in China?

These concerns have direct bearing upon the process of urbanisation as industrial capacity in steel and engineering is closely tied to it. What Xi Jinping is struggling to grip with is to offset distortions arising from the flows of excess capacity into market. Any attempt to moderate the flows of excess capacities will affect the supply of infrastructural factors that go into building construction and transportation thus scaling down the process of urbanisation. Do the urbanisation trends in recent years signal any such scaling down? The evidences available thus far suggest a mixed range of trends from relative deceleration in building construction and at the same time strong upsurge in urban projects. There are three urban development policies symptomatic for their deep ambivalence. Firstly, the central government has issued new regulations restraining the local government in land acquisition for commercial purposes. Earlier the local government at municipal and country level could easily convert farm land for commercial and property development purposes. The forceful eviction of peasant cultivators and home demolitions provoked deep resentment among the affected people. But the processes of forced evictions and home demolitions are still continuing as new reports about real estate development continue in different cities. Thirdly China has entered a building cycle trap where continued urbanisation has become an economic locomotive from which it appears difficult to get out.

## Xi Jinping's Xiong'an: A City for a New Era

The announcement in April 2017 about the establishment of the Xiong'an New Area clearly elaborates how the new cluster model is going to be. On the first of April that year, the CPC Central Committee and the State Council jointly announced a plan to establish the Xiong'an New Area, a designated special economic region in the northern Hebei province. The new city will be located about hundred kilometers southwest of central Beijing and span three counties of Xiongxian, Rongcheng and Anxin in Baoding prefecture. The rationale for Xiong'an as outlined in the joint announcement is two-fold, the first is to transfer those economic sectors and institutions having non-capital functions out of Beijing. The second is to coordinate the economic development of Beijing-Tianjin-Hebei region and thus creating a new growth pole region in northern China. The Xiong'an is advertised as an antidote for not only the urban crises of Beijing but also for regional inequalities between the prosperous southeastern provinces and underdeveloped northern China.

The Xiong'an announcement stirred intense public interest and market speculations outside, but it left reasonable anxiety among the people in the three counties slated be part of the future city. From urban designers, architects, academics to real estate speculators, and local business, Xiong'an has already become a legend but without ever knowing well the finer details of the city. Since Xi Jinping has invested his personal prestige in the project, the city will at any rate be grandiose in style and substance. The provincial leadership has set up a Xiong'an Preparatory Committee to steer the project forward. Xi Jinping has appointed Xu Kuangdi the former Shanghai mayor and an urban planner himself as the chief consultant. The local government even six months prior to the announcement has stopped all property transactions including permission to people to move into their new homes, and processing of new *hukou* applications. In addition to these measure, the government has introduced complete freeze of property market not only to control price speculation, but also to reduce the land and property acquisition costs.

Xiong'an provides us with useful entry points to understand how certain key process will continue to affect the local people. What has been called *domicide* or home destruction where the existing habitat of the people are destroyed to create new space for urban construction will be an impending fate of many locals. The three counties are not barren hinterland or desolate outskirts. They do have significant population and built environment with moderate density. The government has announced that every square meter in the area will be planned before construction begins. This means much of the existing building has to be demolished and residents to be relocated. Therefore, the same set of processes that ravages the people's habitat elsewhere and in the past, will be repeated in these counties perhaps under far tighter security conditions.

The region was, once upon a time, home of the largest wetland in north China. But today after decades of local development it has become ecologically fragile. The famed Baiyangdian lake is heavily polluted from chemical effluents and construction waste. What awaits the Xiong'an planners is the monumental logistical challenges, to chip away the large built environment, clean up the Baiyangdian, relocate a proportion of the local population before the majestic city can rise up and to shine on Xi Jinping's legacy for a long time to come.

## New Technological Paradigm and the Urban Question

To return to the second broad framework discernible from the Congress, there is a new accent on innovation and technological reliance which suggest a new departure from the labour intensive urbanisation model. In recent years the idea of innovation has been circulating indiscriminately in all economic milieu of China in as much as the term has entered the street banners adorning market places to community inner lanes. Innovation is typically being a technological paradigm that makes possible certain breakthrough to overcome those restrictive conditions imposed on an industrial sector or firm and which will be then leading to significant productivity gains. It is very confounding as to why China under Xi Jinping is making the idea of innovation into a popular campaign. In the context of new urban turn what would be the role and purpose of innovation and technological reliance? A few preliminary hypotheses can be advanced.

Xiong'an is predicated to be an innovation city. The urban clusters will strive to become incubators of innovations. What is prompting innovation in urban planning? Is it prompted by concerns arising from the Lewis turn initially identified by Cai Feng as a change in the demographic composition where declining supply of a certain age cohorts of working people leading to wage increases. If interpreted in the context of urbanisation it will imply that China's current demographic composition does not allow a labour intensive model which in fact would also mean low wage road to urbanisation. Therefore productivity gains in urban construction has to search for other factors such as innovation in planning, design and construction methods where the value of equal labour time can be maintained through innovation or by relying on new technologies. Second could be a fatal attraction to techno-managerial fixes to otherwise insurmountable problems created by urbanisation such as pollution, waste, etc. But then can interventions in nature through direct human actions and through new technological paradigm produce qualitatively different outcome? Either way it is difficult to see how the value of equal labour time that go into the urban production processes, can be substituted by innovation induced new technologies.

## Rescuing Nature: Official Environmentalism and its Impacts on Urbanisation

The third aspect is a protective affinity towards nature well elaborated in the Political Report. This can be termed as China's first official environmentalism that recognises the corrosive effect of economic development on the nature and by extension on the quality of life in general. The implications of official environmentalism for urbanisation will be far reaching as it implicitly brings about certain restrictive conditions on urban process. Urbanisation and environment are conditioning factors acting upon each other in cause and effect relationship. Therefore, these two are not separate spheres of the social world. Since Xi Jinping has quite evocatively elaborated the need to protect ecology and promised the CPC's commitment to it, then, we can easily infer that the impending consequence will be a diminishing impact on urbanisation. How does a promise to protect environment, in turn, lead to certain levels of contraction in urban development in the future? Urbanisation does require, unlike in case of other economic sectors such as the services, a portion of the natural world or land for it to complete part of the process, say for example building construction. Often the proportion of urbanisation is corresponding to that proportion of the natural world destroyed, or in other words the land made available for the construction of building and other infrastructures. China's urbanisation has heavily been oriented towards the construction activities because of the supply side dynamics peculiar to China. In the new context where the CPC has owned up China's natural world, whatever is left by now, and called for its protection, the immediate effect will be that of a general deceleration of the processes through which land is made available for further destruction, meaning urbanisation. Henceforth the local governments, unless where the central leadership is actively complicit, will be shying away from any project that requires new land acquisition, or debt financing by the central banks will not come through for such projects.

Although the CPC has brought in certain obstacles to urbanisation through the proxy of environment, it has left some of the crucial questions unattended. In the past, two factors were decisive in driving the local government leaders towards the urbanisation projects. The first was a motivating factor where the local GDP growth rate which was otherwise referred to as development, taken as a criteria for cadre promotion. Second was a compulsion where the new tax regime required the local government to transfer a significantly higher share of the tax revenue to the central government thus leaving them with fiscal burden difficult to surmount. The formation of a growth coalition involving the local government leaders, real estate and construction companies and the bank officials took place in this context. This became an interlocking economic coalition well entrenched in the local economy in course of time. The CPC central leadership has not indicated how to mitigate the economic cost of deflationary tendencies in urbanisation which the new ecology norms is going to precipitate.

## REFERENCES

Chan, Kam Wing. 2013. 'Internal Migration in China: A Dualistic Approach' in Frank N. Pieke and Hein Mallee (eds.), *Internal and International migration: Chinese Perspectives,* New York: Routledge, pp 49–72.

Chen, Xiangmin. 1994. 'The New Spatial Division of Labor and Commodity Chains in the Greater South China Economic Region' in Garry Gereffi and Miguel Korzeniewicz (eds.) *Commodity Chains and Global Capitalism*, London: Praeger, 1994. pp 165–186.

*China Daily USA*. 2017. 'New area to be 'historic' development', 3 April.

Li Keqiang. 2017. 'Report on the work of the government', Delivered at Fifth Session of the 12th National People's Congress of the People's Republic of China, 5 March, For Full Text See, http://www.xinhuanet.com/english/china/2017-03/16/c_136134017.htm

Sassen, Saskia. 2004. 'The Formation of Intercity Geographies of Centrality' in Seng Kuan and Peter G. Rowe (eds.) *Shanghai: Architecture and Urbanism for Modern China*, Munich: Prestel, pp 8–24

Shao, Qin. 2013. *Shanghai Gone: Domicide and Defiance in a Chinese Megacity,* Plymouth, UK: Rowman and Littlefield Publishers, INC.

*South China Morning Post*. 2017. 'Why Xi Jinping put his new city dreams in old hand', 2 May.

———. 2017. 'The polluted lake at the heart of Xi Jinping's new city dream', 23 April.

*The New York Times*. 2017. 'Within hours, plans for a quiet corner of China send home prices soaring', 3 April.

Xi Jinping 2017. 'Secure a decisive victory in building a moderately prosperous society in all respects and strive for the greater success of socialism with Chinese characteristics for the new era', Report to the 19th National Congress of the Communist Party of China, *Xinhua,* 18 October,

*Xinhua*. 2017. 'China is set to establish the Xiong'an new area in the northern province of Hebei', 10 April.

# 18

# Wellbeing and Deepening of Healthcare Reforms

*Madhurima Nundy*

## 'Wellbeing' as Articulated in the 19th Party Congress

Wellbeing has become prominent in policy discourse all over the world and it appears several times in Xi Jinping's speech at the 19th Party Congress. The Political Report delivered by Xi Jinping is lengthy and comprehensive. Xi attempts to cover all aspects of development in the last five years and highlights challenges that face China today. The fact that wellbeing appears 12 times in the report is revealing. Xi consolidates multiple issues under this at various points in his speech.

This paper looks at the idea of wellbeing in the context of the Political Report of the 19th Party Congress. The second part of the paper views wellbeing through the lens of healthcare reforms undertaken in China in the last two decades. It analyses its outcomes and direction it seems to take under Xi, and considers whether this converges with his view on wellbeing in the 19th Congress Report.

Wellbeing of the population gets affected by social, economic, political and institutional factors and has multiple meanings. In Chinese, wellbeing or *fuli* (福利) (as used by Xi Jinping in his Political Report) has several meanings – welfare, happiness, contentment, material benefit and so on. Wellbeing appeared in the 18th Congress Report that was delivered by Hu Jintao, but there is a significant difference in the context in which it was used then and the way it is used in the 19th Congress report. Hu Jintao spoke in more general terms in 2012, while Xi puts it in context and outlines the areas of focus. The usage of tense is different too, where the earlier Report was more on what had already been achieved in terms of wellbeing, Xi looks to the future.

There was much that was conveyed by Xi on the aspect of basic living standards and wellbeing, saying that 'wellbeing of the people is the fundamental goal of development' (Xi 2017: 20). In the section on 'Socialism and basic policy', he said that 'public wellbeing' still faced challenges of poverty alleviation and the rural-urban disparities that still exist. He indicated that Socialism with Chinese characteristics should be upheld and there should be a new practice based on theoretical analysis that would provide, "...policy guidance on the economy, political affairs, rule of law, science and technology, culture, education, the wellbeing of our people, ethnic and religious affairs, social development, and ecological conservation", among others (Xi 2017: 16).

Xi called to strengthen areas of weaknesses and by doing so promote social fairness and justice to improve wellbeing of people's lives. Within this he spoke of improving access to – child care, education, employment, housing, medical services, elderly care, emergency services.

As a prelude to his speech, Xi gave an overview of socio-economic development and that 60 million people had been lifted above poverty. There was emphasis and acknowledgement of the contradictions of Chinese development and growth as a result of unbalanced and inadequate development. The report pointed to large disparities in development between rural and urban areas, between Provinces, in income distribution, and that people faced difficulties in areas of employment, education, healthcare, housing and elderly care (Xi 2017). It clearly stated that quality of growth had to take precedence over speed of growth and though not stated explicitly, it is understood this preoccupation with growth has been at the cost of wellbeing of people.

Xi integrated social security and wellbeing under the section on 'protecting people's livelihood; improving wellbeing and strengthening and developing new approaches to social governance'. The section covered important themes like protecting the rights of education, employment and raising income levels, improving social security systems (social security for children, women, elderly, non-working urban residents, unemployed), alleviating poverty, food security and food safety, better health services, improving environment and strengthening social governance (Xi 2017).

From the speech one gathers that there is a holistic understanding of wellbeing. The sense one gets is that wellbeing is an important philosophy that underpins social, collective and individual ways of living. Wellbeing is not restricted to physical health alone but includes social, economic, environmental, and cultural contexts that influence health of the population.

In the next section, the paper looks at healthcare as an important component of wellbeing. Within healthcare, the paper discusses the components that were discussed in the 19$^{th}$ Congress Report and puts them in the context of how healthcare services have shaped in the past few years with Xi at the helm, and the direction it proposes to take in the coming years. What would this mean for wellbeing of the Chinese people, when seen through the lens of healthcare services?

## Healthcare in China: A component of wellbeing

China had attained enviable health indicators by 1978 because of its universal and comprehensive access to basic services including healthcare. But the health sector was one of the most neglected sector post 1980s, with the breakdown of commune systems and decollectivisation. Inequalities in income across urban and rural areas, access to basic services and high medical costs due to the breakdown of the cooperative medical system resulted in stagnating health indicators. These inequalities peaked during the late 1990s and early 2000s and the poor management of the outbreak of SARS (Severe Acute Respiratory Syndrome) was a reflection of all that was wrong with the health service system. It was during the 16th Party Congress in 2002, after over two decades of economic reforms that there was a call to urgently address access to health services. High cost of medical care had pushed people into poverty especially in rural China (Nundy 2014). Subsequently, the new Party leadership, led by Hu Jintao and Wen Jiabao, acknowledged that increase in GDP did not reflect balanced development. The reforms for the health sector in the early 2000s focussed primarily on provisioning and financing. Reforms in provisioning occurred at the secondary and tertiary level where hospitals were given the autonomy to generate revenue as government subsidies were drastically reduced to 10 percent of the hospital revenue. Therefore, the referral linkages that existed between primary, secondary and tertiary medical institutions were further broken. There was enough evidence to show that there was variation in public hospitals across provinces in terms of facilities, equipment, and human resources. This was largely due to decentralisation and inequalities in finances. Therefore, in poorer areas there were severe shortages of government funding compounded with low capacities for revenue generation which further resulted in poor retention of human resources. In the financial reforms, rural and urban health insurance schemes were launched to improve access to healthcare (Nundy and Baru 2013).

For almost two decades now, the CPC took measures to improve accessibility by universalising coverage to health services through insurance. The insurance attempted to cover most people. These reforms did not converge with provisioning where hospitals were still generating revenue by overprescribing medicines and diagnostic services. Despite insurance cover, an expensive healthcare system was created where costs increased rapidly. Though the percentage of out-of-pocket expenditure reduced, from average of 60 percent in

2002 to 34 percent in 2015, the progress was uneven and in real terms people were still paying significant amounts, out-of-pocket (Liu 2017). The most affected were the rural population, migrants and also within urban population there were disparities between those who were employed with the government and state-owned enterprises (SOEs), as against those residents who were unemployed and dependant. Since the insurance did not resolve the issue of accessibility to healthcare services, new reforms were announced in 2009 to make the services equitable. Before the launch of the new reforms, there was much deliberation between academics, global institutions and policy makers, who were divided in their idea of reforms. These included those who were pro-government, those who were pro-market and those who wished to take a middle ground. To address gaps, the policy makers arrived at a compromise and opted for a middle ground (Yip and Hsiao 2015). The reforms and course correction – included additional investments in public hospitals but did not specify whether these would be public, private or a mix of both; introduced measures to control provider behaviour and stop profit-making through drug mark-ups; and expanded the scope of generic drug use. In addition, there was further expansion recommended for social insurance coverage for the entire population with additional benefits. Another important reform mandate was to rebuild and strengthen primary healthcare to improve access and equity (Hu 2017). While there was a move towards course correction, they came with new perils and challenges.

On the one hand there were steps taken towards course correction to make services equitable, on the other hand health services especially public hospitals moved towards greater commercialisation. In China, public hospitals dominate medical care, with 90 percent of in-patient and out-patient services being provided by public hospitals. Since the 18th Party Congress in 2012, there has been furthering of markets in public hospitals. Domestic and foreign for-profit investors have been allowed to invest in hospitals at the secondary and tertiary level. This has led to the infusion of private capital and expansion of these institutions based on ideas of business and profit models. There are now several public-private partnerships (PPP) based models of hospitals in the first and second tier cities (Baru and Nundy 2017).

In the next section, we look at what Xi has highlighted under healthcare in the 19th Congress Report.

## Healthcare in the 19th Party Congress Report

In the 19th Party Congress Political Report, Xi highlighted some of the following issues under healthcare but it is important to understand what he said, in the context of what has already been implemented in the last five years and the ongoing reforms in the health sector.

> 'We will deepen reform of the medicine and healthcare system, establish distinctively Chinese systems for providing basic healthcare, medical insurance, and quality and efficient healthcare services, and develop a sound modern hospital management system' (Xi Jinping 2017: 43).

*On preventive healthcare*: There was a brief mention of carrying out extensive 'patriotic health campaigns' and preventing major diseases. A significant point made in the report is about ensuring food security and that every plate must be full.

Here, one does not get the sense of what these patriotic health campaigns would entail and how these would be implemented. Post 1978, preventive services had broken down and till the SARS outbreak of 2002–03, no major reforms took place for preventive services. The Report does not give any picture of the burden of diseases. China still faces challenges of managing communicable diseases like tuberculosis and outbreak of influenza viruses; and is now facing an immense burden of non-communicable diseases like cancers, heart diseases, diabetes and so on. But one important point that is made in preventing ill-health is that of food, nutrition security and safety, which are components that one tends to forget when talking of preventive healthcare. Preventive healthcare otherwise becomes more focused on immunisation and other supplements. Access to food security and food safety is a vital determinant of a healthy population and must be integrated with health and wellbeing of a population.

*On primary healthcare:* The Report emphasises on strengthening community health services and increasing the cadre of general practitioners at the primary level.

One aspect of the healthcare system that has received much attention in the last five years has been building of primary level healthcare services. This has been one of the key pillars of reforms and course correction since 2009. The breakdown of primary healthcare and overdependence on tertiary care had led to irrational, expensive and skewed services. People had lost faith in primary level care which was China's backbone till the early 1980s. Since 2015, there has been a process of rebuilding the primary level of care by introducing the family physician as the gatekeeper and first point of contact. China is deficient in human resources in health and there is dearth of general practitioners, especially when most are opting for specialisations. In 2016, the CPC introduced a new policy of training new graduates of medicine as family physicians to increase their number. But one needs to see how this will shape up and whether the flow of patients will get diverted to the primary level in the coming years.

*On public hospital reforms, rise in private investments and privatisation:* One of the major concerns that brought about the 2009 reforms was the 15 percent mark up on drugs that was allowed by hospitals to generate revenue and share profits with doctors. This perverse incentive had raised the cost of medical care despite universal insurance coverage. In the Political Report, Xi reported that the profits made by hospitals by selling overpriced drugs would be stopped. Beyond this the Report does not say much on public hospital reforms explicitly. In one line, Xi stated that the CPC will support private health sector and industries without getting into details.

From this, one gathers that there is acknowledgement that cost of medical care is still a concern and the reforms of 2009 have not had any major impact on reducing it. Rise in medical costs and catastrophic expenditure has been one of the major causes of impoverishment in China. A large proportion of out-of-pocket expenditure constitutes purchase of overpriced and overprescribed medicines. Many public hospitals in China still function commercially despite the 2009 healthcare reforms where one of the pillars of reform was to create a national essential drug list so as to remove all profit mark-ups linked to selling medicines in hospitals and to change provider behaviour. Providers have become deeply entrenched into the 'for-profit' system and the reforms initiated are unable to undo this established behaviour. For changing this behaviour, the government has to think of progressive ways of filling the fiscal gap created after removing profit mark-ups.

In the last two decades, much of the government subsidies have gone towards maintaining the health insurance schemes in order to universalise coverage rather than investments in public hospitals. However, even with the increase in public investment in hospitals, the fiscal gap will remain. To fill this gap, public hospitals are opening up to private sector investments and forging partnerships, because the secondary and tertiary hospitals are dependent on high technology equipment that is capital intensive. It is for this reason that public-private partnerships (PPPs) are being piloted. There is political uncertainty with respect to these partnerships and the private sector recognises the uncertainty of investments in the health sector. The success or failure of these partnerships will be critical in determining whether the process of commercialisation will lead to privatisation of hospitals in China. What is interesting in the PPPs in the health sector is that private investors are first focusing on training the health workforce to adapt to the culture of a private enterprise. The idea is to use the leadership of the teaching hospitals to train doctors and health personnel to acquire the skills and attitude necessary for a business model to succeed. There is an effort in improving the public sector but this is being done by infusing the fund gap with private investments. PPPs as an institutional arrangement reflect the policy indecisiveness of the government regarding the role of the private sector. There is a great deal of scepticism and debate on the fallout of these arrangements for a comprehensive health service system, cost of care and equity of access.

In popular understanding it is generally thought that the private sector in healthcare is not vibrant in China but this has now acquired visible presence across levels of care. Since Xi took up his position in 2012, the private sector has received greater attention. There has been liberalisation of policies to invite private sector investments in many aspects of medical services and this includes establishing wholly owned foreign hospitals at the tertiary level of care in special economic zones (SEZ) of leading cities. These investments have been opened for companies from Macau, Taiwan, Hong Kong and Singapore, to begin with. Before, none of the so-called private hospitals were completely private as they were joint ventures with a government company having at least 30 percent share. The only private network of hospitals was set up by an American woman entrepreneur in the 1990s under the name of the United Healthcare group. Investments by private sector have also opened up for senior citizen care homes from several other countries. The market share in healthcare sector is clearly set to increase under Xi, though entering Chinese market is said to be a laborious process due to which private investors are very cautious of making investments in what they see as a constrained environment.

Medical care is an important area of private growth largely due to excessive demands made on the public sector and the rising expectations of middle class and rich Chinese for 'world class' care. There is evidence of growing pressure on the Chinese government to include select private hospitals as part of the social insurance scheme. Already a few hospitals have been empanelled by some local governments. The growth of SEZ in the hospital sector also shows that there is a demand for such services. The growing private sector has to deal with many uncertainties. These uncertainties are related not only to finances but also to the availability and willingness of medical personnel to work in the private sector. This is one domain that one needs to observe closely and look at the implications of privatisation on access to medical care.

*On elderly care:* In the Report, Xi mentioned fostering a secured environment for the elderly along with integrated health and medical services.

China faces demographic challenges with an increase in the proportion of an ageing population who will need comprehensive care. Elderly care is one of the big challenges for China with population of elderly reaching 30 percent in cities like Shanghai and there is limited support for rural elderly. The elderly are a heterogeneous group with differential needs. The burden of chronic diseases is more in this age group, which puts demands on the healthcare system. This is another area that one will have to observe in the coming years.

## Direction of Healthcare Reforms and what it means for wellbeing

Xi covered in brief the major challenges that must be addressed, but health service system in China has become increasingly complex and fragmented. Four decades of commercialisation of medical care has fundamentally altered the healthcare system. From a comprehensive health services network prior to the 1980s, a fragmented and curative-based system of healthcare has emerged. The social insurance schemes are focused on curative services and do not integrate with other services. Since 2009, there has been an attempt to transform the profit-driven hospital based care to an integrated primary based care that is cost effective and of better quality. But challenges still remain. New policies involving the private sector could derail the system, creating more complex structures with inequities and rising costs, leading to a medical-industrial complex. A joint report by the World Health Organisation (WHO), World Bank and the Ministry of Human Resources and Social Security (MOHRSS) in 2016 on 'Deepening Health Reform in China' has warned China of the increasing costs of medical care that would create a 'high-cost and low-value' system (WHO, World Bank, MOHSS 2016). There is an urgent call for structural reforms to address inequities.

Wellbeing has gained currency in policy debates in the last decade. Leaders and policy makers have sought new frameworks and narratives within which they could challenge the dominance of GDP growth in the wake of financial crisis across the world, irrespective of political ideologies. It has also arisen in the context of the increase in the burden of non-communicable diseases or in other words 'lifestyle' disease and an ageing population. This notion of wellbeing has generally indicated individual wellbeing and behaviour change which is distant from a social and collective view of wellbeing. If Xi's report is taken as a new beginning, entering a new era of socialism, then there is a sense of integration that the state is attempting to achieve, so that wellbeing is not just restricted to the physical aspect of an individual but integrates other areas in a comprehensive way by including education, employment, housing, food security, child care, elderly care, and medical services. Wellbeing has multiple meanings and Xi seems to have alluded to the social determinants of wellbeing and has reinforced its collective and social spirit.

But if we look at wellbeing through the lens of reforms that are taking place in healthcare, the policies are far from being integrated. The rhetoric of collective spirit and call for comprehensive social security policies are present but the health policies being implemented on the ground seem antithetical to it. While overall health might have improved on average, inequities in access to healthcare are on the rise. If wellbeing is the 'fundamental goal of development', policies must be progressive, inclusive and universal, irrespective of where a person stands in material terms. The demands of a transforming society with a rising middle class, and demographic (an ageing population) and epidemiological (increase in chronic diseases) transitions, have put the emphasis on curative and hospital oriented care – a clear shift from a comprehensive, universal and responsive health service for which China was praised in the late 1970s. Even though there are visible contradictions, China's efforts to address and provide universal and equitable healthcare is laudable, in contrast to the low priority given to this subject in India. If anything, we have only regressed by introducing cuts in spending on the social sector and turning a blind eye towards healthcare by underinvesting in the over-burdened public health system and creating a complex and unregulated private health sector that is inaccessible to a large section of the population and impoverishes many who access its services. When the state articulates wellbeing it is important to note what that promise attempts to incorporate.

Health protection in its comprehensive sense has never been a political mandate in India, though policies have attempted to be progressive and comprehensive despite sounding rhetorical. A policy is as good as its implementation and that has been the challenge. While under the United Progressive Alliance (UPA), the National Rural Health Mission launched in 2004 was a clear break from the past, with an effort to strengthen the public health systems at the primary level and encourage community level participation in access to health and health services, the momentum that it had gained during the initial years has stalled. Before they won, the present government had made a new health policy and a health protection scheme a mandate in the electoral manifesto. This led to the National Health Policy 2017 that had received much criticism in its draft form and it was finalised after much contestations from all quarters – the private sector, the right to health movement, academics and policy makers. Though in its final form it has its positives, it lacks clarity while discussing involvement of the private sector to attain public sector goals. The policy had focused on increasing public investments in health in a few years. In the Budget 2018, the government announced a universal health protection scheme (*Ayushman Bharat*) for the poor based on the insurance model which came into force in September 2018 with great fanfare. It chose to follow a framework of public-private partnership whose results in the health sector so far leave much to be desired. In the absence of a strong public health delivery system such programmes cannot achieve their proclaimed objectives. All these newer policies only seem to lead us away from a comprehensive understanding of health and wellbeing.

## REFERENCES

Baru, R and M. Nundy. 2017. 'Public-Private Partnerships in Healthcare: China and India', *ICS Analysis,* Issue No. 51.

Hu Shanlian. 2017. 'Overview of Healthcare Reform in China: Experiences and Lessons', in M. Nundy (ed.) *Health Service Systems in Transition: Challenges in India and China,* ICS Monograph, No. 3, July.

Liu, Gordon. 2017. 'Building a National Health System', *China Economic Quarterly,* 21 (1), 16–23.

Nundy, M and R. Baru. 2013. Recent Trends in Health Sector Reforms and Commercialisation of Public Hospitals in China, *ICS Working Paper.*

Nundy, M. 2014. Transformation of Health Insurance Schemes in China: Lessons for Access, *China Report,* 50: 1, 31–43.

WHO, World Bank and the Ministry of Human Resources and Social Security. 2016. Deepening Health Reform in China: Building High-Quality and Value-Based Service Delivery, China Joint Study Partnership, World Bank Group and World Health Organization.

Xi Jinping. 2017. 'Secure a Decisive Victory in Building a Moderately Prosperous Society in All Respects and Strive for the Great Success of Socialism with Chinese Characteristics for a New Era', 19th National Congress of the Communist Party of China, *Xinhua,* 18 October, http://www.xinhuanet.com/english/download/Xi_Jinping's_report_at_19th_CPC_National_Congress.pdf (accessed on 25 November 2017).

Yip, W. and W. Hsiao. 2015. 'What Drove the Cycles of Chinese Health Sector Reforms?', *Health Systems & Reform,* 1:1, 52–61.

# 19

# Women's Share in the Sky: The Outlook at the 19th Party Congress

*Usha Chandran*

It is claimed that President Xi Jinping in his three and a half hour speech giving the Political Report, with thirty thousand characters covered everything that mattered and there was no scope for anyone to fill in. Ironically the word 'gender' appeared only once in the whole 65 pages report.[1] With Xi Jinping Thought gaining entry to the constitution his status is believed to have been elevated to that of once great leader Mao Zedong. However most would agree that Xi and Mao are fundamentally different in their ways of dealing with the issues of national concern. Xi is a man of action and Mao was a man of slogans; Xi aims to make China a strong nation in the world and Mao was a revolutionary, his revolutionary legacy was successful in guiding the huge Chinese nation on the track in which it is walking now. Even though, Mao has been criticised for several political mistakes, nonetheless, it is widely agreed that post-Mao, China has and is continuing to witness the expansion of social gaps and inequalities. One of the key aspect being gender inequality. The gender question which was once a key agenda in the Party as well as 'Mao's thought', finds no more than a mere mention in the core Party agenda and 'Xi's thought' today.

The outlook before post-liberation China was isolated from the outside world and a closed economy was followed. The government took help of its organisations at various levels and the resources within the country to revive the economy and realise the strategy of industrialisation. The onus of modernisation was mainly put on the shoulders of large-scale human resources. In wake of this, Mao's proclamation 'Women hold up half the sky' is believed to have indicated that women constitute half of the resources. Deng Yingchao[2] while motivating women to join the social production, reminds them about women's contribution in the Communist Revolution, and states that women are capable to put in their every effort and spirit to actively participate in nation building (Cai et al. 1988: 165). The Women's Federation leaders were consistent in emphasising the importance of women's participation in social labour for the successful implementation of women's liberation movement (Tan 1994: 78). There was mass mobilisation of women for the first time in Chinese history which enabled women to realise their subordinate status in the society and provided them with an opportunity to fight against it. A large number of women came out of the four walls of their house and worked hand in hand with men, breaking the stereotypical image of women in China. The idea that, 'women should share equal responsibilities as well as opportunities, thus equal work and equal wages as men', were propagated and encouraged. However, women were concentrated at the lower levels and only in a certain types of jobs (Kelkar 1979: 103). Post-Liberation era to the Reforms era Chinese history is full of accounts of how ACWF[3] was used as a tool to extract this resource. Mao Zedong had once stated, 'we need women to fight the Japanese, we need women in social production, anything under this world will not succeed without women's participation' (Li 1988: 162), of course he took utmost care to avoid mentioning leadership at the highest level.

Women's presence at the highest political level was almost invisible. Except for the exceptional case of Song Qingling (Madame Sun Yet-sen), who was the Vice President (ceremonial post) of PRC from 1949–75, the highest post ever held by women leader is Vice-Premier. Only four women have held this post till date. Most of the few top level women leaders during Mao's period except, Vice Premiers Wu Guixian[4] (1975–77) and Chen Muhua[5] (1978–82), had some or the other family links with the existing top male leaders.[6] The fate of such women leaders are invariably crucially linked to their husband's or relative's. Moreover, most of the time women leaders lead the ACWF and rarely had any presence in the core political leadership. The Women's Federation, which was formed with the aim to act as a bridge between the Party and women, made efforts to solve women's issues through mobilising them and briefing them about national policies in general and on women's issues in particular. However, Women's Federation leaders were far less powerful than the Party leaders. The powers of ACWF leaders were limited, and since women's issues were also entangled with other issues their hands were tied even when it came to problems related to women. (Manning 2006: 588) During Cultural Revolution as the country was slowly plunging into chaos, women's affair no longer remained under the control of Women's Federation leaders. The creation and propagation of the image of 'Iron Girl' came to the fore during this time (Jin 2006: 613). The creation of 'progressive' role models was seen as significant to arouse revolutionary passion. Mao's slogan, "men and women are the same, whatever men can do women can also do", was broadly propagated as the 'supreme instruction' for political mobilisation of women during the Cultural Revolution (Jin 2006: 617). The ideological implication of these slogans resulted in, men being projected as the standard or norm and women were to strive towards achieving that standard, which they were constantly motivated to acquire. Thus, resulting in re-emphasising men's superiority over women. Women's presence at the top leadership continued to be negligible. Very few women reached the top leadership even during the Mao's era (Mohanty 2018: 292). Women could now claim equality, however it came with a price. The condition that women have to do as much as men can do; a prerequisite for women to fight for equal status with men. As long as they can't they will have to take up a subordinate position, thus women's fight for equality takes the shape of being an ongoing one, where women are constantly striving to be as good as men. Therefore, as a result of this fight, even though women continue to be almost invisible in the top political decision making bodies, they constituted half of all township and town level directors and deputy directors during the Cultural Revolution. However, by mid 1980's this figure went down to 10 percent (Howell 2002: 43).

## Women under the Reforms

With the Reform and Opening-up policy implemented by the Chinese Government in 1978, throughout the 1980s China was undergoing a phase of transition from a centrally planned economy to a Socialist market economy. However, profit oriented market viewed women as major chunk of surplus employment. The ACWF leaders like Kang Keqing, noted that, 'too many people are employed in China, but it is wrong to say that just because women shoulder heavy burden at home they should go back home and perform their household duties.' (Kang 1988: 450–74) Nonetheless, the ACWF leaders did not have any power to stop or reduce the actual practice of retrenchment of women workers. As was the trend in the job market, in politics also women were losing their status. Only two out of the 29 ministers were female, female deputies maintained the figure of 21 percent from 1973 to 1993. Out of the 6000 mayors only 500 were women, that is less than 10 percent (Howell 2002: 43–44). One of the *External Reference Material on Union, Youth and Women's Work in China*, published by Peoples Press in 1982, stated that the cultural, scientific and technological level of majority of women workers are relatively low, many of them are still not able to break away from heavy manual work in production, the situation of 'men generals and women soldiers', and 'men doing technical work and women doing menial work', has not yet changed. Similar to the fact that women were mostly taken in jobs which are considered extension of women's familial and social role, women leaders were mostly assigned portfolios related to women and children as well as culture. The work considered less important or sometimes even less prestigious; like health and family welfare.

The underlying existence of gender bias as well as lack of quality and self-confidence among women, stop women's growth in the ladder of politics. There were several ways in which women were made to feel inferior and incapable to men. Proverbs and folklores regarding men's superiority and constantly belittling women's level of social contribution continued to be a part of everyday language and experience. Some of the folklores in circulation were, 'A well sunk by a woman will not draw water', proverbs particularly rejecting women's political participation like, 'it was alright to include women in production, but not in politics, what good could a woman do?' and 'when a women rules the roost everything is in a mess' (Croll 1977: 724).[7] Such, day to day experiences maintained low self-esteem of women which limited them to lower or mediocre level at work. Thus, sometimes women's inferiority complex pave way for men to reach the top level of leadership, this is also reflected in most public and private sector, where women rarely reach the top even today. However, some women like Chen Muhua, China's most powerful woman throughout the reform period, did emerge out of these adversities. An alternate member of the Politburo from 1977–87, she was Vice-Premier, Minister, State Councillor, President of the People's Bank, and full member of the Central Committee since 1973. (Rosen 1995: 318). However, Party Central Committee had a meagre rise from 4.1 (8$^{th}$ CPC) to 6.4 (14$^{th}$ CPC) in female membership.

With the reforms and opening-up, there was an increasing realisation of issues related to women, many scholars felt the need to study the various facets of women's issues and explore various approaches in the West (Min 2005: 274). The women's research group sought to redefine their understanding on 'gender' and 'women's liberation', challenging traditional Socialist ideology on 'gender equality'. The open-door policy made it possible to explore the range of Western scholarships on feminism and gender and what came into existence was the wide conviction that although politics and economics are important, women's liberation also requires the transformation of gender stereotyping. And this process will be much harder than economic reforms (Li 1988 and Min 2005). A closer look at the CPC's women's liberation movement shows that, initially women's participation in Communist Revolution was one of the top priorities, however, it was mainly advocated by the leading male leaders of the Party and thus carried a male perspective to it. Women's political participation was restricted to the mass level, mainly in executing the Party's policies amongst women and mobilising them. The male leaders always formed the chunk of top leadership. Thus the very foundation of women's liberation movement in China was laid with the strong presence of male domination at the core. Based on the

Party's demand from women, and the understanding on women's liberation, women contributed during liberation and anti-Japanese war, women contributed in national construction, they were pushed to contribute their jobs to the market economy, then came a time when women had to sacrifice their unborn babies to the 'One Child policy' and economic development. It is now that the full implication of Mao's statement, 'Women hold up half the sky' has come to light. It actually implies women hold or have to bear half of the duties in nation building. However, in that case what about women's half share over the rights and the fruits, what about their half share in the sky–Isn't that an ongoing fight?

## Sky of Politics: China's highest 'Decision Making' Body

Sky, being at the highest level from the earth, the 'Sky' of politics in a country would then be the highest posts/body which has the power of decision making. In this sense then the Sky in Chinese politics are the posts of President, Premier and Standing Committee of the Politburo. There has never been a women President or Premier, nor a single female member at the Standing Committee, which is the core decision making body, in the history of modern China. Therefore, one can say women's share in the sky is absolutely Zero – 零 (*ling*)

Recent development in 'Greater China' – Hong Kong and Taiwan – have women Heads of State for the first time. This was considered a historical development which also raised hopes of witnessing anything close to this if not similar in mainland China. However, these expectations were not high within China, therefore the complete absence of women in the 19th Party Congress Standing Committee is not at all surprising. Even though there is little doubt that the percentage of women's participation in politics have increased steadily in China over the past few decades. As to exactly where have these numbers gained entry needs a closer look. Only then is it possible to answer the fundamental and most commonly asked questions like, why a country like China, which was a pioneer in implementing gender equality in the world, has never seen a women Head of State or a woman leader at the highest decision making body? Why there seems to be a little chance of any change in this situation, even in the near future? Why women's share in the Sky is Zero?

The Communist Party of China has never publicly explained how the decisions to appoint the Politburo Standing Committee members, is made. As we view the picture top down, the Standing Committee members are selected from the pool of full Politburo members who are not due to retire, the exception being when a young leader is slated to become the Party Secretary or State Premier. Therefore, according to analysts the most important criterion to be appointed as the member of the Standing Committee is perhaps to be the protégé of the current Party Secretary, or a full member of the Politburo and to be below the age of 68. However, there is another important criterion that is rarely discussed in any of the analysis within China, that is, to be appointed as the Standing Committee member one has to be a 'MAN'. No woman has ever been a Standing Committee Member and it is highly unlikely that there might be any change in this in the near or far future. In fact, it will be no less than a miracle if it happens. China's 'Men in Black' will continue to rule!

As for the Politburo, only four women have ever held the post of Vice-Premier till date; Wu Guixian (1975–77), Chen Muhua (1978–82), Wu Yi (2003–08) and Liu Yandong (2012–18). At present there is only one women member at the Politburo. Sun Chunlan was the head of the UWFD until the 19$^{th}$ Party Congress (2014–18). Post 19$^{th}$ Party Congress and followed by the 13$^{th}$ NPC, Ms Sun is one of the vice-premiers. The 18$^{th}$ Party Congress had two members at the Politburo for the first time after the end of Cultural Revolution (Jiang Qing wife of Mao Zedong and Ye Qun wife of Lin Biao). In Fact, Sun Chunlan was the only one even eligible to be slated as a member of the Standing Committee. However as expected this did not happen. Even as Yu Zhengsheng, Chairman of CPPCC is likely to retire, and some view Sun Chunlan to be (technically) the obvious choice but it is unlikely to happen, the sole reason being she is a woman. As speculated, her Politburo membership has been upheld for another tenure. Female representation decreased from 10 percent in the 17$^{th}$ Central Committee to 8.8 percent in the 18$^{th}$ Central Committee. The decline in female full members was even more significant from thirteen (6.4 percent) to ten (4.9 percent). Only ten of the 204 members of the new Communist Party Central Committee are women. The number remains same as the previous congress in 2012. It also means that 95 percent of Central Committee members are men. Li Bin, Minister of National Health and Planning Commission, was the only Central Committee female member, was speculated to be promoted to the Politburo, but she was not. Among the 25 ministers in the State Council, Li Bin is currently the only woman. None of the other Central committee full members (female) rose up to the Politburo of the 19th Party Congress. The first reason being their gender and the other reasons are like age, unfavourable factional identity or since they do not occupy the posts traditionally known to be the stepping stone for being promoted to Politburo. The percentage of women delegates at the 19$^{th}$ Party Congress are at 24.1 percent, an increase from 23 percent in the 18$^{th}$ Party Congress. At the 17$^{th}$ Party Congress it was 20 percent, while the figure was 18 percent at the 16$^{th}$ Party Congress in 2002. At the Provincial Party Secretary level, even though there have been a few female Party Secretaries, currently there is not even a single female Provincial or Municipal Party Secretary, with an exception of Carrie Lam Cheng, who is the Chief Executive of Hong Kong Special Administrative Region (HKSAR). These provincial party positions are considered most important stepping stone for a

Politburo membership. Only 21 percent of all party members are women and only 23 percent of all national-level civil servants are women. Further down the system, little more than 1 percent of village committee chairs are women.

To name a handful of women leaders at the higher level in the provinces; only two women serve as governors: Xian Hui (Hui nationality), Governor of Ningxia and Bu Xiaolin (Mongolian descent) the Governor of Inner Mongolia. Wu Lan (Mongolian descent) is the Hunan Deputy Party Secretary, Chen Yiqin (Bai) is Guizhou Deputy Party Secretary. Cao Shumin (Han), an alternate member of the 18th Central Committee and the former president of the China Information and Communication Research Institute, was recently appointed as to be Mayor and Party Secretary of Yingtan City, Jiangxi Province, Zhang Xiaolan, Member of Provincial Party Standing Committee of Gansu, who was a delegate to the 19th Congress failed to make the CC cut. Interestingly, most of the above-mentioned leaders belong to ethnic minorities. It has been observed that ethnic minority group (8.5 percent) is over-represented, whereas women (48.4 percent) are under-represented. Three out of the ten women at the Central Committee are from the minorities. 12.2 percent of the Provincial Party leaders are from the ethnic minorities group and only 9.2 percent are women. Indicating that it is more difficult for women leaders to get ahead in the Party leadership than the ethnic minorities (especially women). However, on the contrary at the top most level there is at least one women leader at the Politburo, but there is not even a single ethnic minority leader at the Politburo.

Fifth session of the 10th NPC, 2007, decided that the proportion of women representatives shall not be less than 22 percent at the 11th NPC. As a result by 2013 female members at NPC was 23.4 percent. The 13th NPC has 742 women, accounting for 24.9 percent of the total, up 1.5 percentage points from the previous NPC. There have been efforts to implement regulations for having more women representatives in People's Congress, Political Consultative Conference and government at each level including village committee, prefecture and local government. In 2009, the State Council Information Office published the National Human Rights Action Plan of China, requiring that there should be at least one female member in the NPC, Political Consultative Conference and government at each level. In 2010, the Eleventh National People's Congress adopted the new Organic Law of the Villagers' Committees of the People's Republic of China, stipulating that there should be women members in each villagers' committee, and female village representatives shall account for more than one-third of the village assembly attendants. In 2011, the State Council promulgated China National Program for Women's Development (2011–2020), specifying objectives for progressively increased proportion of principal female leaders at all levels of leadership across local governments and authorities at the county (prefecture) level and above, for example, 30 percent in villagers' committee members and 10 percent in villagers' committee heads. However, apart from indirect efforts by ACWF to create gender awareness amongst leaders, there have been very less direct efforts to promote women's presence at the middle and high level of party command. Therefore, the only space where women's presence have increased is at the grassroots level even within the party.

## Ideological and Policy Barrier

The ideological guidance of women's liberation movement advocated by the Communist Party of China was the *Marxist women's theory*[8] (Min 1980: 282). According to this theory the first step to women's liberation was women's employment, thus the issues faced by the movement were not entirely focused on women's liberation but more on women's employment. This manifestation of women' liberation as being the dominant one, became an object of awe even by the Western feminists. So much so that in the initial years following the opening-up, 'the Chinese society symbolised in its situation of womanhood, seem to hold out a utopian promise for the disenchanted Western society in particular for women' (Uberoi 1991: 401).

Nonetheless, there was no awareness nor was there any need felt to spread awareness on women's political participation. Equality between men and women was incorporated in the legal system which largely changed the traditional concept of women. Women gained political, social, economic and legal rights. Even though women's liberation movement promised to wipe away all kinds of subordination against women, however, the deeply ingrained patriarchal value system of life in China, and the challenges of market economy let the inequalities 'resurface' itself during the reforms period. It was obvious that 'the causes of women's liberation was deemed secondary to the important task of socialist transformation' (Kelkar 1986: 960). One would ask did traditional attributes of women ever leave Chinese society? As the word 'resurface' suggests, it was perhaps forced down the water and as soon as the force was relaxed it resurfaced and continued breathing. Can the influence of more than 2000 years of history of patriarchy be undone by a few years of ideological imposition? It could be said that the strong current of Marxist women's theory hovered over the society like the Mediterranean wind bringing along with it rain and thunder storm but it went away as swiftly as the wind, with the change of season.

As women entered the public sphere through employment, where patriarchal rules of the house cannot reach, *private patriarchy* changed into *public patriarchy*, where women started being collectively exploited by the employers. With women's entry into wage labour, patriarchal division of labour at home gets extended to women's employment. By ensuring low-wages for women, they can ensure women are secondary earners, thus women's financial dependency on men could also be ensured. Limiting women's career growth would help in consolidating men's superiority over women. Thus a dominance-dependence relation is created between men and women (Hartmann 1976: 136). The issue of women's increasing presence and power are handled by men as a collective unit in a way so that women are kept away from the highest level of social production as well as decision making. Therefore, in case of China *private patriarchy* turns into *State patriarchy*, and further transforms into *public patriarchy*. As a result in spite of a wide acceptance of women's participation in social production and economic activity there is a strong aversion against women's participation in politics, precisely because it involves decision making. It is widely known in traditional patriarchal thinking that men do not want to be ruled by women. Most people use the argument that women are poor leaders and incompetent to act as principals, and thus they should be family-oriented instead of pursuing political achievements.

Apart from these barriers, there are practical policy based walls, which arguably stems from within the ideological barriers. The pre-reforms 'quota' system which had guaranteed a certain number of positions for women cadres, were not in place anymore.[9] Since cadres engaged in industry or agriculture can produce 'tangible' results visible to all, but in 'softer' jobs, like culture and education, it is more difficult to 'quantify' achievements. Since areas such as education, culture, public health and family planning were mostly given to women there was lack of actual performance records. Most of the studies on women leaders suggests that most women leaders, regardless of their own specialisation, have been mobilised at some point in their careers to do women's work[10] (Rosen 1995: 327). Even now the ACWF's job profile has not changed much. Regulations like different retirement age[11] for men and women as well as higher minimum age for women to compete in chief positions. There have been several cases where women were forced to retire even earlier than the stipulated retirement age (Guo 2008: 91). The five years difference in retirement amounts to 6 percent loss in pension for women, in addition to the loss of 5 years full pay. This has been an issue of debate and discussion in the Women's National Congress since the 1980's, and even up to the 21st century it has not had positive results. The policy of different retirement age is one of the most crucial example of translation of gender discrimination advocated directly by the government. Besides, early retirement of women is welcomed and supported by most of the employers and male colleagues since there is no competition from female colleagues for higher position, due to their early retirement. Therefore, the position of director, head of the department, Party Provincial head and other such high political positions are invariably occupied by men. Another important barrier is the appropriation of women's quantitative rather than qualitative representation by the government, institutionalised bodies, media as well as women's organisations themselves. Due to the deep-rooted ideological barriers and prolonged history of women being kept away from politics there is a serious lack of efficient and talented women leaders. Underlying patriarchal ideology as well as lack of gender-neutral policies limit women's elevation beyond the glass ceiling and also restricts the overall proportion of women in politics in China.

## A Comparison on Women's Share in the Sky in Indian Politics

Jawaharlal Nehru's first cabinet had only one woman minister – Rajkumari Amrit Kaur who was given the charge of Health Ministry. Despite this, the successive years did not see any representation of women. Lal Bahadur Shastri's lean cabinet of 10 ministries had no place for women. Contrary to the image of Indira Gandhi, the 5$^{th}$, 6$^{th}$ and 9$^{th}$ cabinet of India under Indira Gandhi's rule did not see any female union minister. However, the 6$^{th}$ and 9$^{th}$ cabinet included eminent women such as Dr Sarojini Mahishi, Nandini Satpathy, Sushila Rohatgi and Saroj Khaparde as Ministers of State. Rajiv Gandhi's cabinet accommodated only one woman minister – Mohsina Kidwai. Maneka Gandhi was made the Minister of State for Environment & Forests during V.P. Singh's regime. But all these years, percentage of women participation in the cabinet hovered between 0-7 percent. P.V. Narasimha Rao's 13$^{th}$ cabinet only had Mamata Banerjee as Minister of State for HRD, Youth Affairs and Sports, and Women and Child Development. After a long hiatus, Sushma Swaraj was appointed as the Minister of Information and Broadcasting in the first Vajpayee Cabinet. Vasundhara Raje and Uma Bharti were seen in the list of ministers of state. For the first time since independence, the cabinet (2004 to 2009) inducted more than one woman union minister, Meira Kumar, Ambika Soni and Panabaka Lakshmi, taking the percentage of women's representation to 10 percent. That was probably the beginning of the end of under-representation of women in Indian cabinet.

The NDA government walked the talk on women empowerment, six out of a team of 23 ministers of the new cabinet headed by Narendra Modi are women. What needs to be noted is that two of the most challenging portfolios were given to female ministers. Sushma Swaraj, External Affairs Minister and Nirmala Sitharaman, Defense Minister, both portfolios being a male bastion. However, some say it could be both challenging and crippling, since at the time of crisis or important decisions the PM will not be confronted with male ego and resistance, and take up the power of decision making in his hands. Among the 543 MPs elected, 62 are women, making 11 percent of the composition, and of the thirty-one Chief Ministers only three are women. Even though the 30 percent Women's Reservation bill has not yet been passed, this is the highest number of female Cabinet ministers and women MPs elected to the Lok Sabha in any Indian government in history. With over 25 percent of women leaders made part of the country's most important decision-making body, could it be a sign of the reversal of past trends? Even though the proportion of women in the sky of Indian politics is quite high as compared to China, however as we go lower the percentage decreases and takes a complete back seat. Therefore, women's representation in politics is not far reaching enough to make a difference in women's life. The relatively high representation of women at the grassroots level in China and the exact opposite situation in India lets out the fact that even though women do hold high position in India however at the grassroots level, they are still not quite able to make an evident change. Therefore, in the Indian context then it can be argued that the whole struggle and fight for equality post-independence, has been the fight to assert women's presence, make them visible in the spaces of power and making their voices audible to the power holders to make a difference in their lives.

## Conclusion

In China the maximum proportion of women's participation in politics is at the grass-root level which decreases as it goes up the hierarchy, making a pyramid without a definite northern tip, whereas in India its exactly the opposite making a reverse pyramid without a definite southern tip. There is an upper ceiling for women leaders in China, unless there is an exception made by the dominant gender to accommodate and promote women leaders, this situation is unlikely to change for a long time to come. The complete absence of gender issues, perhaps a non-acknowledgement of gender issues being a reality, in Xi's doctrine of 'Socialism with Chinese characteristics in the new era' announced at the 19th Party Congress is a grave cause of concern. He points out that he will bring the Chinese nation to be a 'strong' nation like before.[12] Is this nation going to represent its strength through its masculinity by completely blocking women from the top leadership and by rejecting the very existence of gender discrimination? If so then women holding up half the sky in Chinese politics, is far from reality even in the distant future. Research indicates that the adverse external factors are greatly responsible for women themselves not being able to easily break away from the restrictions of tradition and culture.[13] The collective cultural consciousness of women has not yet been liberated from the paradox of tradition and modernity. Therefore, their socio-political and economic engagement were restricted to the lower and middle level. It may be concluded that reasons for absence of women in politics is three-fold; lack of political awareness, lack of equal access to resources and lack of decision making power. However, many women engaged in spreading gender awareness realise the only way is to continue to fight and change the conditions rather than wait for the favourable conditions to be given in a silver platter.

## NOTES

1. We must adhere to the fundamental national policy of gender equality, and protect the legitimate rights and interests of women and minors. We will improve our systems for social assistance, social welfare, charity, and entitled groups' benefits and services. We will improve the system for supporting and caring for children, women, and elderly people left behind in rural areas'; Report to the 19th National Congress of the Communist Party of China, *Xinhua,* 27 October 2017, 45.
2. Deng was the Chairwoman of the Chinese People's Political Consultative Conference from 1983 to 1988, she was wife of first Chinese Premier, Zhou Enlai.
3. All China Women's Federation
4. China's first women Vice Premier from January 1975 to September 1977.
5. Have held the post of Vice Premier, State Councilor, Minister of Foreign Economic Relations and Trade, Commissioner of the National Family Planning Commission, Governor of the People's Bank of China, and Chairwoman of the All-China Women's Federation. She was an alternate member of the Politburo of the Communist Party of China, one of the few women to have entered China's top decision-making body.
6. Deng Yingchao, wife of Zhou Enlai, first Premier of PRC; Kang Keqing, who served as Vice Chairman of the Chinese People's Political Consultative Conference (CPPCC), Chairman of the All-China Women's Federation, wife of Zhu De, first Vice Chairman of PRC, an active member of the Red Army; Cai Chang, first Chairwomen of ACWF, wife of Li Fuchun, Vice-Premier and Chairman of the State Planning Commission, considered one of the main founders of socialist economy of PRC.
7. For a detailed analysis on women's experience of oppression, covered by '*Women of China*' articles on criticizing Confucius and Lin Biao see Croll 1977: 721.
8. 'Marxist Women's Theory' advocates that women are revolutionary forces, women's liberation is a condition of proletarian revolution and that productive labour is the basic condition of women's liberation and is progressive. Min 2005: 282.
9. A local study, from an internally circulated journal, provides details on decline of rural women party members during the reform period. Qiushineibuwengao, no. 4, February 25, 1991, pp. 28–29.
10. Mobilizing women to execute the national policies. Eg: family planning and effective implementation of the 'One Child Policy'.
11. Female labours are to retire at 50, while male labours retire only at 60. Female cadres and professionals are to retire at 55 while their male counterparts retire only at 60 or sometimes even 65
12. In his report to the congress, Xi suggested that if Mao made China independent, and Deng made it prosperous, he would make it strong again – propelling the country into its 'new era'.
13. Prof Wei Guoying, (Former Director, Women's Studies Centre, Beijing University. A leading Gender Studies scholar in China) expressed in an interview with me, that for women its almost impossible to reach the highest level of politics, or any other field, unless you are Wu Yi (meaning a person like Wu Yi, apart from being bold, one should also be unmarried), even though the maximum level Wu Yi reached was that of Vice-Premier.

## REFERENCES

1982. '中国的工会、青年和妇女工作对外宣传参考材料之二' *Zhongguo de gonghui, qingnian he funu gongzuo, duiwai xuanchuan cankao cailiao zhier,* [External Reference Material No-2, on China's Union, Youth and Women's Work] Peoples Press, 68–69.

2003. *Women Press for Equal Retirement Rights, CCTV.com,*24 August, http://china.org.cn/english/2003/Aug/73131.htm (accessed on 10 October 2017).

2014. Women's Studies Institute of China's, 'Shadow Report of Chinese Women's NGOs on the Combined Seventh and Eighth Periodic Report Submitted by China under Article 18 of the Convention on the Elimination of All Forms of Discrimination against Women', September.

Deng Yingchao. 1988. '学会本领做好工作' *Xuehui benling zuohao gongzuo*' [Learn skill, and do good work], Editorial article in *People's Daily* on 8th March 1950, in Cai Chang, Deng Yingchao & Kang Keqing, 妇女解放问题文选 *Funu jiefang wenti wenxuan,* [Documents on the Question of Women's Movement], Beijing: Peoples Publishing House, pp.165-68.

Guo Huimin. 2009. 'Gender Discrimination in Employment in China', in *New and Emerging Developments in Gender and Law in China*, Compilation of papers and presentations at the China Gender and Law Experts Consultation, 21-24 September, Wellesley Centres for Women, p.91.

Hartmann, Heidi. 1976. 'Capitalism, Patriarchy and Job Segregation by Sex', in Blaxall M and Reagan B, *Women and the Work Place: The Implications of Occupational Segregation*, Chicago: University of Chicago Press, 137–79.

Howell, Jude. 2002. 'Women's Political Participation in China: Struggling to hold up half the Sky', Hansard Society for Parliamentary Government, *Parliamentary Affairs*, Vol-55, 43–56.

Jin Yihong. 2006. 'Rethinking the 'Iron Girls': Gender and Labour During the Chinese Cultural Revolution', (Translated from Chinese by Kimbeley Manning and Chu Lianyun), *Gender and History*, Special issue on translating Feminism in China, Vol-18, No.4, November2006, 613–34.

Kang Keqing. 1988. '奋发自强开创妇女运动新局面' *Fenfa ziqiang, kaichuang funu yundong xin jumian* [Strive to Strengthen Oneself, Start the New Phase of Women's Movement], Kang Keqing's Work report to the Fifth National Women's Congress on 2nd September 1983, in Cai Chang, Deng Yingchao& Kang Keqing 妇女解放问题文选 *Funu jiefang wenti wenxuan* [Documents on the Question of Women's Movement], Beijing: Peoples Publishing House, 450–474.

Kelkar, Govind. 1979. 'China's Women The Change and the Challenge', *Economic and Political Weekly,* Vol. 14, Issue No. 5-6, 100–103.

_____ 1986, 'Policy towards Women before and after Cultural Revolution A Feminist Perspective', *Economic and Political Weekly,* Vol XXI, No 22, 959–60.

Li Xiaojiang. 1988. 夏娃的探索, *Xiawa de tansuo* [Eve's Exploration], Zhengzhou: Henan Peoples Publishing House.

Liang Yu. 2018. 'More women, fewer officials on China's top legislature', *Xinhua*, 24 February, http://www.xinhuanet.com/english/2018-02/24/c_136997333.htm (accessed on 10 August 2018).

Manning, Kimberley Ens. 2006. 'Making a Great Leap Forward? The Politics of Women's Liberation in Maoist China',*Gender and History*, Special issue on translating Feminism in China, Vol-18, No.4, 574–93.

Min Dongchao. 2005. 'Awakening Again: Traveling Feminism in China in the 1980's', *Women's Studies International Forum,* No.28, 274–88.

Mohanty, Manoranjan. 2018. *China's Transformation: The Success Story and the Success Trap*, New Delhi: Sage.

Uberoi, Patricia. 1990. 'Feminine Identity and National Ethos in Indian Calendar Art', *Economic and Political Weekly,* Vol. 25, No. 17, WS41–WS48.

_____ 1991. 'Chinese Woman in the Construction of Western Feminism', *Alternatives: Global, Local, Political.* Vol. 16, No. 4, 387–405.

'Profile of the 16th Lok Sabha', PRS Legislative Research, http://www.prsindia.org/media/media-updates/profile-of-the-16th-lok-sabha-3276/ (accessed on 9 February 2018).

Rosen, Stanley. 1995. 'Women and Political Participation in China', *Pacific Affairs*, Vol. 68, No. 3, 315–341

Shubhojit. 2014. 'Women Cabinet Ministers in India' 1 July, |http://www.elections.in/political-corner/women-cabinet-ministers-india/ (accessed on 9 February 2018).

Tan Shen. 1994. '当代中国职业妇女： 由政府安排工作或进入劳动力市场' *Dangdai zhongguo zhiye funu: you zhengfu anpai gongzuo huo jinru laodong lishi chang'* [Contemporary China's Working Women: Work in service provided by the government or enter the labour market], in Li Xiaojiang, Zhu Hong, XiuYu (eds.) 性别与中国 *Xingbie yu zhongguo* [China and Gender], Beijing: Beijing Sanlian Joint Publishing, 78–92.

Wang, Jane. 2017. 'Women's Federations Join Hands to Embrace 19th CPC National Congress', 10 July, http://www.womenofchina.cn/womenofchina/html1/news/action/1707/1981-1.htm (accessed on 2 February 2018).

# 20

# Protecting China's Environment:
## Changing Party's Attitude and State's Policy

*Rajiv Ranjan*

The deteriorating environmental health of the People's Republic of China has aroused concerns and debates over the cost-benefit analysis of development vs. environment. Abandoning development is no longer regarded as the optimal solution for the developing world. The solution lies in a deeper and comprehensive understanding of the challenges. Apparently, the leadership of the People's Republic of China was never unaware of the environmental aftermath of its imposing development but it chose to deny or rather say it preferred its ambitious development agenda over environment. Considering the multi-dimensional consequences of environmental degradation, even the economic leverage gained over years by the PRC appears to be under threat. While China spends one percent of its Gross Domestic Product (GDP) on environmental preservation, still pollution and environmental degradation annually amount to 8 to 13 percent of GDP. Hence, environmental costs are as high as annual economic growth. The deteriorated environmental situation causes many domestic socio-political problems.

The People's Republic of China was compelled by the alarming consequences of unbridled development to re-consider its strategy. Hence, the Chinese government has gradually strengthened its efforts to control depletion of the national environment. It is evident from the fact that the State has adopted a number of environmental policy and plans, enacted a comprehensive set of national laws and regulations and has established a number of environmental institutions. The 18$^{th}$ Party Congress of CPC has amended Party's constitution to include 'promoting ecological progress' as the fifth component to build socialism with Chinese characteristics, apart from developing socialist market economy; promoting socialist democracy, developing advanced socialist culture; and building harmonious socialist society.

After 25 years, Standing Committee of the National People's Congress (NPC) revised the Environmental Protection Law (EPL) 1989 that was adopted on 24 April 2004 and came into effect on 1 January 2015 (NPC, Environmental Protection Law of China 2004). Revised law departs from the previous established pattern that environmental protection should be coordinated with economic and social development and emphasised that environmental protection should come first. The law enlarged the overall scope of environmental protection and contains 70 articles, while the original law had 45. More importantly, the revised EPL also went through *fourth review*, in April 2014, which the Standing Committee of the NPC was compelled to call – a rarity in Chinese law-making. The departure from previous established pattern and summoning fourth review signifies strengthening of environmental protection on at least two fronts. Firstly, environmental protection voices within have become more vocal and strengthened its positions to influence policy formulations. Secondly, leaders of the Party-State have also realised that growing environmental deteriorations could no longer be neglected to achieve the goal of a 'prosperous China'. So a change in attitude and policy.

In September 2006, State Environmental Protection Administration of China (SEPA) later Ministry of Environment Protection, China[1] and the National Bureau of Statistics of China (NBS) jointly released the first green GDP report. The report indicated that environmental pollution cost China 511.8 billion Yuan (USD 64 billion) in economic losses, accounting for 3.05 percent of the country's GDP in 2004 (The State Council 2004), whereas World Bank report indicates that if the adjusted human capital approach is replaced by the value of a statistical life (VSL) then the amount goes up to about 781 billion Yuan, or about 5.78 percent of GDP (World Bank and State Environmental Protection Administration 2007).

The People's Republic of China could not contentedly pursue the developmental drive and was compelled by the alarming environmental degradation to re-consider its development path and strategy. Hence, the Chinese government has gradually strengthened its efforts to control depletion of the national environment. It is evident from the fact that the state has adopted a number of environmental policy and plans, enacted a comprehensive set of national laws and regulations and has established a number of environmental institutions, for instance Environmental Protection Law 1987 and creations of Ministry of Environment Projection.

The study aims to gauge the strengthening environmental protection efforts in China. First, the chapter briefly outlines the environmental intuitions/ institutions in China. Secondly, the paper examines the revised environmental protection law, 2004 and 13th Five Year Plan to ascertain if China is seriously strengthening environmental protection. Thirdly, the paper studies changes in Party-State attitude towards environmental protection by analysing leader's speech and 'Report to Party Congress', in particular focus on President Xi's speech at the 19th Party Congress (Xi Jinping 2017). Fourthly, the chapter also investigates local leader's promotion as after the economic reform, local leaders (mayors) were also evaluated on deliveries in economic growth, not to discard the weightage of political resume.

## Environmental Institutions in China: An Outline

The 1972 United Nations Conference on the Human Environment (UNCHE), held in Stockholm, first provided impetus for introducing environmental management in China. For more than 30 years, China has established a large bureaucracy within the various ministries, commissions and administrative agencies involved in environmental protection. The State Council is China's Cabinet, representing and leading all agencies of the central government. Its main role in environmental protection is to make vital decisions and coordinate the actions of all relevant agencies.

China's environmental programme was formally introduced in 1973 at a national conference on the environment that was endorsed by Chairman Mao Zedong. However, the policy guidelines that emerged from the conference were non-binding in nature, 'urged rational distribution and overall planning in industry and agriculture; comprehensive utilisation of raw and processed materials, along with recycling; and reliance on the population to abide by laws and regulations and to take the primary responsibility for environmental protection' (Boxer 1989: 680).

**Figure 1: China's Environmental Protection Apparatus**

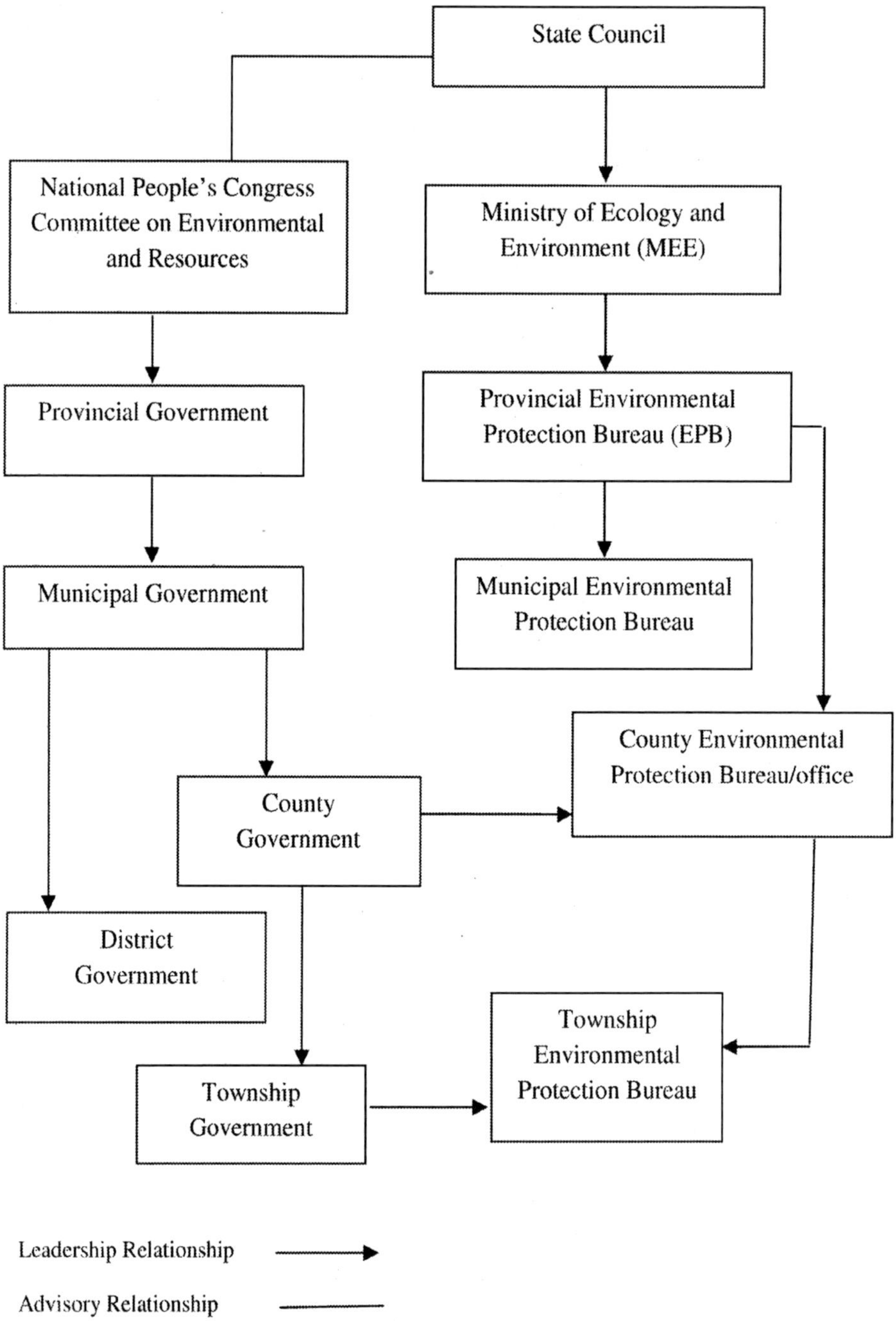


Adapted from Chen 2009: 20.

Premier Zhou Enlai was the driving force behind the conference and China's decision to formally pursue environmental protection as a national policy. China's environmental programme has two main components: ecology and protection. Environmental ecology starts from the premise that national survival requires knowing how to sustain biological productivity, and that protection and conservation of forest, water, air, marine, and other ecosystems are essential to this (Boxer 1989: 681). In the process of establishing and improving the environmental statutory framework, China 'attaches equal importance to environmental law enforcement and environmental legislation' (State Council Information Office 2006).

China has executed an environmental administration system, whereby governments at all levels are responsible for the environmental quality of the areas within their jurisdiction. The competent administrative departments have the power of overall supervision and management. For past 25 years, a range of institutions have been created to promote environmental protection. Indeed, many of these bodies are created under the provisions of Articles 9 and 16 of the 1989 Environmental Protection Law (NPC, Environmental Protection Law of China 1989). It forces local people's governments to establish standards to maintain the quality of the environment in areas under their jurisdiction, and to take measures to improve the quality of the local environment. Interestingly, most environmental disputes are resolved by extra-judicial processes (Palmer 1998: 790).

The most vital organ of institutional structure is the NPC's State Commission on Environmental and Natural Resources Protection (全国人大环境与资源保护委员会 *Quanguo renda huanjing yu ziyuan baohu weiyuan hui)* established in 1993. The responsibility of this body is 'to deal with general policy matters in the area of protection of the environment and natural resources' (Palmer 1998: 793).

It also assists the Standing Committee in its supervision of other environmental agencies. The main purpose of the Commission on Environmental and Natural Resources Protection is to give inputs in the 'drafting of regulations and guidelines on issues of environmental welfare'.

Second, State Council Committee for Environmental Protection 国务院环境保护委员会 (*Guowuyuan huanjing baohu weiyuanhui*) is the Secretariat for the Commission. It is an administrative organ for the Commission which is responsible for 'drafting legislation, producing plans for and reports on environmental protection' (ibid). The State Council also investigates into serious incidents of pollution, handling conflicts over environmental problems between provinces. The Council also conducts environmental inspections in provinces and resolves the problems of provinces through mediations (Zheng 2017). The

Council also works among masses to promote awareness of environmental security.

The Ministry of Ecology and Environment (MEE, 中华人民共和国 生态环境部 *zhonghua renmin gonghe guo shengtai huangjing bu)* the chief organ for formulating and implementing policies was established in 1988 as the National Environmental Protection Agency. It is third in the institutional hierarchy, but many essential jobs have been assigned to it. The Ministry of Ecology and Environment Projection supersedes Ministry of Environment Protection and have been given bigger task to enhance environmental protection by transferring responsibilities of the National Development and Reform Commission on tackling climate change and emission reduction to this ministry (Yang 2018).

The agency functions under the direct leadership of the State Council. The mission of MEE is to 'improve environmental quality and build a beautiful China which enjoys blue sky, green land and clean water' (MEE 2018 Mission). MEE is responsible for 'establishing a sound basic system for environmental protection. Draw up and organise the implementation of national policies, programmes, and plans for environmental protection, draft laws and regulations, and formulate departmental rules.' (MEE 2018 Mandate). Under revamped mandate of the ministry many other specific functions including 'overall coordination, supervision and administration of major environmental problems; for attaining national pollution reduction targets; for contributing opinions on the size and direction of fixed-asset investment, and the allocation of fiscal funds of the central government in the environment sector'; to take precautionary measures against pollution at the source and control pollution and environmental damages on behalf of the State Council, conduct environmental impact assessment of major economic and technical policies, development plans, and major economic programmes, contribute opinions on the environmental impact of draft environment protection legislations, in accordance with national regulations, review and approve the environmental impact of major development regions and development projects; guide, coordinate, and oversee ecological conservation effort; for the supervision and administration of nuclear safety and radiation safety; conduct international cooperation and communications on environmental protection'; organise, guide, and coordinate the environmental communications and education, develop and organise the implementation of the outline on environmental communications and education, launch communications and education on developing ecological civilisation and building an environment-friendly society, and advance the public and social organisations to participate in environmental protection', makes MEE a more influential environmental organisation in China (ibid).

Presently, there are more than 2,500 environmental protection administration departments above the county level with a total staff of 88,000 engaged in environmental administration, monitoring, inspection and control, statistics collection, scientific research, publicity and education (MEP 2002).

## Legal Apparatus of Environmental Protection

The environmental protection 'is a whole system, not only includes technologies of environmental protection, investment of environmental protection and policies of environmental protection, but also involves the establishment and improvement of system of environmental regulation' (Gan 2011: 172).

China has promulgated many specific laws on environmental protection as well as laws on natural resources related to it. They include the Law on the Prevention and Control of Water Pollution 1984, Environmental Protection Law 1989, now revised in 2004, Law on the Prevention and Control of Air Pollution 2000, Law on the Prevention and Control of Environmental Pollution by Solid Wastes 1995, Marine Environment Protection Law 1999, Forestry Law, Grassland Law, Fisheries Law, Mineral Resources Law, Land Administration Law, Water Resources Law, Law on the Protection of Wild Animals, Law on Water and Soil Conservation, and Agriculture Law.

The State, since 1996 has enacted or has formulated or revised laws on environmental protection, such as those on prevention and control of water pollution, marine environment protection, prevention and control of air pollution, prevention and control of noise pollution, prevention and control of solid waste pollution, evaluation of environmental impact, and prevention and control of radioactive pollution, as well as laws closely related to environmental protection, such as those on water, clean production, renewable energy, agriculture, grassland and animal husbandry (White Paper on Environmental Projection 2006).

By the end of 2005, the State had promulgated over 800 national environmental protection standards. In addition, the municipalities of Beijing and Shanghai, and the provinces of Shandong and Henan have promulgated over 30 local environmental protection standards (State Council Information Office 2006, China).

## Strengthening Environmental Protection Governance

The process to amend the EPL 1989 in NPC began in 1995. During 1995 to 2011, 78 proposals were submitted for amendment. The Environment Protection and Resources Conservation Committee of the Standing Committee of the NPC conducted an assessment of implementation of the EPL 1989 during 2008–2010.

Interesting, when the Standing Committee of the NPC began the process to amend the EPL in 1989, the mood was not in favor of a strong EPL. An ambitious initial proposal from the Ministry of Environmental Protection, then SEPA, was rejected. Although, there was need and push for amendment to of 1989 law. The NDRC and the Environmental Protection and Resources Conservation Committee of the NPC, as the most powerful representatives of economic interests, took over, and the latter assumed the drafting responsibility. As a result, the Committee released a first public draft version on 31 August 2012 that was weak in terms of environmental protection.

It was at this time that a broad coalition of proponents of stricter environmental protection voiced their displeasure with the draft. The MEP (now MEE) publicly released a list of 34 arguments against this version. Then, the Environmental Protection and Resources Conservation Committee, which had been previously charged with drafting responsibility, was required to relinquish its drafting duties in favor of the Law Committee of the NPC, which was more environmentally friendly. The second draft version put forward by the Law Committee in mid-2013, clearly reflected the strength of the MEP and the trend towards environmental protection.

Beginning in mid-2013, the environmental proponents grew more vocal, leading an intense debate that delayed the swift approval of the draft. As discussed in the beginning of this chapter, Standing Committee of the NPC revised the EPL, 1989 after the fourth review, in April 2014 (Li 2014), which is very rare in Chinese law-making and adopted a law that is greatly different from what observers had expected in 2011.

This new law contains many provisions that promise to strengthen environmental protection in China. Moreover, the revision process itself signaled the growing influences of environmental considerations and public opinion in Chinese lawmaking. Indeed, the public exerted great pressure on environmental opponents, which was crucial to the success of the new law.

The revised law makes provision for environmental impact assessment and prohibits development plans without environmental impact assessment. The article further emphasises that construction projects without environmental impact assessment shall not be allowed (Article 19, Environmental Protection Law of the People's Republic of China, 2014). Earlier several construction projects were either initiated with faulty EIAs or without EIAs at all. If a project failed to submit an EIA report, the environmental agency could only order construction to stop and the EIA to be completed. A company that did not make up the EIA later could be fined a maximum of RMB 200,000 (Lau 2014). However, large state-owned enterprises and other companies often found it less expensive to pay the fine than to commission an EIA (ibid).

## Changes in Attitude: Environmental Ideology

Evidence from the empirical findings reported earlier shows that China has paid increasing attention to environmental issues from both a domestic and global perspective. China's environmental communiqués (Ministry of Environmental Protection 2004–2009) indicate that China invested 1,636 billion RMB (US$240 billion) in environmental conservation from 2003 to 2008 (Wang & Lin 2010: 1702). The policy shift in China has been due to several reasons.

The ideas and attitudes of China's top leadership have drastically changed over the past decade. The government has become increasingly aware of the urgent need to halt environmental deterioration because of its adverse effects (Huang et al. 2010: 237). For example, the rapidly increasing air and water pollution over recent years have incited environmental conflict and social protests in many regions and have become destabilising factors capturing the attention of the Chinese government (Ho 2001).

The 'Scientific Development Concept' was put forward at the Third Plenary Session of the 16$^{th}$ Communist Party of China (CPC) National Congress in 2003. It is the core of the current CPC ideology and incorporates sustainable development, social security, increased democracy, and ultimately, the creation of a harmonious society. In March 2005, Chinese President Hu Jintao further set the national development goal of constructing a 'resource-saving, environment-friendly' society. Since then, more concerns have been given to environmental sustainability on the political agenda of the central government.

Hu Jintao, at 18$^{th}$ Party Congress 2012, included ecological progress as fifth component of socialism with Chinese characteristics. He further emphasised

> 'promoting ecological progress is a long-term task of vital importance to the people's wellbeing and China's future. Faced with increasing resource constraints, severe environmental pollution and a deteriorating ecosystem, we must raise our ecological awareness of the need to respect, accommodate to and protect nature. We must give high priority to making ecological progress and incorporate it into all aspects and the whole process of advancing economic, political, cultural, and social progress, and work hard to build a beautiful country, and achieve lasting and sustainable development of the Chinese nation' (Hu 2012).

The 18$^{th}$ Party Congress of CPC has amended Party's constitution to include 'promoting ecological progress' as fifth component to build Socialism with Chinese characteristics, apart from developing a Socialist market economy; promoting Socialist democracy, developing advanced Socialist culture; and building harmonious Socialist society (Hu 2012).

## Xi Jinping's thought on 'Socialist Ecological Civilisation'

Xi Jinping while presenting the Work Report of previous five years at the 19th Party Congress emphasised that 'notable progress has been made in building an ecological civilisation'. He further stressed that 'we have devoted serious energy to ecological conservation. As a result, the entire Party and the whole country have become more purposeful and active in pursuing green development, and there has been a *clear shift away from the tendency to neglect ecological and environmental protection (emphasis added)*' (Xi 2017: 4). Xi Jinping also called upon 'to build China into a great modern socialist country that is prosperous, strong, democratic, culturally advanced, harmonious, and beautiful' (ibid). Xi's idea of building 'Socialism with Chinese Characteristics for New Era' is inclusive of 'Socialist concept of ecological civilisation' and promote the formation of a new pattern of harmonious development' (*Xinhua* 2017). The beautiful China, as Xi explained in his speech is to 'create good working and living environments for our people and play our part in ensuring global ecological security' (Xi 2017: 20).

Beautiful China as a concept first appeared in Hu Jintao's Report at 18th Party Congress. Hu Jintao expressed that China 'must give high priority to making ecological progress and incorporate it into all aspects and the whole process of advancing economic, political, cultural, and social progress, work hard to build a beautiful country, and achieve lasting and sustainable development of the Chinese nation' (Hu 2012: 25). What is clear from his remarks that ecological progress is not a stand alone goal but must be carried out together with social and economic progress (Sichuan University 2012). 13th Five Year Plan (2016–2020), further refined the concept and emphasised that China will step up 'ecosystem and environmental protection efforts, ensure that resources are used more efficiently and that more quality ecological goods are available to the public, and simultaneously help the people become prosperous, help the country grow stronger, and build a Beautiful China' (National Development and Reform Commission 2016) In addition, Xi has expanded the concept of beautiful China also to global ecological security and more precisely to China's role in climate change diplomacy. It is yet too been seen if Xi Jinping further expand the scope of Belt and Road Initiative to make 'Green Belt and Road'.

To get a sense of what Xi Jinping achieved in his first five years in environmental protection, report of the *South China Morning Post*, vividly sums it up. The *Post* mentions that Xi has 'pushed through a variety of high profile environmental policies in its first five years: it has moved to ban the ivory trade by the end of 2017, committed to block imports of solid waste such as consumer plastics, increased efforts to tackle air pollution around Beijing, investigated mining operations in nature reserves, blocked plans for hydropower facilities along the country's last free-flowing major river, and made steps towards the creation of a US-style national park system' (Standaert 2018).

Xi, while deliberating on problems remain to be resolved, underlined that environmental protection is one of major areas of focus in times to come. When he calls for the basic policy that uphold and develop socialism with Chinese characteristics in the new era, one of fourteen policies is to ensure harmony between human and nature, 天人合一 *tianren heyi* (Xi 2017: 20). Interestingly, Xi is resorting to traditional Chinese philosophy to infuse renewed efforts in promoting environmentalism in China. Ironically, this dictum was distorted into 人定胜天 *rending shengtian,* meaning 'man must conquer nature' during Mao's Great Leap Forward Era.[2] One can also infer that rising China is not only learning lessons in foreign policy from its pre-Qing dynasty strategic thoughts but also infusing traditional thoughts in contemporary society, culture and even in environmental protection.

Xi optimistically says that in the first stage from 2020 to 2035, developing China into a Modern Socialist country, there will be a 'fundamental improvement in environment and building a beautiful China will be attained' (ibid 24). He is further hopeful that in the second stage from 2035 to the middle of the 21st century, new heights are reached in every dimension of material, political, cultural and ethical, social, and *ecological advancement* (emphasis added).

Xi's speech at 19th Party Congress devotes one full section on 'Speeding up Reform of the System for Developing an Ecological Civilisation, and Building a Beautiful China'. These signals the dawn of the new era in environmental protection in China, making it clear that China will no longer prioritise development over environment. He reiterates that in addition to 'creating more material and cultural wealth to meet people's ever-increasing needs for a better life, we need also to provide more quality ecological goods to meet people's ever-growing demands for a beautiful environment' (Xi 2017: 45).

He also laid out plans to 'restore the serenity, harmony and beauty of nature' (ibid), which were neglected or destroyed during the rapid industrialisation and urbanisation in the past. Firstly, China will promote green development by establishing a legal and policy framework to push for green production and consumption. Xi also highlights that China will 'create a market-based system for green technology innovation, develop green finance, and spur the development of energy-saving and environmental protection industries as well as clean production and clean energy industries' (Xi 2017). More importantly, he also realised that previous model of development has encouraged officials to attain growth while ignoring the environment cost to get promoted in hierarchy, which has been dealt in later part of the chapter. Xi introduces a new yardstick, one can safely infer that, to evaluate the performance of the party cadre and government officials for considerations of promotion, when he says that China will 'launch initiatives to make Party and government offices do better when it comes to conservation, and develop eco-friendly families, schools, communities, and transport services'.

Secondly, Xi reiterates the need for everyone not just government agencies to get involved. He proposes to establish an 'environmental governance system in which government takes the lead, enterprises assume main responsibility, and social organisations and the public also participate'. In other words, environmental protection in China continues to follow a top-down approach and is not going to change. Though, Xi recognises the role of civil society but it has to act as axillary bodies or assisting agencies to government in the environmental governance.

More importantly, Xi stressed that China will actively be part of global environmental governance and honors its commitments on emissions reduction. As a matter of fact, China has voluntarily proposed to reduce by 40–45 percent the intensity of carbon dioxide emissions per unit of GDP by 2020 compared to the level of 2005 paving the way for 'nationally determined contributions', the historic clause of Paris Climate Agreement (Ranjan 2016).

Thirdly, China will intensify the protection of ecosystems. Xi empathised that there will be major projects to 'protect and restore key ecosystems, improve the system of shields for ecological security, and develop ecological corridors and Biodiversity protection networks, so as to strengthen the quality and stability of ecosystems. In addition, diversified market-based mechanisms for ecological compensation will be set up' (Xi 2017: 46–7).

Finally, China will also reform the environmental regulation system by strengthening overall planning, organisation, and leadership for building an ecological civilisation. Regulatory agencies will be established to manage state-owned natural resource assets and monitor natural ecosystems, and improve environmental management systems. Institutional reform is a key to solving the environmental problems. Xi says 'will establish regulatory agencies to manage state-owned natural resource assets and monitor natural ecosystems, and improve environmental management systems. These agencies will, in a unified way perform the duties of the owner of public-owned natural resource assets, the duties of regulating the use of all territorial space and protecting and restoring ecosystems, and the duties of monitoring the discharge of all pollutants in urban and rural areas and conducting administrative law enforcement' (Xi 2017: 47). In fact, by creating Ministry of Ecology and Environment, China has already implemented it, proving that China is seriously redesigning its environmental institutions to provide more efficiently and effectively curb pollutions and improve ecology, which has been dealt in earlier in this chapter.

In addition, Xi also infuses his thoughts to establish a 'Socialist ecological civilisation' and to develop a new model of modernisation with humans developing in harmony with nature. Put it differently, China is establishing a different model of 'ecological modernisation' with Socialist characteristics, whereby Party-State is taking the lead role in environmental protection and civil society and people act as enabler to build Beautiful China.

Xi Jinping, speaking at the National Ecological and Environment Conference, Beijing, held on 18–19 May 2018, reiterated that 'we must consciously integrate economic and social development with the building of an ecological civilisation' and 'building an ecological civilisation is of fundamental importance for the sustainable development of the Chinese nation' (Xi 2018). Further, he stressed that 'ecology and environment is a major political issue for Party's mission and also a major social issue that affects the people's livelihood' (ibid). Therefore, it's urgent to meet public expectations by stepping up the building of ecological civilisation.

Xi expanded the scope to construct 'global ecological civilisation' and advocated getting deeply involved in global environmental governance to come up with a worldwide solution for environmental protection and sustainable development, while guiding international cooperation to tackle climate change (ibid). The US withdrawal from Paris Agreement and increasing commitments from China to tackle climate change and Xi's push for constructing global ecological civilisation indicates that Beijing is rapidly increasing its international profile as a responsible global power.

Apparently, these attitudinal changes in Party-State towards environmental protection clearly demarcate the departure from earlier policy of 'development first' and indicates a new era with focus on simultaneously striving for economic, social and ecological progress.

Firstly, the civil society has become increasingly active in putting pressure on governments to clean up the environment (Huang et al. 2010: 237). Several serious environmental incidents have demonstrated the increasing power of the public in blocking development projects that may cause negative environmental impact in the long run, including the 26 Degree Air-conditioner Energy Reduction Campaign in 2004 (*People's Daily* 2004), the case of Yuanmingyuan Park Water Retaining Project in 2005 (Pu 2007, the Nu River Dam Event in 2005 (Jim 2017) and the Anti-PX Chemical Project Movement at Xiamen City in 2007 (Tang 2008).

Secondly, both WTO accession and the Olympic Games in 2008 pressured the Chinese government to pay more attention to environmental problems. The accession to the WTO in 2001 focussed China's attention on the need to develop sound and transparent environmental regulations while Beijing's successful bid to host the 2008 Olympic Games provided the expected external pressure on the government to clean up the environment (Shi and Zhang 2006: 275 and Liu and Diamond 2005: 1198).

Thirdly, environmental degradations, air and water pollutions are easily visible and felt by residents, thereby higher officials could no longer ignore an unchecked developmental drive. Zhengning Pu and Jiasha Fu in their study meticulously confirm the role of economic growth and environmental sustainability has in Mayor's promotion in China (Pu and Fu 2018). In China, local officials, often have one term of five years or two terms for their current positions. Then officials are evaluated on certain yardsticks to be promoted or not. However, since the 1980s, local economic growth has been one of the key parameters along with political achievement. Interestingly with 'regime shift' (Kahn and Zheng 2017) and growing importance of environmental protection, environmental sustainability is gradually becoming one of the yardsticks on which local leaders are evaluated. Pu and Fu are in view that pollution especially the industrial waste water acts as an obstruction to promotion (Pu and Fu 2018: 458), but not across all regions of China. Therefore, it is becoming inevitable for local leaders in China to give due considerations to environmental sustainability as economic growth is no longer seen as only major indicator of development.

## Conclusion

The ideas and attitudes of China's top leadership have changed drastically over the past decade. These are evident from the top leaders' ever increasing focus on environmental protection. For instance, Hu Jintao's harmonious development and Xi Jinping's emphasis on 'ecological civilisation' and 'Beautiful China'..The government has become increasingly aware of the urgent need to halt environmental deterioration because of its adverse effects. This deepening environment crisis has led China to transform her environmental policy. The civil society has also become increasingly active in putting pressure on governments to clean up the environment. In addition, several major environmental incidents have demonstrated the increasing power of the public in blocking development projects that may cause negative environmental impact in the long term. Thus, these factors have compelled China to adopt comprehensive measures for environmental protection.

The Report to the 19th Party Congress can be seen as heralding new reforms in environmental management, governance, protection and movement. Seeing this commitment coming from core leader Xi Jinping, is not an empty word but as mentioned in the chapter elsewhere and empirical evidence suggests these shift in attitudes are backed by overhauling legal apparatus, reforming existing out dated laws and strong and effective enforcement. The Report to the 19th Party Congress also made it clear that environmental protection in China would continue to be top-down approach. Though, market will be a key instrument in environmental protection but how much space will be shared with civil society only time can tell. Moreover, these lofty goals of ecological reforms are not easy but challenging tasks and if implemented in true spirit then definitely China can achieve its third centenary goal (if one), of ' Socialist Ecological Civilisation'.

## NOTES

1. 11th National People's Congress in its first session replaced State Environmental Protection Administration (SEPA) with Ministry of Environmental Protection of the People's Republic of China (MEP) in March 2008. For more details, see "Hua Jianmin: Ministry of Environmental Protection established to bolster environmental protection effort" (华建敏：组建环境保护部加大环境保护力度), 11 March 2008, *Sina*, http://news.sina.com.cn/c/2008-03-11/152315124637.shtml (accessed on 14 November 2017).
2. For more discussions on 人定胜天 and 天人合一, see, Wang Weiluo, 从中国传统文化看 "人定胜天" 的本意 (*cong zhongguo chuantong wenhua kan rending shengtian de benyi*) People's Daily, 13 January 2005, http://www.people.com.cn/GB/ huanbao/35525/3116590.html (accessed on 25 October 2017).

## REFERENCES


11th National People's Congress in its first session replaced State Environmental Protection Administration (SEPA) with Ministry of Environmental Protection of the People's Republic of China (MEP) in March 2008. For more details, see *Sina*. 2008. 华建敏：组建环境保护部加大环境保护力度, *Hua Jian min: Zujian huanjing baohu bu jia da huanjing baohu lidu* [Hua Jianmin: Ministry of Environmental Protection established to bolster environmental protection effort] , 11 March, http://news.sina.com.cn/c/2008-03-11/152315124637.shtml (accessed on 14 November 2017)

2004. 全国人民代表大会，中国人民共和国环境保护法， *Quanguo renmín daibiao dahuì, zhongguo renmin gongheguo huanjing baohu fa* [National People's Congress, 'Environmental Protection Law of China'], 25 April, http://www.npc.gov.cn/npc/ xinwen/2014-04/25/content_1861279.htm (accessed on 5 September 2017).

2012. 美丽中国, 省会及副省级城市建设水平（2012）研究报告, *Meili zhongguo shenghui ji fu sheng ji chengshi jianshe shuiping (2012) yan jiu baogao* [Sichuan University, "Beautiful China: Provincial Capital and sub-provincial level City Construction Research Report, 'Beautiful China' Evaluation Task Force"], http://media.people.com.cn/ n/2012/1225/c54431-20012648.html (accessed on 2 October 2017).

2014. 中华人民共和国环境保护发自2015年一月一日起施行, *Zhonghua renmin gongheguo huanjing baohu fa zi 2015 nian yi yue yi ri qi shixing* [Ministry of Ecology and Environment, Environmental Protection Law of the People's Republic of China, 2014], 25 April, http://zfs.mep.gov.cn/fl/201404/t20140425_271040_wap.shtml (accessed on 25 October 2017).

Boxer, B. 1989. 'China's environmental prospects'. *Asian Survey*, 29 (7), pp. 669–686.

Chen, Gang. 2009. *Politics of China's Environmental Protection: Problems and Progress* (Vol. 17). Singapore: World Scientific.

Chunmei, W. and Zhaolan, L. 2010. 'Environmental policies in China over the past 10 years: progress, problems and prospects'. *Procedia Environmental Sciences, 2,* pp. 1701-1712.

DuPont, A. 2001. *East Asia Imperilled: Transnational Challenges to Security.* Cambridge: Cambridge University Press, p. 52.

Economy, E. C. 2010. *The River Runs Black: The Environmental Challenge to China's Future.* New York: Cornell University Press.

Gan Kaipeng. 2011. *Proceedings of the 8th International Conference on Innovation & Management.* November 30-December 2, Kitakyushu, Japan, p. 172

Ho, Peter. 2001. 'Greening Without Conflict? Environmentalism, NGOs and Civil Society in China', *Development and Change,* 32(5): pp.893–921

Hu Jintao. 2012. Full text of Hu Jintao's Report at 18th Party Congress, *People's Daily Online,* 8 November, http://en.people.cn/90785/8024777.html (accessed on 5 September 2017).

Huang X, Zhao D, Brown, C.G., Wu Y and Waldron, S. A. 2010. 'Environmental issues and policy priorities in China: a content analysis of government documents', *China: An International Journal, 8*(02), p.237.

Information Office of the State Council of the People's Republic of China. 1996. 'Green GDP Accounting Study Report 2004, issued', http://www.gov.cn/english/2006-09/11/ content_384596.htm (accessed on 11 March 2008).

Information Office of the State Council of the People's Republic of China. 1996. '*Environmental Protection in China (1996-2005)',* http://www.china.org.cn/english/2006/Jun/170355.htm#3 (accessed on 26 October 2016).

Information Office of the State Council of the People's Republic of China. 2002. 'Environmental Protection in China', 9 July, http://www.fmprc.gov.cn/mfa_eng/topics_665678/3711_665954/t18990.shtml (accessed on 25 October 2016).

Information Office of the State Council of the People's Republic of China. 2006. '*White Paper* on Environmental Projection 1996-2005', http://www.china.org.cn/english/MATERIAL/170257.htm (accessed on 11 March 2008).

Jahiel, A. R. 1998. 'The organization of environmental protection in China', *The China Quarterly, 156,* pp.757–787.

Kahn, M.E. and Zheng S. 2016. *Blue Skies over Beijing: Economic Growth and the Environment in China.* Princeton University Press.

Liu Jianguo and Diamond, J. 2005. 'China's Environment in a Globalizing World', *Nature,* 435 (7046).

Li Yang. 2014. 'Protect environment by allowing public litigation', *China Daily,* 18 April, http://www.chinadaily.com.cn/opinion/2014-04/18/content_17446560.htm (accessed on 5 October 2017).

Lau Lynia. 2014. 'China's Newly Revised Environmental Protection Law', *Clyde & Co,* 24 April, https://www.clydeco.com/insight/article/chinas-newly-revised-environmental-protection-law (accessed on 5 October 2017).

National People's Congress of People's Republic of China. 1989. 'Environmental Protection Law of the People's Republic of China', http://www.npc.gov.cn/englishnpc/Law/2007-12/12/content_1383917.htm (accessed on 15 March 2018).

National Development and Reform Commission. 2016. 'The 13th Five-Year Plan For Economic and Social Development of the People's Republic of China, (2016-2020)', http://en.ndrc.

gov.cn/newsrelease/201612/P020161207645765233498.pdf (accessed on 5 September, 2017).

Palmer, M. 1998. 'Environmental regulation in the People's Republic of China: The face of domestic law'. *The China Quarterly, 156*, pp.788–808.

*People's Daily*. 2004. '*26-degree Campaign* launched to save energy in Beijing', 27 June, http://en.people.cn/200406/27/eng20040627_147675.html (accessed on 7 October 2017).

Pu Yufei. 2007. 'Transparency and Public Participation in Water Resources Management in China', State Information Centre, http://siteresources.worldbank.org/INTEAPREGTOPENVIRONMENT/Resources/ReportwatergovernancePuYFEN662007Edited.pdf (accessed on October 7, 2017).

Pu Z. and Fu J. 2018. 'Economic Growth, Environmental Sustainability and China Mayors' Promotion', *Journal of Cleaner Production*, 172, pp.454–465.

Ranjan, Rajiv. 2016. 'Paris Climate Agreement: Triumph for Developed Nations, Compromise for Developing Ones', *The Dialogue*, 13 April, http://www.thedialogue.co/paris-climate-agreement-triumph-developed-nations-compromise-developing-ones/ (accessed on 5 December 2017).

Shi Han and Zhang L. 2006. 'China's environmental governance of rapid industrialisation'. *Environmental Politics*, 15 (02), pp.271–292.

Standaert, Michael. 2017. 'Have Chinese missed the takeaway from Xi Jinping's environmental message?' *South China Morning Post*, 12 November, http://www.scmp.com/week-asia/politics/article/2119391/have-chinese-missed-takeaway-xis-environmental-message (accessed on 23 January 2018).

Tang Hao. 2008. 'Xiamen PX: a turning point?', *China Dialogue*, 16 January, https://www. chinadialogue.net/article/1626-Xiamen-PX-a-turning-point (accessed on 7 October 2017).

Wang Weiluo. 2005. 从中国传统文化看"人定胜天"的本意, *Cong zhongguo chuantong wenhua kan "rendingshengtian" de benyi* [Understand the meaning of 'Man must conquer Heaven' from Chinese Traditional Culture], *People's Daily*, 13 January, http://www.people.com.cn/GB/huanbao/35525/3116590.html (accessed on March 5, 2018).

World Bank. 2007. 'Cost of pollution in China: Economic Estimates of Physical Damages', Washington.

Xi Jinping. 2017. 'Secure a Decisive Victory in Building a Moderately Prosperous Society in All Respects and Strive for the Great Success of Socialism with Chinese Characteristics for a New Era', Delivered at the 19th National Congress of the Communist Party of China, 18 October, http://www.xinhuanet.com/english/download/Xi_Jinping's_report_at_19th_CPC_ National_Congress.pdf (accessed on 14 November 2017).

*Xinhua*. 2017. 习近平指出，加快生态文明体制改革，建设美丽中国, *Xi Jinping zhichu, jia kuai shengtai wenming zhidu gaige, jianshe meili zhongguo* [Xi Jinping pointed out to speed up the reform of ecological civilization system and building a beautiful China], 18 October, http://news.xinhuanet.com/politics/19cpcnc/2017-10/18/c_1121820882.htm (accessed on 22 October 2017).

*Xinhua*. 2018. 习近平出席全国生态环境保护大会并发表重要讲话, *Xi Jinping chuxi quanguo shengtai huanjing baohu dahui bing fabiao zhongyao jianghua* [Xi Jinping attended the National Conference on Ecology Environment Protection and delivered an important speech], 19 May, http://www.gov.cn/xinwen/2018-05/19/content_5292116.htm (accessed on 5 June 2018).

Yang, Wangli. 2018. 'New ecological environment ministry is a milestone', *People's Daily*, 17 March, http://www.chinadaily.com.cn/a/201803/17/WS5aacdb1da3106e7dcc142418.html (accessed on 23 March 2018).

Yardley, Jim. 2005. 'Seeking a Public Voice on China's 'Angry River', *The New York Times*, 26 December, http://www.nytimes.com/2005/12/26/world/asia/seeking-a-public-voice-on-chinas-angry-river.html (accessed on 7 October 2017).

Zheng, Jinran. 2017. 'Provincial pollution checks uncover problems', *China Daily*, 31 March, http://www.chinadaily.com.cn/china/2017-05/31/content_29553812.htm (accessed on 5 December 2017).

# IV. ETHNIC QUESTION

# 21

# Nationality Work under the Fifth-Generation Leadership:
## The Xinjiang Question

*Debasish Chaudhuri*

Territorial sovereignty and national as well as inter-ethnic unity are continued to be an important aspects of Chinese politics due to persistent threat to national security and stability posed by ethno-national movements in Xinjiang and Tibet, Taiwan issue, and protests against PRC's policies in Hong Kong. The knife attack in Kunming railway station and series of violence in Xinjiang since 2013 gave clear indication to the new leadership that neither interethnic relations nor security situation improved since the Lhasa riots and months-long unrests in the Tibetan areas in other provinces in 2008 and Urumqi riots in 2009. In this backdrop the fifth generation leadership in China time to time expressed their determination that territorial sovereignty and national integration would not be compromised under any circumstance. Importance of national unity (*minzu tuanjie*) has been given utmost priority in official minority discourse following the Central Nationality Work Conference in 2014.

It is believed in China that Xi Jinping's vision of rejuvenation of Chinese nation and realisation of "China dream" (*Zhongguo meng*) effectively embrace 56 ethnic groups of the country and increase cohesion of Chinese nation (*Zhonghua minzu*). The millennium dream of national revival also encapsulated Hu Jintao's concept of national glory and humiliation in socialism (*shehui zhuyi rongruguan*). Xi Jinping's another visionary plan of building global connectivity through 'one belt one road' (OBOR) projects is also considered to be an effective antidote of some of the protracted ethno-national movements in China's border lands especially in Xinjiang, which has been designated as the 'core' region in the Silk Road Economic Belt' in the 13$^{th}$ Five Year Plan. In order to bring positive change in the present state of affairs in minority regions, Xi Jinping also emphasise poverty alleviation and building of well-off society. 'Xi Jinping Thought on Socialism with Chinese Characteristics for a New Era', enshrined in the newly amended constitution in the recently concluded 19th Party Congress suggests that new opportunities would be created for the minorities and minority areas. The main focus of the paper is to examine nationality work under the fifth generation leadership and highlight important points addressed in the 19th Party Congress in October 2017. The paper takes Uyghur case to substantiate arguments regarding effectiveness of ethnic policy under the present leadership.

## Nationality Work since 1949

Without having much knowledge about the non-Han population, the Communist Party of China in the initial years of its history uncritically accepted the Soviet style debate on the right to self-determination of minorities and federalism. The 'Sinification' of Marxism in China and evolution of CPC's thinking of national condition (guoqing) changed CPC's earlier position. The system of ethno-regional autonomy was devised and a host of new institutions dealing with minority affairs came into existence. Despite conscious efforts to formulate ethnic policies suitable for Chinese condition, the Soviet legacy, especially the latter's experience of denationalising minority regions through revolutionary means and confining national minorities within designated geographical area, identification of national minorities and minority languages on the basis of Joseph Stalin's definition of nation have had lingering effects on the Party's thinking on Nationality Work.

Being the ultimate authority to formulate theoretical foundation on National Question and determine course of nationalities work, the CPC adopted strategic approach to deal with the vast swath of peripheral land occupied by various non-Han national minority groups. And its ethnic policies increasingly came under the influence of Han supremacy, revolutionary excesses, cultural pretensions as well as genuine efforts for welfare of the masses. The scholars and experts working on the field played marginal role of researcher, interpreter and propagator whereas Party cadres and top leadership took charge of taking decision in the minority affairs and minority regions practically without even trying to make any consensus with the former.This situation changed to a certain extent in the reform period that allowed scholars from different disciplines of social sciences to revisit and even challenge the existing ethnic policies.

The Nationality Work in the PRC can be divided into following phases:

**1949-1957:** The main concern during this period was to win the trust of national minorities and gradualism was considered to be an accepted norm of handling issues related to minorities and the minority dominated areas of

China. The Party leadership was equally critical of local nationalism and Han chauvinism.

**1957-1965:** There was growing impatience towards 'special characteristics' of minorities.

**1966-1971:** Revolutionary integration and assimilation were emphasised and most of the original ideas of the National Question and Nationality Work were repealed. The religious and cultural traditions of national minorities suffered maximum repression during this phase.

**1971-1977:** Intensity of repression began to subside and more tolerant approach to minorities made a gradual return.

**1978-1989:** With the dilution of Socialist ideology in the reform ear, the CPC focused on performance in economic development and wanted to gain political legitimacy by mobilising every section of the population including minorities in the process of economic modernisation. This is widely seen as a phase of accommodative nationalities and religious policy. The national economic development was planned in accordance to Deng Xiaoping's concept of *liang ge daju* (two general situations) and the minority dominated interior provinces were asked to take interest in the development as a whole and have patience for their turn until the coastal Provinces achieved a certain level of development. The consequence of this policy was however not evident until the late 1980s. Protests and riots broke out for the first time in the reform period in Tibet in September 1987 which made coercive approach to be part of Nationality Work again. The accommodative phase of minority policies virtually came to an end following the massacre of demonstrators in the Tian'anmen in1989.

**1990-till date:** This phase is characterised by conservative treatment of ethnic dissent, coercion, and increasing development gaps between regions, between urban and rural areas as well as among various social and ethnic groups. The central leadership acknowledged growing complexity in the relations between national minorities vis-à-vis the Chinese Party-State and the Han majority. To meet the challenge the government planned to hold Central Nationality Work Conferences on regular intervals. During the tenure of Jiang Zemin two Nationality Work Conferences were held in 1992 and 1999 and one was held under the leadership of Hu Jintao in 2005. The Party acknowledged that Nationality Work was a complex and protracted affair. Speedy economic development, expansion of social institutions, and self-reliance for development in the minority regions were given priority. The ethno-regional autonomy was projected as an important component of Chinese political system. The highest Party cadres called for fostering large number of ethnic cadres. This period was also marked by some of the major national and international incidents like rise of separatist violence in Xinjiang, subsequent strike hard measures, world-wide anti-terrorist war following 9-11 incidents in 2001 and riots in Lhasa and Urumqi in 2008 and 2009 respectively.

## Academic Debates

One of the most prominent academic discourses on Nationality in the reform period was Fei Xiaotong's theory of "Plurality and Unity in the Configuration of the Chinese people" (*"Zhonghua minzu duoyuan yiti geju" lilun*). This theory stresses the unity of Chinese nation of all nationalities with the Han at the centre and expounds that cohesive force (*ningjuli*) of the national identity lies in the historical development of the Han nation. This further emphasises primordial ties between ancient ethnic confederation (*minzu gongtongti* or *minzu jituan*), *Huaxia* and the present Han people. It is argued that ethnic confederation developed into a single entity (*yiti*) from a number of smaller groups. The presence of smaller ethnic groups within the single entity is what Fei Xiaotong described as plurality (*duoyuan*). Fei Xiaotong provided theoretical basis of the official discourse of national unity and Han centric Chinese nation (*zhonghua minzu*) (Fei 1988).

In the face of deteriorating inter-ethnic relations and separatist violence in Xinjiang since 1990s, a section of Chinese academics and scholars of ethnology began to probe into the existing ethnic policies in the country since late 1990s. This scholarly debate was focussed around the following issues: excessive Soviet influence on the ideological orientation of ethnic policies and Nationality Work; definition of Chinese terms 'nation' (*minzu*) and 'ethnic group' (*zuqun*); whether 55 ethnic minorities in China are equivalent to nation; lessons from the Soviet disintegration and improvement in race relations in America; increasing sensitivity towards political rights, territorial segmentation and demographic segregation of all minorities; dilution of political consciousness, promotion of exchanges, interactions and blending among national minorities; effectiveness of ethno-regional autonomous system; individual rights of the citizens and collective rights of individual ethnic groups; conflict of interests among masses; consolidation of Chinese nation (*zhonghua minzu*); depoliticisation of minority policy and promotion of culturalism; need for Second Generation of National Minority Policy (Ma 2014).

There was however another section of scholars who questioned the validity of these arguments. It has been observed by some that the Soviet Union broke down into smaller Nation-States within a short span of seventy years because it came into existence as a united multinational Socialist Republic only in 1922. In contrast, China has been a unified country of numerous ethnic groups for over two thousand years; therefore it would not collapse the way the former did. Moreover, ethno-regional autonomous system in China is not modelled after the federalism practised by the erstwhile Soviet Union. The problem lies not in the existing autonomous system of China but in the implementation of the autonomy law. However, it is commonly acknowledged that preferential treatment of ethnic minorities is the most questionable component of ethnic policy in China. In fact, inequality among various national minorities is the source of many problems. There will be wide range of inter-ethnic interactions, harmony and ethnic blending only when disparity between the Han and ethnic minorities will be eliminate in the real sense. Merely defining all minorities of China in terms of culture will neither resolve nationality problem nor depoliticise ethnic policies. Finally, the proposed second generation minority policy trivialises both cultural plurality and national identity among many ethnic communities in China (Chang 2013: 7-9).

The scholars belonging to both sides of the debate endorsed that the nationality problem will be resolved in the process of China's development and all non-Han nationalities and the Han will be blended with each other and emerged as the closely connected, unified and monolithic entity of Chinese nation. In this regard both draw inspiration from Fei Xiaotong's theory of plurality and unity of the Chinese people. The proponents of culturally oriented ethnicity appear to be impatient in resolving national problem and their urge of depoliticising ethnic policy obviate the presence of ethno-national groups with strong sense of national identity in China.

However, it needs to be noted that twenty-two of the total fifty-five national minorities are small in terms of population size[1] and the political significance of each of them is mainly based on the official narrative of their contribution in making Socialist China and their role in building a unified Chinese nation. Though State ethnic policy stress on equality among nationalities, at the policy level, importance of individual minorities varies in respect to geographical proximity with the border, demographic size, area of territory under their jurisdiction, ethnic capital, relations with previous regimes at the centre, history of resistance against the central authorities in China and separatist tendency, cultural and religious affiliation, amount of symbolic value, and other domestic and international factors. The perceived role of a particular group as a unifying agent determines how the State deals with the group and the region they belong to at any specific time. In terms of relative importance, the Uyghur and Tibetan are much ahead of other minorities of China and considered to be serious threat to political stability, national security and glory of the Chinese nation.

## Under Xi Jinping's Leadership

Born in a family of cadres of the CPC and brought up in the turbulent years of Mao's radical politics in the 1960s and 1970s, Xi and most of his princeling comrades in the Party, government, bureaucracy and military have strong faith on 'Communist ideals with Chinese characteristics' and have enough wisdom 'to resist being blinded by the extreme left'. Among the princeling faction of the party, Xi Jinping enjoys special place because of the legacy of his father Xi Zhongxun who suffered under both Mao and Deng for his candid and outspoken nature. The familial connection with the Party not only inculcated in Xi Jinping a sense of filial piety to ensure continuity of the Party rule but also to purify Chinese politics from the menace of corruption, revive its Socialist tradition, and ascertain Party's grip on power (Andrésy 2016: 15-19, 36-7, 77-84). Moreover, as the first head of State from the princeling generation he needed to prove his credential as a wise, powerful and decisive leader.

Unlike his predecessor, Xi Jinping did not have experience of working in the minority regions during his previous appointments. In the beginning of his career as the head of Party, State and military, there were conjectures by some experts that Xi would inherit his father's moderate approach in dealing with national minorities. The elder Xi was respected by both Uyghurs and Tibetans for resolving a difficult ethnic conflict without bloodshed in Xinjiang during the early years of 1950s and for taking personal initiative in cultivating relations with the Dalai Lama and other leaders of the community. He first participated in the 'liberation' of Tibet and later took charge of Tibetan affairs in two phases at the centre. Until now Xi Jinping however did not deviate from the existing official line (Andrésy 2016: 112-14). On the contrary, Xi's highly idealistic vision of rejuvenation of the Chinese nation and the Chinese dream offers very little space for individual minority nationalities (*minzu geti*), especially the groups who have strong sense of national identity. Moreover, it is difficult to ignore the fact that Chinese national dream is not possible without optimum realisation of aspirations of different sections of Chinese society including national minorities.

Nationality Work during the last five years of Xi Jinping's rule will be discussed on the basis a number of important conferences, high level visits of central leadership to minority areas and major appointments of minority cadres and leadership structure in the autonomous regions and prefectures.

## *Conferences on Ethnic Affairs*

Three important conferences, namely, Second Xinjiang Work Forum, Fourth Central Nationality Work Conference and Sixth Tibet Work Forum were held in Beijing between May 2014 and August 2015. The Tibet Work Forums and Nationality Work conferences were already in place since 1980s and 1990s respectively. It was after the Urumqi riots in 2009 that the central leadership felt the urge of having better insight of the problems in Xinjiang and decided to hold Xinjiang Work Forum in 2010 and continue to carry out the Forum every four years. The purpose of the Second Xinjiang Work Forum was to evaluate the achievements of some policies outlined in the previous form. The event turned out to be more significant for the fifth generation leadership because of some violent incidents in Xinjiang and other parts of China since 2013.

The Second Xinjiang Work Forum made following decisions specific to Xinjiang (*Tianshannet* 2016) for proper handling of Xinjiang Work (nationality and religious work) was a major task for the entire Party machinery as well as the whole nation; the central leadership validated Party's Xinjiang policy since 1949 as correct; Xinjiang problem was the most difficult and long-lasting problem; Xi Jinping called for severe blow to terrorist activities in Xinjiang.

The Central Nationality Work Conference deliberated on the on-going academic discussion on ethnic policies in China. The official position clearly endorsed Party's ideological and theoretical discourse on the National question and Nationality Work as well as ethno-regional autonomy and State policies towards minorities. This conference marked the end of open academic debate on the subject. It appeared from the mood of the conference that the leadership was reluctant to tolerate personal opinion of individuals on the issues of State affairs and emphasised on unified thinking on ethnic matters.

The sixth Tibet Work Forum underlined following issues: consolidation people's feelings in TAR and Tibetan areas in four other provinces; ruling Tibet according to law; having complete grasp on the primary condition and particular contradiction of the Tibetan society for building over-all well-off society; carry out long term construction and make Tibet rich and prosperous.

The official release summed up deliberations in these three conferences as Xi Jinping's minzuguan, which stressed following points: Nationality Work was linked to general situation (*daju*) of China and has great significance in the face of new circumstances; national unity is the lifeline of all ethnic groups; proper handling of Nationality Work was crucial for the Party and the people; Socialism with Chinese characteristics was essentially the way to resolve ethnic problem in China; and rapid development is the key to strengthen national unity (*Xinhuanet* 2015).

### *Footprints of Leading Comrades*

The Party leadership under Xi Jinping mostly followed decades-old practice of developing personal rapport with minority cadres and common people through regular meetings and high profile tours to minority areas. In absence of ideological charm of the Party and charisma of the first generation of CPC leaders, this kind of interactions in the reform period, especially since the Party abandoned accommodative policies in 1990s, served the limited purpose of displaying economic achievements in the minority regions, harmonious relations among various ethnic groups and capacity and determination of central government to maintain political stability by fighting against all forms of separatist tendencies. It appears that the visits of fifth generation leaders to minority areas have been restricted to a great extent because of some highly symbolic violent attacks by a section of Uyghur community in 2013 and 2014 including bomb explosion and knife attack at the Urumqi railway station just hours after Xi Jinping concluded his visit to Xinjiang on 30 April 2014. After this incident, apart from Chairperson of CPPCC Yu Zhengsheng, no member of Politburo Standing Committee visited Xinjiang and Tibet.

In the last five years, the visits of the top leadership were mainly restricted to the poverty stricken minority areas of Inner Mongolia, Ningxia, Guangxi, Guizhou, Yunnan, Sichuan, Hunan, and Heilongjiang. Besides visiting Uyghur dominated Kashgar, Xi Jinping travelled to areas inhabited by Dongxiang, Mongol, Bai, Korean, Tujia, Miao, Hui and Hezhe ethnic groups. Interestingly, a small village of Hezhe ethnic group named Bacha, situated in Tongjiang township of Heilongjiang Province was visited by both President Xi Jinping and Premier Li Keqiang. Hezhe is one of the smallest ethnic groups living in eastern fringes of China. After gaining control over a vast territory under a border agreement with Russia in 2008, China has initiated various development projects in this area, as result relative importance of this ethnic group has increased. Bacha also received special attention of the central leadership because of a devastating flood in 2013 summer. Poverty stricken Xiangxi Tujia-Miao Autonomous Prefecture in Hunan Province was another destination of both Xi Jinping and Yu Zhengsheng in 2013 and 2015 respectively. The official discourse on building of well-off society in the minority areas trace personal initiative of President Xi in poverty eradication of Chixi, a village inhabited by She ethnic group in Ningde prefecture (Fujian) when he served as Party chief in the prefecture.

The most important message conveyed by the top leadership during their visits to the minority areas are: national unity and stability are blessings, and separatism and unrest are a curse; poverty alleviation is the major task of the Party and government and none of the minorities will be excluded from China's modernisation process; counter-support system for the border regions needs to be continued; instructions for cadres to act more in accordance to the popular will and give priority to livelihood issue; giving confidence to minority nationalities in preservation and development of their culture; Socialism with Chinese character is the correct path in resolving China's ethnic problem and everyone should have unswerving faith on the party's leadership.

### *Appointments and Participation of Minority Cadres*

While the CPC leadership always value recruitment and training of large number of minority cadres for propaganda purpose and inclusion of increasing number of minority elites within the system, selection and appointments of minority leaders in important positions is still a controversial issue because of deep rooted mistrust and prejudice about non-Han political elites in the Party. Selections of a few minority leaders in the high places in the Party and appointments in the top level administrative position since 18th Party Congress are projected as Xi Jinping's determination to break away from the rising tendency of Han chauvinism. It was during the initial years of the PRC that Mao Zedong warned about both local nationalism and big Han tendency in the Party. There was however no genuine effort to curb this since the Cultural Revolution. Yang Jing's elevation in the Secretariat of the 18th Central Committee and appointment as the Secretary General of State Council, promotion of former Xinjiang Governor Nur Bekri as Deputy Director of NDRC and Director of National Energy Administration, and selection of Cui Yuying, a female Tibetan cadre as Vice Minister of Central Propaganda Department are usually cited as proof of fair treatment towards capable minority cadres (*Duowei News* 2015). Bayanqolu (Mongolian) and Chen Qiufa (Miao), Party secretaries of Jilin and Liaoning are the only two leaders of ethnic origin holding powerful position in the regional Party committees since 2014 and 2017 respectively. Xi is possibly interested to recruit more minority cadres and officials in important positions in order to check dissatisfaction among loyal and efficient minority elites, but he does not want to make alteration in decades old power imbalance at the local levels.

In this regard following quantitative and qualitative information are quite revealing. The national minority delegates in the 19th Party Congress has increased to 262 (11.4 percent) from 248 (10.9 percent) in the previous Congress in 2012. The percentage of minority representatives in the Congress is more than that of the national population, but representation of individual groups is not necessarily proportionate to their population. Moreover, member of ten out of fifty-five national minorities did not participate in both 18th and 19th Congresses. Achang, Dongxiang, Jing, Pulang and Lisu each have one representative in the last two Congresses (Table 1). It is evident that slight increase of number of delegates in two successive Congresses does not indicate improvement of status of minority elites.

The ethnic make-up of leadership structure in the five ethnic autonomous regions according to the latest data clearly shows dominance of Han cadres both in the regional Party Committees and governments. Number of local cadres in the government of Tibet Autonomous Region is somewhat more than the Han cadres (Table 2).

**Table 1: Minority Delegates in the 18th and 19th Party Congresses and Rank in Population**

| *Name* | *Rank* | *18th* | | | *19th* | | | *Name* | *Rank* | *18th* | | | *19th* | | | *Name* | *Rank* | *18th* | | | *19th* | | |
|---|---|---|---|---|---|---|---|---|---|---|---|---|---|---|---|---|---|---|---|---|---|---|---|
| | | *total* | *m* | *f* | *total* | *m* | *f* | | | *total* | *m* | *f* | *total* | *m* | *f* | | | *total* | *m* | *f* | *total* | *m* | *f* |
| Zhuang | 1 | 17 | 12 | 5 | 18 | 8 | 10 | Li | 16 | 4 | 3 | 1 | 3 | 1 | 2 | Daur | 33 | 1 | 1 | 0 | 1 | 0 | 1 |
| Hui | 2 | 38 | 18 | 20 | 38 | 21 | 17 | Kazakh | 17 | 3 | 3 | 0 | 4 | 2 | 2 | Sala | 34 | 1 | 1 | 0 | 1 | 1 | 0 |
| Manchu | 3 | 34 | 22 | 12 | 32 | 12 | 20 | Dai | 18 | 2 | 1 | 1 | 1 | 1 | 0 | Pulang | 35 | 1 | 0 | 1 | 0 | na | na |
| Uyghur | 4 | 12 | 8 | 4 | 13 | 10 | 3 | She | 19 | 3 | 0 | 3 | 5 | 0 | 5 | Tajik | 37 | 1 | 1 | 0 | 1 | 0 | 1 |
| Miao | 5 | 9 | 5 | 4 | 13 | 10 | 3 | Lisu | 20 | 1 | 0 | 1 | 0 | na | na | Achang | 39 | 0 | na | na | 1 | 0 | 1 |
| Yi | 6 | 8 | 5 | 3 | 8 | 3 | 5 | Dongxiang | 21 | 0 | na | na | 1 | 1 | 0 | Nu | 40 | 1 | 0 | 1 | 1 | 0 | 1 |
| Tujia | 7 | 11 | 5 | 6 | 18 | 13 | 5 | Geluo | 22 | 2 | 2 | 0 | 2 | 1 | 1 | Ewenki | 41 | 1 | 0 | 1 | 1 | 1 | 0 |
| Tibetan | 8 | 30 | 21 | 9 | 33 | 19 | 14 | Lahu | 23 | 1 | 0 | 1 | 2 | 2 | 0 | Jing | 42 | 0 | na | na | 1 | 0 | 1 |
| Mongol | 9 | 27 | 16 | 11 | 21 | 13 | 8 | Wa | 24 | 1 | 0 | 1 | 1 | 0 | 1 | Yugu | 47 | 1 | 0 | 1 | 1 | 1 | 0 |
| Dong | 10 | 4 | 1 | 3 | 3 | 1 | 2 | Shui | 25 | 1 | 1 | 0 | 3 | 0 | 3 | Menba | 49 | 1 | 0 | 1 | 1 | 0 | 1 |
| Buyi | 11 | 3 | 1 | 2 | 2 | 0 | 2 | Naxi | 26 | 1 | 0 | 1 | 2 | 2 | 0 | Oroqen | 50 | 1 | 0 | 1 | 1 | 0 | 1 |
| Yao | 12 | 3 | 2 | 1 | 6 | 1 | 5 | Qiang | 27 | 2 | 1 | 1 | 2 | 1 | 1 | Dulong | 51 | 1 | 1 | 0 | 1 | 1 | 0 |
| Bai | 13 | 8 | 6 | 2 | 4 | 3 | 1 | Tu | 28 | 1 | 0 | 1 | 1 | 1 | 0 | Hezhe | 52 | 1 | 1 | 0 | 1 | 1 | 0 |
| Korean | 14 | 5 | 3 | 2 | 9 | 4 | | Xibo | 30 | 2 | 1 | 1 | 3 | 1 | 2 | Gaoshan | 53 | 1 | 1 | 0 | 1 | 1 | 0 |
| Hani | 15 | 1 | 1 | 0 | 1 | 0 | 1 | Kyrgyz | 31 | 1 | 1 | 0 | 1 | 0 | 1 | Luoba | 54 | 1 | 0 | 1 | 1 | 1 | 0 |

*Source:* Six Census Data and List of Delegates in the 18th & 19th Party Congresses

**Table 2: Han and Minority Cadres in Party Committee and Governments in Autonomous Regions**

| *Name* | *Total Han* | *Han Female* | *Total Minorities* | *Ethnic Composition* | *Minority Female* | *Cadres Han/Minority* |
|---|---|---|---|---|---|---|
| Guangxi Zhuang AR (20) | 14 | 1 | 6 | Zhuang 4; Hui 1; Yao 1 | Hui 1 | 7:3 |
| Inner Mongolia AR (19) | 12 | 0 | 7 | Mongol 7 | Mongol 3 | 12:7 |
| Ningxia Hui AR (18) | 14 | 0 | 4 | Hui 4 | Hui 1 | 7:2 |
| Tibet AR (23) | 10 | 0 | 13 | Tibetan 12; Miao 1 | Tibetan 1 | 10:13 |
| Xinjiang Uyghur AR (21) | 13 | 1 | 8 | Uyghur 5; Kazakh 1; Dongxiang 1 | Nil | 13:8 |

*Source:* Data of Regional Party and Government Personnel, http://district.ce.cn/zt/rwk/index.shtml (19-11-2017)

It is evident from the change of ratio between Uyghur and Han, and between Tibetan and Han in regional Party Committees and governments of XUAR and TAR after 2015 that the fifth generation leadership is, on contrary keen to make relatively important ethnic groups numerically insignificant in the political institutions (Table 3).

**Table 3: Change of Ethnic Structure in XUAR and TAR**

| *Categories/units* | *Ratio of between Uyghur and Han and between Tibetan and Han Members* | |
|---|---|---|
| | *Before 2015* | *After 2015* |
| Regional Party Committee of XUAR | 6:15 | 5:15 |
| Regional Party Committee of TAR | 7: 15 | 6: 15 |
| Leaders in XUAR Government | 6:11 | 5:10 |
| Leaders in TAR Government | 8:15 | 8:16 |

*Source:* Gu 2016:193.

## The 19th Party Congress – Document and Doctrine

Xi Jinping in his Report to the 19th Party Congress declared the beginning of new era of Socialism with the Chinese characteristics and stressed the need for addressing 'major conflicts' and contradictions. The document discusses that 'the principal contradiction facing Chinese society in the new era is that between unbalanced and inadequate development and the people's ever-growing needs for better life' (p. 9-10). He emphasised functional aspect of movements of contradiction that leads to social advancement. The Report categorically points out that struggle is needed to confront contradiction and in order to unite and lead people the Party has 'to effectively respond to major challenges, withstand major risks, overcome major obstacles, and address major conflicts, it must undertake a great struggle with many new contemporary features' (p.13). The struggle here has much deeper implications but it definitely means struggle against separatism as well as other anti-State, anti-Party elements. Xi Jinping urged fellow Chinese in the both sides of the Straits to oppose all form of separatist activities. The text does not offer any new formula to improve inter-ethnic relations other than reiteration of usual dictum on ethnic separatism, religious extremism, and other disruptive activities.

Xi also talks about cultural needs and demands for democracy, rule of law, fairness, security, and a better environment. Nevertheless it is clear that the authority intends to reduce all sources of conflicts and contradictions to the economic matters and ensure completion of building moderately prosperous society in China. The Report provides a road map for coordinated regional development strategy which might help the Party State to reduce some major contradictions between and within regions, between rural and urban areas, and between various social and ethnic groups.

## Dealing with Xinjiang Problem

The recent developments in Xinjiang give some idea how the Party-State under the present leadership will practice its Nationality Work in the coming years. Appointment of Chen Quanguo as Party Secretary of Xinjiang in August 2016 in place of Zhang Chunxian and former's elevation to the new Politburo suggests that the central authority was not quite pleased with Zhang's performance in curbing violence in the region. It is widely acknowledged that Chen successfully contained self-immolation in TAR and maintained stability in Tibet and he would be able to use his innovative style to fight against Uyghur separatism and terrorism in China's western frontier. Some observers however believe that this reshuffle was mainly because of factional infighting. There is possibly some truth in it though it is not clear what sort of power play leads to the unceremonious exit of Zhang from a troubled region.

On the basis of various reporting it appears that there were clear tendency of reduction of frequency and intensity of ethnic violence in Xinjiang after it experienced highest casualties of over 450 in 2014. In March 2016, Zhang claimed significant drop of violent incidents in the region and expressed his intension to continue 'high-pressure' security crackdown. Number of violent incidents also began to reduce according to the international media including in Radio Free Asia's Uyghur service in the early 2016 (COI Compilation 2016: 51-2). Increasingly tighter security mechanism and round the clock surveillance in the Uyghur areas since the Urumqi riots is certainly responsible for the containment of separatist violence in the region. Change of leadership when relative peace just started in the region reflected central leadership's intention to destroy the roots of all problems in the Xinjiang and bring an end to the 'people's war' against protracted violence led by the Uyghur community.

Further securitisation is happening in Xinjiang and display of military strength in the form of regular flag march has become a part of life across the region since Chen Quanguo became Party boss. Since the second half of 2016, the Regional Authority has stepped up social control through the following security measures: building convenience police station across cities and rural areas; strengthening everyday policing through mobilisation of ordinary people to assist the authority by reporting about suspicious elements and watching each other's household activities under the 'double-link household system'; imposing restrictions on foreign trips of some citizens by keeping their passports in the police custody; instructing the people to install GPS tracking devices in the private vehicle; mass collections of DNA samples; greater restrictions on religious activities, cultural practices and social customs of the Uyghurs including banning of religious names for the new born children.

On the basis of the results of repressive policies in the region and renewed coercive polices under Chen, it is doubtful whether party's pacification tactics through overall development would be successful in eradicating the spirit of independence and separatist sentiments in Xinjiang and other areas.

## NOTE

1. The population of twenty-two ethnic groups in the 2000 census was less than 10 thousand.

## REFERENCES

Andrésy, Agnès. 2016. *Xi Jinping Red China, the Next Generation*. Lanham: University Press of America.

Chang, Bao. 2013. 转型与反思中的中 国民族政 策与民族理论 – 对中国当代民族研究的 一点体会和评论, *Zhuanxing yu fansi zhong de Zhongguo minzu zhengce yu minzu lilun – dui Zhongguo dangdai minzu yanjiu de yi dian tihui he pinglun* [Transformation and reflection on Chinese ethnic policy and theory of ethnicity], *Sociology of Ethnicity*, Issue no. 134, 30 April, 1-9.

COI Compilation. 2016. 'China: Situation of Uyghurs', Austrian Centre for Country of Origin & Asylum Research and Development, April, www.ecoi.net (accessed on 29 November 2017).

*Duowei News*. 2015. 习近平用人破大 汉主义少数民族崛起, *Xi Jinping yong ren po dahanzhuyi shaoshu minzu jueqi* [Xi Jinping gets rid of Han chauvinism through official recruitments], March, http://www.wenxuecity.com/news/2015/03/01/4067808.html (accessed on 26 April 2015).

Fei Xiaotong. 1988. 'Plurality and Unity in the Configuration of the Chinese People', *The Tanner Lectures on Human Values, Delivered at the Chinese University of Hong Kong*, 15 and 17 November, 166–221. http:// tannerlectures.utah.edu/_documents/a-to-z/f/fei90.pdf (accessed on 21 May 2006).

Gu Mingzhang. 2016. 中国民族问 题与习近平的治理政策, *Zhongguo minzu wenti yu Xi Jinping de zhili cezheng* [Chinese nationalities problem and Xi Jinping's administrative policies], *Taiwan International Studies Quarterly*, Vol. 12, No. 4, 181-208.

Ma Rong 马戎. 2014. 旗帜不变，稳住陈脚，调整思路，务实改革 - 对中 央民族工作会议的解读, *Qizhi bu bian, wen zhu chenjiao, tiaozheng silu, wushi gaige – dui zhongyang minzu gongzuo huiyi de jiedu* [Interpretation of central nationalities work form – continuation of political stand, readjustment of thought, and pragmatic reform], *Sociology of Ethnicity*, Issue no. 172, 30 November, 1-3

*Tianshannet*. 2016. 习近平对做好新疆民族工作重要讲话精神, *Xi Jinping dui zuo hao Xinjiang minzu gongzuo zhongyao jianghua jingshen* [Spirit of Xi Jinping's speech at the Xinjiang nationalities work forum], 31 May, http://china.chinadaily.com.cn/2016-05/31/content_25560156.htm (accessed on 28 August 2017).

*Xinhuanet*. 2015. 习近平的民族观, *Xi Jinping de minzuguan* [Xi Jinping's view on Ethnicity], 24 August, http://news.xinhuanet.com/politics/2015-08/24/c_128160466_3.htm (28-08-17).

# 22

# Tibet Policy in Xi Jinping's 'New Era'

*Tshering Chonzom*

To the relief of the Chinese leadership, the six day long 19th Congress of the Communist Party of China (CPC) concluded successfully on 24 October 2017 without incident. To recall, three Tibetans self-immolated on the eve of the 18th Party Congress (Bhutia 2013) and one on the very day of the Congress, bringing the total number of self-immolations that week to 11 (International Campaign for Tibet 2012).[1] So, what might be in store for China's Tibetan population following the 19th Party Congress?

To a large extent, much of the work on Tibet, while being dealt with separately through mechanisms such as the various Tibet Work Forums, fall under the broad rubric of 'nationality[2] work'.[3] Currently, not only is there a lack of clarity about Xi Jinping's position on Tibet related issues, he has not fully disclosed his views on where he stands on debates within China on the need to reform nationality related policies. Owing to this uncertainty, there has been a tendency between groups on the different poles of the so called '2nd generation ethnic reforms' debate[4] to project Xi's support for their respective positions. For example, Leibold (2014) saw a tendency between the two opposing camps to appropriate Xi's speech at the nationality conference that was held on 28–29 September 2014.

Xi's Political Report to the 19th Party Congress (Xi 2017) does not yet provide any clear lead into his thinking on the matter of nationality or Tibet. People and groups are anyway not singled out for mention in such Reports.[5] Minority nationality related points in Xi's Report appear with respect to a few inter-related themes – such as 'ethnic' unity, united front work, western region development, religious work, and so on. This paper undertakes a critical review of some of these themes in more detail relating it to some of the trends actually observed during the first term of Xi Jinping's leadership.

Apart from relevant secondary materials, the research will refer to the many congregations on nationality work and Tibet work held at the national level,[6] speeches of Chinese leaders during these events and during other important occasions, such as anniversaries and so on. It will also refer to relevant regulations and official documents[7] that concern nationality or Tibet work where available. The paper is a review of the overall ground situation in Tibet during the Xi era to determine the direction of his future Tibet policy.

## Strike Hard Against 'ethnic separatist activities'

While Xi mentioned the term 'ethnic' only 15 times in his Political Report to the 19th Party Congress as opposed to 25 in Hu Jintao's Report to the previous Congress, he specifically mentioned the term 'ethnic separatist activities'. 'Ethnic separatist activities' is a term that came to be used frequently by the regional leadership of the Tibet Autonomous Region (TAR) since a few years. In a September 2015 interview to a newspaper affiliated with the Ministry of Human Resources and Social Security, then regional Party chief, Chen Quanguo (who is now Party chief of Xinjiang) elucidated the scope of 'ethnic separatist activities' (Li 2015). Among others, 'going on overseas pilgrimages to worship the Dalai Lama and attending prayer sessions and lectures, or sending their children and relatives to schools linked to his clique' – that are basically located in India – constitute as separatist activities. He also elaborated some aspects of the punishment to be meted out for such activities: such as disqualification from recruitment to the Party's echelons. The rules issued by local authorities would punish not just current cadres 'holding religious beliefs', but also those who aspire to join the Party in the future by excluding them.

The new rules targeted at the 'Dalai clique' internally indicates a more nuanced understanding as to who the Chinese authorities consider belonging to the so called 'clique'. Not only is there a distinction in terms of the various actors who comprise it, but the authorities also seem to have decided upon a disaggregated strategy of dealing with the respective members of the 'clique', inside and outside. 'Ethnic separatist activities or 'ethnic separatism', therefore, would denote activities by the supposed members of the 'clique' inside Tibet.

Introduction of travel restrictions and arduous new procedures in the procurement of international passports for Tibetans in TAR since April 2012 (*Radio Free Asia* 2013) has been one of the ways to curb the activities of the supposed 'ethnic separatists'. These guidelines were issued following the travel of many Tibetans to Bodh Gaya in Bihar, India's eastern state, to attend the Kalachakra religious gathering presided over by the Dalai Lama (For a comprehensive report on this theme, see *Human Rights Watch* 2015 and *International Campaign for Tibet* 2015). According to these two reports, there has not been a single case in the TAR since 2012 where a Tibetan has been issued an ordinary passport in lieu of the one surrendered following his or her return from India; nor has any new applications for passports been processed. Reportedly, travel restrictions are in place also between the TAR and the other Tibetan areas. Passport curbs and recalls, including travel restrictions were later imposed in parts of Xinjiang as well (*Human Rights Watch* 2016) and are still in place in both Tibet and Xinjiang. The thinking behind restriction on passports as a way to tackle 'ethnic separatist activities' was simple – lack of contact with Tibetans outside would reduce and limit exchange of information, ideas and interactions which would in turn bring down the number of self-immolations and protests. The Chinese state views immolations as the handiwork of outside forces, the 'Dalai clique'.

The TAR was labeled as 'a major battleground against separatism' (Li 2015) by Chen Quanguo on 11 November 2015. Hence, apart from imposing restrictions on Tibetans from travelling within Tibetan areas and abroad, especially to India, the authorities have implemented a new security policy inside the TAR, which involved the setting up of 'convenience police stations … for community based policing' (Zenz and Leibold 2017). According to a *South China Morning Post (SCMP)* report, these stations comprise of 'one-or two-storey concrete structures (that) are stocked with wheelchairs, first aid kits, repair tools, umbrellas and even phone chargers for public use (*SCMP* 2016). They also come equipped with surveillance cameras and guards on 24-hour 'seamless' patrols and can be quickly turned into checkpoints if needed'. Adrian Zenz and James Liebold cite the Ministry of Public Security (Shek 2012) to explain, 'By August 2012, Lhasa had established 161 of these concrete structures with a distance of no more than 500 meters between stations' (Zenz and Leibold 2017). By 2016, the number had increased to 700 according to them. A 2016 *SCMP* report however, cites a lesser number at 156 with 'closest two only 15 meters apart' (*SCMP* 2016). It further mentions that '81,140 units of double-linked households have been formed, covering more than three million residents' across Tibet. Zenz and Leibold further inform that such a method of surveillance in Party parlance is known as 'grid style social management', a practice that segments urban communities into geometric zones so that security staff can systematically observe all activities with the aid of new technologies. In their view, such an approach to securitisation is probably the most 'sophisticated'. Chen, on being transferred to Xinjiang in August 2016, replicated the security policies that had been tried and tested in TAR. Zenz and Leibold (2017) who carried out a comprehensive and empirical analysis of the security personnel recruitment process in TAR and Xinjiang, conclude that the security build-up in Xinjiang will soon surpass that of TAR – during his first year, they have recorded an announcement of 91,000 security related positions compared to 38,000 by all of Xinjiang's private sector.

Xi's thoughts seem to be in consonance with what has transpired on the ground in Tibet. In his Political Report, his mention of 'ethnic separatist activities' figured alongside problems of similar nature to be tackled: such as 'acts of infiltration, subversion, and sabotage, as well as violent and terrorist activities … and religious extremist activities'. All of the above were mentioned under the section on 'national security', taking nationality work a notch higher. Xi stressed the need to work towards maintaining 'ethnic unity' in the face of attempts to 'split China' and 'undermine… social harmony and stability'.

As per a latest report in the *SCMP*, the China Commission for Discipline Inspection, the CPC's anti-graft watchdog, held a closed-door meeting in Beijing in January 2018, heralding a renewed national campaign against organised crime (Mai 2018), commonly known as the 'strike hard campaign' that began in the 1980s and pursued vigorously under the leadership of Jiang Zemin (in 1996 and 2001) as well as during the Hu Jintao period in 2010. The latest call was followed up more than a week later by authorities in Tibet adapting the campaign to suit the local agenda, which has primarily been focused on cracking down on 'separatism'.

The three target groups identified for crackdown were: 'triads' who promoted 'the middle way', 'Dalai surrogates' who operated under the banner of 'culture and environmental protection', as well as those 'who called for the protection of the mother tongue' (Mai 2018). The report, if true, formally targets Tibetans not just on political grounds, but also for speaking out in support of their language and environmental protection. Earlier the government targeted those who propagated 'Tibet independence', the targets now are people supporting the Dalai Lama's 'middle way' approach (MWA), which seeks 'genuine autonomy' within the Chinese State. The authorities do not feel the need to call for crackdown on independence proponents either owing to its sense that it doesn't constitute a majority/threat or they would like to build a narrative around it.[8]

## Religion in China must be Chinese in Orientation

The People's Republic of China, the Nation-State that came about in the mid-20th century is not only 'multi-national', but also multi-religious. Incidentally, its two problematic nationality groups, Uyghurs and Tibetans, are also devotedly religious Muslims and Buddhists respectively. Compared to three mentions in Hu's 2012 Report to the 18th Party Congress, Xi's Report to the 19th Party Congress had six mentions about religion/religious work.

The leadership in Beijing seems to see itself facing a 'new situation and new problems in the Party's religious work', as this is what was stated by Xi in his speech at the national religious work conference in September 2016. New situations obviously would demand newer or innovative policy approaches and especially since these are packaged as problems, counter measures have to be developed in accordance. Xi's solution is to call upon all to study and develop 'socialist religious theory with Chinese characteristics' (*Xinhua* 2016).

According to a *Global Times* report, Xi, in his speech at the religion conference, offered government support to 'sinicise foreign faiths' (Kou 2016). There is however a stark difference in the way news outlets like *Xinhua* interpreted and translated Xi's speech at the religion conference. Notably, the official translation of Xi's Political Report to the 19th Party Congress by *Xinhua* refrain from using the term 'sinicise' – a politically more loaded term – and instead uses the term 'reorient' and 'adapt'. The usage of the term sinicise or sinicisation connotes a comparatively more negative and conservative approach. In his political report to the 19th Party Congress, Xi maintained the need to 'uphold the principle that religions in China must be Chinese in orientation' and must 'adapt themselves to socialist society'. He avowed that 'we will fully implement the Party's basic policy on religious affairs'.

Either owing to translation issues or otherwise, again, another *Global Times* report mentions about a forum that was held on 6 September 2017, very close to the 19th Party Congress, with the theme 'Chinese culture and religious sinicisation'. It was held in Beijing and was attended by leaders of five major religions in China – Buddhism, Taoism, Islam, Catholicism and Christianity (*Global Times* 2017). In a similar meeting earlier in 2015 of 700 representatives of Muslim, Buddhist and Christian religious communities (*SCMP* 2015), Zhang Chunxian,[9] the then Party Secretary of Xinjiang too is said to have called for 'sinicisation' of religions in China. This report by the *SCMP*, like the *Global Times* and *Xinhua* report is in English and hence, there is no way of corroborating with the actual Chinese term used and to verify if anything was lost in translation.

Nevertheless, the statements on the need to adapt/orient/sinicise/localise religions in China convey an overbearing sense of control and imposition. Add to this the comment by Zhang Yijong at a UFWD (United Front Work Department) press conference on 21 October 2017, held alongside the 19th Party Congress, where he stated that Tibetan Buddhism 'originated within China' and 'didn't come in from the outside'. Zhang's comments by implication, portends a more assertive and aggressive policy in China's religious work at home and abroad. Notably, the term religion/religious figured 29 times during his press conference. The national religion conference was also convened after almost a decade – the last one was held in 2001 during Jiang Zemin's leadership – signaling a concerted focus on religious work, in what is termed as a 'new era of Buddhist work' by the Buddhist Association of China (*Xinhua* 2017a).

The implications, along with the revised regulation on religion (See *Xinhua* 2017c) that was promulgated earlier last year on 26 August 2017, are going to be far reaching. To be implemented from 1 February 2018, the new regulation was promulgated again in the context of what is seen as 'changing situations at home and abroad' (*Xinhua* 2017c), something Xi reiterated in his Report to the 19$^{th}$ Party Congress as well. Though it is not clear what the Chinese leadership has in mind when referring to 'changing situations', the following discussion may provide some clues.

Zhang Chunxian for instance, at the 2015 meeting, called for 'sinicisation' of religions in response to 'destructive activities' of 'hostile forces' such as separatism, extremism and illegal religious activities (*SCMP* 2016). Zhu Weiqun, in the *Global Times* report mentioned earlier, was forthcoming in elaborating the 'new religious situations and problems' faced by China as – 'the increasing number of religious people, religious extremism, and foreign forces' infiltration in China through religions' (Kou 2016). The increase in the number of religious believers in China is something that has been discussed internationally too. The Tibetan leadership in exile, including the Dalai Lama, has consistently dwelled on the positive implication of such trends – increase in the number of Buddhist followers in China – under the assumption that a religiously inclined population would be open-minded and just. It is interesting that leaders like Zhu Weiqun who is in charge of religious affairs in the CPPCC have recognised this trend and are advocating counter measures.

With respect to Tibetan Buddhism, a number of measures have been implemented already to deal with these perceived challenges. In mid January 2016, the Buddhist Association of China launched an online database[10] containing 'profiles of 870 verified Living Buddhas' (Cao 2016).[11] The announcement about the creation of such a database was made in December 2015 by none other than Zhu Weiqun himself citing fake rinpoches as a threat to China's 'national security, as they use(d) money they collect to sponsor illegal or even separatist activities in Tibet' (Cui and Luo 2015). Subsequently, about 400 more names were added (*International Campaign for Tibet* 2016) in the late April 2016.

Earlier, on 18 July 2007, the Chinese government's State Administration for Religious Affairs (SARA) issued a regulation known as Order No. 5, to be effective from 1 September 2007, with the explicit aim to exclude 'any foreign organisation or individual' from the reincarnation selection process. In this case too, it is evident that the measure was brought out to counter a perceived external actor. The 2007 regulation basically outlines a number of eligibility conditions, application procedures and the government and religious institutions to be approached for approval, depending on the level of 'impact' of the reincarnated 'monk' (Congressional Executive Commission on China 2007; for the translated document, *International Campaign for Tibet* 2007). Both the above measures would have a bearing on the Dalai Lama's succession, which has been an issue of major debate (Bhutia 2015) for quite some time now.

In the coming years, it would be interesting to see what it means for China's religious communities and nationalities to have to orient and adapt their religious beliefs to Chinese culture.

## Coordinated Regional Development Strategy for Stability and Security

In many ways, Xi seems to be interested in continuing with the dual approach of emphasising economic development and stability/security maintenance – a policy that was adopted since the early 1990s as TAR was opened wider in response to unrelenting protests in the late 1980s. Xi had reiterated this policy when he visited the TAR as the Vice President during the 60th anniversary of the 'peaceful liberation of Tibet'. In a somewhat circular way, he had stated, 'To speed up development holds the key to resolving all issues in Tibet' and 'Social stability provides the very basis for leapfrog development' (*Xinhua* 2011b).

Xi's repeated mention of 'large disparities...between regions' in his Report to the 19th Party Congress is of significance for China's nationalities that inhabit the western part of China. The western region is also co-terminus with other areas that found special mention in Xi's report – 'old revolutionary base areas, areas with large ethnic minority populations, border areas, and poor areas'. While arguing that regional development has become more balanced, he emphasised the need to 'strengthen measures to reach a new stage in the large scale development of the western region'.

In a full section on the aspect of 'Implementing the coordinated regional development strategy', Xi indicated his plans for the same. Apart from promising 'more energy to speeding up the development' of the aforementioned areas, he called for the need to 'put in place new, effective mechanisms to ensure coordinated development of different regions'. Therefore, the strategy of 'coordinated regional development' was seen as necessary in order to truly achieve a 'moderately prosperous society in all respects' by 2020. This would probably involve revisiting the western development programme/strategy put in place since 1999 during the leadership of former top leader Jiang Zemin. We can also expect more 'collaboration on poverty alleviation between the eastern and western regions' as envisioned by Xi in his Report.

To a large extent, Xi would like to approach the national questions in these areas, namely the restive western region, by opening it up 'wider' and sending 'talent' there. As Xi says in the Report:

> 'We will encourage and guide people with talent to work in remote poor areas, border areas with mainly ethnic minority populations, and old revolutionary base areas, as well as in communities and on the frontlines.'

The sending of talent[12] would be part of the aid-cadre and pairing up policy. Both Xi and Zhang Yijong mention these policies of the Chinese government; in the TAR they have formally been in place since the 3rd Forum on Work in Tibet in 1994. Under this scheme, prosperous eastern cities that are tied up with cities in the TAR, among others, provide finance, infrastructure, education, technical, health, and human resource assistance. Economic development for stability maintenance of frontier regions in Xi's schema is linked to 'border security'. Xi avowed in quite a resolute tone, 'We will accelerate development in the border areas, and ensure their stability and security'.

While the Tibetan areas outside the TAR do not fit into the classical definition of a border area, however, their close cultural, social and political linkage with the TAR and its capital Lhasa, the core symbol of Tibetan identity, ensures their inclusion in the leadership's agenda of 'border security' and by extension, China's 'national security'. Since the 5th forum on work in Tibet (2010), which avowed a common/coordinated approach to all Tibetan areas in China, many Tibetan areas in Qinghai and Sichuan[13] too have been paired up with prosperous eastern cities and municipalities. Furthermore, pairing up has been carried out at the intra-provincial level between better off cities and minority areas within Sichuan. It has to be seen if the concerned authorities, primarily the Development Reform Commission, has considered the criticisms against the pairing up policy by officials within China (Jin 2015).

## 'Patriotic United Front' – a Magic Weapon

One of the overbearing rubric under which nationality work and Tibet Work is carried out in China is through the CPC's United Front Works Department (UFWD). A full section of Xi's Political Report was devoted to 'consolidating and developing the Patriotic United Front', as had been done in the previous Political Report by Hu Jintao. The UFWD handles nationality, religious and overseas Chinese affairs, including non-CPC intellectuals and personages.[14] It also uses another organisation called the Chinese People's Political Consultative Conference (CPPCC), an advisory body, to carry out its united front activities.

It has been an important institutional contact for the Tibetan leadership in exile during the three decades long intermittent Sino-Tibetan dialogue process that formally commenced in 1978. Within the UFWD organisational structure, the 7th Bureau is tasked with work related to Tibet and headed by Sithar, a Tibetan national who is due to retire soon. It would be interesting to observe who takes his place as Sithar (along with Zhu Weiqun) had acted as interlocutor from the Chinese side during the Sino-Tibetan dialogue process. The talks stalled owing to lack of a meeting ground and 2010 was the last time that the two sides met.

At a press conference on 21 October 2017 on the sidelines of the 19th Party Congress (UFWD 2017), the UFWD leadership saw itself as an important player in Xi's formulation of a 'new era' (*Xinhua* 2017a). Indeed, at the national religious work conference that was held from 22 to 23 April 2016 (*Xinhua* 2016), Xi called upon the UFWD to take the lead in coordinating responsibilities with various organisations. In his Report to the 19th Party Congress, Xi likened united front work to a 'magic weapon' that will 'ensure the success of the Party' (*Xinhua* 2017b). Under his leadership, China convened the 21st 'CPC Central Committee's Conference on United Front Work' from 18 to 20 May 2015 after a hiatus of about nine years.[15]

Further, highest level of CPC leadership – the PBSC – initiated an effort to draft regulations for its united front work, encompassing delineation of its 'principles, frameworks, priorities and progress' (CPPCC 2015).[16] The regulation finally came into effect from 18 May 2015 and is touted as being historic, marking the entry of united front work into a 'new stage'. Subsequently, China set up a Central Committee leading group on united front work on 30 July 2015 (*Xinhua* 2015) confirming interest and attention on United Front Work at the highest echelons of the leadership. The leading group is tasked with supervision of local Party departments to ensure implementation of 'central leadership's policies on the United Front' (*Xinhua* 2015). Further, as commanded by Xi, the authorities are to pursue 'people of all walks of life, including non-CPC elite, young people from the private sector and overseas Chinese' (*Xinhua* 2015) to enhance and increase support for United Front Work.

Among these target groups, the united front work among overseas Chinese or *huaqiao* (including '*new huaqiao*', implying Chinese citizens living abroad) has come under increased attention recently. Three prominent research articles on the theme of China's United Front Work abroad appeared in 2017 (Brady 2017, Kynge 2017 and Beaumelle 2017). Additionally, there have been news reports discussing China's United Front activities with concern in Australia (Feng 2017), New Zealand (Edwards 2017) and Canada (Blanchfield 2017) among others. While the analysis of the above is beyond the scope of this paper, it may be stated that the UFWD would continue work abroad not just among the *huaqiao* and the *new huaqiao*, it would also expand its 'foreigner management' (Brady 2017) work. As far as Tibet is concerned, 'overseas Tibetans' and Tibet supporters would also be included within this outreach and propaganda work abroad.

Notwithstanding the overseas dimension of its work, from an institutional point of view, Xi, in his Political Report called upon the UFWD to 'encourage more exchanges and interactions among different ethnic groups'. 'Ethnic and religious' work are taken as inter-related, for valid reasons, and hence, early on in his Report, Xi mentions that the 'patriotic United Front' has already accomplished its task in the 'work related to ethnic and religious affairs' with the adoption of 'new approaches'. However, it is clear that the Party realises that there is still much left to be done. Hence, in the area of nationalities work, Xi calls upon the UFWD to assist the different nationalities of China to 'remain closely *united like the seeds of a pomegranate'* that stick together, and work jointly for common prosperity and development'. In its United Front Work, the Party must 'uphold the principle that religions in China must be Chinese in orientation' and help religions in China to 'adapt themselves to Socialist society'.

Interestingly, in March 2018, following the National People's Congress meeting, the CPC released a plan to deepen reform of the Party and State institutions, with the stated aim of engendering collaboration between the Party and State bodies and increasing overall efficiency (*Xinhua* 2018). The plan involved reform in eight main areas, the first being in the CPC Central Committee institutions. Out of the 19 items listed under it, three of them pertain to the UFWD. In this context, the reform measures manifest and are a logical culmination of the leadership's understanding about the inter-relation between nationality and religious work. As a result, even while the State Ethnic Affairs Commission (SEAC) is retained as a department in the State Council, it is to be headed by the UFWD. The State Bureau for Religious Affairs, which was under the State Council, was completely disbanded and merged with the UFWD.[17] As a result, along with overseas Chinese affairs work, the Party body UFWD has now been vested with immense authority in the twin affairs related to nationality and religious work in the new era.

## Conclusion

The discussion in the preceding sections attempted to analyse the various trends in China's nationality policy and Tibet policy in the last few years and gauge the priorities in the coming years, also drawing from latest leadership pronouncements during and following the 19th Party Congress and the expanded role certain institutions (like the UFWD) are slated to play. While Chinese intellectuals and some in the policy circle debated the contours of China's nationality policy in the face of growing unrest in the minority areas such as Tibet in 2008 and Xinjiang in 2009, Xi refrained from openly siding with any camp leaving room for interpretation and adaptation.

On the ground however, efforts have been on to recalibrate in what is viewed as a new and changed internal and external situation, be it in nationality work or religious work in China. As such, not only has the UFWD's authority expanded following the CPC's plan to deepen reform of the Party and State institutions, the various State security apparatus have increasingly found a role in tackling China's nationality problems. Given Xi's emphasis on 'national security' and 'border security', that came up repeatedly in his 19th Party Congress Political Report, it is not likely that there will be a relaxation on this front any time soon. To elaborate, Xi called for 'rigorous' protection against 'ethnic separatist activities' as essential not just for internal stability and 'ethnic unity', but also for safeguarding the country's 'national security'. Xi held such a view much before he took on the top leadership position in China.

For instance, in 2011, in a speech in Lhasa on the 60th anniversary of the signing of the 17 points agreement or what Chinese know as the 'peaceful liberation' of Tibet, Xi, then Vice President, announced, 'Tibet serves as an important national security screen' (*Xinhua* 2011a). Reference to importance of borders and the need to secure it, reinforces the approach of passport curbs implemented in many parts of China now. With the restriction on movement of people out of the restive areas, along with the focus on tackling the 'ethnic' and internal nature of 'separatism', it seems that the authorities are setting priorities on the basis of what they consider as most urgent. They are also being more systematic in their approach. Another important agenda that follows from the traditional approach of clubbing stability maintenance and development work seems to be to focus on opening the western region wider and pushing for more economic development and infrastructure build-up there.

## NOTES

1. Out of the total six immolations in 2017, four were between March and May and two after the 19th Party Congress on 26 November and 23 December (See International Campaign for Tibet 2017 for an updated list of all immolations since 2009).
2. This paper uses the term 'nationality' instead of 'ethnic', which used to be the official and generally accepted nomenclature to refer to groups such as Tibetans in China – such that it was common to see statements like 'China is a multinational country' or terms like 'minority nationality', 'Tibetan nationality' and so on in the Chinese Constitution, official White Papers and so on. This changed in the 1990s and the term being used in all official statements and documents (in the English language), including in academic writing from inside China, is 'ethnic' groups and not nations or nationalities. The Chinese term minzu, however, has remained the same. For example, the Regional National Autonomy Law issued in 1984 abbreviated as RNAL was changed to REAL as a result. The complications arising out of the change in nomenclature is reflected in the confusion over names of institutions such as universities or government departments, as also academic journals that had 'nationality' in their English titles. For example, outside the gate of the newly inaugurated campus of the Southwest Minzu University in Chengdu, Sichuan, there is a huge display embedded on the wall of the gate that reads – Southwest University for Nationalities.
3. 'Nationalities work' is the application of the theory of 'national question'. 'National question' in turn is a term emerging out of Marxist-Leninist theory, which defines a methodology for dealing with specific questions concerning the status of communities

called nations or nationalities (Moseley 1966). The author's use of the terms 'Tibet work' or 'Tibet question' are inspired by the above formulation, though devoid of the ideological component.

4. With one group basically terming the regional national autonomy system being practiced in the People's Republic of China since its inception as archaic and proposing a 'melting pot' approach.
5. With the exception of Hong Kong, Macao and Taiwan who are discussed under a separate section on 'Upholding 'One Country, Two Systems' and Moving toward National Reunification'.
6. To elaborate, since Xi Jinping took office in October 2012, three major conferences have been held in the domain of China's nationalities work, namely, the Central Nationalities Work Conference (September 2014), Conference on United Front Work (May 2015) and Conference on Religions (September 2016). Tibet specific conferences have also been organized, such as the 6th Tibet Work Forum (August 2015) and the 5th Tibet Development Forum (July 2016).
7. China issued a number of White Papers since the 18th Party Congress: three on Tibet, 'Tibet's Path of Development is Driven by an Irresistible Historical Tide' (April 2015), 'Successful Practice of Regional Ethnic Autonomy in Tibet' (Sept 2015), 'Development and Progress of Tibet' (Oct 2013); three white papers on Human Rights were issued consecutively from 2012-14.
8. The Tibet White Paper in 2015 titled 'Tibet's Path of Development is driven by an Irresistible Historical Tide' for example had a full section denouncing the MWA. This is in stark contrast to older White Papers that categorically targeted Tibetan independence as the primary issue of concern.
9. Zhang Chunxian is now a member of the CPC's powerful 25 member Politburo following the 19th Party Congress reshuffle.
10. Here is the link http://hf.tibet.cn/ to what is described as 'Rinpoche check system in Tibetan Buddhism' available on the website of the China Tibet Online http://eng.tibet.cn/ The other places where the link has been mandated to appear are on the websites of the Chinese Buddhist Association and SARA.
11. For a rare criticism of China's religious policy in the context of the database by a Tibetan academic, Jamphel Gyatso, from the Chinese Academy of Social Sciences in Beijing, see International Campaign for Tibet 2016)
12. In mid 2017, already 1,500 teachers were present in Tibet and Xinjiang as a part of the aid programme. The government had plans to dispatch 10,000 more teachers to support local education in the two regions (Xinhua 2017e).
13. The information is as per the author's field findings. The author does not have information about whether these have been implemented in Gansu and Yunnan as well.
14. To get a sense of UFWD work responsibilities within a University system, which also demonstrates the penetrative nature of the institution, not just in politics but also academic life, see: http://eng.cumt.edu.cn/11/b1/c990a70065/page.htm
15. The last one, that is the 20th UFWD Conference during Hu Jintao's rule was held in 2006. The 19th UFWD conference during Jiang Zemin's rule was held in 2000. According to Gerry Groot (2015), 'the citation of the Central Committee in the title of the latest edition of the conference gave it status equal to other CCP central-level work conferences'.
16. The date of commencement of this project and its duration of completion is not clear from the website report as on the one hand it says that the total exercise took one year and five months, on the other, it says that research, field investigation and others were begun since 2012.
17. Likewise, the Overseas Chinese Affairs Office of the State Council was also dissolved and merged into the UFWD.

## REFERENCES

Website of SARA, http://www.sara.gov.cn/

Website of the CPPCC, http://www.cppcc.gov.cn/

Website of the UFWD, http://www.zytzb.gov.cn/tzb2010/index.shtml

Website of the Buddhist Association of China http://www.chinabuddhism.com.cn/

Beaumelle, Marcel Angliviel de la. 2017. 'The United Front Work Department: 'Magic Weapon' at Home and Abroad', *China Brief*, Jamestown Foundation, Vol. 17, No. 9, July, https://jamestown.org / program / united-front-work-department-magic-weapon-home-abroad/ (accessed on 18 September 2017).

Bhutia, Tshering Chonzom. 2013. 'Self-immolations, the Tibet Question and the Way Forward', ICS Analysis, Institute of Chinese Studies, No. 7, March, http://www. icsin.org/ uploads/2015/04/06/8e8fd25536ebc696ea436417afb23d9e.pdf (accessed on 18 February 2018).

Bhutia, Tshering Chonzom. 2015. 'The Dalai Lama's Reincarnation Debate: Unraveling Hype, Identifying Interests', *China Report*, Vol. 51, No. 3, August, http://journals.sagepub.com/doi/abs/10.1177/0009445515587399 (accessed on 12 November 2017).

Blanchfield, Mike. 2017. 'Beware effects of China's 'united front' in Canada: former envoy', *The Canadian Press*, 8 December, https://www.ctvnews.ca/politics/beware-effects-of-china-s-united-front-in-canada-former-envoy-1.3712754 (accessed on 18 January 2018).

Brady, Anne-Marie. 2017. 'Magic Weapons: China's political influence activities under Xi Jinping', 18 September, Kissinger Institute on China and the United States, Wilson Center, https://www.wilsoncenter.org/article/magic-weapons-chinas-political-influence-activities-under-xi-jinping (accessed on 22 December 2017).

Buddhist Association of China. 2017. '中国佛教协会学习十九大精神培训班在京开班' *Zhongguo fojiao xiehui xuexi shijiu da jingshen peixun ban zaijing kai ban*, ['Chinese Buddhist Association begins training classes to learn the spirit of the 19th CPC National Congress at Beijing'], 21 November, http://www.chinabuddhism.com.cn/e/action/Show Info.php?classid= 506&id=38908 (accessed on 21 December 2017).

Cao, Siqi. 2016. 'China launches Living Buddha database to curb impostors', *Global Times*, 19 January, http://www.globaltimes.cn/content/964339.shtml (accessed on 15 September 2017).

Congressional Executive Commission on China (CECC). 2006. 'Communist Party Adds Tibetan Affairs Bureau to the United Front Work Department', 3 October, http://www.cecc.gov/publications/commission-analysis/communist-party-adds-tibetan-affairs-bureau-to-the-united-front (accessed on 18 October 2017).

Congressional Executive Commission on China. 2007. 'Measures on the Management of the Reincarnation of Living Buddhas in Tibetan Buddhism (ICT Translation)', 18 July, http://www.cecc.gov/resources/legal-provisions/measures-on-the-management-of-the-reincarnation-of-living-buddhas-in-0 (accessed on 2 August 2007).

CPPCC. 2015. '中国共产党统一战线工作条例（试行）' 诞生记' *Zhongguo gongchandang tongyi zhanxian gongzuo tiaoli (shixing)' dansheng ji* ['The Birth of the Communist Party of China United Front Work Regulations (Trial)' ], 3 June, http://www.zytzb.gov.cn/tzb2010/tzyw/201506/373ef491cd1548e7af44fbc4dadd0856.shtml (accessed on 15 November 2017).

Cui, Jia and Luo Wangshu. 2015. 'Database of Living Buddhas to help spot fake from real', *China Daily*, 8 December, http://www.chinadaily.com.cn/china/2015-12/08/content_22654676.htm (accessed on 22 October 2017).

Edwards, Bryce. 2017. 'Political Roundup: China's 'magic weapons' in NZ', *New Zealand Herald,* 12 December, http://www.nzherald.co.nz/nz/news/article.cfm?c_id=1&objectid=11958211 (accessed on 15 January 2018).

Feng, Chongyi. 2017. 'How the Chinese Communist Party exerts its influence in Australia: detained professor', *ABC News,* 6 June, http://www.abc.net.au/news/2017-06-06/how-china-uses-its-soft-power-strategy-in-australia/8590610 Originally published as 'Academic Chongyi Feng: profits, freedom and China's 'soft power' in Australia', *The Conversation,* 6 June, http://theconversation.com/academic-chongyi-feng-profits-freedom-and-chinas-soft-power-in-australia-78751 (accessed on 24 October 2017).

*Global Times.* 2017. '5 main religions in China agree to sinicize', 7 September, http://www.globaltimes.cn/content/1065265.shtml (accessed on 19 November 2017).

Groot, Gerry. 2015. 'The Expansion of the United Front Under Xi Jinping', *The China Story Yearbook,* Australian Centre on China in the World, Australian National University, https://www.thechinastory.org/yearbooks/yearbook-2015/forum-ascent/the-expansion-of-the-united-front-under-xi-jinping/ (accessed on 18 February 2018).

*Human Rights Watch.* 2015. 'One Passport, Two Systems: China's Restrictions on Foreign Travel by Tibetans and Others', 13 July, https://www.hrw.org/report/2015/07/13/one-passport-two-systems/chinas-restrictions-foreign-travel-tibetans-and-others (accessed on 17 November 2017).

*Human Rights Watch.* 2016. 'China: Passports Arbitrarily Recalled in Xinjiang', 21 November, https://www.hrw.org/news/2016/11/21/china-passports-arbitrarily-recalled-xinjiang (accessed on 19 November 2017).

International Campaign for Tibet. 2007. 'New State Regulations on Recognition of Tibetan Reincarnates', ICT Briefing Document, 25 September, http://www.savetibet.de/fileadmin/user_upload/content/berichte/Briefing_Papier_Reinkarnationsgesetz.pdf (accessed on 11 September 2017).

International Campaign for Tibet. 2012. 'China's new leadership and Tibet', 16 November, http://www.tibetpolicy.eu/china-s-news-leadership-and-tibet/ (accessed on 27 November 2017).

International Campaign for Tibet. 2015. "'A policy alienating Tibetans' – the denial of passports to Tibetans as China intensifies control," ICT Special Report, 13 July, https://www.savetibet.org/policy-alienating-tibetans-denial-passports-tibetans-china-intensifies-control/ (accessed on 22 September 2017).

International Campaign for Tibet. 2016. 'The 'poisonous fruit' of Tibet's religious policy as China publishes 'Living Buddha' database', 2 May, https://www.savetibet.org/the-poisonous-fruit-of-tibets-religious-policy-as-china-publishes-living-buddha-database/ (accessed on 15 October 2017).

International Campaign for Tibet. 2017. 'Self-immolations by Tibetans', 27 December, https://www.savetibet.org/resources/fact-sheets/self-immolations-by-tibetans/ (accessed on 15 January 2018).

Jin, Wei. 2015. 'Tibet as Recipient of Assistance and Its Sustainable Development', *China Policy Institute Policy Paper,* No. 9, https://www.nottingham.ac.uk/iaps/documents/cpi/policy-papers/cpi-policy-paper-2015-no-9-jin-wei-final-051015.pdf (accessed on 18 September 2017).

Kou, Jie. 2016. 'Meeting calls for religions with Chinese characteristics', *Global Times,* 25 April, http://www.globaltimes.cn/content/979899.shtml (accessed on 8 December 2017).

Kynge, James, Lucy Hornby and Jamil Anderlini. 2017. 'Inside China's secret 'magic weapon' for worldwide influence', *Financial Times,* 26 October, https://www.ft.com/content/ fb2b3934-b004-11e7-beba-5521c713abf4 (accessed on 17 February 2018).

Leibold, James. 2014. 'A Family Divided: The CCP's Central Ethnic Work Conference', *China Brief*, Vol. 14, No. 21, Jamestown Foundation, 7 November, https://jamestown.org/program/a-family-divided-the-ccps-central-ethnic-work-conference/ (accessed on 22 September 2017).

Li, Ruohan. 2015. 'Officials warned of Dalai worship', *Global Times*, 11 November, http://www.globaltimes.cn/content/951991.shtml (accessed on 1 October 2017).

Moseley, George, ed. 1966. *The Party and the National Question in China*. London: MIT Press.

*Radio Free Asia*. 2013. 'Tibetans Face Passport Dilemma', 20 January, https://www.rfa.org/english/news/tibet/passports-01202013213254.html (accessed on 13 January 2018).

*Reuters*. 2017. 'China says no excuses for foreign officials meeting Dalai Lama', 1 October, https://www.reuters.com/article/us-china-congress-tibet/china-says-no-excuses-for-foreign-officials-meeting-dalai-lama-idUSKBN1CQ057 (accessed on 22 February 2018).

Shek, Chung. 2012. 'Twenty-six new convenience police stations have been put into operation in Lhasa, Tibet', *People's Public Security News*, 12 August, http://www.mps.gov.cn/n2255079/n2255804/n2255808/c3872620/content.html (accessed on 14 November 2017).

*South China Morning Post* (*SCMP*). 2015. ' 'Sinicise' religion to combat 'hostile forces': Chinese official', 16 June, http://www.scmp.com/news/china/policies-politics/article/1822607/sinicise-religion-combat-hostile-forces-chinese (accessed on 17 August 2017).

*South China Morning Post* (*SCMP*). 2016. 'Passports taken, more police ... new party boss Chen Quanguo acts to tame Xinjiang with methods used in Tibet', 12 December, http://www.scmp.com/news/china/policies-politics/article/2053739/party-high-flier-uses-his-tibet-model-bid-tame-xinjiang (accessed on 14 December 2017).

TCHRD. 2015. 'China engages in political purge in the name of anti-corruption drive in Tibet', Tibetan Centre for Human Rights and Democracy, 2 February, http://tchrd.org/china-engages-in-political-purge-in-the-name-of-anti-corruption-drive-in-tibet-2/ (accessed on 17 September 2017).

UFWD. 2017. '10月21日 "党的统一战线工作和党的对外交往" 记者招待会' *Dang de tongyi zhanxian gongzuo he dang de duiwai jiaowang' jizhe zhaodai hui*, [Press Conference on CPC's United Front Work and External Exchanges'], 21 October, http://live01.people.com.cn/zhibo/Myapp/Html/Member/html/201710/9_103964_59e9a30d58bdc_quan.html (accessed on 18 March 2018).

Xi Jinping. 2017. 'Secure a Decisive Victory in Building a Moderately Prosperous Society in All Respects and Strive for the Great Success of Socialism with Chinese Characteristics for a New Era', 19th National Congress of the Communist Party of China, *Xinhua*, 18 October, http://www.xinhuanet.com/english/download/Xi_Jinping's_report_at_19th_CPC_National_Congress.pdf (accessed on 18 November 2017).

*Xinhua*. 2011a. 'Full text of speech by Xi Jinping at Tibet's peaceful liberation anniversary conference', 19 July, http://www.china.org.cn/china/2011-07/19/content_23023375.htm (accessed on 12 October 2017).

*Xinhua*. 2011b. 'China's Xi vows to speed up Tibet's development while fighting separatism', 19 July, http://www.globaltimes.cn/content/666873.shtml (accessed on 15 November 2017).

*Xinhua*. 2015. 'China founds central leading group to pool support', 30 July, http://news.xinhuanet.com/english/2015-07/30/c_134464393.htm (accessed on 17 December 2017).

*Xinhua*. 2016. 'China Focus: Xi calls for improved religious work', 23 April, http://news.xinhuanet.com/english/2016-04/23/c_135306131.htm (accessed on 18 October 2017).

*Xinhua*. 2017a. 'Confident Xi begins second term with ambitious promises for 'new era'', 26 October, http://english.qstheory.cn/2017-10/26/c_1121858049.htm (accessed on 11 January 2018).

*Xinhua*. 2017b. 'Full text of Xi Jinping's report at 19th CPC National Congress', 3 November, http://news.xinhuanet.com/english/special/2017-11/03/c_136725942.htm (accessed on 16 January 2018).

*Xinhua*. 2017c. 'China revises regulations on religious affairs', 7 September, http://news.xinhuanet.com/english/2017-09/07/c_136592391.htm (accessed on 19 January 2018).

*Xinhua*. 2017d. 'Confident Xi begins second term with ambitious promises for 'new era'', 26 October, http://english.qstheory.cn/2017-10/26/c_1121858049.htm (accessed on 25 January 2018).

*Xinhua*. 2017e. 'China to select 10,000 volunteer teachers to Xinjiang, Tibet', 16 June, http://www.xinhuanet.com/english/2017-06/16/c_136371362.htm (accessed on 28 January 2018).

*Xinhua*. 2018. 中共中央印发《深化党和国家机构改革方案 *Zhonggong zhongyang yinfa "shenhua dang he guojia jigou gaige fang an"* ['The Central Committee of the Communist Party of China issued a Plan to Deepen the Reform of the Party and State Institutions'], 21 March, http://www.xinhuanet.com/politics/2018-03/21/c_1122570517.htm (accessed on 29 March 2018).

Zenz, Adrian and James Leibold. 2017. 'Chen Quanguo: The Strongman Behind Beijing's Securitization Strategy in Tibet and Xinjiang', *China Brief*, Vol. 17, No. 2, Jamestown Foundation, 21 September, https://jamestown.org/program/chen-quanguo-the-strongman-behind-beijings-securitization-strategy-in-tibet-and-xinjiang/ (accessed on 19 December 2017).

# V. IDEOLOGY, CULTURE AND HISTORY

# 23

# Xi Jinping Thought and China's 'New Era': Ideological Line of the 19th Congress

*Manoranjan Mohanty*[*]

## The Proclamation of Xi Jinping Thought

Analysts around the world who had seen the reforms in China as a set of pragmatic measures launched by Deng Xiaoping in 1978 to gain wealth and power by all possible means were again confronted with an articulate ideological formulation at the 19th Congress of the Communist Party of China (CPC). It is called "Xi Jinping Thought on socialism with Chinese characteristics in the new era" (新时代的中国特色社会主义习近平思想 *xin shidai de zhongguo tese shehui zhuyi xi jinping sixiang*). It was spelt out in the Political Report to the Congress in great detail as 'thought' （思想 *sixiang*） and was incorporated into the Party Constitution on 24 October 2017 as 'Xi Jinping Thought'. Thereafter, many Party documents have made it a common part of their reports and analysis. For example, Premier Li Keqiang in his Work Report to the 13th Session of the National People's Congress (NPC) on 5 March 2018 started his presentation saying:

> At its 19th National Congress, the Party established the position in history, of Xi Jinping Thought on Socialism with Chinese Characteristics for a New Era, and mapped out an inspiring blueprint and a programme of action for securing a decisive victory in building a moderately prosperous society in all respects and for striving for the success of socialism with Chinese characteristics for a new era. This is of great immediate significance and far-reaching historical significance (Li Keqiang 2018: 1).

[*] I am grateful to Ravi Bhoothalingam for his challenging comments on an earlier draft of the paper which helped me greatly in clarifying and reformulating many of the ideas.

It is important to note that the ideological line of the CPC, though stated in the formulations of Xi Jinping Thought, also very much flowed from the various policy perspectives outlined in the Political Report itself and other documents published before regarding, for example, the economy, state and party governance, military, global initiatives, culture and above all the vision of the future envisaged by the Xi leadership. The Central Committee (CC) Communiques of the preceding Party Plenums, the Premier's Work Report to the annual sessions of the NPC, besides the speeches of Xi Jinping himself and above all the two volumes on China's Governance provided enough formulations that finally got into the announcement of Xi Jinping Thought (Xi 2014; 2016; 2017). Yet it was not certain that this big ideological proclamation would be made at the end of the first term of a leader as it is customary to do so at the end of the two terms to bring about a leadership transition and codify the contribution of the outgoing leader in theoretical terms. Theoretical contribution, it should be stressed, is regarded as the highest form of contribution to the historical process in the Marxist tradition. It is also true that posterity may not acknowledge that and is free to reject, ignore or under-emphasise its significance. That Xi Jinping leadership decided to take this extraordinary step at the end of the first term showed a political strategy that was unfolding in China to establish firm leadership to steer a line of development.

When the PRC Constitution was amended in March 2018 ending the two term limit of the President and the Vice-President this political process took even more concrete shape. It showed that Xi Jinping had been able to carry a large section of the Party to accept his personal leadership in steering China in course of the next many years through a set of bold policies on both domestic and global fronts. It also was a major political strategy to package those policies in the form of 'Thought for the New Era'. It should be pointed out that Xi in his Political Report uses not his own name but 'Thought in the New Era'. As the political process unfolded in the subsequent period it became clear that the 19th Congress presented an ideological line that has been described in Chinese press as a landmark in the history of not only the CPC but also the PRC. Whether these assertions represented an ideological legitimation of a powerful leadership of the time which have had parallels before or indeed they amounted to be a major new perspective having implications for policies in all sectors only future would reveal. My hypothesis is advanced even if the latter was the case. In other words, even if Xi's new initiatives give a fresh orientation to the whole range of policies in relation to the economy, society, state, culture, ecology and global affairs this path of development generated a set of problems.

## The Argument

Besides examining the key elements in the ideological line and comparing them with earlier formulations, I argue that though they represented a powerful response to some of the challenges emerging out of the four decades of reforms in China and trends in the global situation, they did not amount to inaugurating an alternative path of transformation for China and the world. The New Era perspective of Xi Jinping and the 19th Party Congress continued the overall focus on achieving economic growth and military strength while improving people's livelihood conditions that was the main orientation of the four-decade old Reforms and Open Door initiated by Deng Xiaoping in 1978. Deng's strategy was based on a clear commitment to the essential features of the two hundred year old path of European industrial revolution including its character in the new stage of globalisation. This model no doubt produced China's success story as it achieved remarkable economic success making China the second largest economy of the world having vastly improved infrastructure and much progress in people's living conditions. But it produced social inequalities and regional disparities that continued to rise, environmental degradation and climate change that caused new suffering for people and social alienation and corruption that continued to acquire new forms.

The interesting thing is that these very problems were recognised by the Chinese regimes both under Hu Jintao and more so by Xi Jinping. Both initiated many serious measures. But the irony is that these problems persisted despite these measures. This is 'China's Success Story and the Success Trap' (Mohanty 2018a). Is it possible that Xi Jinping and his colleagues were determined to grapple with this even more strongly than their predecessors and take China out of the success trap by the ideological, political and organisational initiatives that they had taken? Behind the lofty goal of Building Socialism in the 21st century, fulfilling the goals of the two centenaries – 2021 and 2049 – there may actually be a set of clear challenges economic, social, political and international.

Rather than going for a creative development of socialism in the 21st century that should evince a deep interest in a vision that gave priority to working towards equality of individuals, groups and regions across class, race, religion, ethnicity and gender which has emerged as the central concern in the 21st century, the growth-centric objective to build a strong country seemed to re-emerge as the principal goal of the Xi Jinping regime. Nor does it take people's rights to self-governance at every level as its key principle. Centralised state management of society under direct control and supervision of the Party has got a renewed emphasis both at the 19th Congress and the 13th NPC in March 2018. One does not see any serious commitment to working for achieving dignity and equal respect for all cultures, languages, religions at home and abroad. Even though sustainability and a new relationship between humans and nature did figure in the Political Report the core emphasis was not on this aspect. The new development philosophy while trying to present a multidimensional vision – political, economic, social, cultural and ecological was a positive perspective but it did not explicitly address material, political, cultural, aesthetic and moral needs of human beings. Paradoxically, there was more explicit reference to Marxism and ideological education and party conduct in the 19th Congress documents, but the focus on building strength of China and securing material development were the principal goals which were justified as the nationalist agenda of realising the Chinese Dream of 'great rejuvenation'. This was presented as 'building socialism in the 21st century'.

The main thesis of my paper is that the New Era ideological line of the CPC strengthens the building of a capitalist economy and society in China under the leadership of the CPC and the state structure and the military led by it under the 'core leadership' of Xi Jinping. With new modes of management and legitimation the leadership uses not only traditional elements of power used in the history of the CPC but also modern technological and cultural tools in a global scale. With the removal of term limits by an amendment of the PRC Constitution in March 2018 this development strengthens Xi's ideological and political power at the centre of China's governance system. Centralisation of political power backed by an attempt to legitimise it in the name of Xi Jinping Thought is sought to be justified in the name of completing the agenda set by the preceding Party Congresses. And Xi presenting a view of the changed conditions at home and abroad presented his line of thinking putting it at a high pedestal.

Put in the framework of China's Success Story and the Success Trap, I visualise that the next decades will see more of the successes in China's economic growth even at a medium or a lower rate, continuous improvement in livelihood especially of the middle classes, very advanced infrastructure and increasing global influence that has already attracted global responses. But together with all this China will still be in a trap, unable to overcome the problems of inequality, disparity, alienation and ecological decay and perhaps facing even more unanticipated new problems (Mohanty 2018b). China will no doubt achieve the three landmark goals – 'moderately prosperous society in all respects' by 2020 as set by the Jiang Zemin leadership, 'completing modernisation by 2035' and 'building a strong, modern, socialist country by 2049' as set by Xi Jinping at the 19th Congress. Contrary to many western commentators' speculation, these policies and the ideological line, will most likely keep China united, militarily and industrially strong as the world's leading power. But the irony is that these very policies would maintain the Success Trap even while regime after regime recognised it and tried to initiate measures to move out of it as did Hu Jintao and Xi Jinping thus far (Mohanty 2014). The main reason is that growth-centric economic model with the aim of turning China into a great power and the centralised all-encompassing Party to steer that process, overwhelm all the other goals indicated in the Party programme.[1]

It may be said that the major initiatives on environment and energy and science and technology, especially Xi Jinping's enormous focus on building a digital economy and society may actually address some of these problems more effectively than before. Xi's address to the Chinese Academy of Sciences and Chinese Academy of Engineering on 28 May 2018 in Beijing where he called for efforts to build China as a world leader in science and technology gave clear indications of his line of thought on this issue. That would be the evidence for Xi having successfully led China out of the 'success trap' – a trap that saw the coexistence of high growth with inequality, regional disparity, alienation, corruption etc. in course of implementing Deng Xiaoping's Reform and Open Door policy for four decades. In that sense the jury is out whether Xi Jinping's New Era initiatives would successfully solve these problems to a satisfactory extent. But historical experience with this pattern of growth both in Europe, the US and China shows that preoccupation with growth generates a process of accumulation that is not compatible with basic norms of equality and sustainability.

## Thought (*Sixiang*), Theory (*Lilun*), Outlook (*Guan*) and Ism (*Zhuyi*)

For about a year before the 19th Congress there was speculation that something like Xi Jinping Thought may be announced at the Congress. Especially after the Sixth Plenum of the Central Committee had declared Xi as the 'core' in October 2016 and had stressed the need for the entire Party to function 'in alignment' with the core leadership. Until the Congress, there was the call to everyone to act according to the policies embodied in the 'Xi Jinping's major addresses, new vision, thinking and strategies for China's governance' (Li Keqiang 2017: 11). The declaration of 'core' and the subsequent adoption of 'Xi Jinping Thought' could be explained as a response to the existence of dissidence and opposition to his policies within the party which he wished to defeat. At the same time, seen in a positive frame, they were meant for giving a fresh impetus to China's comprehensive development just as Xi's announcement of 'Chinese Dream for national rejuvenation' did in 2012 November. Together with the sustained anti-corruption campaign and the reorganisation and replacement of military command, these indicated Xi Jinping's method of not only consolidation of his personal leadership over the Party, armed forces, state and society but also pushing forward an agenda of China's development into a new stage. This was not the first time that such an ideological exercise was done.

When Mao Zedong's theoretical advisers wrote an ideological draft using the term 'Maoism' (毛泽东主义 *Mao Zedong Zhuyi*) he struck down *Zhuyi* (主义) and wrote 'Thought' (思想 *sixiang*) instead. He gave the status of 'Ism' (*zhuyi*) to the founders of communist theory and socialist revolution, Marx and Lenin. The history of this ideological process in China from 1945 till the Cultural Revolution when it was raised to the level of a cult is well known (Mohanty 1977). The architect of China's reforms, Deng Xiaoping, did not announce a theory when he was in direct command formulating and directing reform policies from 1978 till 1992. The momentous formulation of 'Reform and Open Door' (改革开放 *gaige kaifang*) was attributed to the historic 'Third Plenum' of the 11th Central Committee in December 1978 and 'socialist market economy' to the 13th Congress of the CPC in 1987 and 'socialism with Chinese characteristics' (*zhongguo tese shehui zhuyi*) thereafter. This was what led to the characterisation of Deng Xiaoping leadership as a superb pragmatist. Only after his death in February 1997, the 15th Party Congress in September that year, adopted the formulation 'Deng Xiaoping Theory on Building Socialism with Chinese Characteristics'. Clearly the formulation was in the offing while he was alive and he may have approved the term 'theory' (理论 *lilun*) rather than 'thought' (*sixiang*) for his ideas. His line of thinking was manifest in his famous saying: 'wading through the water by touching the stones' (shaping policies as the situation needed from time to time). Many analysts point at this formulation to emphasise the 'pragmatism' of Deng Xiaoping. But actually this was his way of adopting capitalist and other innovative practices while building socialism.

Jiang Zemin's 'important thought on Three Represents' (重要思想三个代表 *zhongyao sixiang sange daibiao*) was adopted into the Party Constitution in 2002 at the time of his retirement and Hu Jintao's 'Scientific Outlook on Development' (科学发展观 *kexue fazhan guan*) added in 2012 when he handed over the leadership to Xi. These formulations though reiterated ritually in Party documents are seen today as less significant than Xi Thought. That line of thought was retained by Xi Jinping who affirmed the concept of a 'new development philosophy' that stressed high quality development rather than high speed and high quantity growth. This perspective very much grew out of Hu Jintao's 'scientific outlook on development'. For Xi Jinping, the 'new normal' was proclaimed as a reduced rate of growth with greater focus on the integrated achievement in all five dimensions – economic, political, social, cultural and ecological, simultaneously. Hence the current adoption of Xi Jinping Thought should not be seen as undermining or delegitimising the formulations of Jiang Zemin and Hu Jintao as many commentators have done.

After every Party Congress there is a wave of discussion on the recent formulations and their significance. Thus the scale of emphasis on the 'newness' of the current formulation which appears to be more than the usual, is to be understood in perspective. However, it is clear that ideological and political claim to stress the special status of Xi Thought has acquired unprecedented focus. Xi Jinping Thought is now placed in the public consciousness in China next to Mao Zedong Thought and Deng Xiaoping Theory, sometimes even omitting the latter.

In social sciences theory is a higher form of generalisation than ideology and concepts such as outlook, strategy, policy and tactics are lower in order of temporal and spatial application. Tactics for example is a very temporary arrangement to address a particular situation and strategy is more general than that. In natural sciences, there is even stricter standards of generality based on the requirements of evidence-based verification. Though the debates on positivist science have opened new notions of science as well. In ideological and political context, especially in the traditions of the communist movement these terms have to be judged in the context of the emergence and legitimation of a particular leadership. Indeed, they are part of the strategy of political management of the top leader who together with his intellectual advisers, in this case at the CPC's Central Party School decide on the nomenclature of the ideological statement. 'Naming' or 'rectification of names' or authoritative characterisation of a body of ideas in Chinese philosophical tradition since Confucius has been a serious exercise with much implications. Thus the choice of 'Thought' may have been carefully done to make Xi Jinping's status in the history of the CPC next only to Mao Zedong.

The context of the new formulation was outlined in Xi Jinping's Political Report in October 2017 thus:

> The achievements of the past five years have touched every area and broken new ground; the changes in China... have been profound and fundamental. For five years, our Party has demonstrated tremendous political courage and a powerful sense of mission as it has developed new ideas, new thinking, and new strategies,.. solved many tough problems that were long on the agenda but never resolved, and accomplished many things that were wanted but never got done. With this, we have prompted historic shifts in the cause of the Party and the country (Xi Jinping 2017: 7).

It is this act of addressing unsolved problems such as corruption with political courage demonstrated by many dismissals and reorganisation in military and taking multiple initiatives at home and globally during the first five years of Xi Jinping leadership which has led to 'historic shifts' in the context of China's own development and the fast changing global historical process and hence the talk of the 'new era' and new tasks.

## What is the New Era?

According to Xi Jinping the mission of the CPC has entered a new stage of 'national rejuvenation' which was the Chinese Dream. When Mao Zedong declared from the ramparts of Tiananmen Square on the inauguration of the People's Republic of China on 1 October 1949: 'China had stood up' (中国站起来 *Zhongguo zhanqi lai* !) it had achieved national independence and it could not be bullied by imperialism any more. Deng Xiaoping led the 'great new revolution of reform and open door' which achieved a moderately prosperous society. The popular formulation on this is because of the reforms 'China had become a rich country' (中国富起来 *Zhongguo fuqi lai* !). The new era now referred to 'building China as a strong country' (中国强起来 *Zhongguo qiangqi lai* !).

| | | |
|---|---|---|
| CHINA HAD STOOD UP | *Zhongguo zhanqi lai* | 1921–1949 |
| CHINA HAD BECOME RICH | *Zhongguo fuqi lai* | 1978–2020 |
| CHINA MUST BE STRONG | *Zhongguo qiangqi lai* | 2020–2035–2049 |

Changing with the times had been a constant refrain of Xi Jinping's addresses right from the time he took over. To face new challenges before China, he put great emphasis on the role of the CPC and therefore party-building had been one of his main preoccupations. The anti-corruption campaign was meant to make the party an efficient instrument to play this new role in full conformity with the new line of thought. In the Political Report he again and again spoke of the 'great mission' of the party to accomplish the goals of the new period. Changing with the times and facing the tasks of a new era became the recurrent theme of all discourses from the 19th Party Congress right through the months leading to the convening of the 13th NPC and thereafter.

Analysing the Political Report we can discern three features of this new era. First was an acknowledgement of the realisation of the goal set for 2020, namely 'well-off or prosperous society in all respects'. This happened to be on the eve of the first centenary of the foundation of the CPC, therefore acquired much ideological and political significance. Lifting all the population currently below the poverty line – eliminating poverty – by 2020 and doubling the per capita income of 2010 by 2020 besides many other indicators of development were the evidence of this. The second feature was the agenda for achieving the goal for the second centenary – the one-hundredth anniversary of the founding of the PRC. That goal was to make China a great modern socialist country that is prosperous, strong, democratic, culturally advanced, harmonious, and beautiful (Xi Jinping 2017a: 11). This goal had been the focus of the 19th Congress with a two phase plan – one from 2020 till 2035 and another for the period till 2049. Here out of all the descriptions of the projected goal building a 'strong China', economically and militarily using the innovation, technology and people's mobilisation in the cyber era drew prominent attention. Efforts on all fronts were to be geared towards that. The third feature is the challenges that the party faced domestically and externally. This was analysed in some detail in the Political Report. Domestic challenges were captured in the articulation of the new 'principal contradiction' between 'unbalanced and inadequate development and people's rising needs'. This acknowledged the existence of many problems not only in various sectors of the economy but also in society, culture and above all in environment. The 'four comprehensives' and a series of specific measures to improve governance were the response to them. The external dimensions, namely global challenges and the strategy to cope with them were the highlight of the 19th Congress. In earlier party congresses, the foreign policy and initiatives on global issues were a much smaller component and were never the focus. In the 19th Congress Xi Jinping clearly wanted the Chinese people to consciously see themselves as citizens of a rising nation with the aim of becoming a leading power by the mid-21st century and sent the message to the world accordingly. Many of the foreign policy doctrines which were announced from time to time during the first five years by Xi Jinping were refined and presented at the 19th Party congress. Three of them were most conspicuous and now formed what was called the 'new type of international relations' or the diplomatic line during the New Era. They were: Major country relationship in the 21st century, the working for common destiny of the humankind and the Belt and Road Initiative.

What was significant was the thrust given to the 'New Era' tasks. Xi emphasised that the old mind set would not do and everyone, every institution must be determined to 'emancipate their thought', cope with the challenges of the 'New Era' and show performance. It was like Deng Xiaoping's drive in the first years of reforms to eliminate the ideological impact of the Cultural Revolution doctrines. While acknowledging the great achievements of the past four decades – calling the 'reform and open door' as the second great revolution – he squarely pointed out how there were many things 'long on the agenda but not done' and his regime accomplished them. That set the tone for the performance criteria for the 'new era'.

Did the formulations at the 19th Congress adequately comprehend the main features of the 'new era' or the manifest and latent issues in contemporary China and the world and the near future of the next three decades? That is open to debate at least on three grounds. First, domestically, the causes of alienation of people which were economic, political, cultural and ecological; Second, the key feature of the global process was the affirmation of autonomy of people, nations and cultures all over the world. The economic and political doctrines in the new global perspective announced in the 19th Congress did not seem to seriously address that. The third, perhaps the most significant issue globally is the environmental challenge of the Anthropocene era with serious policy implications for domestic policies and international relations (Falk et al. 2017). The new Chinese strategy mainly seemed to use investment and trade in a 'win-win' framework as the driving force for 'shared future of humankind'.

The 19$^{th}$ Congress will be remembered for its proclamation of the recognition of a 'New Era'. It is to face the challenges of the New Era that the 19$^{th}$ Congress announced the Xi Jinping Thought.

## Xi Jinping Thought – Eight Principles and Fourteen Points

Interestingly, neither Mao Zedong Thought nor Deng Xiaoping Theory were spelt out in such detail as the presentation of Xi Jinping Thought in the Political Report at the 19$^{th}$ Congress. In Section III, the Report 'makes clear' eight affirmations and then states fourteen points to guide policies on various fronts thus presenting a comprehensive framework of theory and practice for the new era.

The eight clarifications are in the nature of statement of principles guiding policies and they had been talked about in bits and parts on various occasions during the previous five years. They are stated as follows in the Political Report (Xi 2017a: 15–17).

- A two-step approach to build 'a great modern socialist country' (till 2035 and then till 2049).
- Principal contradiction was between unbalanced and inadequate development and the people's ever-growing needs for a better life; promote people-centered, well-rounded human development.
- The five-sphere integrated plan (economic, political, social, cultural and ecological), and the four-pronged comprehensive strategy (comprehensively achieve well-off society, deepen reforms, promote rule of law and enforce strict self-governance of the party).
- Deepening reform in every field
- Socialist rule of law
- Building a strong military; world-class forces that obey the Party's command, can fight and win
- Major country diplomacy with Chinese characteristics aims to foster a new type of international relations and build a community with a shared future for humankind.
- Party leadership as the highest force for building Socialism with Chinese Characteristics in the New Era.

These eight principles are clearly stated as the constituent elements of Xi Jinping Thought which, as the Political Report puts it, 'represents the latest achievement in adapting Marxism to the Chinese context and encapsulates *the practical experience and collective wisdom* of our Party and the people'

(Xi 2017a: 17 Emphasis added). This resonated with the way Mao Zedong Thought was presented before.

These principles are complemented by a set of fourteen points which further clarify the meaning of the guiding principles and are perhaps intended to facilitate implementation of them on the ground (Xi 2017a: 17-25). They are:

1. Ensuring Party leadership over all work
2. Committing to a people-centered approach
3. Continuing to comprehensively deepen reform
4. Adopting a new vision of development that is innovative, coordinated, green, open and shared development that benefits everyone
5. Ensuring that the people run the country – organic unity of Party leadership, people-centered governance, and law-based governance
6. Ensuring that every dimension of governance is law-based, practicing socialist rule of law with Chinese characteristics
7. Upholding core socialist values, (creative evolution and development of fine traditional Chinese culture, revolutionary culture, and developing an advanced socialist culture, cherishing our cultural roots, drawing on other cultures, and being forward-thinking, fostering a Chinese spirit, Chinese values, and Chinese strength to provide a source of cultural and moral guidance for our people)
8. Ensuring and improving living standards through development (promote social fairness and justice, make steady progress in ensuring people's access to childcare, education, employment, medical services, elderly care, housing, and social assistance)
9. Ensuring harmony between human and nature (Building an ecological civilisation – fundamental national policy of conserving resources and protecting the environment, develop eco-friendly growth models and ways of life, sustainable development featuring increased production, higher living standards, and healthy ecosystems, continue the Beautiful China and play our part in ensuring global ecological security)
10. Pursuing a holistic approach to national security (Ensure both development and security, put national interests first, take protecting people's security as the mission and safeguarding political security as a fundamental task, and ensure both internal and external security, traditional and non-traditional security, and China's own and common security. Enhance capacity-building for national security, and resolutely safeguard China's sovereignty, security, and development interests)
11. Upholding absolute Party leadership over the people's armed forces (Obeying the Party's command, to fight and win, and maintain excellent conduct, strategically important to achieving the two centenary goals and national rejuvenation )

12. Upholding the principle of 'one country, two systems' and promoting national reunification
13. Promoting the building of a community with a shared future for humankind (The dream of the Chinese people is closely connected with the dreams of the peoples of other countries; the Chinese Dream can be realised only in a peaceful international environment and under a stable international order. Foster new thinking on common, comprehensive, cooperative, and sustainable security. We will pursue open, innovative, and inclusive development that benefits everyone; safeguard world peace, contribute to global development, and uphold international order.
14. Exercising full and rigorous governance over the Party (We must focus on oversight over leading officials, uphold democratic centralism, impose strict Party discipline, and strengthen internal oversight, develop a positive and healthy political culture in the Party, resolutely correct misconduct in all its forms, and show zero tolerance for corruption.)

On the face of it the eight-fourteen statement contains a very wide range of areas of society and people's lives and may even have some major point on each of the 'material, political, cultural, aesthetic and moral needs of human beings' about which we raised questions. Through 'people-centric governance, environment-oriented policy to build a beautiful country, focusing on socialist values Xi Jinping may have outlined a comprehensive programme, thus proposing 'an alternative paradigm of development'. This manifold listing is an empiricist method of putting down everything that looks relevant at a particular time rather than deciding on a key set of points that makes a difference. In fact, most of this we have seen stated and applied during the Hu Jintao period and Xi's first term. Moreover, permeating the eight-fourteen statement there is a thrust that overrides the other dimensions. That becomes clear when we examine the core principles of Xi Jinping Thought.

## The Core of the 8-14 Framework

The elaboration of Xi Jinping Thought in the Political Report was more an attempt to ensure that all the policy initiatives that Xi had taken during his first term were put clearly as constituting his way of taking China forward in the period ahead. It gave legitimacy and ideological backing of Chinese Marxist tradition which has remained a major method of building popular support through mass mobilisation. This approach also allowed the central leadership to pass down to the grass-roots cadres the policy package with the aura of a new ideological framework.[2]

In fact, the eight principles are a cluster of a wide range of policies and perspectives whereas a systematic statement of 'Thought' is generally a succinct statement of core principles. Mao Zedong Thought had theory of people's democratic revolution and socialist construction guided by class struggle as core principles (Mohanty 2012: 15). Deng Xiaoping Theory had stressed combining market economy with state and opening to the world as basic principles. In this case a wide range of policies, principles and affirmations are put together in a package that is proclaimed as Xi Jinping Thought. It contains such fundamental elements as a formulation on the principal contradiction at the present juncture and the reiteration of the traditional principle of Party leadership over the armed forces or the formulation on 'one country two systems' which Deng Xiaoping worked out to facilitate Hong Kong's reintegration with China.

However, if one takes the kernel of Xi Jinping Thought it appears that three interdependent dimensions form its basic elements. They are (a) the principal contradiction, (b) Party-led national rejuvenation and (c) the global perspective. Actually, the last two grow out of the first. Xi Jinping regime is likely to be fully engaged in pursuing this three-point agenda.

The principal contradiction is stated as the second clarification or assertion, the first being the goal of building the moderately prosperous society by 2020 and strong modern socialist country by mid-21$^{st}$ century which are the two centenary goals. It is now as *between unbalanced and inadequate development and the people's ever-growing needs for a better life.* This should be put against two earlier formulations on which there were many sharp debates in China. One was the 1956 formulation as the one between 'advanced superstructure and backward productive forces' – a formulation that became the central premise of the post-Mao reforms. The principal contradiction articulated during the Cultural Revolution was stated in terms of class struggle between proletariat and the bourgeoisie, especially between proletarian culture versus persisting bourgeois elements in the economy. The 'shift of focus 'announced by the Third Plenum of 1978 was from class struggle to 'economic construction'. From that point on the CPC's political line of Reforms and Open Door allowed no relaxation on the new focus. For example, in the wake of the Tiananmen Demonstrations Deng Xiaoping not only reiterated this, he announced his famous 'one centre, two points' (一中两点 *yizhong liang dian*) in which one centre was economic construction and the two points were reform and open door and four cardinal principles.

Does the new formulation strike a balance between the two? That could be one interpretation if the ideological stress on Marxism and the talk of 'socialism in the twenty first century' are taken into consideration. Hosting the World Marxism Congress in 2017 and the Global Conference in Beijing in June 2018 to celebrate the 200th birth anniversary of Karl Marx may also suggest an accent on Marxism in contemporary China (Butcher 2018). This contradiction is put together with the 'new development philosophy' and integrated multi-dimensional development as well as stress on building an 'ecological civilisation'. All this is consistent with the new issues of socialism in the twenty first century.

But the overall character of the eight-fourteen framework of Xi Jinping Thought becomes explicit when we read this together with the other two, namely the programme of Party-led national rejuvenation and the global strategy. They demonstrate a firm commitment to maintaining a steady growth of the economy and military strength and building China as a leading world power through the instrumentality of Party-led governance system.

Is it a purposive, deliberately designed, dual strategy that Xi leadership has formulated? It uses the new development philosophy to address domestic problems of inequality, environmental crisis and so on and the growth strategy aiming at steady development of productive forces with the help of the latest digital technology of the 'fourth industrial revolution' for promoting the global role of China evident in the BRI, SCO, BRICS and more. My assessment puts them in conflict with each other – each requiring the other to serve the overall aspiration of China to emerge as a 'great modern socialist country' where building economic and military strength trumps all other objectives. Therefore, the latter two elements, Party-led national rejuvenation programme and global perspective give us some idea about China's emerging future.

## Xi Jinping Thought and the Emerging Future

These are, no doubt significant interventions to maintain a tempo of economic growth. In theory there is attempt to maintain a balance between growth, equity and sustainability. Prosperity and modernisation remain core objectives for the coming decades for which the Party had to ensure stability with pro-people governance. No wonder that both the volumes of selected speeches of Xi Jinping are titled *The Governance of China* (Xi Jinping 2017b). That is how the 'Chinese dream of national rejuvenation' is envisaged. The goal of building a 'strong and prosperous country' by 2050 makes growth, even at the 'new normal' of medium rate, the central focus. The class situation in contemporary China adds some critical meaning to understand the politics of this strategy. For realising the rejuvenation goal the role of Chinese entrepreneur class and the middle class which are already global and fairly powerful in Chinese society remains central. This is so even when the CPC presence is expanded and consolidated in every sector of Chinese society and polity under Xi Jinping. It is not possible that they will allow any change in the growth focus of the Chinese economy. These classes emerged as the major social forces in course of the reforms and ultimately becoming the drivers of China's reform strategy during the past four decades. Therefore, there is a contradiction between the 'new development philosophy' that is so much welcomed by the migrant labourers, farmers and workers and the agenda of building a 'strong, modern, socialist' country relying on the digital economy. The Party's role in reconciling these conflicting objectives in a situation of one-Party rule with nominal consultative role of non-communist parties is bound to be a big challenge.

The 'national rejuvenation' strategy actually shapes China's new global perspective under Xi Jinping. Besides many new initiatives on multilateral cooperation and more pronounced role in world oganisations, Xi has charted a steady path of modernisation and reorganisation of the PLA to make it a 'world class force to fight 21st century battles and win wars'. Among the new initiatives the Belt and Road Initiative launched in 2013, Xi Jinping's signature programme with US$ one trillion allocation has unfolded as a China-initiated framework for a new model of international cooperation. In fact, Xi Jinping said so in his address at the International Forum on BRI in May 2017. Indeed, it is more than a connectivity promotion project. It allows Chinese capital to invest abroad. Through this Chinese manufacture and modern digital products will cater to the world market with even more attractive terms. Geostrategic features as in case of the China-Pakistan Economic Corridor (CPEC) are bound to invite a variety of reactions as indicated by the Indian objections to CPEC. The path of CPEC in the part of Jammu and Kashmir under the control of Pakistan is questioned by India which claims that part as its territory. That such issues could have been handled with timely consultation involving China, India and Pakistan that respects concerns of all parties was not considered. BRI is growing in significance as representing an alternative global system of political, economic and cultural interaction and it cannot be ignored by any country. The challenge for China is to pursue it as a mutual cooperation project based on the principle of 'equality and mutual benefit' – a core principle in Panchasheel (Five Principles) and Bandung Declaration and allay the fears of some countries about it being a project of global hegemony.

The 'new type' of international relations that Xi advocates and speaks of in all global forums that he addresses is a major element of Xi Jinping perspective. In it he defends economic globalisation, champions open trade and investment which in fact have worked to China's advantage during the past four decades. It is interesting to note that rather than transforming the current unequal international political and economic order, China now defends the present system. Though on certain occasions such as BRICS annual meetings the declarations did carry some references to that kind of agenda. 'New type of great power relations' that Xi Jinping had announced first when he had met President

Obama in 2013 in California took many different forms. It is more often stated as 'new type of major power relations' as mentioned during the SCO meeting in Qingdao in May 2018 referring to the relations between China, India and Russia. The principles of mutual respect, common interest and win-win cooperation are the basic ideas governing this approach and should be generally welcomed. But it has to work in tandem with the UN Charter principles of equality of all countries big and small.

The Chinese model of state-led market economy following an independent path was recommended by Xi Jinping for other countries in his address at the 19th Congress: "[The Chinese model] offers a new option for other countries and nations who want to speed up their development while preserving their independence, and it offers Chinese wisdom and a Chinese approach to solving the problems facing mankind." This showed a new sense of self-confidence about the path that Chinese reforms went through that Xi thought he could publicise even though Deng Xiaoping had constantly stressed 'Chinese characteristics' in the programme of socialist construction.

The 'common destiny of humankind' that Xi Jinping has put forth indeed has many laudable elements. At a time when the world is beset with outbreaks of violent incidents, refugee crisis, environmental and health hazards besides numerous humanitarian crises the discourse on common human destiny has many positive implications. These have to be concretised and made a part of all strategic initiatives of all countries, only then it would have some substantial meaning for humanity, especially the disadvantaged people across the world.

But if these policies aim at legitimising the Chinese policies at home and abroad then they would have limited credibility. If they promote the Chinese model of growth globally it is likely to produce the same kind of results in other countries that emulate the Chinese model – economic success with social and environmental problems which Xi Jinping is trying hard to address. Xi Jinping's global vision, lofty as it may be, is very much based on the Chinese reform model that has produced the paradox of success and the problems.

The firm commitment to the reform strategy, the focus on a tightened, Party-led governance system together with the global initiatives in a grand scale may add up to a path with many new possibilities. It is this package of policies and governance model that led to the bold announcement of not only Xi Jinping Thought but also to the amendment in the PRC Constitution by the 13th NPC in March 2018 ending the two term limits for President and Vice-President of China making it possible for Xi to continue for a third term in 2023 and beyond. Even though it conveyed a negative message that reversed a democratic political initiative taken by Deng Xiaoping earlier many people in China seem to have accepted this as an institutionalised leadership arrangement to face the formidable challenges that Xi Jinping faced at home and globally.

The placement of Xi Jinping Thought in discourses of political philosophy has led many to compare it with Confucianism citing the stress on the appeal to virtues and values guiding the ruler and the masses. But that is only an aspect of the Xi perspective. Parallels have been drawn with the Legalists because of the reference to rule of law and curbs on discretion that led to corrupt practices. But the Party's all-encompassing role has meant the overriding role of collective wisdom of the party centre rather than procedures leading to judgement. The meritocratic political system is another reference point for some which has been in the making since the beginning of the reforms. But the innovation drive in digital age puts a certain kind of elite, the technocratic elite in critical role but under political leadership. Even the CPC's traditional formulation of 'red and expert' character of cadres, let alone 'meritocracy' does not fully explain the present orientation. The comparison with Mao in some periods when mass line politics and nationalism and proletarian internationalism were pronounced too does not adequately characterise the Xi regime. It certainly is not a 'functional dystopia' breaking new grounds on so many fronts. We can only say that it has elements of utopias of many leaders and thinkers of China and the world. That is why the world will continue to closely watch if Xi Jinping's new initiatives will be able to strengthen China's success story while taking China out of its success trap. If they do then Xi Jinping Thought would acquire a theoretical status in the history of socialist thought. But as of now it appears that China's Success Trap would continue for many decades (Mohanty 2018b).

## NOTES

1. This has created an 'agency trap' because the Party which enjoys enormous legitimacy from its legacy of the Chinese revolution and the economic successes of the reforms is also an efficient and well-organised instrument of policy formulation and implementation. Without the participation of people at different levels in decision-making and adequate forums of debate and discussion the 'agency' is likely to carry on the overall strategy without fundamental alteration of the course of growth that is needed to tackle the serious problems (Mohanty 2018a: 134).
2. In early 2018, the CPC Propaganda Department produced a daily diary for the Party cadres for use in training classes in which one clarification or one principle out of the eight-fourteen framework was explained in detail.

## REFERENCES

Butcher, Asa. 2018. 'Xi Jinping speech honours Karl Marx's 200th birth anniversary', *Global Times,* 4 May, https://gbtimes.com/xi-jinping-speech-honours-karl-marxs-200th-birth-anniversary (accessed 12 August 2018)

Falk, Richard, Manoranjan Mohanty and Victor Faessel (eds.). 2017. *Exploring Emergent Global Thresholds: Towards 2030.* New Delhi: Orient BlackSwan.

Li Keqiang. 2018. *Report on the Work of the Government.* Delivered at the First Session of the 13th National People's Congress of the People's Republic of China on March 5, 2018, Full Text: http://en.people.cn/n3/2018/0403/c90000-9445262.html (accessed 19 July 2018).

Mohanty Manoranjan. 2012. *Political Philosophy of Mao Zedong.* New Delhi: Aakar Books. (Original edition 1977, Macmillan).

____. 2014. *Ideology Matters: China from Mao Zedong to Xi Jinping.* New Delhi: Aakar Books.

____ . 2018a. *China's Transformation: The Success Story and the Success Trap.* New Delhi: Sage Publications

____. 2018b. 'China Stuck in a Success Trap', *Asia Global* (Hong Kong), 17 May.

Xi Jinping. 2016. *The Governance of China I.* Beijing: Foreign Languages Press.

Xi Jinping. 2017a. *Secure a Decisive Victory in Building a Moderately Prosperous Society in All Respects and Strive for the Great Success of Socialism with Chinese Characteristics for a New Era*' Delivered at the 19th National Congress of the Communist Party of China, October 18, 2017, Full Text at http://www.xinhuanet.com/english/ download/Xi_Jinping's_report _at_19th_CPC_National_Congress.pdf (accessed on 19 July 2018).

____. 2017b. *The Governance of China II.* Beijing: Foreign Languages Press.

# 24

# Xi Jinping and the Politics of Culture

*Sabaree Mitra*

In the run up to the 19th Congress of the Communist Party of China (CPC), there had been speculation about the manner and extent of the change it would usher in, while there was little doubt that it would consolidate Party's General Secretary Xi Jinping's position, stature and power. Newly designated as 'core leader', with his 'Thought' enshrined in the Party's Constitution, Xi Jinping has reinvented and redefined ideological and theoretical formulations; in doing so he has showcased an admirable appropriation of ideas across history, influencing how well-known concepts will be applied in the new context of China. Many viewed this as 'Xi Jinping's coming out party' and yet the outcome has gone far beyond the domestic scene, going on to influence China's regional and the international status. It has not only impacted the Chinese population much more than was anticipated, it has also generated deep interest among China academics and the international public. Particular interest has been aroused in cultural issues, ranging from creative pursuits and productions to social norms and interactions, as also in political culture inculcated through an amalgamation of values, and above all through the construction of a strong, committed and confident Chinese people.

Looking back, Xi Jinping's speech delivered in October 2014 at a highly publicised Culture Forum, was regarded by many as comparable to the *Yan'an Talks on Literature and Art* delivered by Mao Zedong in 1942. As Xi admonished against 'becoming the slave of the market'; his concern for ideological values clearly came through. Many others have viewed this speech as an effort to integrate China's contradictory goals of adhering to the core socialist values and at the same time making the most of the market forces in the realm of culture. Even Deng Xiaoping in his speech to the writers and artists in 1979, much like Xi in 2014, had emphasised that at the core of creativity of the progressive writers and artists lie their 'intimate ties with the people'. On many occasions since 2014 Xi has given evidence of his rather conservative ideals in the way he envisioned culture and its role in all sense of the term. Among these, particularly important are the speeches delivered by Xi Jinping in September 2014 on the 2,565th anniversary of Confucius, at China's cultural revival project initiated by the CPCCC and the State Council in early 2017, as also the policies of *Wujin* (五进, literally meaning 'Five Introductions') and *Wuhua* (五化, literally meaning 'Five Transformations'), originally initiated by Xi as an experiment when he was the Party Secretary of Zhejiang Province (2002-07).

It is evident that China's domestic situation and concerns have changed over the decades as its society has witnessed extensive transformation in the wake of economic reform and open-door policy. The diversity of artistic choice, plurality of cultural discourse and the emergence of popular culture, all indicate the existence of a plural, multilayered cultural arena that is predicated upon the creation of a cultural market. The nature and type of cultural productions have changed, so have the cultural expectations of the leadership and the people. No less important is the fact that in the recent decades growing cultural interaction between China and the rest of the world, especially the West, has, on one hand given rise to new desire for cosmopolitanism and on the other, it has bred an aspiration to come out on top. In other words, it is natural under the circumstances that both the Chinese leadership and people should be keen on China emerging as a 'cultural superpower'. In the context of the 19th Congress of the CPC, which consolidated Xi's stature at par with Mao and Deng and perhaps more, this paper will try to address the following questions: Does Xi Jinping conceptualise culture differently from earlier leaders? In a continued effort to use culture as a tool of the State and the Party, is Xi creating a new political constituency?

## Importance of Culture: Experience of the Chinese Party-State

Mao Zedong had delivered his famous 'Talks on Literature and Art' in May 1942, primarily with the objective to settle the long-debated issues of role of literature and art in society and how they are located in relation to politics. Subsequently, the Talks, delivered even before the Party-State was established in 1949, assumed a canonical status in the cultural discourse of the Mao period. Though there have been occasional formulations and debates especially in the realm of literature, such as Qin Zhaoyang's essay 'Realism – The Broad Road' in 1956, or call for 'middle man' characters by Shao Quanlin, Zhao Shuli, Kang Zhuo and others, the tightening of political control during Anti-Rightist Movement and Cultural Revolution managed to put a straightjacket on all those who wanted to put on their thinking caps in the domain of culture. In other words, on one hand the Talks became the foundation of cultural policy in the

PRC, on the other the efforts of all sections of cultural practitioners to interpret or develop the Talks into a more comprehensive theoretical framework suitable for a post-revolutionary socialist society met with very little encouragement or success.

After the fall of Gang of Four the renewed hope of the masses in general and the intellectuals in particular, was strengthened by the changes culminating into the Third Plenum of the $11^{th}$ Party Congress in 1978. Though there were disappointment and perhaps disillusionment in the aftermath of the crackdown on the short-lived Democracy Wall movement in 1978, the shift of focus away from politics and the new leadership's emphasis on the importance of knowledge and intellectuals gradually instilled faith and encouraged the stride towards a relatively freer atmosphere of creativity. In the 1980s, the framework for economic development was further strengthened to call for greater individual autonomy and to dismantle the collective ethos, to keep pace with the opening to the outside world as well as with increased pace of economic and cultural globalisation. Yet, the domain of culture and academia witnessed campaigns against 'Spiritual Pollution on the Ideological Front' and 'Bourgeois Liberalisation' more than once in the 1980s. However, the experience of the campaigns, especially the one against 'Bourgeois Liberalisation' in 1987, indicated that they were not directed at any community, but at erring individuals who were practicing and spreading ideas that could challenge the authority of the leadership and supremacy of the Socialist system. For instance, while the controversial documentary 河殇 (*He Shang*) (translated as *River Elegy*) was banned in November 1988, those involved in its production did not suffer any serious damage in the immediate aftermath.

It is well documented that by the mid-1990s Chinese society displayed a pluralistic, multi-layered, market-oriented dimension. It was natural that all aspects of human development, including culture, reflected this transformation, bringing in variety of shades in cultural creativity and theoretical debate. As early as 1991, when the crew of the spectacularly popular TV serial 渴望 (*Kewang*) (translated as *Aspirations* or *Yearnings*) was received by Li Ruihuan to Zhongnanhai, the residential and work complex of Chinese leaders, adjacent to the Forbidden City. Li, a Politburo member responsible for ideological work, appreciated the entertainment value of the serial and acknowledged that entertainment was an important function of art. In fact in the keynote address to the Sixth Congress of the Federation of Writers and Artists and the Fifth Congress of the Chinese Writers Association in December 1996, Jiang Zemin recognised the important role played by the writers and artists in improving moral and cultural qualities of the Chinese people and in providing spiritual nourishment to the people. On the whole, the official response to culture, especially to literature and art, through the 1990s indicate that the regime has adopted an increasingly tolerant, pragmatic stance, balancing between keeping pace with changing requirements of the Chinese society, and retaining and asserting (whenever needed) its leadership role and control over cultural productions.

Since then, the new millennium has witnessed further cultural fragmentation in China; especially with the gradual rise of strong popular cultural trends and plurality of discourse, the earlier concept of mainstream culture with political value and social relevance got replaced by availability of multiple cultural choices, thus giving rise to a robust cultural market. In this connection it must be mentioned that Hu Jintao's report to the 17$^{th}$ CPC Congress in 2007, while having a section on 'Promoting Vigorous Development and Prosperity of Socialist Culture', did not go beyond rhetorical generalities that is often the hallmark of official speech and pronouncements of the CPC leaders. But it is relevant to note that Hu actually called for protection of cultural heritage and promotion of Chinese culture worldwide, as well as cultural innovation and popularising development of non-profit cultural programmes and facilities across the country. In many ways, Hu's essay in 求实 (*Qiushi*) in 2012 drew world-wide attention develops his ideas of China's cultural rise much more assertively; to the extent that it links the desire to deepen the impact of China's soft power with increasing comprehensive national strength.

In fact after Xi Jinping took over the reins of the CPC, one of the significant speeches in the first few months was during his visit to the exhibition on 'Road to National Rejuvenation' 复兴之路 (*fuxing zhilu*) in Beijing on 29 November, 2012. Frequently quoted by Chinese commentators, this speech provides a comprehensive picture of Xi's world view and his 'Chinese dream' and had a strong cultural connotation.

## Xi Jinping's Tryst with Culture

While drawing a parallel with Mao Zedong, several scholars have tried to analyse how Xi Jinping has drawn from the lessons of the Cultural Revolution, or for that matter how Xi's pursuit of 'absolute power' may lead to catastrophe both for him and China. Notwithstanding Xi's call for the 'great renewal of the Chinese nation', it is apparent that he has been unwavering in his effort to instill loyalty and obedience across the board. To that end, he has drawn unhesitatingly from multiple sources to shape a unifying ideology that is not without a strong popular constituency. It is obvious in the way Xi Jinping has been courting the superstructure of culture to consolidate and expand its role and utility, taking it from the domestic to the international in a manner that manifests an unprecedented confidence. Going through his political journey from Zhejiang to

Beijing, one would try to read and analyse his /speeches delivered at different occasions: 1) Xi's experimental formulations of 五进 (*Wujin*) and 五化 (*Wuhua*) as the Governor of Zhejiang Province (2002-2007), 2) Speech delivered by Xi Jinping on the occasion of 2,565$^{th}$ anniversary of Confucius in September 2014, and 3) Xi's speech delivered in the Culture Forum held in October 2014.

### (1) *Xi's experimental formulations of 五进 (Wujin) and 五化 (Wuhua)*

*Wujin* and *Wuhua,* literally meaning 'five penetrations/five introductions' and 'five transformations', were first introduced in the Zhejiang Province by Xi Jinping as an experiment to Sinicise external cultural/religious influence, such as Christianity. The policy of *Wujin* consisted of introduction of laws and regulations into churches; bringing in health facilities and medical treatment into churches; extending support to the needy, as well as promoting popular science into churches; and ideas of inculcating harmony into churches. *Wuhua* includes localisation of churches, regularisation of church management, indigenisation of theology, transparency in church funding and finance, and rendering church doctrines compatible. Reading between the lines, it does not take much imagination to understand that while on one hand it is an effort to integrate the Christian population to the mainstream, on the other, it is a clear diktat to follow the social and political order of the day. Above all, there is no doubt that, in an adaptation from the earlier times, these formulations were meant to transform the often-belligerent church community under the scrutiny of neighborhood organisations and hold it accountable to the spirit and utility of people's bodies. Moreover, the benefits, such as healthcare and transparency, that this transformation promised to the community were not small incentives at a time when Chinese society was beginning to face deepening issues of inequality brought about in the wake of de-collectivisation and privatisation.

### (2) *Speech delivered by Xi Jinping on the occasion of 2,565$^{th}$ anniversary of Confucius in September 2014.*

In September 2014, the Fifth Congress of the International Confucius Association was held in Beijing to commemorate the 2,565$^{th}$ birth anniversary of Confucius. The theme of the conference was 'Confucianism: World Peace and Development'. The keynote address was delivered by President Xi Jinping, in which he discussed at length the enduring relevance of Confucianism as the major tenets of his thought could continue to be source of wisdom in contemporary China. To quote: 'The ideology and culture of today's China is a continuation and sublimation of traditional Chinese ideology and culture. To understand present-day China, to know the present-day Chinese, one must delve into the cultural bloodline of China, and accurately appreciate the cultural soil that nourishes the Chinese people.' He went on to say that Confucianism is key to 'understanding the national characteristics of the Chinese as well as the historical roots of the spiritual world of the present-day Chinese. Confucianism has morphed with the times, and evolved in accordance with corresponding conditions, constantly refreshing itself while responding to demands of the times. This is why it has had such lasting vitality.' Xi further underscored that 'Confucianism has emphasised giving play to culture's educational and enlightening functions in cultivating worthy personalities, and combined the cultivation of individuals' and society's moral qualities with management of state affairs.' He also held the banner of civilisational discourse high when he said 'The world has become what it is today amid the exchanges and mingling between different civilisations. Promoting such exchanges and mingling as well as mutual learning and reference is indispensable path toward a better world and better lives for people of all countries.... The civilisation of each country and nation is rooted in its soil, with its own characteristics and virtues.... Differences between the civilisation of one's own country and that of others should be handled rationally, with awareness that every civilisation is unique' (Xi 2014).

It can be argued, it was perhaps the first open acknowledgement of the centrality of Confucian thought in Chinese culture in several decades. What is more, coming from the topmost leader of the land, the pronouncements acquired political significance by far outdoing the well-known academic point made by numerous scholars of Chinese history. More important, however, is to understand that the present ideological discourse is not ashamed to and certainly will now re-appropriate all those aspects and elements of China's cultural past that would help in consolidating power of the current regime and in strengthening its ideological authority.

### (3) *Xi's speech delivered in the Beijing Culture Forum held in October 2014*

Delivered within a month after his speech on the occasion of 2,565th anniversary of Confucius, Xi Jinping's speech in Culture Forum in October 2014, in many ways, followed an expected trajectory of reclaiming China's cultural past to strengthen the management of state affairs. Yet, the format of the speech is strongly reminiscent of Mao's seminal Yan'an Talks delivered in 1942 Though released a year later in October 2015, the official translation had not been made public. Divided into sections, the speech addresses five important themes, namely, 1) Realisation of Chinese people's great rise requires prosperous flourishing of Chinese culture, 2) Produce excellent works worthy of our times, 3) Persist in following the creative direction with people at the core, 4) Chinese spirit is the soul of Socialist literature and art, and 5) Strengthen and improve Party's leadership on literary and artistic work. While the themes addressed are self-explanatory and clear in implication, some specific elements need particular attention. For instance, Xi provides a historical chronological survey of China's cultural history, where he runs through the whole panorama of cultural icons from ancient Chinese thinkers such as Confucius, Mencius, etc. to Li Bai, Du Fu, etc. to Cao Xueqin to pillars of May Fourth literature such as Lu Xun, Guo Moruo, Mao Dun, Ba Jin etc. to modern Chinese artists of different art forms such as Mei Lanfang, Xu Beihong, etc. Further, he rationalises this reclaiming of China's past by mentioning how the pantheons of thinkers, writers and artists through history of a particular people (actually mentioning French and Indian) collectively reflect the essence of that people's culture. Finally, Xi argues that the construction of Chinese spirit is inextricably bound to Chinese literature and art.

Xi Jinping pointed out that excellent works of literature and art are so because of their 'ideological profundity, artistic exquisiteness and product superiority'. He acknowledged that the period since reform and opening up has witnessed unprecedented diversity in cultural production; at the same time, he cautioned, cultural practitioners must resist being completely market driven. With rising living standard of the Chinese people, their demands for quality cultural products have also risen. He pointed out that every age has its unique characteristics; literature and art workers, as engineers of the souls, 'should be able to enlighten thoughts.... reflect the Socialist core value system in their works.' While addressing the last issue, Xi Jinping emphasised that only those cadres, who are both able and honest, must be made responsible for correctly implementing the Party's spirit in literature and art; while doing so, they must respect the creative individuality and creative labour of literature and art, and create a good atmosphere for development of literature and art criticism.

## Xi Jinping's Political Report: Building Stronger Cultural Confidence and Helping Socialist Culture to Flourish

The speech delivered by Xi Jinping in the 19$^{th}$ National Congress of the CPC, was a mammoth exercise as it summed up the 'original aspiration and the mission of the Chinese Communists.' In reality it was an effort at putting forth a comprehensive framework for building 'Socialism with Chinese characteristics for a new era' in order to 'realise the Chinese dream of national rejuvenation'. Divided into thirteen sections, it covered a range of issues perceived to be of utmost importance to the continued authority and leadership of the CPC. One of the sections (VII) was titled 'Building Stronger Cultural Confidence and Helping Socialist Culture to Flourish' that delved into various aspects of building a Socialist culture with Chinese characteristics and the role it was expected to play. He said: 'Culture is a country and nation's soul. Our country will thrive only if our culture thrives, and our nation will be strong only if our culture is strong.... Socialist culture with Chinese characteristics is derived from China's fine traditional culture, which was born of the Chinese civilisation and nurtured over 5,000 years; it has grown out of the revolutionary and advanced socialist culture that developed over the course of the Chinese people's revolution, construction and reform under the Party's leadership; and it is rooted in the great practice of Chinese Socialism with Chinese characteristics.... To develop Socialist culture with Chinese characteristics means to develop a Socialist culture for our nation – a culture that is sound and people-oriented, that embraces modernisation, the world, and the future, and that both promotes Socialist material wellbeing and raises Socialist cultural-ethical standards. In developing this culture, we must follow the guidance of Marxism, base our efforts on Chinese culture, and take into account the realities of contemporary China and the conditions of the present era. We should ensure that this culture serves the people and serves Socialism' (Xi 2017).

Xi further held that ideology must play its role in guiding culture in the right direction. He said that a distinction must be made 'between matters of political principle, issues of understanding and thinking, and academic viewpoints', but all erroneous views must be resisted with a clear stand. He said that China's fine traditional culture must evolve with time and its vision, concepts, values and moral norms must be adapted in accordance to the need of the hour, so that Chinese culture maintains its appeal. Xi also spoke at length about the importance of ideals and morality, and asserted that 'We must promote credibility building, institutionalise volunteer services, and heighten people's sense of social responsibility, awareness of rules, and sense of dedication' (Xi 2017). Referring specifically to Socialist literature and art, Xi said that 'writers and artists should take a people-centered approach and draw inspiration from everyday life and experiences of the people to produce works that do justice to our times (Xi 2017); he also said that 'originality and experimentation with new approaches' in literary and artistic creativity will be encouraged. Lastly, Xi Jinping asserted that in order to provide people with rich intellectual nourishment during their pursuit for a better life, new mechanisms of cultural production must be explored. The cultural sector must be developed and more popular cultural activities launched. In this last section he dwelt on the necessity of improving China's cultural capacity for engaging in international exchanges so as to enhance China's cultural soft power.

In this context it is relevant to mention that in the last few years on several occasions Xi Jinping has talked about 文化自信 *(wenhua zixin)*, roughly translated as 'cultural confidence', calling it one of the 'four confidences' (道路自信，理论自信，制度自信，文化自信 *daolu zixin, lilun zixin, zhidu zixin, wenhua zixin)* that is confidence in the path, theories, system and culture which must be adhered to by the Party. In the speech delivered on the occasion of the 95th anniversary of the founding of the CPC in 2016, Xi said: '文化自信，是更基础、更广泛、更深厚的自信' *(wenhua zixin shi geng jichu, geng guangfan, geng shenhou de zixin)* (Xi 2016a). It is the content of this 'cultural confidence' that includes the entire cultural and civilisational past of China, which has been visualised by Xi Jinping to be one of the key forces behind the great revival of the Chinese people (中华民族伟大复兴 *zhonghua minzu weida fuxing*). In his speech delivered on the occasion of the 10th National Congress of China Federation of Literary and Art Circles and the 9th National Congress of China Writers Association on November 30, 2016, Xi discussed the concept of cultural confidence in detail, linking it with the role the writers and artists are expected to play. He said 'The realisation of national rejuvenation requires us to have confidence in the path, theories, system and culture of Socialism with Chinese characteristics. A good understanding and strong confidence in China's profound culture are the prerequisites for the creation of excellent works with distinct national features and unique personal style.... Culture is the soul of both a country and a nation.... Confidence in culture is basic, deep-rooted, and reaches far and wide; it is a force that is more fundamental, stable and persistent. Increasing confidence in our own culture is critical to the prospects of our country, to our cultural security, and to the independence of our national character' (Xi 2016b: 378). He further added, 'We need to complete a creative transformation in cultural inheritance, and try to surpass those from whom we learn. We hope to create excellent works that embody the essence of the Chinese culture, reflect the Chinese people's aesthetic pursuits, spread the values of contemporary China, and are in line with the world's progressive trends. We have to present our literature and art in the international arena with distinct Chinese features, in a distinctive Chinese style and Chinese ethos' (Xi 2016b: 381).

## Conclusion: Some Highlights

The hallmarks of the 19th Congress were: 'forgetting not the initial intent' (不忘初心 *buwang chuxin*), 'keeping always the mission in mind' (牢记使命 *laoji shiming*), 'holding high the banner' (高举旗帜 *gaoju qizhi*), and 'forging ahead in unity' (团结奋进 *tuanjie fenjin*). Reiteration of 'forgetting not the initial intent' (*buwang chuxin*) (which was enshrined in the caption of Xi's keynote speech at the 19th Congress), is an effort to remind all about the original intention and mission of the Chinese Communists in seeking happiness for the Chinese people and seeking rejuvenation of the Chinese nation. We may add to it Xi's 2018 New Year greeting delivered on 31 December 2017 in which he said that all officials of the Party and Government must 'think what the people are thinking' (想群眾之所想 *xiang qunzhong zhi suo xiang*) and 'get busy for what people think is urgent' (急群眾之所急 *ji qunzhong zhi suo ji*) so that 'people can enjoy greater prosperity and happiness' (讓人民生活更加幸福美滿 *rang renmin shenghuo gengjia xingfu meiman*). In fact, wholeheartedly thinking for the people is regarded by many Chinese commentators as the salient feature of Xi's political culture and the message of the 19th Congress.

Xi Jinping's rise as a predominant Chinese leader pre- and post-19th Congress is the corollary of the interplay of two scenarios. On one hand, the prolonged peace, stability and prosperity of China as well as the universal elevation of people's living standard stimulated the popular desire for a higher spiritual atmosphere and richer cultural life. The information revolution and the quick expansion of knowledge and wisdom through the smart gadgets, internet and social media added more fuel to this new trend. On the other hand, Xi Jinping has emerged as a visionary and missionary statesman firmly rooted in realism, and yet full of ideas and ideals – as a 'great dreamer' in Rabindranath Tagore's words. If the Mao Zedong Era could be characterised as 'Politics in Command' which was replaced by Deng Xiaoping Era's 'Economics in Command', then, Xi Jinping's China is characterised by 'Culture in Command' for sure. Culture, as a matter of fact, is the trend of doing things and the energy of getting things done. Xi Jinping, in the past five years, has had such a culture in tow.

In conclusion, the following points emerge as the highlights of Xi Jinping's perception and use of culture: While Xi's conceptualisation of culture is different from that of Mao Zedong, he has not underestimated the importance of culture, like many of his predecessors did. He has realised that the potential and utility of culture are far more complex and diverse in contemporary times; to this end he conceived of its role to include the social, political, and philosophical into a composite whole. Moreover, though Mao Zedong did ponder over the question of the national character of literature, Xi had the breadth of vision to take that concept forward, and straddling across time and space, he has further strengthened the utilitarian aspect of culture for the present.

Xi Jinping, for the first time perhaps in the history of CPC, has openly acknowledged the wealth of cultural traditions found in China's long journey through history. By doing so, he has reclaimed China's ancient past and then gone on to create an amalgamation of the classical and the popular, the ancient and the modern, the conservative and the revolutionary to the post-revolutionary, which he has called Chinese culture. In the process he has not only broadened the utility of culture by many measures, but has also expanded the constituency that now includes a wide range of cultural products and cultural practitioners hitherto marginalised.

The Chinese word *Yichan* (遗产), often used to denote cultural legacy, signifies that culture is a heritage accumulated over centuries and generations from the wisdom and practices of forefathers. It is this sense of the term that gets reflected in the way Xi Jinping has innovatively drawn from China's cultural past. Interestingly, the word used for culture in most Indian languages, *Samskriti*, has its origin in Sanskrit words *sam* (a prefix literally meaning 'together') and *kriti* (a noun derived from the verb *kri*, literally meaning 'to do', 'to cultivate', 'to refine' etc.); broadly based on these, the word *Samskriti* refers to a collective value system shaped over time through a process of cultivation and refinement. In this the concept of culture is very similar in Indian and Chinese civilisations. While efforts of using culture as a tool or weapon in twentieth century, especially post-May Fourth 1919, China often focused on negating the civilisational connection, Xi Jinping has successfully appropriated and utilised that connection this time.

It is clear that from Xi's perspective, the utilitarian role of culture does not necessarily have to be confined to China's domestic politics but can be extended to the international arena where rules of engagement has changed over time to include many unconventional strategies, including culture. That this aspect of culture has come to influence the Chinese psyche of late, has already been evident in the way Chinese state and the Chinese people have been projecting its stature in the context of international literature and art awards. The interest generated in the Chinese media and among the people on the eve of Mo Yan's Literature Nobel was a case in point. Xi Jinping's formulations on culture has taken cognisance of such trend and tried to maximise the utility of culture in the cause of defining Chinese national identity and 'cultural supremacy'.

Many China watchers have felt that there is a continuity from Mao Zedong to Xi Jinping in the way they have seen culture as a tool to impose 一言堂 (*yi yan tang*) a 'one-voice chamber'. But Xi Jinping has gone beyond just ensuring 'monoculture'; he has actually attempted to expand the ambit of culture and its role very innovatively so as to make it appear more inclusive, appealing and assertive. But how will Xi's formulations impact some other facets of culture such as religion, education etc., will have to be studied at length.

It is true that culture was always assigned an important status and role in the discourse of the Communist Party of China. But it can be argued that the contribution of Xi Jinping in taking this discourse forward is unprecedented and incomparable to any other Chinese leader in the past as culture is now being projected at the core of *Chineseness* or Chinese people's identity. What is more, such projection would be much more readily acceptable even to an ordinary Chinese like no law or policy would be, encouraging him/her to do the utmost to 'conquer the world'.

## REFERENCES

China Copyright and Media, 'Hu Jintao's Article in Qiushi Magazine-translated' https://https://chinacopyrightandmedia.wordpress.com/2012/01/04/hujintaos-article-in-qiushi-magazine-translated/ (accessed on 16 October 2017).

China Copyright and Media, 'Xi Jinping's Talks at the Beijing Forum on Literature and Art', https://chinacopyrightandmedia.wordpress.com/2014/10/16/xi-jinpings-talks-at-the-beij ing-forum-on-literature-and-art/

Hu Jintao, 'Hold High the Great Banner of Socialism with Chinese Characteristics and Strive for New Victories in Building a Moderately Prosperous Society in all', Report to the 17th National Congress of the Communist Party of China, October 15, 2007, china.org.cn, http://www.china.org.cn/english/congress/229611.htm (accessed on 23 November 2017).

胡锦涛，'坚定不移走中国特色社会主义文化发展道路，努力建设社会主义文化强国' *Hu Jintao: jianding bu yi zou zhongguo tese shehui zhuyi wenhua fazhan daolu nuli jianshe shehui zhuyi wenhua qiangguo*, [Hu Jintao: Unswervingly Keeping to the Road of Socialist Culture with Chinese Characteristics and Working Hard to Build a Socialist Cultural Power[ (2011年10月18日)《求实理论网》，http://www.qstheory.cn/zywz/201201/t2012 0101_133218.htm (accessed on 16 November 2017).

毛泽东，'在延安文艺座谈会上的讲话' *Mao Zedong zai Yan'an wenyi zuotanhui shang de jianghua*, [Mao Zedong,Talks at the Yan'an Forum on Literature and Arts], 《毛泽东选集》第三卷，人民出版社，北京, 1968年, (804-835叶)

Ma Jian. 2016. 'Xi Jinping – a son of the Cultural Revolution', *The Japan Times*, May 10, 2016, https://www.project-syndicate.org/commentary/china-xi-jinping-mao-zedong-parallels-by-ma-jian-2016-05?barrier=accessreg

Gardels, Nathan. 2014. 'Xi Launches Cultural Counter-Revolution To Restore Confucianism As China's Ideology', *The World Post*, 文化自信是更基本 *wenhua zixin shi geng jiben* [Cultural Confidence is more basic],《陕西画报》, ?1994-2017 China Academic Journal Electronic All rights reserved. http://www.cnki.net

Willy Lam. 2016. 'Xi Jinping uses 'traditional culture' to launch a new Cultural Revolution', *AsiaNews.it.*, http://www.asianews.it/ index.php?l=en&idn=1&art=36661 & mag= visualiz zaperlastampa (accessed on 23 May 2017).

习近平：在文艺工作座谈会上的讲话，*Xi Jinping; zai wenyi gongzuo zuotanhui shang de jianghua*, (Xi Jinping: Talks at the Forum on Literary and Artistic Work), 新华社北京2014 年10月14日电，http://news.xinhuanet.com/politics/2015-10/14/c_1116825558.htm (accessed on 12 November 2017).

习近平: 文艺不能在市场经济大潮中迷失方向，*Xi Jinping: wenyi buneng zai shichang jingji dachao zhong mishi fangxiang*, [Xi Jinping: Literature and art can't be lost in the market economy, cannot be a slave in the market] http://news.xinhuanet.com/politics/2014-10/15/c_1112840544.htm (accessed on 23 May 2017).

习近平谈文化自信，*Xi Jinping tan wenhua zixin*, [Xi Jinping discusses cultural confidence],《宝鸡社会科学 2016.04》, ?1994-2016 China Academic Journal Electronic All rights reserved. http://www.cnki.net

Xi Jinping. 2014. 'Speech at the Opening Ceremony of the International Conference in Commemoration of the 2,565th Anniversary of Confucius' Birth and the fifth Congress of the International Confucian Association', September 24, 2014, available at http://library.chinausfocus.com/article-1534.html (accessed on 21 November 2017).

'Xi Jinping's Culture Wars', *A ChinaFile Conversation* by Stanley Rosen, Michael Berry, Jindong Cai, Sheila Melvin, November 12, 2014, http://www.chinafile.com/conversation/xi-jinpings-culture-wars (accessed on 23 May 2017).

Xi Jinping, 'Speech at a Ceremony Marking the 95th Anniversary of the Founding of the Communist Party of China', July 01, 2016, English Edition of *Qiushi* Journal October-December 2016. Vol. 8, No. 4, Issue No.29. Updated: 2016-Dec-20 17:13, http://english.qstheory.cn/2016-12/20/c_1120042032.htm (accessed on 25 May 2018).

Xi Jinping. 2016. 'Confidence in Chinese Culture' (November 30, 2016), *Xi Jinping: The Governance of China II*, Beijing: Foreign Language Press, 2017, pp. 378-381.

Xi Jinping, 'Secure a Decisive Victory in Building a Moderately Prosperous Society in All Respects and Strive for the Great Success of Socialism with Chinese Characteristics for a New Era' Delivered at the 19th National Congress of the Communist Party of China, October 18, 2017, Full Text of Xi Jinping's Report at 19th CPC National Congress, available at http://www.xinhuanet.com/english/download/Xi_Jinping's_report_at_19th_CPC_National_Congress.pdf (accessed on 26 December 2017)

'学习贯彻习近平参观《复兴之路》展览讲话述评' *Xuexi guanche Xi Jinping canguan "fuxing zhilu" zhanlan jianghua shuping,* [Studying and Implementing Xi Jinping's Speech on the Exhibition of "The Road to Rejuvenation"] 中央政府门户网站 www.gov.cn 2012年12月06日 17时43分 来源：新华社，http://www.gov.cn/jrzg/2012-12/06/content_2284276.htm (accessed on 03 February 2018).

Zi Yang, 'Xi Jinping and China's Traditionalist Restoration', *China Brief,* Vol. 17, issue 9, https://jamestown.org/analyst/zi-yang/

# 25

# Understanding Xi's China through the Civilisational Prism

*Tan Chung*

*(This reflective essay by the evergreen Professor Tan Chung was written in January 2018. It serves as a fine personal end-piece to this volume, by a great historian and scholar of China-India relations and a humanist).*

The title of this essay on the recent 19th Congress of the Communist Party of China (CPC), held in October 2017 might lead the reader to wonder why I place Xi Jinping's China in terms of the country's past. I am the oldest contributor to this volume, and perhaps I am obsessed with China's history, but I seek your indulgence to consider a historian's answer and let you draw your own conclusion.

It so happened that this great event – the 19th Party Congress – coincided with the publication in Beijing of the Chinese version of my book, *China: A 5000 Year Odyssey*. When I traveled to Beijing for the book release, the 19th Congress dominated the news across the country. On the Hainan Airline plane from Boston to Beijing on 26 October 2017, all the Chinese newspapers carried extra-large photographs of Xi Jinping beaming at the passengers, as if welcoming everybody to a new China over which he is set to preside for another five years or more. I saw this new China (especially the ruling elite) sitting behind closed doors studying the refreshing messages of the 19th Congress. Banqueting at public expenses had disappeared in recent years. Extravagant restaurants had shut down. People gathered round the frugal (not so frugal) dinner tables discussing Xi Jinping – mostly appreciative, but amidst varying shades of dark innuendo. One smelt in Beijing an air of tremendous self-confidence, while sunshine warmed the hearts in freezing temperatures. The media had been worked up – something big was coming.

I spoke on various occasions on my new book which seeks to view China through the prism of civilisation. I reminded my audiences that, long before the appearance of humans, the two great rivers, the Yangtze (the third longest of the world) and the Huanghe (the fifth longest), drew the contours of China on earth and created a 'common entity of geography'. Then, people living in the Yangtze and Huanghe valleys transformed that geographical entity into a 'common entity of civilisation', which in turn became a 'common entity of political system'. That development made China a 'civilisation state', especially during the famous Han, Tang and Song dynasties. All of them were common entities of destiny. During the Song dynasty, China was the most advanced country on earth, at the same time indulging in hedonistic pacifism and merrymaking, and ignoring national defence. China was like a gigantic glass fishbowl with fish swimming merrily inside while gluttonous cats waited beside it ready to jump in at any moment. In 1127, the Nurchen troops stormed the Northern Song capital, Bianjing, and looted the city, taking away the Song Emperor and his imperial father, his Queen and the entire imperial harem, and 100,000 civilians, in addition to uncountable treasures. This marked the end of the first phase of the Song Dynasty. Then, in 1279, the second phase, the Southern Song, ended when 100,000 soldiers and civilians jumped into the sea along with the last Song Emperor, to avoid captivity at the hands of the invading Mongol troops. These two pathetic tragedies buried all the good memories of China's 'common entity of destiny'. After that, with the exception of the Ming Dynasty, China was transformed into a kind of 'nation state', with racial repression on the one hand and territorial expansion on the other, under the rule of the Mongol (Yuan) and Manchu (Qing) dynasties. Then there came the challenge from the sea, which became the 'gunboat road' dominated by the Western imperialist powers. China was reduced to the status of a 'sub-colony'.

Only after the establishment of the People's Republic of China (PRC) in 1949 and the initiation of economic reforms some thirty years later did China return to its normal course along the civilisational highway. On the one hand, China returned to the true 'Common entity of destiny' typified by the prosperous Tang and Song dynasties, with the unmistakable revival of hedonistic pacifism and merrymaking. On the other hand, the PRC has also inherited from the Mongol and Manchu dynasties an accent on military might, and embraced their enlarged territories much beyond the contours carved out by the two great rivers. According to the moral standards of our contemporary world of 'nation-states', such a development is perfectly normal. However, readers must remember that China is essentially a 'civilisation state'. May I suggest that, with the passage of time, it will abandon the bad behaviour of the 'nation-state', like a youngster recovering from German measles?

In my book, I told the story of China as an *insider*, to both foreigners and Chinese, neither of whom fully understand the true nature of Chinese civilisation. My book's narrative is steeped in my love for China, but I don't view its past as a 'great tradition'. The well-known American sinologist, John King Fairbank, had famously highlighted the development of China in terms of a 'great tradition' followed by a 'modern transformation', as though everything good in China was due to the 'modern transformation', while everything bad was due to Chinese 'tradition'. Unlike Fairbank, I personally fail to see a so-called 'great tradition' in China, for the great tragedies of the 12th and 13th centuries in Chinese history do not make me entirely optimistic. On the positive side, however, though foreigners could easily overrun China time and again, China's civilisation could never be destroyed. Unlike the ancient Babylonian, Egyptian, Greek and Roman civilisations, Chinese civilisation is like the legendary phoenix, always reborn from the ashes. Today, China is surely closer than ever to that odyssey along the civilisational highway than it had been during the Tang and Song dynasties stretching from the 7th to the 12th century, while the gluttonous cats that once eyed the huge fishbowl of China have gone their own way.

The characteristics of Tang and Song China are now combined with the vibrant energy of wealth creation. Along with this surge, China has embraced to its advantage the current trajectory of 'Anglobalisation' (led by the U.S., followed by Europe, Australia and Canada with their multinational corporations as flag-bearers). From the 1980s China had positioned itself as a nation of goods' producers-cum-sellers, aptly described as the 'factory of the world'. Regrettably, however, the hedonism of past dynasties had returned with a vengeance.

How does the 'Anglobal' (Anglo-global) world receive the PRC? There was a time when the advanced world was shedding its 'sunset industries', while China became an enthusiastic taker. China invested excessively in infrastructure and laid bare its scenic land to the ferocious pollution that accompanies heavy and chemical industries. China allowed its cheap labour to be ruthlessly exploited by the multinational companies for processing their products, reducing costs and enhancing their profits. Thus 'Made in China' became an integral part of the economic life of much of the world.

Starting from the regime of Jiang Zemin, the CPC has worked hard for a quarter of a century to show that this country of over a billion people is worthy of recognition and respect. When China is given a chance to show its best, it lives up to the expectations. There is the famous observation in the Chinese classic *Book of Change* ('*Yijing*' 易经): 'The greatest virtue of Heaven and Earth is creation' (天地之大德曰生 *tiandizhi da de yue sheng*). The people of China are enthusiastic and creative, and the CPC has done its best to encourage and promote these 'Chinese characteristics' from the early 1980s. It has opened the Party to entrepreneurs. Today, more than 40 percent of China's leading 'Capitalists' are CPC members. The quarter-century old banner of 'new Socialist villages' (社会主义新农村 *shehui zhuyi xin nongcun*) flies high on Xi Jinping's watch, metamorphosing poverty and backwardness into prosperity and modernity, with local Party units leading farm hands towards developing capitalistic enterprises. Innumerable CPC leaders at the grassroots wear hats as CEOs in China's rural areas. In the last five years, the Xi Jinping administration has built extensive modern highways in the countryside, linking more than 99 percent of China's villages and townships with motor transportation arteries. Considering China's vast territory and rugged landscape, this is a great transformation in mobility and rural development. Moreover, by June 2016, China's netizens in the rural areas made up almost 30 percent of the population as against over 60 percent in urban areas. This puts urban China in the front row in the developed world, and rural China far ahead of other developing societies in our information era.

Industry, commerce and services are booming in urban China, catching up with the highest world standards. On the surface, it is miraculous. In reality, it is a result of tremendous hardwork, sacrifice, and dedication. For China, being globalised means being Westernised and Anglicised. However, such a development suits China well and helps China return to its odyssey along the civilisational highway. Today, Xi Jinping's China is an homogenous synthesis of a heterogeneous Chinese thesis with an Anglicised antithesis. It is not the unity of diversity, but the unification of diverse forces, systems, traditions, institutions and styles. Such a chemical process of unification may indeed cause intense struggle, David Shambaugh, the Director of the China Policy Programme at George Washington University, had predicted, in an influential doomsday essay titled 'The Coming Chinese Crackup' published in *The Wall Street Journal* on 6 March 2015. Clearly, Shambaugh was unable to appreciate the unification energy of Chinese civilisation, thus paradoxically elevating global awareness of the crisis-management capability of Xi Jinping and his team.

Like Shambaugh, many commentators regard Xi's China as an odd man out in the modern democratic mainstream, though China's persistent economic growth is on a fast track that no other country can match or overtake. Immediately after the 19$^{th}$ Congress, the important Annual All-China Conference on Economic Work (中央经济工作会议 *zhongyang jingji gongzuo huiyi*) met in December 2017. It set the goal that China must ensure greater quantitative economic growth than the U.S. growth in 2018. Another important decision of the Conference was to ensure smooth economic development in 2018, free from unanticipated risks like the global financial crisis of 2008. This testifies to China's confidence in its present economic strength as an unshakable pillar in our fragile global economic situation, no longer on the receiving end of accusations and apprehensions. Countries and peoples the world over have begun to respect and admire how China is shaping up internally and externally.

During my post-19th Congress sojourn in Beijing, I gathered the impression that Xi Jinping's focus at the 19th Congress is the rounded and balanced development of China, in contrast with the desperate emphasis on pushing up China's GDP growth in the three decades under the previous regimes of Deng Xiaoping, Jiang Zemin and Hu Jintao that had produced substantial damage to the Chinese natural, cultural and socio-political ecology. The 'China breaking up' chorus would have hit the nail on its head, had not the Xi Jinping administration taken timely corrective measures. In fact, for many years, Xi Jinping has advocated an alternative development path and his message has now been driven home with its elevation at the 19th Congress to the status of 'Xi Jinping Thought' (习近平思想 *Xi Jinping sixiang*). My readers must be aware of the enduring Chinese obsession with the so-called 'rectification of names/terminology' (正名 *zheng ming*). Before the 19th Congress there were only the three 'rectified' or officially codified Chinese terms: 'Marxism' (马克思主义 *Makesi zhuyi*) 'Mao Zedong Thought' (毛泽东思想 *Mao Zedong sixiang*) and 'Deng Xiaoping Theory' (邓小平理论 *Deng Xiaoping lilun*). When the term 'Mao Zedong Thought' was codified during the 1940s and 1950s, it was Mao Zedong himself who had strongly objected to the initially proposed terminology of 'Maoism' (毛泽东主义 *Mao Zedong zhuyi*), preferring the more modest denomination of 'Mao Zedong Thought'. I am told that a similar situation emerged during the 19th Congress. When the proposal of 'Xi Jinping Thought' was mooted, it was Xi himself who was reluctant to have his 'thought' elevated to the level of 'Mao Zedong Thought'. The compromise formulation is the addition of an eleven-character qualification, 'Socialism with Chinese Characteristics in a New Era' (新时代中国特色社会主义 *xin shidai zhongguo tese shehui zhuyi*) – making 'Xi Jinping Thought' a hyphenated version of 'Mao Zedong Thought'.

Do we then see a return of the personality cult of the Mao Zedong era? I should advise against a hasty conclusion in this regard. On the contrary, I see a need for a correction of the poverty of revolutionary ideology over the past three decades. In the absence of a revolutionary ideology, extravagant lifestyles, detrimental to the long-term health of Chinese civilisation, had become rampant. My readers may recall that under the banner of 'Mao Zedong Thought' there was scope for China to develop a type of socialism to guide the PRC's political practices free from Western interference, and giving full play for the millennial wisdom of Chinese civilisation. The greatest contribution of Mao Zedong Thought to the development of Socialism in China (or 'Socialism with Chinese characteristics') was its total rejection of the Eurocentric Marxian bias against 'rural idiocy' (*via* the 'Communist Manifesto'). Mao Zedong was himself one of Marx's so-called 'rural idiots' who, along with millions of other 'rural idiots', created a new China with the earth-shaking phenomenon of peasant uprising or '*fanshen*' (翻身) (i.e. from the down-trodden to the upright position in social standing). Xi Jinping's China is *of, by and for* the prosperity of the billion-plus *fanshen* peasants, but Karl Marx was completely blind to the fact that China was a civilisation whose industry and commerce were built on agriculture long before Europe distinguished itself in these essential ingredients of modern economic life. This was the essential and 'characteristic' base of Chinese civilisation.

While Mao Zedong had seriously focused on 'Chinese characteristics' without explicitly advocating them, Xi Jinping has now made 'Socialism with Chinese characteristics' the landmark of his administration. For me, this is the prominent message of the 19$^{th}$ Congress. When I discovered this after I landed in Beijing in October 2017, I realised this vital omission in my book on 5000 years of Chinese civilisation. My book was nothing but a discourse on 'Chinese characteristics', but these words were absent from the pages. That realisation prompted me to give a talk at the Renmin University, Beijing, titled 'From 5000 to 2050'. The number '5000' is drawn from the title of my book, while the number '2050' is the target date for Xi Jinping's new movement that aims to create a splendid Socialist country 'with Chinese characteristics'. I can easily imagine that if Xi Jinping's 'dream' were to come true, China would have reclaimed the global status that it had enjoyed during the best years of the Tang Dynasty. That is to say, by 2050, China would excel in both economic development and science and technology, with substantial military power as well, thereby enjoying high prestige in the comity of nations. I think this is the picture drawn by the 19$^{th}$ Congress, and many of my friends in China were clearly thrilled by this 2050 prospect.

If my reader is non-Chinese, do you look forward to the day when this Chinese dream materialises? Or are you worried that a new and mysterious hegemon is going to turn out to be like the proverbial bull in the china shop? I speak of a 'mysterious hegemon' for the reason that we can find no trace of a 'Chinese hegemon' in world history. After a comprehensive survey of China's 5000 year odyssey, I am convinced that China is not cut out for the role of a world hegemon. In fact, the 19$^{th}$ Congress emphatically reiterates antipathy towards hegemony and, to the contrary, highlights the ideal of a 'common destiny for humanity' (命运共同体 *mingyun gongtongti*). This 'common destiny for humanity' is exactly the message of my book.

It has been the convention of the previous Party Congresses to limit the tenure of the top leader to two five-year terms. By that convention, the shadow of Xi Jinping's successor should have been evident among the new members of the Standing Committee of the Politburo of the CPC elected by the 19$^{th}$ Congress. The impression I gathered from my inquiries in Beijing is the likelihood of a substantial change in the conventional succession system. That change is not unrelated to the projection of 'Xi Jinping Thought'. It is possible that there will be a substantial revision of the rules during the 20$^{th}$ Congress: that is, the Chairmanship of the CPC (of which Xi Jinping would be the first incumbent), would have an unlimited tenure, while the two-term succession convention for the Chairman of the PRC will continue. If that happens, China would return to the Mao Zedong era which had different chairmen for the Party and the country respectively – Mao Zedong as the Chairman of the CPC, and Liu Shaoqi as the Chairman of the PRC. At that time, China was enjoying a period of 'Hundred Flowers Blossoming'– 'democratic' and relaxed. Unfortunately, the Cultural Revolution wrecked that ephemeral episode.

Whatever should be the case, it is certain that there will be a maximisation of Xi Jinping's reputation and influence in China (of course also in the world) in the coming five years, and perhaps even beyond, with Xi Jinping assuming the role of supremo like Deng Xiaoping until he breathed his last. My readers may remember that when Deng Xiaoping assumed that role he was not so much a dictator but a guarantor, as it were, for China's smooth entry into the Anglobal world. Thus, as a future supremo, Xi Jinping might see to it that China works itself into a new arena now vaguely described by the 19$^{th}$ Congress as achieving the victory of 'Socialism with Chinese characteristics in a new era'. This description is being spelled out by some Party ideologues like Gao Shangquan (高尚全) as the satisfaction of the increasing demand of the Chinese people in respect of their economic, political, cultural, social and environmental concerns. In his Political Report to the 19$^{th}$ Congress, Xi Jinping has defined the main contradiction of Chinese society today as that between insufficient and uneven economic development and the increasing universal demands of the Chinese people for a good life such that, by the year 2050, China would become a country in which the majority, if not the entirety, would live like the middle and upper middle classes of the developed countries. Is this aspiration just empty talk or a serious goal? I believe it is the latter. Gao Shangquan tells us that for the last five years the Xi Jinping administration has taken some 1500 reform measures and that Xi's drive for reform shows no sign of relaxation. When the 20$^{th}$ Party Congress meets in 2023, we shall be in a better position to judge this.

Some may ask about the difference between the 'good life' projected by the 19$^{th}$ Congress and the 'hedonistic merrymaking' that I had earlier referred to. For me the goal of a universal 'good life' discussed in the 19th Congress indicates prosperity in a positive sense, while 'hedonistic merrymaking' is an extravagant indulgence by the privileged minority at the expense of the welfare of the majority. The Xi Jinping administration favours the former. We may understand the two scenarios better through a quote from my book on what the Tang Emperor Taizong (唐太宗 626-49), had said: 'people enjoying living means the officials' life is not good' (民乐则官苦 *minyue zeguan ku*) and 'the officials enjoy living means people are troubled' (官乐则民劳 *guanyue ze minlao*). I don't know whether Xi Jinping has ever used these words, but he has said that those who want to enjoy life have no place in the government. In my survey of China's 5000-year odyssey I regard hedonistic merrymaking as a fatal weakness of Chinese civilisation, and am concerned about its potential reemergence. Xi Jinping's disapproval is reassuring in this regard.

Xi Jinping's great achievement is, of course, his ruthless campaign against corruption during his first five years. Not only has it been unprecedentedly vigorous, but it has been projected as a hallmark of the vibrant energy of Chinese civilisation. To my great surprise and delight, a book titled *The Concise History of Anti-corruption in China* (简明中国反贪史 *jianming zhongguo fantan shi*) was brought out in 2015 by a historian of the Chinese Academy of Social Sciences, Wang Chunyu (王春瑜). The book surveys Chinese political history from a new perspective, and concludes that all the major dynasties in China rose through campaigns against corruption, but could not sustain them. Finally, it was corruption that brought about their downfall. That book has become a basic text of China's anti-corruption campaign, highlighting the natural tendency of corruption in China's political environment, and the structural necessity of constant and sustained 'anti-corruption struggle' (反贪斗争 *fantan douzheng*). Thousands of corrupt officials, high and low, were cleansed from Xi's government in these five years. These included 17 members and another 17 candidate members of the Party Central Committee, plus six members of the Commission for Discipline Inspection (which is the headquarters of China's anti-corruption campaign). Cynics used to describe anti-corruption efforts in pre-Xi China as an exercise in 'killing the flies but not hurting the tigers'. No longer. In his Political Report to the 19th Congress, Xi reiterated that both 'flies' and 'tigers' are targeted, adding a third category: the 'foxes'. This is a hint that, howsoever shrewd a corrupt official may be, he or she will ultimately be brought to book.

Xi's anti-corruption campaign actually forms an important part of his reform programme, which has both destructive and constructive elements. It visualises a three-stage construction of China's political culture with specific targets. The initial stage is to ensure that officials 'have no guts for corruption' (不敢腐 *bugan fu*). The second stage is to 'give them no way for corruption' (不能腐 ***bunengfu***); the final stage is to transform them to having 'no intention of corruption' (不想腐 ***buxiangfu***). In other words, initially the emphasis is on stringent punishment with 'zero tolerance', making the officials think twice before tasting the forbidden fruit. Gradually, the rules and regulations become comprehensive enough to prevent corruption. Finally, a new culture of honesty and integrity emergesin Chinese politics, so that corruption has no soil on which to grow. Once again, Chinese civilisation would favour Xi Jinping, who must have been inspired by an observation of Mencius that the true spirit of a Chinese 'won't be corrupted by wealth' (富贵不能淫 ***fu gue buneng yin***), 'won't be diminished by poverty' (贫贱不能移 ***pinjian buneng yi***), and 'won't be humiliated by external forces' (威武不能屈 ***weiwu buneng qu***). Xi Jinping is indeed building 'Socialism with Chinese characteristics', relying on genuine Chinese wisdom.

An important measure of Xi Jinping's anti-corruption campaign is to send the 'central inspection team' (中央巡视组 *zhongyang xunshizu*) to Provinces, state-owned enterprises, and major universities for intensive investigation of the functioning of the organisation and its personnel. Since last year, the scope of inspection expanded to include judicial institutions and law courts. In the course of 12 inspections in five years, the inspection teams received 1.59 million letters from the public exposing malpractices in the inspected institutions, which led to the resolution of 8,200 administrative problems and bottlenecks. This is an innovation much needed for a huge country like China, with a vast intermediary layer of socio-political interests, insulating the top leadership from the masses. There are always bad elements preventing the resonance between the leader's concern for the welfare of the people, and the people's desire for a judicious and people-friendly administration. The fact-finding inspection teams help the central government to demolish the intermediary barriers.

I must tell you that these anti-corruption reforms and innovations are drawn from the experience of China's odyssey along the civilisational highway. During historical times, there were episodes of courageous imperial 'censors' (监察御史 *jiancha yushi*), i.e. young toppers of the imperial examinations, exposing the corruption and malpractices of powerful provincial governors. Dr. Sun Yat-sen (Father of the Republic of China) concluded that in addition to the triple division of government functions (legislative, executive and judiciary), the Chinese political system required two additional and functionally important aspects, namely 'examination' (考试 *kaoshi*) and 'censorial/supervisory' (监察 *jiancha*). In a vast country like China with many layers of governing authorities there is always a situation, popularly summed up as: 'The emperor is as far away as the heaven is high above' (天高皇帝远 *tiangao huangdi yuan*). Only the government can efficiently supervise the government and ensure judicious and honest governance.

'The green mountains and rivers are our mountains of gold and silver' (绿水青山就是金山银山 *Lushui qingshan jiushu!*) This is a famous adage of Xi Jinping. He reiterates it in his Report to the 19th Congress, adding the advice: 'treating our environment like treating our life' (像对待生命一样对待生态环境 *xiang duidai shengming yiyang duidai shengtai huanjing*). Xi Jinping's political ideal is as 'green' as that of any world 'Green Party' leader. People who live in the big cities like Beijing and Shanghai do enjoy unprecedented freedom to breathe freely, but merely the freedom to breathe dirty air! If my memory is correct, during the 18th Congress when Xi Jinping attended a group discussion of scientists, he was told that people in the streets of Beijing were making fun of Mao Zedong's great poem, '*Snow*' (雪 *xue*). Mao wrote in the poem:

'O, my country,
What an enchanting bride,
For countless heroes who woo her with craving eyes!'
江山如此多娇，以无数英雄 尽境折腰！
*Jiangshan ruci duo jiao, yin wushu yingxiong jinjing zheyao*

The Beijing residents who breathed dirty air paraphrased:

'O, the air,
What a filthy mess in the skies,
For countless beauties who cover their faces up to the eyes!'
空气如此糟糕，引无数美女戴口罩
(*kongqi ruci zaogao, yin wushu meinu dai kouzhao*)

In the above poem Mao used the two Chinese words 'rivers and mountains' (江山 *jiangshan*) as a symbol for China. People in China are eager to see the beauty of their country restored, and Xi Jinping's call for the creation of a 'beautiful China' has generated overwhelming enthusiasm everywhere.

But what is the meaning of 'Socialism with Chinese characteristics'? Some people would say that it is self-evident that everything in China has a Chinese appearance, taste and flavour, i.e., 'Chinese characteristics'. However, highlighting '*Socialism* with Chinese characteristics' by the 19th Congress does have specific connotations which must not be ignored. For me, from an historical perspective, 'Socialism with Chinese characteristics' is the concretisation of the age-old Chinese civilisational ideal of 'grand harmony of all under Heaven' (天下大同 *tianxia datong*). In Xi Jinping's Report to the 19th Congress, he reiterates that there must be 'nurture for the young' (幼有所育 *you you suoyu*), 'teaching for the learner' (学有所教 *xue you suojiao*), 'wage for the labour'

(劳有所得 *lao you suode*), 'medicine for the sick' (病有所医 *bing you suoyi*)', 'care for the old' (老有所养 *lao you suo yang*), 'accommodation for the resident' (住有所居 *zhu you suoju*), and 'support for the weak' (弱有所扶 *ru you suofu*). While this flowery language is an unmistakable echo of the text of the classical 'Essay on grand harmony' (大同篇 *datongpian*) in the *Liji* (礼记, Book of Rites), we can see that in this narrative Xi Jinping has already spelled out 'Socialism with Chinese characteristics'. Let me quote another sentence from the 19th Congress Report (my translation): Xi says that China should 'dig deep into the excellent culture of the quintessential Chinese civilisation' (深入挖掘中 华优秀传统文化 *shenru wajue zhonghua youxiu chuantong wenhua*) as well as 'satisfy the demand of the times' (结合时代要求 *jiehe shidai yaoqiu*). I think this is the real meaning of 'Socialism with Chinese characteristics'.

The 19th Congress also marked the re-emergence of what one might call 'civic sense' (社会公德 *shehui gongde*), that is, a combination of 'professional ethics' (职业道德 *zhiye daode*), 'family values'(家庭美德 *jiating meide*) and 'individual morality' (个人品德 *geren pinde*) in a social atmosphere of 'high and virtuous thinking' (向上向善 *xiang shang xiang shang*), 'filial respect for parents and love for the near and dear' (孝老爱亲 *xiao lao ai qin*), 'loyalty to the fatherland' (忠于祖国 *zong yu zu guo*) and 'dedication to the people' (忠于人民 *zong yu renmin*). The emphasis on 'filial piety' (孝) is exquisite! What is the use of celebrating 'Father's/Mother's Day' in the absence of filial piety? 'Filial piety', an ideal now re-established by Xi Jinping, is an inherited cultural treasure that had been lost in China–first damaged by the 4 May, New Culture Movement, then destroyed by the Cultural Revolution. At the 19th Congress, the new 'Chinese dream' is formulated as: 'creating in the middle of this century a powerful Socialist country, rich and strong, democratic, civilised, harmonious, and beautiful' (在本世纪中叶建成富强民主文明和谐美丽的社会主义现代化强国 *zai ben shijie zhongye jiancheng fuqiang minzu wenming hexie meili shehui zhuyi xiandai hua qiangguo*). The reiteration of 'powerful' and 'strong' may seem to confirm the international impression of an assertive China evoking 'fear', not 'love', among others, especially China's neighbours. This aspect has always been my concern. I have advocated for decades that the best image for China should be 'respect and love' (敬爱 *jing ai*), not 'respect and fear' (敬畏 *jing wei*). This advice did create some effect in China, but my limited contactsdid not go far enough – after all, one little swallow does not make a summer.

In saying this, I do not view the 19th Congress' 'Chinese dream' in a negative sense. In fact, the essential truth of my book is a lament on the want of awareness of the need for a 'strong country', especially during the Song Dynasty. Ironically, the world has complimented China for inventing gunpowder, which it never in fact invented. This false compliment misled Georg Friedrich Hegel, the famous 19th century German thinker, to highlight the Chinese incompetence in depending on the European Jesuits' help to make their first cannon a millennium after they had invented gunpowder. Hegel should have known, and the world should have known, that the Chinese invention by its Chinese name, '*huoyao*' (火药) is a 'concoction for fire'. During the Song Dynasty, this fireworks-powder was easily available all over China. It was Genghis Khan who set up a special unit in his ever-victorious army with captured Chinese soldiers directed to use this fireworks-powder for the purposes of blasting defensive barriers (in fact, scaring the enemy to death) in Eurasia. Thus was born the concept of 'gunpowder', courtesy of the Mongols, not the Chinese.

If the concept of gunpowder were the brain-child of the Chinese, would not the people of the Song Dynasty have taken advantage of the *made-in-China* fire-powder to repulse the inroads of the horsemen of the Khitan, Nurchen and Mongol nation states, and emerged victorious? Would that not, then, have changed the entire course of world history? It was not Chinese stupidity, but China's odyssey along the civilisational highway (coupled with the carefree merrymaking of the Song ruling elite) that resulted in the two great tragedies of the 12th and 13th century. Viewed from this historical perspective, the 19th Congress's determination to make China a powerful country is unexceptionable. Simultaneously, the 19th Congress has also announced to the entire world that neither would China import a foreign model, nor would it export the Chinese model of development, and that China would never become a world hegemon. That is reassuring. Of course, when China is not yet the strongest country on earth, China's non-hegemonic pledge has only symbolic value. Only when China is militarily peerless (which surely would not happen within a quarter of a century) can people be in a position to determine if the pledge is true or false. Right now, what we can say is that China is rather relaxed in its coexistence with the current hegemon of the world – the U.S.A., which ceaselessly makes provocative gestures in China's territorial waters. China is fundamentally different from the erstwhile Soviet Union that joined the fierce armaments race with the U.S. and ultimately destroyed itself. China has no intention of following such a course. China's creation of its *assertive* image was primarily due to its hawkish public opinions and knee-jerk reactions to controversial issues concerning territory and territorial waters. If Xi's China continues to send out peaceful and conciliatory signals and messages, the people of other countries, especially in China's neighbourhood, will sleep better.

I think my readers have already a full plate from me! Do you find sufficient food for thought in this plate, dear readers?

# APPENDICES
# Some Relevant Information on Party, State Structure and Personnel

*Bhim B Subba*

## Appendix I

### CPC Congress and Membership, 1921-2017

| Party Congress | Year | Party Leader | Total Membership |
|---|---|---|---|
| 1st | 1921 | Chen Duxiu | 57 |
| 2nd | 1922 | Chen Duxiu | 195 |
| 3rd | 1923 | Chen Dixiu | 420 |
| 4th | 1925 | Chen Duxiu | 994 |
| 5th | 1927 | Chen Duxiu | 57967 |
| 6th | 1928 | Xiang Zhongfa | 40000 |
| 7th | 1945* | Mao Zedong | 1,211,128 |
| 8th | 1956 | Mao Zedong | 10,734,384 |
| 9th | 1969 | Mao Zedong | 20,000,000 |
| 10th | 1973 | Mao Zedong | 28,000,000 |
| 11th | 1977 | Hua Guofeng | 35,000,000 |
| 12th | 1982 | Hu Yaobang | 39,650,000 |
| 13th | 1987 | Zhao Ziyang | 46,000,000 |
| 14th | 1992 | Jiang Zemin | 51,000,000 |
| 15th | 1997 | Jiang Zemin | 58,000,000 |
| 16th | 2002 | Hu Jintao | 66,000,000 |
| 17th | 2007 | Hu Jintao | 73,000,000 |
| 18th | 2012 | Xi Jinping | 82,000,000 |
| 19th | 2017 | Xi Jinping | 89,000,000 |

**Note*: From 1945 till 1976 Mao Zedong was the Chairperson of the CPC. At the 11th Congress in 1977 Hua Guofeng was elected as the Chairperson. The office of the Chairperson was replaced by that of General Secretary at the 12th Congress in 1982.

*Source:* Mohanty, Manoranjan. 2014. *Ideology Matters: China from Mao Zedong to Xi Jinping*. New Delhi: Aakar Books. p.xx.
*People's Daily Online*. http://english.cpc.people.com.cn/
http://www.xinhuanet.com/english/2017-06/30/c_136407371.htm
http://cpc.people.com.cn/GB/64162/64168/64556/index.html

# Appendix II

## CPC Membership of Women and Minorities (1949–2017)

| Years | Total Membership | Women (persons) | % | Minorities (persons) | % |
|---|---|---|---|---|---|
| 1949 | 4,488080 | 532287 | 11.86 | 0 | 0.00 |
| 1956 | 12,504332 | 1,306110 | 10.45 | 458746 | 3.67 |
| 1960 | 17,406054 | 2,101524 | 12.07 | 781560 | 4.49 |
| 1965 | 18,710353 | 2,155245 | 11.52 | 827334 | 4.42 |
| 1973 | 30,123826 | 3,779207 | 12.55 | 1,381222 | 4.59 |
| 1978 | 36,981346 | 4,975923 | 13.46 | 1,758724 | 4.76 |
| 1982 | 40,243432 | 5,399335 | 13.42 | 1,997771 | 4.96 |
| 1987 | 47,755319 | 6,768226 | 14.17 | 2,606568 | 5.46 |
| 1992 | 52,792746 | 7,883829 | 14.93 | 3,018837 | 5.72 |
| 1997 | 60,417384 | 9,836462 | 16.28 | 3,647672 | 6.04 |
| 2002 | 66,941180 | 11,917708 | 17.80 | 4,231021 | 6.32 |
| 2007 | 74,152876 | 15,116028 | 20.38 | 4,787032 | 6.46 |
| 2010 | 80,268615 | 18,029833 | 22.46 | 5,337685 | 6.65 |
| 2012 | 85,127000 | 20,269000 | 23.81 | 5,802000 | 6.82 |
| 2017 | 89, 564000 | 23,888200 | 26.70 | 6,510000 | 7.30 |

*Sources*: Various official sources.

# Appendix III

## Biographical Profiles of the 19th Politburo Members
(as of 20 August 2018)

**Xi Jinping (习近平)**

- Born on 15 June 1953, Beijing
- 2012—present, General Secretary of the Communist Party of China (CPC)
- 2013—present, President of the People's Republic of China (PRC)
- 2012/13—present, Chairman of the Central Military Commission (CMC)
- 2013—present, Chairman, National Security Commission
- 2012—present, Head of the Central Leading Groups (中央领导小组)
    - 2012- Taiwan Affairs
    - 2013- Comprehensively Deepening Reforms
    - 2013- Foreign Affairs and National Security
    - 2014- Network Security and Information Technology
    - 2014- Deepening Reforms of National Defence and the Military
- 2016—present, Commander in Chief, Joint Operations Command Centre of the PLA
- 2017—present, Chairman, Central Military and Civilian Integration Development Committee
- 2012—present, Chairman, Central Financial and Economic Affairs Commission
- 2007—present, Politburo Standing Committee (PBSC) Member
- 2002—present, Full member of the CPC Central Committee

**Li Keqiang (李克强)**

- Born on 1 July1955, Anhui Province
- 2013—present, Premier, State Council
- 2013—present, Vice-Chairman, National Security Commission
- 2013—present, Deputy head, CLG for Comprehensively Deepening Reforms
- 2013—present, Deputy head, Central Financial and Economic Affairs Commission
- 2013—present Head, State Energy Commission;
    - State Council Leading Group for Western Region Development

   - State Council Leading Group for Rejuvenating the Northeast Region & other old Industrial Bases
   - National Leading Group for Climate Change and for Energy Conservation & Reduction of Pollution Discharge
- 2007—present, Politburo Standing Committee Member
- 1997—present, Full member of the CPC Central Committee

**Li Zhanshu (栗战书)**

- Born on 30 August 1950, Hebei Province
- 2017—present, Politburo Standing Committee Member
- 2018—Chairman, 13th National People's Congress Standing Committee
- 2012—present, Director, General Office, CPC Central Committee
- 2012—present, Director, Office of the National Security Commission
- 2012—present, Member of the Politburo
- 2012—present, Full member of the CPC Central Committee

**Wang Yang (汪洋)**

- Born on 12 March 1955, Anhui Province
- 2017—present, Politburo Standing Committee Member
- 2018—Chairman, Chinese People's Political Consultative Conference (CPPCC)
- 2013-18: Vice Premier, State Council
- 2007—present, Member of the Politburo;
- 2007—present, Full member of the CPC Central Committee
- 2007-12: Party Secretary of Guangdong Province

**Wang Huning (王沪宁)**

- Born on 6 October 1955, Shanghai
- 2017—present, Politburo Standing Committee Member
- 2017—present, Executive Secretary, Party Secretariat, CPC Central Committee
- 2017—present, Member, LSG for Internet Security and Informationisation
- 2013—present, Secretary General, General Office, LSG for Comprehensively Deepening Reforms
- 2007—present, Member of the Politburo
- 2002—present, Director, Central Policy Research Office of the CPC Central Committee

**Zhao Leji (赵乐际)**

- Born on 8 March 1957, Qinghai Province
- 2017—present, Secretary, Central Commission for Discipline Inspection (CCDI)
- 2017—present, Member of the Politburo Standing Committee
- 2012-17: Director, Central Organisation Department, CPC Central Committee
- 2012—present, Deputy Director, LSG for Party-Building, CPC Central Committee
- 2012—present, Member of the Politburo
- 2002—present, Full member of the CPC Central Committee

**Han Zheng (韩正)**

- Born in April 1954, Shanghai
- 2017—present, Member of the Politburo Standing Committee
- 2018—Executive Vice-Premier, The State Council (*government budget, social security, environment*)
- 2012—present, Member of the Politburo
- 2012—17: Party Secretary, Shanghai Municipal Committee, CPC
- 2002—present, Full member of the CPC Central Committee
- 2018-present, Chairman, Central Coordination Group for Hong Kong and Macau Affairs

**Ding Xuexiang (丁薛祥)**

- Born in September 1962, Jiangsu Province
- 2017—present, Member of the Politburo
- 2017—present, Director, General Office, CPC Central Committee
- 2017—present, Member, Party Secretariat, CPC Central Committee
- 2012-17: Alternate member, 18th CPC Central Committee

**Wang Chen (王晨)**

- Born in December 1950, Beijing
- 2017—present, Member of the Politburo
- 2018—Executive Vice-Chairman, 13th NPC Standing Committee
- 2008-13: Director, State Council Information Office
- 2002—present, Full member of the Central Committee

**Liu He (刘鹤)**

- Born on 25 January 1952, Beijing
- 2018—Vice-Premier, State Council (*finance, S&T, SMEs, major international economic relations*)
- 2017—present, Member of the Politburo
- 2013—present, Director, General Office, CLG for Financial and Economic Affairs
- 2012—present, Full member of the CPC Central Committee

**Xu Qiliang (许其亮)**

- Born in March 1950, Shandong Province
- 2012—present, Vice-Chairman of the CMC (General rank)
- 2012—present Member of the Politburo
- 2007-12: Commander, PLA Air Force
- 2002—present, Full member of the CPC Central Committee

**Sun Chunlan (孙春兰)**

- Born on 24 May 1950, Hebei Province
- 2018—Vice-Premier, State Council (*education, health, sports & veteran affairs*)
- 2012—present, Member of the Politburo
- 2014-17: Head, CPC United Front Work Department
- 2012-14: Party Secretary, Tianjin Municipality
- 2007—present, Full member of the CPC Central Committee

**Li Xi (李希)**

- Born on 16 October 1956, Gansu Province
- 2017—present, Member of the Politburo
- 2017—present, Party Secretary, Guangdong Province
- 2015-17: Party Secretary, Liaoning Province
- 2012—present, Member, CCDI
- 2012-17: Alternate member of the 18th CPC Central Committee

**Li Qiang (李强)**

- Born in July 1959, Zhejiang Province
- 2017—present, Member of the Politburo
- 2017—present, Party Secretary, Shanghai Municipality
- 2016-17: Party Secretary, Jiangsu Province

- 2013-16: Governor, Zhejiang Provincial Government
- 2012-17: Alternate member of 18th CPC Central Committee

**Li Hongzhong (李鸿忠)**

- Born in August 1956, Liaoning Province
- 2017—present, Member of the Politburo
- 2016—present, Party Secretary, Tianjin Municipality
- 2012—present, Full member of the CPC Central Committee
- 2010-16: Party Secretary, Hubei Province

**Yang Jiechi (杨洁篪)**

- Born in May 1950, Shanghai
- 2017—present, Member of the Politburo
- 2017—present, Director, Office of the CPC Foreign Affairs Work Commission
- 2017—present, Deputy Director, CLG for Hong Kong, Macao and Taiwan Affairs
- 2013-18: State Councilor, State Council
- 2007—present, Full member of the CPC Central Committee

**Yang Xiaodu (杨晓渡)**

- Born in October 1953, Shanghai
- 2017—present, Member of the Politburo
- 2018—present, Director, National Supervision Commission
- 2016—present, Minister of Supervision
- 2014—present, Deputy Director, CCDI
- 2012—present, Full member of the CPC Central Committee

**Zhang Youxia (张又侠)**

- Born in July 1950, Beijing
- 2017—present, Member of the Politburo
- 2017—present, Vice-Chairman, Central Military Commission (General)
- 2012-17: Member, Central Military Commission
- 2007—present, Full member of the CPC Central Committee

**Chen Xi (陈希)**

- Born in September 1953, Fujian Province
- 2017—present, Member of the Politburo

- 2017—present, Director, CPC Organisation Department
- 2017—present, President, Central Party School, Beijing
- 2012—present, Full member of the CPC Central Committee

**Chen Quanguo (陈全国)**

- Born in November 1955, Henan Province
- 2017—present, Member of the Politburo
- 2016—present, Party Secretary, Xinjiang (Uygur) Autonomous Region
- 2012—present, Full member of the CPC Central Committee
- 2011-16: Party Secretary, Tibet Autonomous Region

**Chen Min'er (陈敏尔)**

- Born on 29 September 1960, Zhejiang Province
- 2017—present, Member of the Politburo
- 2017—present, Party Secretary, Chongqing Municipality
- 2015-17: Party Secretary, Guizhou Province
- 2012—present, Full member of the CPC Central Committee

**Hu Chunhua (胡春华)**

- Born in April 1963, Hubei Province
- 2018—Vice Premier, State Council (*agriculture, rural work, poverty alleviation, natural disaster*)
- 2012-17: Party Secretary, Guangdong Province
- 2012—present, Member of the Politburo
- 2007—present, Full member of the CPC Central Committee

**Guo Shengkun (郭声琨)**

- Born in October 1954, Jiangxi Province
- 2017—present, Secretary, CPC Central Committee, Political and Legal Affairs Commission
- 2017—present, Member of the Politburo; State Councilor (2013-18)
- 2017—present, Member, Party Secretariat, CPC Central Committee
- 2012-17: Minister of Public Security
- 2012—present, Full member of the CPC Central Committee

**Huang Kunming (黄坤明)**

- Born in November 1956, Fujian Province
- 2017—present, Member of the Politburo

- 2017—present, Director, CPC Central Committee Propaganda Department
- 2017—present, Member, Party Secretariat
- 2012-17: Alternate member, 18th CPC Central Committee

**Cai Qi (蔡奇)**

- Born in December 1955, Fujian Province
- 2017—present, Member of the politburo
- 2017—present, Party Secretary, Beijing Municipality
- 2014-16: Executive Director, General Office, Central National Security Commission
- 2013-14: Vice-Governor, Zhenjiang Provincial Government
- 2017—present, Full member of the CPC Central Committee

# Appendix IV

## 19th CPC Central Committee Organisational Chart

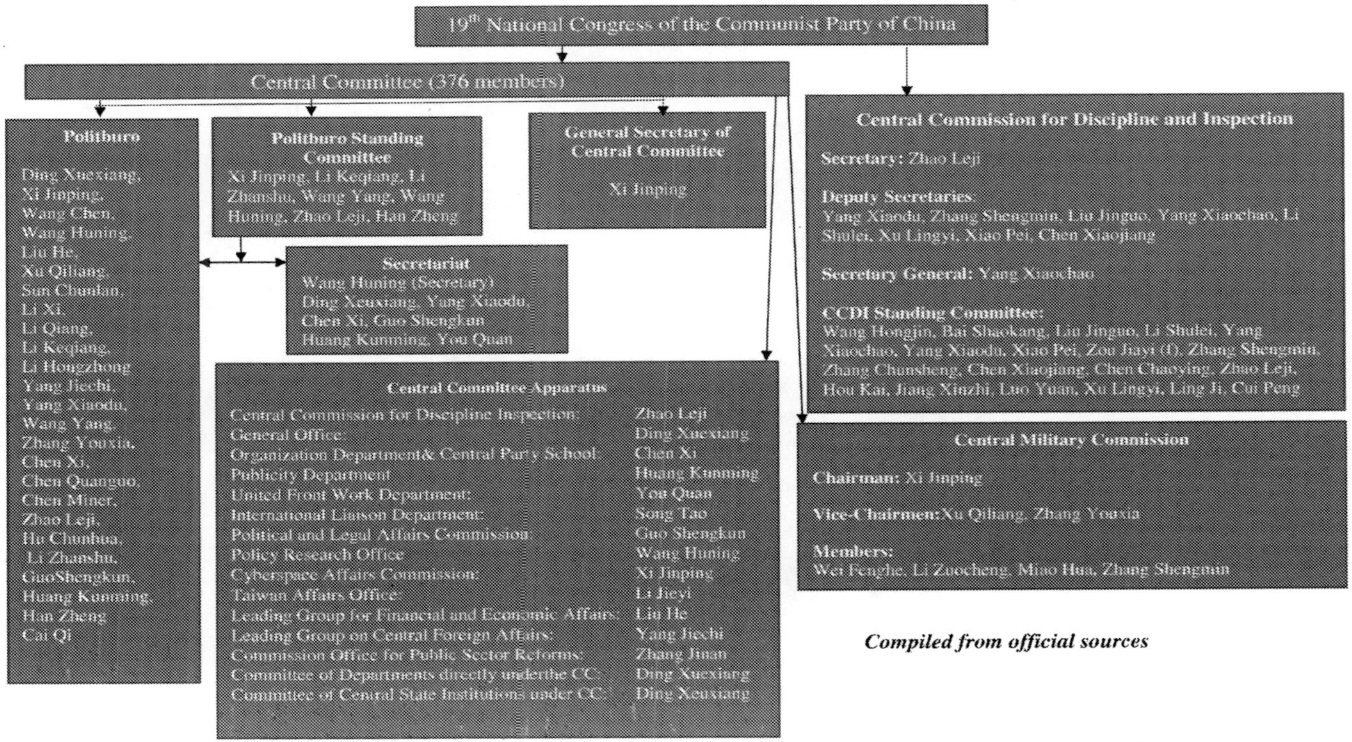


***Compiled from official sources***

# Appendix V

## 13th National People's Congress Organisational Chart

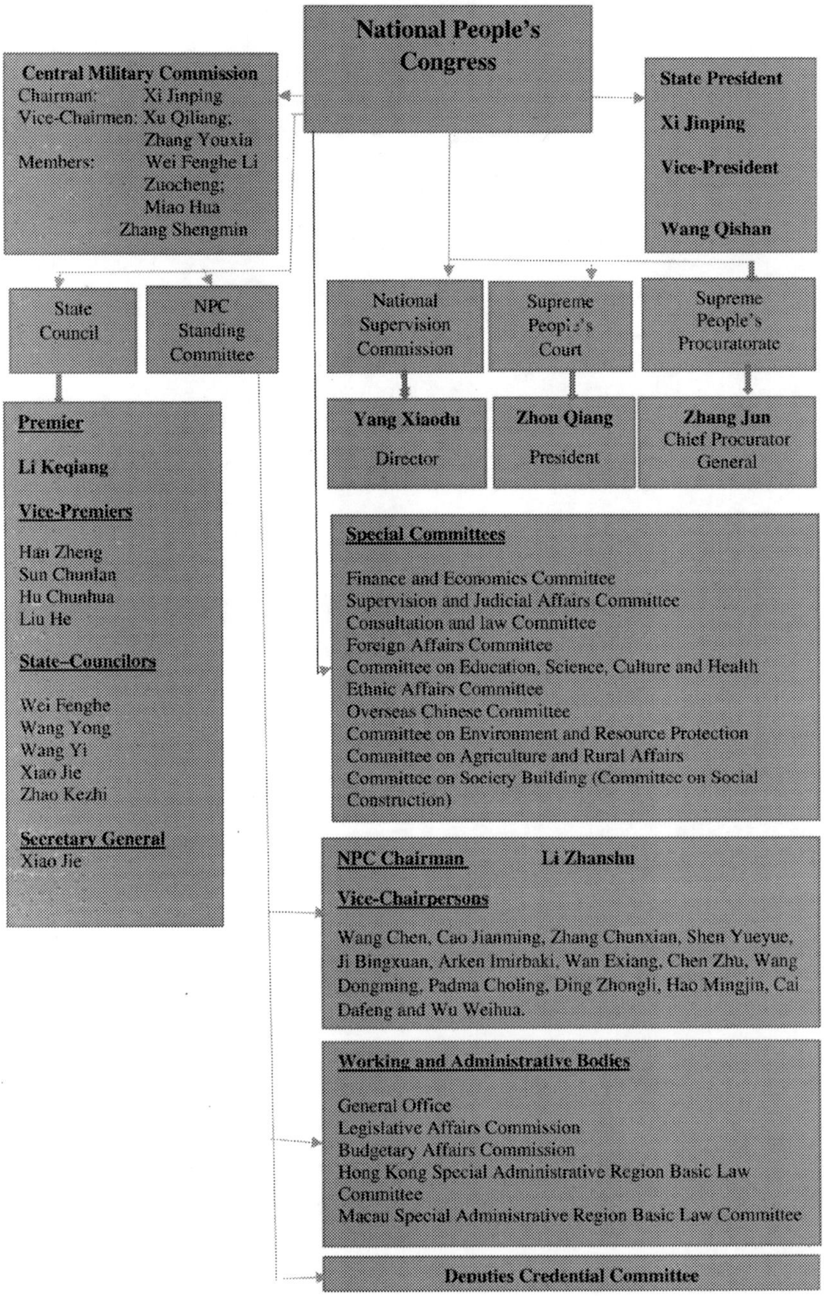

# Appendix VI

## 13th State Council Organisational Chart

**The State Council (国务院)**

*also known as*

**Central People's Government (中央人民政府)**

| **Premier** | **Vice-Premiers** | **State-Councilors** | **Secretary General** |
|---|---|---|---|
| Li Keqiang | Han Zheng<br>Sun Chunlan<br>Hu Chunhua<br>Liu He | Wei Fenghe<br>Wang Yong<br>Wang Yi<br>Xiao Jie<br>Zhao Kezhi | Xiao Jie |

**General Office of the State Council (国务院办公厅)**

| **Ministries/Departments and Incumbent Heads** | |
|---|---|
| Minister of Foreign Affairs: Wang Yi, State Councilor | Minister of Defence: Wei Fenghe, State Councilor |
| Nat. Development & Reform Commission: He Lifeng | Minister of Education: Chen Baosheng *(State Language Commission)* |
| Minister of Science & Technology: Wang Zhigang *(State Administration of Foreign Experts Affairs)* | Minister of Industry & Information Tech: Miao Wei *(China National Space Administration & China Atomic Energy Authority)* |
| Minister of State Ethnic Affairs Commission: Bate'er | Minister of Public Security: Zhao Kezhi |
| Minister of State Security: Chen Wenqing | Minister of Civil Affairs: Huang Shuxian |
| Minister of Justice: Fu Zhenghua | Minister of Finance: Liu Kun |
| Minister of Human Resource & Social Security: Zhang Jinan | Minister of Natural Resource: Lu Hao *(State Oceanic Administration)* |
| Minister of Ecology & Environment: Li Ganjie *(National Nuclear Safety Administration)* | Minister of Housing & Urban-Rural Development: Wang Menghui |
| Minister of Transport: Li Xiaopeng | Minister of Water Resource: E Jinping |
| Minister of Agriculture & Rural Affairs: Han Changfu | Minister of Commerce: Zhong Shan |

| Minister of Culture & Tourism: Luo Shugang | Minister of Nat. Health Commission: Ma Xiaowei |
|---|---|
| Minister of Veterans Affairs: Sun Shaocheng | Minister of Emergency Management: Wang Yupu |
| Governor of the People's Bank of China: Yi Gang | Auditor-General, National Audit Office: Hu Zejun |
| | |

| ***Special* Organisation directly under the State Council (国务院质素特设机构)** |
|---|
| State-owned Assets Supervision and Administration Commission (SASAC)<br>国有资产监督管理委员会 |

| **Organisations *directly* under the State Council (国务院直属机构)** | |
|---|---|
| *General Administration of Customs* | *State Administration of Taxation* |
| State Administration for Market Regulation<br>*(PRC Standardisation Administration & PRC Certification and Accreditation Administration)* | State Administration of Radio & Television |
| General Administration of Sport | National Bureau of Statistics |
| State International Development Cooperation Agency | State Medical Insurance Administration |
| Counselor's Office of the State Council | National Government Offices Administration |
| State Press & Publication Administration (National Copyright Administration)[(a)] | State Administration for Religious Affairs[(b)] |

| **Administrative Offices under the State Council (国务院办事机构)** | |
|---|---|
| Hong Kong & Macau Affairs Office | Research Office |
| Overseas Chinese Affairs Office [(b)] | Taiwan Affairs Office [(c)] |
| Cyberspace Administration of China [(d)] | State Council Information Office [(a)] |

| **Institutions directly under the State Council (国务院直属事业单位)** | |
|---|---|
| Xinhua News Agency | Chinese Academy of Sciences |
| Chinese Academy of Social Sciences | Chinese Academy of Engineering |
| Development Research Center | China Media Group |
| China Meteorological Administration | China Banking & Insurance Regulatory Commission |
| China Securities Regulatory Commission | Chinese Academy of Governance [(e)] |

| State Administrations & Bureaus Under the Ministries and Commissions (部委管理的国家局) | |
|---|---|
| *Ministries/Commissions* | *State Administrations & Bureaus* |
| General Office of the State Council | State Bureau for Letter and Calls |
| National Development and Reform Commission | 1. State Grain & Reserves Administration<br>2. National Energy Administration |
| Ministry of Industry and Information Technology | 1. State Administration of Science, Technology & Industry for National Defense<br>2. State Tobacco Monopoly Administration |
| Ministry of Public Security | State Immigration Administration *(PRC Exit and Entry Administration)* |
| Ministry of National Resources | State Forestry and Grassland Administration *(National Park Administration)* |
| Ministry of Transport | 1. National Railway Administration<br>2. Civil Aviation Administration of China<br>3. State Post Bureau |
| Ministry of Culture and Tourism | State Administration of Cultural Heritage |
| National Health Commission | State Administration of Traditional Chinese Medicine |
| People's Bank of China | State Administration of Foreign Exchange |
| Ministry of Emergency Management | State Administration of Coal Mine Safety |
| State Administration for Market Regulation | 1. State Intellectual Property Office<br>2. State Drug Administration |
| CPC Central Committee Organisation Department | State Bureau of Civil Servants (CPC CC Archives) |
| CPC Central Committee Archives | State Archives Administration |
| CPC Central Committee General Office | National Administration for the Protection of State Secrets *(same as Office of the CPC CC Secrets Protections Commission)* |
| CPC Central Committee General Office | State Cryptography Administration *(same as Office of the CPCCC Leading Group for Encryption Administration)* |

*Notes:* (a) These functions are performed by CPC Central Committee Propaganda Department

(b) Functions performed by CPC Central Committee Unite Front Work Department

(c) CPC Central Committee Taiwan Work Office (same)

(d) CPC Central Committee Cyberspace Affairs Commission (same)

(e) Same as CPC Central Committee Party School (中共中央校)

(f) Ministry of Supervision, which was founded as People's Supervisory Commission and renamed as Minitry of Supervision in 1954. However, it was dissolved in April 1959 to be re-established in July 1987.However, in March 2018, this Ministry was dissolved again to be merged with National Bureau of Corruption Prevention to form a new body—National Supervision Commission. Yang Xioadu, a Politburo member and Executive Deputy-director of CCDI is the head of this newly established body.

*Sources:* 国务院机构和部委管理的国家局设置信息， 据国法 (2018) 6 号 和国法 (2018) 7号文件 *guowuyuan jigou he buwei guanli de guojia ju shezhi xinxi, ju guofa (2018) 6 hao he guofa (2018) 7 hao wenjian* [The State Council Institutional, State Administrations and Bureau under the Ministries and Commissions Establishment Information Documents, *Guofa* (2018) No.6 & *Guofa* (2018) No. 7.] http://www.gov.cn/zhengce/content/2018-03/24/content_ 5277123. htm (accessed on 19 August 2018)

'Bilingual State Council Organisation Chart' *NPC Observer,* https:// npcobserver.com/ bilingual- state-council-organizational-chart/ (accessed on 20 August 2018)

国务院: 国务院组织机构, *guowuyuan: guowuyuan zuzhi jigou* [Organisation Structure of the State Council], http://www.gov.cn/guowuyuan/zuzhi.htm (accessed on 20 August 2018)

# Appendix VII

## 13th CPPCC National Committee

**13th Chinese People's Political Consultative Conference (CPPCC) National Committee**

Standing Committee of CPPCC National Committee

300 members

**Special Committees**

Committee on Handling Proposals
Committee on Economic Affairs
Committee on Agri. & Rural Affairs
Committee on Population Resources and Environment
Committee on Education, Science, Health and Sports
Committee on Social and Legal Affairs
Committee on Ethnic and Religious Affairs
Committee on Culture, History and Study
Committee on liaison with Hong Kong, Macau, Taiwan and Overseas Affairs
Committee on Foreign Affairs

General Office

**Chairperson**

Wang Yang

**Vice Chairpersons**

Zhang Qingli
Liu Qibao
Pagbalha Geleg Namgyal
Tung Chee-hwa,
Wang Gang
Edmond Ho Hua Wah
Lu Zhangong
Wang Zhengwei
Ma Biao
Chen Xiaoguang
Leung Chun-ying
Xia Baolong
Yang Chuantang
Li Bin
Bate'er
Wang Yongqing
He Lifeng
Su Hui
Deng Jianbang
Gu Shengzu
Liu Xincheng
He Wei
Shao Hong
Gao Yunlong

**Secretary General**

Xia Baolong

# Appendix VIII

## CPC Central Leading Groups (领导小组 *Lingdao Xiaozu*), 2018

| *Sl. No* | *Issue* | *Chinese Title* | *Area* | *Estb.* | *Chair* |
|---|---|---|---|---|---|
| 1. | Comprehensively Deepening Reform * | 中央全面深化改革领导小组 | General | Dec. 2013 | Xi Jinping |
| 2. | Taiwan | 中央台工作工作领导小组 | External Affairs & Security | Jul. 1954 | Xi Jinping |
| 3. | Economics & Finance* | 中央财经工作领导小组 | Economy | Mar. 1980 | Xi Jinping |
| 4. | Foreign Affairs / National Security* | 中央外事工作领导小组/ 中央国家安全领导小组 | External Affairs & Security | 1981 | Xi Jinping |
| 5. | National Defence & Troop Reform | 中央军委深化国防和军队改革领导小组 | External Affairs & Security | Mar. 2014 | Xi Jinping |
| 6. | Cybersecurity & Informatisation* | 中央网络安全和信息化领导小组 | External Affairs & Security | Feb. 2014 | Xi Jinping |
| 7. | National Security Commission | 国家安全委员会 | External Affairs & Security | Nov. 2013 | Xi Jinping |
| 8. | Central Military & Civilian Integration Commission | 中央军民融合发展委员会 | Society | Jan. 2017 | Xi Jinping |
| 9. | Hong Kong & Macau | 中央港澳工作协调小组 | External Affairs & Security | Aug. 1978 | Han Zheng |
| 10. | Tibet | 中央西藏工作协调小组 | External Affairs & Security | Pre-2012 | Wang Yang |
| 11. | Xinjiang | 中央新疆工作协调小组 | External Affairs & Security | 2000 | Wang Yang |
| 12. | Party Building | 中央党的建设工作领导小组 | Domestic Politics | 1988 | Wang Huning |
| 13. | Propaganda & Thought Work | 中央宣传思想工作领导小组 | Domestic Politics | Jan. 1988 | Wang Huning |
| 14. | Ideological Infrastructure | 中共中央精神文明建设指导委员会 | Society | Apr. 1997 | Wang Huning |
| 15. | Central Supervision Work | 中央巡视工作领导小组 | Domestic Politics | Nov. 2009 | Zhao Leji |

| *Sl. No* | *Issue* | *Chinese Title* | *Area* | *Estb.* | *Chair* |
|---|---|---|---|---|---|
| 16. | Secrets & Society | 中央保密委员会/中央密码工作领导小组 | Domestic Politics | Feb. 1929 | Li Zhaozong |
| 17. | Institutional Reform in Culture | 中央文化体制改革和发展工作领导小组 | Society | Jun. 2003 | Huang Kunming |
| 18. | Legal Reform | 中央司法体制改革领导小组 | Domestic Politics | May 2003 | Guo Shengyu |
| 19. | Agriculture & Rural Areas | 中央农村工作领导小组 | Domestic Politics | Mar. 1993 | Hu Chunhua |
| 20 | Talent Recruitment | 中央人才工作协调小组/中央西部地区人才开发协调小组 | Domestic Politics | 2003 | Chen Xi |
| 21. | Anti-Corruption | 中央反腐败工作协调小组 | Domestic Politics | Jan. 1996 | *Un-known* |
| 22. | United Front | 中央统一战线工作领导小组 | Domestic Politics | Jul. 2015 | *Unknown* |
| 23. | Mass Line Education | 中央党的群众路线教育实践活动领导小组 | Domestic Politics | May 2013 | *Unknown* |

*Note:* *These four leading groups (小组 ***xiaozu***) have been upgraded to Commissions (委员会 ***wei yuan hui***) in March 2018.

Similarly, among the other three leading groups: Anti-Cult (610 Office) 中央防范和处理邪教问题领导小组 has been absorbed into Ministry of Public Security Central Political and Legal Affairs Commission (CPLAC)and Social Management & Comprehensive Governance (中央社会治安综合治理委员会) is absorbed to Central Political and Legal Affairs Commission (CPLAC); and Maritime Affairs (中央海洋权益工作领导小组) absorbed into Central Foreign Affairs Commission).These reforms and restructuring of the party agencies was taken under the new "Deepening Party and State Institutional Reform Plan" 《深化党和国家机构改革方案》 issued by the CPC Central Committee in March 2018.

# Appendix IX

## Amendments of the CPC Constitution
## Excerpts/sections of amended articles and clauses

**Constitution of the Communist Party of China**

*Revised and adopted at the 19th National Congress of the Communist Party of China on October 24, 2017*

***Compiled from the official document released by Xinhua***

**I. General Program**

"The Communist Party of China uses Marxism-Leninism, Mao Zedong Thought, Deng Xiaoping Theory, the Theory of Three Represents, the Scientific Outlook on Development, and *Xi Jinping Thought on Socialism with Chinese Characteristics for a New Era* as its guides to action."

"Since the Party's 18th National Congress, Chinese Communists, with Comrade Xi Jinping as their chief representative, in response to contemporary developments and by integrating theory with practice, have systematically addressed the major question of our times – what kind of socialism with Chinese characteristics the new era requires us to uphold and develop and how we should uphold and develop it, thus giving shape to Xi 3 / 28 Jinping Thought on Socialism with Chinese Characteristics for a New Era. The Thought is a continuation and development of Marxism-Leninism, Mao Zedong Thought, Deng Xiaoping Theory, the Theory of Three Represents, and the Scientific Outlook on Development. It is the latest achievement in adapting Marxism to the Chinese context, a crystallisation of the practical experience and collective wisdom of the Party and the people, an important component of the theoretical system of socialism with Chinese characteristics, and a guide to action for the entire Party and all the Chinese people to strive for the great rejuvenation of the Chinese nation, and must be upheld long term and constantly developed. Under the guidance of Xi Jinping Thought on Socialism with Chinese Characteristics for a New Era, the Communist Party of China has led the Chinese people of all ethnic groups in a concerted effort to carry out a great struggle, develop a great project, advance a great cause, and realise a great dream, ushering in a new era of socialism with Chinese characteristics" (p.3).

"All party members must have firm confidence in its path, theory, system, and culture, implement the Party's basic theory, basic line, and basic policy, and strive to fulfill the three historic tasks of advancing modernisation, achieving China's reunification......... achieve the two centenary goals, and realise the Chinese Dream of national rejuvenation" (p.3).

At the present stage, the principal contradiction in Chinese society is that between the ever-growing needs of the people for a better life and unbalanced and inadequate development."............ The Party must commit to a people-centered philosophy of development and pursue the vision of innovative, coordinated, green, and open development that is for everyone" (p.3–4).

In accordance with the five-sphere integrated plan and the four-pronged comprehensive strategy for the cause of socialism with Chinese characteristics, the Party must promote coordinated economic, political, cultural, social, and ecological advancement, and coordinate efforts to finish building a moderately prosperous society in all respects, comprehensively deepen reform, fully advance the law-based governance of China, and strengthen Party self-governance in every respect" (p.4).

... "developing a quality work force, the innovation-driven development strategy, the rural vitalisation strategy, the coordinated regional development strategy, the sustainable development strategy, and the military-civilian integration strategy....... draw on advances in science and technology, improve the quality of the country's workforce, and ensure higher-quality and more efficient, equitable, and sustainable development of the economy" (p.4).

... "Party should improve the scientific nature of reform-related decision making, pursue reform in a more systematic, holistic, and coordinated way, and pioneer new approaches through practice"........ The Party shall promote the synchronised development of new industrialisation, information technology application, urbanisation, and agricultural modernisation, and shall build a new socialist countryside, take a new path of industrialisation with Chinese characteristics, and build China into a country of innovation and a global leader in science and technology" (p.5).

... "work to build a community with a shared future for mankind.... It shall follow the principle of achieving shared growth through discussion and collaboration, and pursue the Belt and Road Initiative" (p.7–8).

... "To lead the Chinese people of all ethnic groups to achieve the two centenary goals and realise the Chinese Dream of national rejuvenation,...... in the spirit of reform and innovation, make comprehensive moves to press ahead with the great new project of Party building. It must take enhancing its political building as the overarching principle and make comprehensive efforts to ensure that the Party's political work is stressed, ideology is strengthened, organisations are consolidated, conduct is improved, and discipline is maintained, institutional development is always emphasised, and the fight against corruption keeps going, thus building the Party more effectively in all respects" (p.8).

... "In its own work, the Party shall follow the mass line, seeing that everything is for the people and everything relies on the people, exercising the principle of "from the people, to the people," and translating the correct ideas of the Party into the voluntary action of the people" (p.9).

... "All Party members must keep firmly in mind the need to maintain political integrity, think in big-picture terms, uphold the leadership core, and keep in alignment, and firmly uphold the authority and centralised, unified leadership of the Central Committee with Comrade Xi Jinping at the core, so as to ensure the solidarity, unity, and concerted action of the whole Party and guarantee the prompt and effective implementation of the Party's decisions. The Party shall strengthen and regulate political activities within itself; make intraparty political activities more politically oriented, up-to-date, principled, and effective; cultivate a positive and healthy intraparty political culture; and foster a sound political ecosystem featuring honesty and integrity within the Party" (p.9).

... "The Party shall ensure self-governance is carried out in accordance with regulations and both symptoms and root causes of problems are addressed. The Party must give top priority to ensuring compliance with Party discipline, help its members become more organisation conscious and have a stronger sense of discipline, and work to see that every member is equal before Party discipline. The Party shall ensure the principal and oversight responsibilities for the Party's self-supervision and self-governance are fully assumed; oversight of leading Party organs and of Party members in leadership positions, particularly those holding principal leadership positions, is strengthened; and the internal oversight system is constantly improved. The Party shall step up efforts to improve conduct, build integrity, and combat corruption; apply a zero-tolerance policy on corruption; and establish effective mechanisms to ensure officials do not dare, are not able, and have no desire to be corrupt. ...Leadership of the Communist Party of China is the most essential attribute of socialism with Chinese characteristics, and the greatest strength of this system. The Party exercises overall leadership over all areas of endeavour in every part of the country" (p. 9–10).

**Chapter I. Membership –** ***No Amendments***

**Chapter II. The Party's Organisational System**

**Article 14:** The Party's Central Committee and committees of provinces, autonomous regions, and municipalities directly under the central government shall implement the discipline inspection system, and shall, ... *"within their term of office, carry out inspections of the Party organisations of all localities, departments, enterprises, and public institutions under their jurisdiction"* (p.15–16).

**Chapter III. Central Party Organisations**

**Article 23:** ...... "Members of the Central Military Commission of the Party are decided on by the Central Committee; Chairperson of the Central Military Commission assumes overall responsibility over the work of the Commission (p. 18).

**Chapter IV. Local Party Organisations – *No Amendments***

**Chapter V. Primary Level Party Organisations**

**Article 32.** (2): "to organise Party members to conscientiously study Marxism-Leninism, Mao Zedong Thought, Deng Xiaoping Theory, the Theory of Three Represents, the Scientific Outlook on Development, and Xi Jinping Thought on Socialism with Chinese Characteristics for a New Era; regularise and institutionalise the requirement for all Party members to study the Party Constitution, Party regulations, and General Secretary Xi Jinping's major policy addresses and to meet Party standards; study the Party's lines, principles, policies, and resolutions; acquire a fundamental knowledge of the Party; and improve their general, scientific, legal, and professional knowledge" (p.20).

**Article 33:** "The leading Party members groups or Party committees of state-owned enterprises shall play a leadership role, set the right direction, keep in mind the big picture, ensure the implementation of Party policies and principles, discuss and decide on major issues of their enterprise in accordance with regulations" (p.21).

..."Primary-level Party organisations in social organisations shall communicate to the public and carry out the Party's lines, principles, and policies, exercise leadership over trade unions, Communist Youth League organisations, and other people's group organisations, guide and manage their Party members, lead and serve the people, and advance the cause of the Party" (p.22).

**Chapter VI. Party Officials**

**Article 36.** (1): "Have the necessary understanding of Marxism-Leninism, Mao Zedong Thought, Deng Xiaoping Theory, the Theory of Three Represents, and the Scientific Outlook on Development to be able to perform their duties; take the lead in applying Xi Jinping Thought on Socialism with Chinese Characteristics for a New Era; endeavour to use Marxist positions, viewpoints, and methods in analyzing and solving practical problems; demand of themselves commitment to study, political integrity, and rectitude; and be able to stand the test of any hardship or difficulty" (p. 22–23).

**Chapter VII. Party Discipline**

**Article 40:** "Party discipline mainly consists of political and organisational discipline and discipline regarding integrity, the public, work, and life.

Party organisations shall reprimand and educate, or take disciplinary action against, members who have violated Party discipline, depending on the nature and seriousness of their mistakes, in keeping with the principle of learning from mistakes to prevent recurrence, treating the illness to save the patient, exercising strict discipline enforcement, holding every violator accountable, and discovering problems early and correcting them when they are nascent. The four forms of oversight and discipline enforcement shall be exercised, ensuring that those who have committed minor misconduct are made to "redden and sweat"; that penalties and organisational adjustments to official positions are employed as important means of Party self-supervision and self-governance; and that those who have committed serious disciplinary and/or criminal violations are expelled from the Party" (p.24).

**Article 42:** .... "Any decision to give a member or alternate member of the Central Committee a warning or severe warning shall be examined by the Standing Committee of the Central Commission for Discipline Inspection and then submitted to the Central Committee for approval. Any decision to give a member or alternate member of a local Party committee at any level a warning or severe warning shall be submitted to the commission for discipline inspection at the next level up for approval and reported to the Party committee at the same level as the commission to be put on record" (p.24–25).

**Chapter VIII. Party Organs for Discipline Inspection**

**Article 46:** The Party's commissions for discipline inspection at every level are bodies specifically charged with the responsibility of conducting internal oversight, ..... The Party's commissions for discipline inspection at every level are bodies specifically charged with the responsibility of conducting internal oversight, ...... they shall oversee the performance of duty and exercise of power by Party organisations and Party members in leadership positions, accept and handle complaints and reports made by both Party members and the general public" (p.26).

.... "If it is necessary to file a case, should simultaneously report the matter to the Party committee at the corresponding level and the commission for discipline inspection at the next level up; if a member of the standing committee of the Party committee is involved, the case shall be reported to and subject to preliminary verification by the commission for discipline inspection at the next level up and, if it is necessary to investigate the case, the commission for discipline inspection in question should then report it to the Party committee at the corresponding level for approval" (p. 27).

**Chapter IX. Leading Party Members Groups**

**Article 48:** "to strengthen leadership over Party building within its danwei and fulfill its responsibility for exercising strict Party self-governance in every respect; to discuss and make decisions on matters of major significance within its *danwei,* to manage officials to proper effect; to discuss and decide on important issues including adjusting the setup of primary-level Party organisations, admitting new Party members, and disciplining Party members; to encourage non-Party officials and the people in fulfilling the tasks entrusted to them by the Party and the state; and to exercise leadership over the work of the Party organisations of the *danwei* and those directly under it. ; to discuss and decide on important issues including adjusting the setup of primary-level Party organisations, admitting new Party members, and disciplining Party members; to encourage non-Party officials and the people in fulfilling the tasks entrusted to them by the Party and the state; and to exercise leadership over the work of the Party organisations of the *danwei* and those directly under it" (p. 27).

**Chapter X. Relationship between the Party and the Communist Youth League of China – *No Amendments***

**Chapter XI. Party Emblem and Flag – *No Amendments***

# Appendix X

## Amendments of the PRC Constitution
## Excerpts/Sections of Amended Articles and Clauses

### Amendment to the Constitution of the People's Republic of China

*(Adopted by the 1st Session of the 13th National People's Congress on March 11, 2018)*

**Preamble**

**Seventh Paragraph**

......***amended as*** "the guidance of Marxism-Leninism, Mao Zedong Thought, Deng Xiaoping Theory, the important thought of Three Represents, *the Scientific Outlook on Development, and the Xi Jinping Thought on Socialism with Chinese Characteristics for a New Era."*

...... ***amended as*** "improve the socialist *rule of law*"

...... ***inserted as*** "apply a new vision of development"

..... ***amended as*** "promote the coordinated development of the material, political, spiritual, social and *ecological civilisations,* to turn China into a strong modern socialist country that is prosperous, democratic, culturally advanced, harmonious, and beautiful, and to realise the great rejuvenation for the Chinese nation."

**Tenth Paragraph**

...... ***amended as*** "In the long years of revolution, construction, *and reform*"

...... ***amended as*** "which embraces all socialist working people, all builders of socialism, all patriots who support socialism, and all patriots who stand for the reunification of the motherland and endeavor *to revitalise the Chinese nation*".

**Eleventh Paragraph**

... ***amended as*** "Socialist relations of equality, unity, mutual assistance, and *harmony* have been established among the nationalities and will continue to be strengthened."

**Twelfth Paragraph**

... ***amended as*** "China's achievements in revolution, construction, and *reform* are inseparable from the support of the people of the world"

... ***inserted as*** "follows a path of peaceful development, and pursues a mutually beneficial strategy of opening up"

... ***amended as*** "in developing diplomatic relations and economic and cultural exchanges with other countries and working to build a community with a shared future for mankind"

**Chapter I General Principles**

**Article 1. Paragraph 2**

***... inserted as*** "The defining feature of socialism with Chinese characteristics is the leadership of the Communist Party of China."

**Article 3: Paragraph 3**

***... inserted as*** "All administrative, *supervision,* adjudicatory and procuratorial organs of the State are created by the people's congresses to which they are responsible and by which they are supervised."

**Article 4: Paragraph 1**

***... amended as*** "The State protects the lawful rights and interests of the minority nationalities and upholds and develops a relationship of equality, unity, mutual assistance, *and harmony* among all of China's nationalities."

**Article 24: Paragraph 2**

***... amended as*** "The State champions core socialist values and advocates the civic virtues of love of the motherland, of the people, of labor, of science and of socialism."

**Article 27: Paragraph 3**

***... new paragraph added as*** "State functionaries shall take *a public oath of allegiance to the Constitution when assuming office."*

**Chapter II: Fundamental Rights and Duties of Citizens — *No amendments***

**Chapter III: The Structure of the State**

**Section I: The National People's Congress**

Article 62:

***... new item added as*** "The National People's Congress exercises the power *to elect the Chairperson of the State Supervision Commissio*n."

**Article 63:**

***... new item added as*** "The National People's Congress has the power *to remove from office the Chairperson of the State Supervision."*

**Article 65: Paragraph 4**

***... amended as*** "No one on the Standing Committee of the National People's Congress shall hold office in any of the administrative, *supervision,* adjudicatory or procuratorial organs of the State."

**Article 67:**

***... amended as*** "The Standing Committee of the National People's Congress exercises the functions and power to supervise the work of the State Council, the Central Military Commission, *the State Supervision Commission......"*

### Section II: The President of the People's Republic of China

**Article 79: Paragraph 3**

... ***amended as*** "The term of office of the President and Vice President of the People's Republic of China is the same as that of the National People's Congress." *(two consecutive terms removed)*

### Section III: The State Council

**Article 89:**

... ***amended as*** "The State Council exercises the following functions and powers, to direct and administer economic affairs and urban and rural development, *as well as the building of an ecological civilisation;"*

... ***amended as*** "to direct and administer civil affairs, public security, judicial administration, and other related matters." *("supervision power" of the State Council removed)*

### Section V. The Local People's Congresses and Local People's Governments at Various Levels

**Article 100: Paragraph 2**

... ***new paragraph added as*** "The people's congresses of cities divided into districts and their standing committees may adopt local regulations in accordance with the provisions of law, provided that they do not contravene the Constitution, laws, administrative regulations, and the local regulations of the corresponding provinces or autonomous regions, and they shall take effect after being reported to and approved by the standing committees of the people's congresses of the corresponding provinces or autonomous regions." (See 2015 Legislation Law).

**Article 101: Paragraph 2**

... ***amended as*** "Local people's congresses at or above the county level elect, and have the power to recall, chairpersons of supervision commissions, presidents of people's courts and chief procurators of people's procuratorates at the corresponding level."

**Article 103: Paragraph 3**

... ***amended as*** "No one on the standing committee of a local people's congress at or above the county level shall hold office in State administrative, *supervision,* adjudicatory and procuratorial organs."

**Article 104:**

... ***amended as*** "supervises the work of the people's government, supervision commission, people's court and people's procuratorate at the corresponding level."

**Article 107: Paragraph 1**

... ***amended as*** "Local people's governments at or above the county level, within the limits of their authority as prescribed by law, conduct administrative work concerning the economy, education, science, culture, public health, physical culture, urban and rural development, finance, civil affairs, public security, nationalities affairs, judicial administration and family planning in their respective administrative areas; issue decisions and orders; appoint or remove administrative functionaries, train them, appraise their performance and reward or punish them." *(Local Congress has no authority on supervision matters).*

**Section VII. The Supervision Commissions – *Newly added***
**(Article 123–127 deals with supervision commissions)**

**Article 123:** The supervision commissions of the People's Republic of China at various levels are the supervision organs of the State.

**Article 124:** The People's Republic of China establishes the State Supervision Commission and local supervision commissions at various levels.

A supervision commission is composed of the Chairperson; several Vice Chairpersons; and several members.

The term of office of the Chairperson of a supervision commission is the same as that of the people's congress at the same level. The Chairperson of the State Supervision Commission shall serve no more than two consecutive terms. The organisation and functions and powers of the supervision commissions are prescribed by law.

**Article 125:** The State Supervision Commission of the People's Republic of China is the highest supervision organ.

The State Supervision Commission directs the work of the supervision commissions at various local levels, and supervision commissions at higher levels direct the work of those at lower levels.

**Article 126:** The State Supervision Commission is responsible to the National People's Congress and its Standing Committee. Supervision commissions at the various local levels are responsible to the organs of state power which created them and to the supervision commissions at higher levels.

**Article 127:** The supervision commissions exercise supervision power independently, in accordance with the provisions of law, and not subject to interference by any administrative organ, public organisation or individual.

**Section VIII. The People's Courts and the People's Procuratorates**
**(Articles 128–140**

*Section 7 is accordingly changed to Section 8, and articles 123–128 are accordingly changed to article 128–140.*

**Chapter IV: The National Flag, the National Anthem, the National Emblem and the Capital — *No Amendment***

**Articles 141-43**

*Source:* **Constitution of the People's Republic of China (2018 Amendment)**
http://www.pkulaw.cn/fulltext_form.aspx?Gid=311950
https://npcobserver.com/2018/03/11/translation-2018-amendment-to-the-p-r-c-constitution/
(accessed on 15 October 2018)

# Appendix XI

## Socio-economic Indicators 1980–2017

| Categories | 1980 | 1985 | 1990 | 1995 | 2000 | 2005 | 2010 | 2015 | 2017 |
|---|---|---|---|---|---|---|---|---|---|
| Gini Index | 0.3 | 0.31 | 0.327 | 0.382 | 0.407 | 0.49 | 0.48 | 46 | 0.4 |
| GDP (USD in billions) | 306.17 | 309.84 | 394.57 | 734.52 | 1,211.35 | 2,286.69 | 6,101.34 | 11,063.07 | 12237.7 |
| HDI (rank) | NA | NA | 103 | 101 | 87 | 81 | 89 | 90 | 86 |
| HDI (trends) | 0.407 | 0.452 | 0.495 | 0.547 | 0.59 | 0.637 | 0.689 | 0.743 | 0.752 |
| GDP per capita (USD) | 194.805 | 294.459 | 317.885 | 609.657 | 959.372 | 1753.418 | 4560.513 | 8069.213 | 8643.11 |
| Life expectancy | 66.843 | 68.451 | 69 | 69.9 | 71.7 | 71.9 | 73.5 | 76 | 76.4 |
| Birth rate | 18.21 | 21.04 | 21.06 | 17.12 | 14.03 | 1240 | 11.9 | 12.1 | 11.7 |
| Death Rate | 6.34 | 6.78 | 6.67 | 6.57 | 6.45 | 6.51 | 7.11 | 7.11 | 7.4 |

*Sources:* *People's Daily Online*, 2018. UNDP: Human Development Reports, World Bank Data, National Bureau of Statistics of China

Mohanty, Manoranjan. 2018. *China's Transformation: the Success Story and the Success Trap*. New Delhi, Sage, 7-8

# Contributors

**Alka Acharya** is Professor at the Centre for East Asian Studies, School of International Studies, Jawaharlal Nehru University, New Delhi, teaching Chinese Foreign Policy and Political Economy and guiding research since 1993. She was Editor of *China Report* (New Delhi) from 2005-2013 and Director and Senior Fellow of the Institute of Chinese Studies, Delhi from April 2012 to March 2017. She was nominated to the India-China Eminent Persons Group (2006-2008) and was a member of the National Security Advisory Board of the Government of India during 2006-2008 and 2011-2012. (E-mail: alka.acharya@ gmail.com)

**Ritu Agarwal** is an Associate Professor at Centre for East Asian studies, School of International Studies, JNU. She holds a PhD in Chinese studies from the University of Delhi. She completed her M.A. in Political science, JNU. Her research interests are: rural political economy, urbanisation, gender studies and provincial politics. Dr Ritu Agarwal studied Mandarin Chinese from Beijing Language and Culture University, Beijing. She was a visiting scholar to Yunnan Academy of Social Sciences, Kunming, Jinan University, Guangzhou, Chinese University of Hong kong and was affiliated to East Asia Institute, National University of Singapore, Singapore. (E-mail: ritu10agarwal@gmail.com)

**P K Anand** is a Research Associate at the Institute of Chinese Studies, Delhi. He received his PhD in Chinese Politics from the Centre for East Asian Studies, Jawaharlal Nehru University, New Delhi. He is a recipient of the China India Scholar Leaders Fellowship (second cohort, 2018-20) of the India China Institute, at New School, New York. Anand was also formerly a Visiting Fellow at the Harvard-Yenching Institute, Cambridge, Massachusetts, USA in 2016-17. (E-Mail: anand.p.krishnan@gmail.com)

**Ravi Bhoothalingam** studied Experimental Psychology at Cambridge University under the guidance of noted scientist and Sinologist, Prof. Joseph Needham. After holding senior positions in industry in India and overseas, Ravi serves as an Independent Director on corporate boards. He is Treasurer and Honorary Fellow of the Institute of Chinese Studies, Delhi and a regular commentator on business and culture in China and High Asia. He is a Fellow of the Royal Geographical Society, London. (E-mail: sush.ravi@gmail.com)

**Tshering Chonzom Bhutia** is an Associate Fellow at the Institute of Chinese Studies. She received her PhD in Chinese Studies from Jawaharlal Nehru University, India in 2014. She is currently a China India Scholar-Leaders Initiative (CISLI) Fellow, 2018-20. Her areas of interest include negotiation theory, diversity and inclusion in India and China, Tibet question in China and internationally. Her recently completed ICSSR funded research project comparing the Indian and Chinese government's minority policies will soon be published as ICS Monograph. (E-mail: tsheringjnu@gmail.com)

**Sreemati Chakrabarti** was Professor (Chinese Studies) at the Department of East Asian Studies, University of Delhi. She had been Head of the Department for 3 terms and Dean, Faculty of Social Sciences of Delhi University. She holds a Master's degree from Harvard University and a PhD from Columbia University. Her publications include *China and the Naxalites,Mao, China's Intellectuals and the Cultural Revolution* and a National Book Trust document China. She is Vice-Chairperson and Honorary Fellow, Institute of Chinese Studies. (E-mail: sreemati@gmail. com)

**Usha Chandran** is an Assistant Professor at the Centre for Chinese and South East Asian Studies,School of Language, Literature and Culture Studies, Jawaharlal Nehru University, New Delhi. She teaches Chinese Language, Literature, Translation, Interpretation and Chinese History. Her interests lie in the role of gender in literature, language, society and politics in China and its comparison with India. Presently working in a UPE project on role of language in travelling and translation of feminist theories from the West and gender expressions and characters in Chinese language shaping gender power relations and gender identity in China. E-mail: ushachen75@gmail.com,

**Debasish Chaudhuri** is an independent researcher and an Adjunct Fellow of the Institute of Chinese Studies (ICS) specialising in Chinese politics and society. Chaudhuri is the author of *Xinjiang and the Chinese State – Violence in the Reform Era.* He held positions of Associate Fellow and Research Fellow at ICS and Vivekanand International Foundation. The current focus of his research include Chinese ethnic policies and local responses, political economy of minority regions, Shanghai Cooperation Organisation, impact of the Belt and Road Initiative in the peripheries, Chinese nationalism as well as collective actions and dissident movements. (E-mail: chaudhuri. debasish@gmail.com)

**B R Deepak** is a professor at the Centre for Chinese and Southeast Asian Studies, Jawaharlal Nehru University was trained in Chinese language, literature, history and India-China relations at the Peking University and Chinese Academy of Social Sciences,Beijing, at Jawaharlal Nehru University, New Delhi and University of Edinburgh,UK. Deepak's latest publications include *China's Global Rebalancing and the New Silk Road* by Springer (2018), *My Tryst With China* (2017), *India and China: Foreign Policy Approaches and Responses* (2016), *India and China 1904-2004: A Century of Peace and Conflict* (2005) and *India-China Relations in first half of the Twentieth Century* (2001). (E-mail: deepak110@ yahoo.com)

**Jabin T Jacob** is Associate Professor at the Department of International Relations and Governance Studies, Shiv Nadar University, Greater Noida and Adjunct Research Fellow at the National Maritime Foundation, New Delhi. He was formerly Fellow and Assistant Director at the Institute of Chinese Studies, Delhi and Associate Editor of the journal *China Report.* Jacob holds a PhD in Chinese Studies and has spent time as a student/researcher/faculty in Taiwan, France and Singapore. His research interests include Chinese foreign policy, Sino-Indian border areas, Indian and Chinese worldviews, and centre-province relations in China. As part of his research, Jacob has travelled in many of India's border states and visited parts of the country's disputed borders with China and Pakistan as well as the international borders with Myanmar and Bangladesh. Jacob's latest work is a co-edited volume, *China and its Neighbourhood: Perspectives from India and Vietnam* (2017) and he is currently working on a manuscript on India's policymaking on China. (E-mail: jabinjacob@gmail.com)

**Tilak Jha** is a PhD researcher on China and Chinese media at the Centre for East Asian Studies, School of International Studies, Jawaharlal Nehru University, New Delhi. Earlier, Mr. Jha was a Bai Xian Scholar at the Zhejiang University, Hangzhou, China on the Asian Future Leaders Scholarship from 2014 to 2016. Tilak has several publications in books, journals and newspapers of global repute – all on China. His most recent publication is a chapter on India's Act East policy in a volume published by Routledge in 2018. (E-mail: tilakjha@gmail. com)

**Atul Kumar** is an Adjunct Research Fellow at the Griffith Asia Institute of Griffith University in Brisbane, Australia. Atul has previously taught International Politics at the University of Queensland in Brisbane and at Monash University in Melbourne. Atul writes for *firstpost.com* and has published journal articles on China's Joint War Doctrine, 'China-Turkey's strategic relations', 'Australia's relevance as a member in the QUAD' besides other topics. He is currently working on his book titled *China's Joint War: Emergent Expeditionary Capabilities.* (E-mail: atulkumar06@gmail.com)

**Sabaree Mitra,** Honorary Fellow in the Institute of Chinese Studies, is a Professor of Chinese Language, Literature and Culture in Jawaharlal Nehru University. Her research interest includes contemporary Chinese Literature and Criticism, Chinese Cultural History, India-China Cultural Relations and Regional Interaction. Her major publications are *Purbadiganter Kabita: Samakaleen tin china kabir ek jhalak* (2002), a collection of contemporary Chinese poetry translated into Bengali, *Literature and Politics in 20th century China: Issues and Themes (2005)*, *Chinese Women Writers and Gender Discourse (1976-1996)* (2008). In 2017, she was honored with the prestigious Special Book Award of China. (E-mail: sabareem@gmail.com)

**Manoranjan Mohanty,** a political scientist, China scholar and a peace and human rights activist with special interest in China, India and global transformation, is a retired Professor of Delhi University, Honorary Fellow and former Chairperson of the Institute of Chinese Studies (www.icsin.org) and Distinguished Professor, Council for Social Development, New Delhi (www.csdindia.org) and Chairperson, Development Research Institute, Bhubaneswar. His latest publication: *China's Transformation: The Success Story and the Success Trap.* (E-mail: mmohantydu@gmail.com)

**Raviprasad Narayanan** is Associate Professor, Center for East Asian Studies, School of International Studies, Jawaharlal Nehru University, New Delhi. He has taught courses on Research Methods in International Relations and The State in Modern China in JNU since 2015. He was earlier an Associate Research Fellow with the Institute on International Relation, National Chengchi University, Taipei, Taiwan. He has published several chapters in books and research articles in the *China Report, Asian Perspective, Tibet Journal, World Focus* and other journals. He has also edited a book published by Springer (2015) along with Dr Chen Mumin and Dr GVC Naidu. (E-mail: raviprasad.narayanan @gmail.com)

**Madhurima Nundy** is an Associate Fellow and Assistant Director at the Institute of Chinese Studies, Delhi. She holds a PhD in Public Health from the Centre of Social Medicine and Community Health, Jawaharlal Nehru University, New Delhi. She was a Technical Consultant with the National Commission on Macroeconomics and Health. Her areas of interest include comparative health service systems, health policies and inequalities in health. She has several publications to her name. Her forthcoming book, which she has co-authored along with Prof. Rama V. Baru, is titled *Commercialisation of Medical Care in*

*China: Changing Landscapes*. At ICS she leads the comparative health resource centre. (E-mail: madhurima. nundy@gmail.com)

**Santosh Pai** is a corporate lawyer and has been advising clients in the India-China corridor since 2010. His areas of interest include Chinese investments in India, India-China comparative law and policy, cross-cultural business negotiations and board governance. He holds B.A., LL.B. (Hons.) degree from NLSIU, Bangalore, LL.M. (Chinese law) from Tsinghua University, Beijing and an MBA from Vlerick University, Belgium at its Peking University campus. Santosh is currently a partner at Link Legal, an Indian law firm. He teaches a India-China business course and volunteers at NGOs in his free time. (E-mail: santoshkpai@gmail.com)

**Kishan S Rana,** Emeritus Fellow, Institute of Chinese Studies, Delhi, is a retired career diplomat. He joined the Indian Foreign Service in 1960 and has served as Ambassador/High Commissioner to Algeria, Czechoslovakia, Kenya, Mauritius, and Germany. He is also currently Professor Emeritus, DiploFoundation and Archives By-Fellow, Churchill College, Cambridge. He holds a BA (Hons.) degree and an MA economics degree from St Stephen's College, Delhi. He has authored and edited eleven books on diplomatic studies and related subjects and written extensively in academic journals and newspaper columns. (E-mail: kishanrana@gmail.com)

**C V Ranganathan** is a retired diplomat and currently the President of The Asia Centre in Bangalore. He joined the Indian Foreign Service in 1959. His various postings have been in the Ministry of External Affairs in Delhi including as Joint Secretary in charge of Northern and East Asia Divisions; Commissioner of India to Hong Kong, Ambassador of India to Ethiopia, Deputy Chief of Mission in the rank of Ambassador in Moscow, Ambassador of India to China and Ambassador of India to France. An Emeritus Fellow of the Institute of Chinese Studies, he has coauthored a book on *India and China-The Way Ahead* with Ambassador V C Khanna. (E-mail: cvranganathan@gmail.com)

**Rajiv Ranjan** is an Assistant Professor at the College of Liberal Arts, Institute of Global Studies, Shanghai University, Shanghai, China, teaching graduate courses on Chinese Foreign Policy and New World Order. He is also Adjunct Fellow of the ICS Delhi. He is trained in Chinese language and his research interests include Government and Politics in China, Chinese Foreign Policy, Chinese Society and Culture, New World Order. His publications have appeared in *Millennium: Journal of International Studies, Contemporary International Relations, Political Studies Review, China Report, International Affairs*. (E-mail: mrajivranjan@gmail.com)

**Bhim B Subba** is a Research Associate at the ICS. He has earned his PhD from the Department of East Asian Studies, University of Delhi. He was an ICS-HYI Visiting Fellow at Harvard University for his doctoral research (2016-17). From 2015-16, he was affiliated with National Taiwan Normal University, Taipei, ROC where he pursued language study and independent research. He also received Confucius Institute Scholarship in Harbin Normal University, Heilongjiang, PRC pursuing Mandarin language training. His research interests include comparative political theory, Chinese politics and India-China comparatives. (E-mail:subba.eas@ hotmail.com)

**T G Suresh** is an Associate Professor in the Centre for Political Studies, (CPS), Jawaharlal Nehru University (JNU), New Delhi. He has earned his PhD in Chinese Studies from JNU and M A in Politics and International Relations from Mahatma Gandhi University, Kottayam in Kerala. His research interests include comparative globalisations and political economy of India and China. He has published articles in *China Report*, and *Journal of Asian Public Policy*. Suresh has been a Visiting Research Fellow at the Asia Research Institute, (ARI), National University of Singapore (2012), Asia Fellow of the Asian Scholarship Foundation (Bangkok) to Chengdu and Shanghai ( 2008), and Fellow of the Fulbright American Studies Institute, University of Delaware, US (2004). (E-mail: tgsuresh@mail.jnu. ac.in)

**Tan Chung** is Consultant and Visiting Professor of Yunnan University, Honorary Academician of Yunnan Academy of Social Sciences, Special Senior Researcher of the Chongyang Institute of the Renmin University of China and Special Consultant of the Pangu Think Tank, Beijing. He spent 45 years (1955-1999) of his life in India. He is a vociferous promoter of India-China friendship and understanding. In 2010, he received Padma Bhushan from the Indian President and an award for contribution to China-India friendship from the Chinese Premier. (E-mail: tanchungh@ gmail.com)

**Anurag Vishwanath** is a columnist with *Financial Express* (Delhi). Her book Finding India in China: Travels to the lesser known was published in Singapore, in 2015. She has a PhD in Political Science from the University of Delhi, India. She has also more than 100 articles in *Bangkok Post, Prachatai and Nation* (Thailand), *Far Eastern Economic Review* (Hong Kong) and *Journal of Contemporary Asia* (Manila). Within India, she has written in *Economic and Political Weekly* (Mumbai), *Global Affairs* (Mumbai) and *Indian Management* (Delhi). She was a regular writer at *Business Standard* (Delhi) from 2007-2011. (E-mail: anurag.m.viswanath@ gmail.com)

**Aravind Yelery** is the Senior Research Fellow at Peking University HSBC Business School (PHBS). Before joining PHBS, Aravind was associated with the Institute of Chinese Studies (ICS) in the capacity of Assistant Director and Associate Fellow. He holds a PhD in Chinese Studies from the School of International Studies, Jawaharlal Nehru University, New Delhi. Aravind's research interests include China's foreign policy, Chinese business, Chinese manufacturing trends, urbanisation and Chinese Government and politics. He contributes on China-related issues in several Indian newspapers. He has been interviewed by leading Indian and Global media. (E-mail: aravind.yelery@gmail.com)

# Glossary and Abbreviations

| | |
|---|---|
| ACFTU | All-China Federation of Trade Unions (中华全国总工会 zhonghua quanguo zonggonghui) |
| ACWF | All-China Women's Federation (中华全国妇女联合会 zhongguo funu lianhe hui) |
| AIIB | Asian Infrastructure Investment Bank |
| Anti-corruption struggle | fantan douzheng 反贪斗争 |
| baquan | 霸权 Hegemony |
| bianjiang | 边疆 a border area, frontier region |
| Building a Socialist rule of law state | jianshe shehui zhuyi fazhi guojia 建设社会主义法治国家 |
| CC | Central Committee (中共中央 zhonggong zhonyang) |
| CCDI | Central Commission for Discipline Inspection (中央纪律检查委员会 zhongyang jilu jianch weiyuanhui), a party's discipline agency elected by the Party Congress |
| Central Financial Institutions | zhongyang jinrong xitong 中央金融系统 |
| Central State Organisations | zhongyang guojia jiguan 中央国家机关 |
| CPC Organisation Department | zuzhi bu 组织部 |
| chang hong da hei | 唱红打黑 singing red songs and strike hard the criminals |
| Chinese Dream | Zhongguo meng 中国梦 Announced by Xi Jinping in November 2012 calling for rejuvenation of the Chinese nation |

| | |
|---|---|
| CMC | Central Military Commission (zhongyang junshi weiyuanhui 中央军事委员会) |
| Collective bargaining | jiti tanpan 集体谈判 |
| Collective consultation | jiti xieshang 集体协商 |
| Communist Youth League faction | tuan pai 团派 sometimes referred as 'populist' faction |
| CPC | Communist Party of China (zhongguo gongchandang 中国共产党) |
| CPPCC | Chinese People's Political Consultative Conference (zhongguo renmin zhengzhi xieshang huiyi 中国人民政治协商会议) |
| daguo waijiao | 大国外交 'great power diplomacy' |
| dang jianshe | 党建设 party-building or construction |
| dangzheng fenkai | 党政分开 separation of party and government functions |
| danwei | 单位 an administrative or organization unit |
| DOHRSS | Department of Human Resource and Social Security |
| fa da ... dang da | 法大...党大 the superiority of the law ... the superiority of the Party |
| fazhi ... renzhi | 法治 ...人治 rule of law ... rule of men |
| FDI | Foreign Direct Investment (外商直接投资 waishang zhijie touzi) |
| fenqing | 愤青 'angry youths' who are extremely nationalistic |
| Five Anti Campaign | wufan 五反 (bribery, tax evasion, theft of state property, rigging bids and stealing of state economic information) |
| Four Comprehensives | 四个全面 sige quanmian, one of the corner stones of Xi Jinping's thought |
| fuhe remin liyi | 符合人民利益 accord with the interests of the people |
| gaige kaifang | 改革开放 'reform and opening up' (the political line adopted at the 3rd Plenum of 11th Central Committee in 1978 |
| gaoju qizhi | 高举旗帜 holding high the banner |

| | |
|---|---|
| GDP | Gross Domestic Product (国内生产总值 guonei shengchang zongzhi) shengchan zongzhi |
| GLP | Great Leap Forward (大跃进 dayuejin) – a multi-pronged development strategy aiming at quick results based on mass mobilization in 1958 |
| gongxue jiehe | 工学结合 Work-study model combining school education with on the job training |
| GPCR | Great Proletarian Cultural Revolution or Cultural Revolution (无产阶级文化大革命 wuchan jieji wenhua da geming) wenhua geming (in short) |
| guanxi | 关系 inter-personnel connections |
| heping jueqi | 和平崛起 'peaceful rise' expounded under Hu Jintao leadership |
| He shang | 河殇 translated as River Elegy, a popular but controversial documentary banned in November 1988 |
| HKSAR | Hong Kong Special Autonomous Region (香港特别行政区 Xianggang tebie xinzhengqu) |
| hong zhuan | 红专 Red and Experts (revolutionary and professionals) |
| hukou | 户口 Household registration system – a residency certificate that entitle a resident to access public goods such as education, health, housing and welfare facilities |
| hulian wang qunzu xinxi fuwu guanli | 互联网群组信息服务管理规定 Regulations on the guiding Information Service of Internet Groups |
| jing ai....jing wei | 敬爱 ... 敬畏 respect and love ... respect and fear |
| jiuhuo duizhang | 救火队长 fire-brigade chief, trouble shooter, Wang Qishan known as Xi Jinping's trouble shooter |
| ke wang | 渴 望 translated as Aspirations or Yearnings, popular TV serial |
| Intellectual Property (IP) | (zhihui chanquan 智慧产权) |
| Labour Dispatch | 劳务派遣 laowu paiqian, temporary agency work is a growing phenomenon of non-regular employment, whereby, dispatch agencies provide enterprise managements with employees according to the latter's needs and demands |
| laoji shiming | 牢记使命 always keeping the mission in mind |

| | |
|---|---|
| liang ge yibai nian | 两个一百年 Two Centenaries: CPC 100th anniversary in 2021 and PRC's 100th anniversary in 2049 |
| MAC | Military Affairs Committee |
| minzu gongtong ti | 民族共同体 Ethnic confederation |
| minzu quyu zizhi zhidu | 民族区域自治制度 ethnic regional autonomy system |
| minzu tuanjie | 民族团结 unity of nationalitites |
| MOHRSS | Ministry of Human Resource and Social Security (Zhonghua Renmin Gonghe Guo Renli Ziyuan he Shehui baozhang bu 中华人力资源和社会保障部) |
| Nanxun | 南巡 Southern Tour by Deng Xiaoping in 1992 |
| NBS | National Bureau of Statistics, (Guojia tongji ju 国家统计局) is under the State Council with the responsibility of collecting and releasing data on economy, society and population |
| NDRC | National Development and Reform Commission (Guojia Fazhan he Gaige Weiyuanhui 国家发展和改革委员会) |
| New socialist villages | shehui zhuyi xin nongcun 社会主义新农村 |
| NFWC | National Financial Work Conference (Quanguo Jinrong Gongzuo Huiyi 全国金融工作会议) |
| NPC | National People's Congress (全国人民代表大会 Quanguo Renmin Daibiao Dahui) |
| NSC | National Supervision Commission (Guojia Jiancha Weiyuanhui 国家监察委员会) established in March 2018 |
| OBOR/BRI | One Belt, One Road/Belt and Road Initiative (yidai yilu 一带一路) a signature project of Xi Jinping |
| Party Congress | National Congress of the Communist Party of China (中国共产党代表大会 Zhongguo Gongchandang Daibiao Dahui) |
| Party Core | hexin 核心, party's 'core', Xi Jinping became the core since the Sixth Plenum of the 18th Central Committee |
| Party Plenum | Refers to the plenary session of the Central Committee of the CPC (dang zhongyang quanhui 党中央全会) |
| PB | Politburo (中共中央政治局 zhonggong zhongyang zhengzhiju) |

| | |
|---|---|
| PBSC | Politburo Standing Committee (zheng zhengzhiju changwu weiyuanhui 政治局常务委员会) |
| Petroleum gang | shiyou bang 石油邦 one of faction under former PBSC member Zhou Yonkang who is serving prison sentence |
| PLA | People's Liberation Army (Renmin Jiefangjun 人民解放军) |
| PRC | People's Republic of China (Zhonghua Renmin Gongheguo 中华人民共和国) |
| qi shang ba xia | 七上八下 seven up, eight down (convention of retirement rules of the Chinese leaders i.e. at the eve of the Party Congress, if an incumbent is 67 years of age, then he/she can be promoted, but if 68 years, then must retire from leadership position) |
| Qiushi | 求实 Seeking Truth, bimonthly periodical published by the CPC Central Committee |
| quyu fazhan chaju | 区域发展差距 disparities in regional development |
| rending shengtian | 人 定胜天 man must conquer nature, one of the slogan during the Great Leap Forward |
| Revitalizing the Chinese nation | zhenxing zhonghua 振兴中华 |
| R & D | Research and Development (研究与发展 yanjiu yu fazhan) |
| RMB | Renminbi (人民币), Chinese currency |
| Road to National Rejuvenation | fuxing zhilu 复兴之路 (Xi Jinping's speech in Beijing on 29 November 2012) |
| Samskriti | In Sanskrit, it refers to a collective value system shaped over time through a process of cultivation and refinement |
| SARA | State Administration for Religious Affairs (guojia zongjiao shiwu ju 国家宗教事务局) |
| SARS | Severe Acute Respiratory Syndrome (Yanzhong jixing huxi zonghe zheng 严重急性呼吸综合征) |
| Scientific Outlook on Development | kexue fazhan guan 科学发展观, Hu Jintao's ideological canon enshrined in Party charter in 2012 |

| | |
|---|---|
| secretaries gang | mishu bang 秘书帮, political group or factions who rose up the top leaderships ranks who served as secretaries. |
| SEZ | Special Economic Zones (经济特区 jingji tequ) |
| Shanxi gang | Shanxi bang 山西 邦, political elites who had served or born in Shanxi. Ling Jihua, former Chief of Staff of Hu Jintao was one of the prominent patrons of this group |
| Socialist Education Movement | shehui zhuyi jiaoyu yundong 社会注意教育运动 (1963-66) |
| shuanggui | 双规 'double requirements' – a discipline measure when an official suspected under supervision is to give an account if his wrong doings within prescribed time and in a required place |
| Sina Weibo | 新浪微博 one of China's most popular social media platforms with more than 431 million active users |
| SMEs | Small and Medium Enterprises (zhong xiao qiye 中小企业) |
| SOEs | State-owned enterprises (guo you qiye 国有企业) |
| Social Security | shehui baozhang, 社会保障 as an inclusive concept to cover all types of social arrangements for social care and support |
| Social Welfare | shehui fuli 社会福利, referred to as assistance and services to the vulnerable sections of the society |
| State Council | Guowuyuan 国务院 – China's Council of Ministers |
| taoguang yanghui | 韬光养晦 'hide capacities and bid time', part of 24-character strategy of Deng Xiaoping for conducting foreign relations |
| TAR | Tibet Autonomous Region (西藏自治区 Xizang zizhiqu) |
| Theory of Three Represents | 三个代表 sange daibiao, an ideological canon attributed to Jiang Zemin that required the party to represent advanced productive forces, advanced culture and interests of the masses |
| Three Anti Campaign | 三反 sanfan (corruption, waste & red tape) |
| Three spends | sange xiaofei 三个消费 excesses such as vehicles, banquets and trips of cadres |

| | |
|---|---|
| tiangao huangdi yuan | 天高皇帝远 the emperor is as far away as the heaven is high above |
| tuijin fazhi zhongguo jianshe | 推进法治中国建设 promoting a construction of rule of law in China, Third Plenum, November 2013 |
| UNFWD | United Front Work Department (统一战线工作部 tongyi zhanxian gongzuobu) |
| WeChat | 微信 (Weixin) Chinese multi-purpose messaging, social media and mobile payment app developed by Tencent in 2011 |
| weihu xianfa falu quanwei | 维护宪法法律权威 safeguard the authority of the constitution and laws |
| WHO | World Health Organisation (世界卫生组织 shijie weisheng zuzhi) |
| WTO | World Trade Organisation (世界贸易组织 shijie maoyi zuzhi) |
| wujin..... wuhua | 五进 五化 Wujin and Wuhua, literally meaning 'five penetrations/five introductions' and 'five transformations', were first introduced in the Zhejiang Province by Xi Jinping as an experiment to Sinicise external cultural/religious influence, such as Christianity |
| xiang qunzhong zhi suo xiang | 想群众之所想 think what the people are thinking |
| xiao zu | 小组 (Leading) Small group |
| Xi fensi tuan | 习粉丝团 Xi Fan Club |
| xin shidai de zhongguo tese shehui zhuyi xi jinping sixiang | 新时代的中国特色社会主义习近平思想 Xi Jinping Thought on Socialism with Chinese characteristics in the New Era |
| xin siren bang | 新四人帮 New Gang of Four |
| XUAR | Xinjiang Ugyhur Autonomous Region (新疆维吾尔自治区 Xinjiang Weiwu'er zizhiqu) |
| xuexi cidian | 学习词典 – dictionary with a total of 110 terms related to the Party's new thinking, concepts and strategies that cadres must know in September 2017 |
| yi yan tang | 一言堂 'one-voice chamber' denotes culture as a tool from Mao Zedong to Xi Jinping |

| | |
|---|---|
| xin yi dai lingdao jiti | 新一代领导集体 new generation collective leadership |
| yifa zhiguo | 依法治国 governing the country according to law |
| yishi xingtai lingyu douzheng | 意识形态领域斗争 struggle in ideological sphere |
| yong yuan zai lu shang | 永远在路上 Always on the Road – a CCTV-1 documentary featuring anti-corruption campaign accused confessing to their crime |
| zaguo dang | 砸锅党 cauldron destroyers |
| zengqiang fazhi jingshen | 增强法治精神 strengthen consciousness about the rule of law |
| zhanling xinxi chuanbo zhi gao dian | 占领信息传播至高点 occupying the commanding heights of information dissemination |
| zhanlue bushu | 战略部署 strategic deployment of media |
| Zhongguo fuqi lai | 中国富起来 China had become a rich country (1978-2020) |
| Zhongguo qiangqi lai | 中国强起来 building China a strong country (2020–49) |
| Zhongguo tese shehui zhuyi | 中国特色社会主义 Socialism with Chinese characteristics, Deng Xiaoping's ideological cannon |
| Zhongguo zhanqi lai | 中国站起来 China has risen or stood up (1921–49) |

# Index